A Particular Condition in Life

A Particular Condition in Life

Self-Employment and Social Mobility in Mid-Victorian Brantford, Ontario

DAVID G. BURLEY

McGill-Queen's University Press
Kingston & Montreal • London • Buffalo

© McGill-Queen's University Press 1994
ISBN 0-7735-1199-7

Legal deposit fourth quarter 1994
Bibliothèque nationale du Québec
Printed in Canada on acid-free paper

This book has been published with the help of a grant from the Social
Science Federation of Canada, using funds provided by the Social
Sciences and Humanities Research Council of Canada. Publication has
also been supported by the University of Winnipeg and by the Canada
Council through its block grant program.

Canadian Cataloguing in Publication Data

Burley, David G.
    A particular condition in life: self-employment and social mobility in
    mid-Victorian Brantford, Ontario
    Includes bibliographical references and index.
    ISBN 0-7735-1199-7
    1. Social mobility – Ontario – Brantford – History – 19th century.
    2. Brantford (Ont.) – Social conditions – History – 19th century.
    3. Labor market – Ontario – Brantford – History – 19th century.
    I. Title.
    HN110.B63B87 1994   330.9713'4802   C94–900178–3

Typeset in Baskerville 10/12 by Caractéra production graphique inc.,
Quebec City.

Contents

Tables   vii

Acknowledgments   ix

Introduction   3

1 Business Enterprise and Social Relations in a
   Mid-Victorian Town   19

2 Who Was Self-Employed?   62

3 Credit and Debt   103

4 The Structure of Wealth   127

5 The Making of the Self-Made Man   170

6 Social Change and Urban Politics   198

Conclusion   234

Appendix: Occupational Categories   241

Notes   245

Bibliography   277

Index   301

Tables

1.1 Self-Employment by Occupational Group, 1852–81   25

1.2 Capital, Employment, and Production of Industrial Firms, 1861–71   38

1.3 Classification of New Businesses by Economic Sector, 1861–81   50

2.1 Birthplace of the Self-Employed and Wage-Labouring Adult Male Population, 1852–81   70

2.2 Religion (Major Protestant Denominations Only) by Birthplace, 1852–81   74

2.3 Rates of Self-Employment by Religion (Major Protestant Denominations Only) by Birthplace, 1852–81   75

2.4 Categories of Partnership by Religion, 1842–81   77

2.5 Occupational Groups by Birthplace, 1852–81   79

2.6 Rates of Self-Employment by Birthplace and Age Group, 1852–81   90

2.7 Average Number of Children by Length of Time in Business (Married Couples Only), 1852–81   92

2.8 Characteristics of Women in Business, 1852–81   100

3.1   Reliability of the Mercantile Agency's Credit Reports, 1850–70   113

3.2   Percentage of Businessmen Receiving Credit Ratings by Percentile Rank in Distribution of Assessed Wealth, 1851–81   116

3.3   Credit Ratings by Percentile Rank in Distribution of Assessed Wealth, 1851–81   117

3.4   Number of Businessmen Receiving Negative Credit Ratings, Selected Occupations, 1851–81   119

3.5   Index of Relative Mortgage Debt by Percentile Rank, 1851–81   121

3.6   Index of Relative Mortgage Debt by Age Group, 1851–81   121

3.7   Economic Mobility and Mortgage Debt, 1851–81   122

3.8   Mortgage Indebtedness of Businessmen, 1851–81   123

3.9   Rates of Persistence in Business for Mortgage-Indebted and Unindebted Property Owners, 1851–81   124

3.10 Average Value of Mortgage Debt by Selected Occupations, 1851–81   125

4.1   Real and Personal Property/Income Assessments of Business Population as Per Cent of Total, 1851–80   135

4.2   Distribution of Assessed Wealth by Percentile Rank, 1851–80   137

4.3   Real Estate Holdings of Ignatius Cockshutt, 1847–80   139

4.4   Economic Rank of Rental Property Owners, 1851–80   140

4.5   Tenure of Business and Residential Accommodation, 1851–80   144

4.6   Mortgage Investment: Selected Statistics, 1851–80   147

4.7   Relative Wealth for Economic Sector, Occupational Groups, and Selected Occupations, 1851–80   150

4.8   Value of Probated Estates by Occupational Group, 1860–90   162

4.9   Distribution of Wealth by Age Group, 1851–80   166

4.10 Indices of Relative Concentration of Real Property and Personal Property/Income by Age Group, 1851–52 and 1880–81 168

4.11 Rate of Real Property Ownership by Age Group, 1851–80 168

4.12 Indices of Relative Wealth for Canadian and Immigrant Men in Business Less than Ten Years, 1851–80 169

5.1 Rates of Business Discontinuations, 1851–80 175

5.2 Business Discontinuations and Transiency: Percentage of Men Quitting Business Who Left Town, by Economic Rank and Sector, 1851–80 177

5.3 Economic Mobility of Persistors, 1851–80 181

5.4 Direction of Mobility by Economic Rank, 1851–80 182

5.5 Property Seizures and Insolvencies, 1851–81 189

6.1 Occupation and Economic Rank of Brantford Investors in the Buffalo and Brantford Railway, 1850 203

6.2 Occupation of Voters in Selected Polls, 1878 231

Acknowledgments

Historical research is frequently, like mid-Victorian independence, dependent on mutual self-help. Over the years that this project has absorbed, I have been fortunate to benefit from the help and encouragement of many people. No acknowledgment can fully indicate my obligation to them and my gratitude for their confidence in the enterprise.

First of all, David Gagan introduced me to social history and quantitative methods. He has generously borne with this book, reading its several versions and offering guidance and perceptive criticism. To him is my greatest debt. Other of my friends at the University of Winnipeg, Victor Batzel, Peter Brown, John Hample, Herb Mays, Jim Naylor, and Nolan Reilly, have read sections of the manuscript and confronted me with its strengths and weaknesses. Though he has probably forgotten it by now, Peter George originally suggested the topic and was responsible at a critical juncture for its continuation. John Weaver and Gerry Tulchinsky continued to challenge and encourage me in the project. Finally, some of the most enjoyable hours in the research were spent with John Fierheller, discussing methodology and staring at tables of numbers in pursuit of meaningful trends.

As well, I thank the staffs of the National Archives of Canada, the Archives of Ontario, the Baker Library of Harvard University, and the Office of the City Clerk of the City of Brantford, for their patience and assistance.

In a different form, chapter 3 appeared as "'Good for All He Would Ask': Credit and Debt in the Transition to Industrial Capitalism – The Case of Mid-Nineteenth Century Brantford, Ontario," *Histoire sociale – Social History* 20 (May 1987): 79–100, and is published here with the journal's permission.

My thanks are also due to McGill-Queen's University Press and in particular Philip Cercone, Donald Akenson, Peter Goheen, Ann Quinn, and Joan McGilvray for their commitment to the book. Special thanks are due to Judy Williams for her care in editing the manuscript.

Without financial assistance from the Aid to Scholarly Publications Programme, using funds from the Social Science and Humanities Research Council of Canada, this book could not have been published. The University of Winnipeg generously provided an additional subvention for publishing costs.

Edith protests that I have thanked her enough by "getting the damn thing finished," and so, I shall not offend her further by offering platitudes.

A Particular Condition in Life

Introduction

In 1884 Thomas Cowherd, a tinsmith self-employed in Brantford, Ontario, for more than forty years, realized a long and deeply felt ambition by publishing a volume of his own poetry. Much of *The Emigrant Mechanic and Other Tales in Verse* had been conceived and composed over the many years he had toiled at his bench. Some poems had been printed before in the local newspapers or had been read by the "Tinsmith Rhymer," as Cowherd was known in Brantford, before gatherings in the Mechanics' Institute or in the town hall, but publication preserved his work as a testimony to his life's achievements. Though he confessed to some licence in embroidering the details of his life, he maintained that the essentially factual basis of his writing authenticated his art.

Cowherd's poetry recorded his own "pilgrim's progress" through life. His ambitions and identity were wrapped up in his trade, so that transitions in his work conformed to changes in his life course, and vice versa. Cowherd was "born in one of the humblest ranks in life" in Westmoreland in England's Lake District about 1817, and his father confronted some difficulty in arranging an apprenticeship for his son. Apprenticeship challenged young Tom not just to learn a trade, but also to forge a good and moral character. Though subjected to rude tricks and pranks, even vicious abuse, by some of the journeymen in the workshop, he refused as he matured in life and craft to adopt the behaviour of the worst of his workmates. He worked diligently to learn his trade, he claimed; he "did maintain / A due respect for those above him placed"; he avoided the temptations of idleness and drunkenness during holidays; and "in his eighteenth year, / He did as Christian, publicly appear." His "Master's confidence" rewarded him for "his sober and industrious conduct."

While an apprentice, he became fascinated by the immigration literature which promised opportunities for advancement to those coming to British North America. When he finished his training, he and his parents left for Canada in 1837. Initially Cowherd laboured on a bush farm in the Brantford area, but finding agricultural work not to his liking, he became a travelling tinker. Despite his itinerancy, Tom remained connected to a Brantford congregation of Independentists, a Methodist schismatic sect. He fell in love with one of its members, but despaired of marrying until another member of the congregation lent him money to set up his own shop in Brantford. With his achievement of independence and full maturity, "The Emigrant Mechanic" ends.

Married and independent at his craft, Cowherd found great joy in his family and in his garden. His poetry describes his domestic life, the pain of losing his first wife, his pride in and love for his children and friends, and the quiet pleasures of his home, but it reveals little of his work after marriage. Nonetheless, non-domestic themes remained important. For example, "Stanzas. Written Immediately after Seeing the 'Huron' Locomotive, for the First Time, at Cainsville, January 6, 1854" celebrated the material progress of his adopted home, at the same time as it entreated the town's boosters not to "forget the poor ... / For do they not, with constant toil, such works as this complete?" In a similar vein, in November 1857, he wrote "Winter's Ravages. An Appeal to the Rich on Behalf of the Poor" to solicit help for the unemployed "skilled mechanics [who] want the means of life." Taking up their cause, Cowherd expected workingmen to be worthy of his defence and the aid and respect which they might receive as a result. His poems exhorted, "Put thy shoulder to the wheel," "Mechanics, use your utmost skill, and ply each brawny arm" to make Brantford prosper. In celebrating these achievements, "Let all our conduct ... be orderly and quiet, / And none lay out a single cent in drunkenness and riot." Cowherd's writing defended the social contract between the responsible and the respectable which he saw as the basis for a Christian community.[1]

Was it sheer vanity which led Thomas Cowherd to think that the readers of the 1880s would be interested in and might profit from the example of his early life and his social commentary of thirty years before? If so, Cowherd did not preen alone. A surprising amount of biography and autobiography, and other instructive literature, was written or published in Brantford around the same time.

Thomas S. Shenston, formerly a harnessmaker and later Brant County registrar and loan company president, authored several collections of spiritual advice, wrote moral stories on social issues for the local newspaper, and submitted letters to the editor which gave his own example as a lesson to workingmen dissatisfied with their lot.[2] The *History of the County of Brant*, published in 1883 by the Toronto firm of Warner, Beers and Co., contained biographies of more than sixty businessmen in Brantford. In 1888 the Brantford *Expositor*, which from the 1870s had highlighted the achievements of local self-made men, published more fulsome articles on the city's most successful men, "Our Folks. Men whom We Delight to Honor."[3] The crowning work in this genre was *The Canadian Album: Men of Canada; or, Success by Example*, a five-volume work put out by the Brantford firm of Bradley, Garretson and Co. between 1890 and 1896. The first four volumes were edited by the Rev. William Cochrane of Brantford's Zion Presbyterian Church.[4]

The books, biographical dictionaries, local histories, and newspaper articles that appeared from the 1870s expressed a pride in personal and collective achievements, both material and moral. Brantford's exemplars of success through independence and self-initiative had realized the ambitions of many of those immigrants who had selected British North America as a promising new home. Yet Cowherd, Shenston, and others could not help but be aware of how fundamentally their community and social relationships within it had changed over their lifetimes. Indeed their testimonies implicitly communicated that awareness. They evinced a sincere desire to understand the social transformations in very personal terms. Their life histories and prescriptions for advancement by others constituted not mere didacticism, though clearly they remained convinced that their own lives offered object lessons. But each *apologia pro vita sua* also sought understanding and validation from others. By suggesting that what they had achieved could be attained by others, they denied that their lives had been exceptional and sought to reduce the social distance which their success had produced between themselves and others. To understand themselves and to lead others to understand, they put their memories into writing.

What provoked such literary effusion is a matter for speculation at best. Zygmunt Bauman has maintained that memory is a critical element in class formation: "Memory is the after-life of history. It is through memory that history continues to live in the hopes, the ends, and the expectations of men and women as they seek to make sense of the business of life, to find a pattern in chaos, to construe familiar solutions to unfamiliar worries. ... In its after-life, history reincarnates as a Utopia which guides, and is guided by, the struggles of the present."[5] Cowherd, Shenston, and Cochrane believed something had changed. They were all well into their sixties in the 1880s, and it seemed to them that their generation was passing. They also were surely aware that the opportunities open to their generation no longer were presented to those who followed. Industrial capitalism was restructuring Canadian society, and an immigrant society in which ambitious newcomers might achieve independence through self-employment, as Cowherd and Shenston had done, for example, was being replaced by one in which recourse to wage labour in factories and large commercial enterprises was becoming for more and more men a lifetime condition of work.

Just as one might refer to the making of the working class during this period, so too it is fitting to write of the making of the bourgeoisie. Industrial capitalism had as profound an impact upon mid-nineteenth-century Canadian businessmen as it did upon workers. If Brantford, Ontario, was in any way representative of broader social and economic developments, then in the 1860s and 1870s business became a more restricted and elitist activity, and class relations and class structure became more clearly defined. This study concentrates upon one salient dimension of change, the restructuring of self-employment in business as a social activity.

Self-employment, or "working on one's own account," to use the common mid-nineteenth-century phrase, refers in this study to those people who held, through ownership or tenancy, the means of producing and distributing goods and services. The concern has been to identify all of those people – overwhelmingly men as it turned out – who on some occasion during a particular year were self-employed in business in the production and/or distribution of goods and services.

Not dealt with, since they were salaried employees, were the three or four bank managers and the Grand Trunk Railway superintendent in Brantford in any cross-section year. Significantly, the fortunes of managers were not tied to place, but to a corporation whose activities transcended any place. An important theme of the book, explored by studying the contemporary discourse on independence, is the community-based nature of manly independence and the contemporary perception that changes associated with the transition to industrial capitalism diminished the control that the self-employed had over their community. The presence of managers represented an alternative career path to that of self-employment. Nor were lawyers considered among the self-employed in business, since education determined entry into the professions in a way that was not experienced by those in business.

The occasionally self-employed subcontractor, the carpenter or plasterer who might take a contract but also on occasion worked for wages, however, was included, since his contracting demonstrated an autonomy, albeit in some cases brief and of necessity, from the wage labour relationship which was inherent in the transition to industrial capitalism. Intermittent self-employment or self-employment at the same time as waged work was judged significant not because the carpenter who took a single contract (and in several years they have nearly all been identified) had joined a new class, but because if he sustained that particular condition over time he would belong to a particular class, might become conscious of membership in that class, and be recognized by others as holding that identity. Self-employment, then, must be joined with persistence in business to define the objective features of class membership. Starting by identifying the self-employed casts a wide net for potential class membership which can then be narrowed by an analysis of persistence. Class as experience must perforce be dynamic and contingent.

Self-employment in the 1840s and 1850s was so pervasive in Brantford, and within the capacity of so many men, that its meaning in defining class distinctions was imprecise. In 1852 one of every three men twenty-one years of age or older had been, was, or would be self-employed in at least one of the six decadal cross-section years from 1830 to 1881 for which it has been possible in this study to identify the self-employed. (How many more of the men in Brantford in 1852 were in business in years not examined or in places other than Brantford is beyond estimation.) Wage workers could be thought of either as men who simply had not yet accumulated the experience or capital to be their own bosses or as men who had already been self-employed and might well be so again. As a social boundary, self-employment was permeable to crossings in both directions several times in a man's life, and so probably conformed as much to a stage in life, another manifestation of social maturity, as to class division. Recognizing that a man might cross that boundary several times should force a rethinking of class membership.

Most efforts to define class have employed static criteria to determine position and identity at any point in time rather than over time. For scholars of the working class, debates over class have seldom questioned the boundaries of membership, since wage labour easily marks the property relationship which relegates some but not others to the proletarian condition. Rather, concern has been directed to the experiences, the practice, the culture, which have brought some workers, as E.P. Thompson has explained, to "feel and articulate the identity of their interests as between themselves, and as against other men whose interests are different from (and usually opposed to) theirs."[6] According to Marx, as R.S. Neale has reminded us, class exists latently in itself, objectively defined, but awaits history to awaken its action for itself.[7] History, the passage of time, produces the realization of class, which is the real importance of class. As Eric Hobsbawm has put it, "class in the full sense only comes into existence at the historical moment when classes begin to acquire consciousness of themselves as such."[8] Since, from the Marxist perspective at least, the working class is the revolutionary class, it is its realization of its own identity through struggle which has become the most important problem for historical inquiry. As Neale has too bluntly declared, "the problem of class consciousness is essentially a question of the class consciousness of the proletariat."[9] Less attention, therefore, need be directed to opposing classes and the problem of their consciousness.

Recent interest in the other classes has followed from the study of the working class and has confronted theoretical and methodological challenges in studying what, as Geoffrey Crossick and Heinz-Gerhard Haupt among others have regretted, appears at times as the social residuum.[10] Scholars have encountered considerable difficulty in trying to find, *ex post facto*, the criteria which best describe those who are left over in society once the working class has been extracted. Too many variations in condition appear to exist to permit easy treatment of everyone else as a class, even a highly stratified one.

Stanislaw Ossowski raised the possibility of defining an intermediate class by pointing out that Marx's two relational dichotomies defining class – those who sold their labour power and those who purchased it; those who owned the means of production and those who did not – do not necessarily have the same social boundaries. In the middle are those who own the means of production but hire no labour.[11] Yet the purity of such a definition of the middle has seemed to some to focus empirical study on too small a group. Thus, Crossick and Haupt, like Bechhofer and Elliott, have maintained that some petits bourgeois may employ labour, but only on so limited a scale that, like those who hire none, their livelihoods remain mainly dependent upon their capital and their own labour and that of their families. But, even if this qualification makes the historian more comfortable in dealing with petty property holders as a group, it confuses the issue of an intermediate class, since it remains empirically impossible to demarcate the limits of the petite and haute bourgeoisie. Scholars must then decide if the petite bourgeoisie is still a class or merely a stratum. Bechhofer and Elliott, for their part, have decided that the upward blur of definition renders the petite bourgeoisie a stratum, not a class, though Crossick and Haupt suggest that it is the marginality and lack of clarity that offer the most interesting and profitable study. The latter position, if taken a step further, comes close to Peter Stearns's suggestion that social class, especially when applied to the middle class, is not so much a thing living in history as a useful "heuristic device" needed to sort out "subtleties in power relationships and outlook."[12]

Additional complications were posed by Geoffrey Crossick's earlier contention that those in the new white collar occupations of the nineteenth and twentieth century, most notably clerks, but also managers, commercial travellers, school teachers, and even shop assistants, ought to be considered part of the lower middle class. "A genuine definition of the lower middle class ... must take ... account of both self-ascription and the effective stratification that is demonstrated through the evidence of social relationships." In other words, to be lower middle class required that one think that one was lower middle class and that one associate with others who one thought were also lower middle class.[13] Once the significance of wage labour has been set aside for those whose work kept their hands clean, it becomes possible to abandon opposing interests as grounds for class definition and even, as Stuart M. Blumin has recently argued, to posit that classes may be aware of themselves yet unaware of others. Without the necessity of relationships to other classes, class then for Blumin can be defined by the convergence of shared social experiences of work, consumption, residence, voluntary association, and family organization and strategy. While work constitutes the most important dimension of social experience in Blumin's schema, the fundamental characteristic of work is the distinction between manual and non-manual labour, not the sale of labour power or the ownership of capital.[14]

Emphasizing the manual/non-manual work dichotomy and avoiding the others conveniently removes the contradiction between the white collar worker's wage labour relationship and his frequent espousal of bourgeois values. Ideology can then reinforce class membership. For example, though Michael Katz, Mark Stern, and Michael Doucet have advanced a two-class, rather than three-class, model of the social organization of early industrial capitalism, they have decided that those in white collar occupations ought to be considered members of the capitalist class because of their presumed affinity with those owning the means of production.[15] The authors took no note of Gregory Anderson's explanation of the source of Victorian clerks' loyalty to their employers. Paternalism, close working contact with employers, and their own desire for self-employment led clerks to attribute hardships to personal failings. Either that, or they believed that forces beyond their employers' control, and to which they both were subject, explained their low wages, diminishing opportunities for advancement, and unpleasant conditions of employment.[16] In the end, the selective combination of criteria is unsatisfying: why should ideological conformity be sufficient to convey bourgeois status to non-manual, but not manual, workers? Surely ideology has cloaked opposing class interests rather than reinforced class identity.[17]

The problems of such quantifiers and empiricists as Katz and Blumin in framing an empirically useful definition of class reveal a more general theoretical limitation. A research design which assumes that at any moment all individuals can be assigned a class position fails to recognize that individual consciousness takes time to form. (One could, of course, avoid the problem by claiming to study structures rather than individuals and their consciousness, but this seems methodologically too convenient.) At any moment in time, society can be partitioned to place all men and women in the workforce on one side or the other of some line of demarcation; the next moment in time may find those formerly on one side now on the other. There is a danger in allowing the successful research procedure – the ability to determine any individual's relationship to the means of production – to become the interpretation itself. Class is an experience which, again as Thompson has argued strenuously, an individual lives over time, not just at the moment for which data survive to permit cross-sectional analysis.[18] Nor does identity change as soon as the boundary is crossed. Charles Stephenson has maintained that frequently working-class rather than bourgeois values led men to cross the line, to become self-employed. "A quest for dignity – an effort to flee from the arbitrariness of the capitalist employer," or perhaps to achieve security in old age, motivated workers to open shops or ply their trades on their own account. [19]

Acceptance of the temporal dimension of class should be a necessary component of the conceptualization and analysis of the bourgeoisie. Neither the bourgeoisie nor the working class was born fully formed, as has been implied by Katz and company; for them class formation is anterior to their study, occurring prior to 1850, a proposition which few other Canadian social historians would like to defend. Does this mean that class in itself, if not for itself, was absent in mid-nineteenth-century Ontario society? Not necessarily; it was in a process of becoming, not being.

While working-class historians have easily accepted the notion of class as a process of becoming, historians of the petite bourgeoisie have been more reluctant to admit change into their definition, suspicious, perhaps, of the Marxist assertion that the lower middle class is an inessential and transitional class, destined to disappear as classes become polarized. When such historians do admit change, it is change that has produced a continuity of the middle; Arno J. Mayer, for example, has argued for a "second 'making of the lower middle class'" in the mid-nineteenth century with the proliferation of service, technical, and professional occupations. That the first lower middle class was self-employed, while the second engaged in wage labour, was of significance, but 'a thick ideational cement fills the cracks in the structure of common economic interests.'[20]

Once one accepts that everyone need not be consigned to a particular class at each and every moment in time, that men and women are in social motion, advancing and falling, then one can avoid some of the awkward and contradictory propositions in middle-class historiography and quantitative methodology. Thus, self-employment need in the first instance be no more than one possible relationship to the means of production in a society. Certain historical circumstances and social processes may lead people in that sort of relationship to become conscious of their class membership. Thus, persistence in self-employment, rather than self-employment itself, ought to be the precondition for the definition of a bourgeoisie.

Adding persistence in self-employment as a dimension of bourgeois identity does not resolve the problem of the great disparity in status between the small shopkeeper and the extensive wholesaler, or the master artisan and the manufacturer. It does, however, explore the reproduction of petite and haute bourgeoisie and the rigidity of lines between them, for failures in any stratum created openings either to be engrossed by those already in positions of advantage or to be seized by those eager to move up the social scale. The first step was self-employment, which qualitatively distinguished businessman from worker. From among those who had achieved that condition in life, the processes of persistence in business and acquisition of wealth acted to form the bourgeoisie over time.

This study endeavours first to analyse the ways in which self-employment was experienced at several cross-sections in time, 1830, 1842, 1851–2, 1861, 1871, and 1880–1[21] and over time from cross-section to cross-section, and second to examine the ways in which individuals sought to understand their own position within changing social and class definitions and to act with others in the same position. The intent is to combine an analysis of an objective feature of class with its subjective awareness. History and memory, then, figure prominently in the formation of class.

Any inquiry seeking to generalize from the individual to the social must necessarily decide upon the most appropriate social boundaries. The decision to examine class formation within a community, and in Brantford, Ontario, in particular, is not founded on the assumption that the universe reveals itself in its smallest parts. Nor does it contend that Brantford was representative of general social change in Victorian Canada, though obviously it was not unique. Rather, in a society largely populated by immigrants, perceptions of business and personal opportunity arose most commonly from perceptions of place. If a man were to immigrate, where might he find success? Immigration literature and gazetteers offered plenty of suggestions. As well, the municipal boosterism of so many Ontario urban centres from the 1830s to the 1850s sought to maximize locational advantages through transportation facilities, which might capture the flow of commerce. Thus, if people tied their fates to places, then community ought to provide the best framework for a study of the extent to which aspirations were realized.

Some places, of course, won, and others lost, enhancing or compromising the ambitions of those who located there. Cobourg went bankrupt competing with Port Hope; Kingston failed to acquire an abundant hinterland. Hamilton never displaced Toronto as the province's leading commercial centre. Brantford's promoters had no exceptional ambitions, though their schemes may have been grander than some. Brantford typified those western Ontario towns and small cities which, John McCallum argued, grew from the agricultural prosperity of their immediate hinterlands.[22] The prospect of staple-based prosperity induced the town's boosters to improve the transportation infrastructure essential to realize their ambitions. Though their village numbered only three hundred residents in 1830, they joined in the promotion of the Grand River Navigation Co. to improve water connections with Lake Erie and the Welland Canal. By 1852 the town had grown to a population of 3,877, and the promise of more extensive growth based on the transport of staple commodities by rail from the continental mid-west through the town to the American seaboard led to municipal support for the Buffalo, Brantford, and Goderich Railway. Weighty indebtedness following the crash of 1857 and lingering stagnation thereafter ended dreams of commercial empire.[23] The disenchanted left Brantford, reducing its population from 7,266 in 1857 to 6,251 in 1861.

Through the 1860s and 1870s, local attention focused on the possibilities of industry as a foundation for the urban economy. The demand of farmers in Brantford's immediate hinterland for implements encouraged the development of a number of farm equipment and metal fabricating industries, while the town council's willingness to bonus major employers attracted other industries, most notably the Grand Trunk Railway's car shops. The prospect of factory employment attracted people to the town, and its population rose from 8,107 in 1871 to 10,555 in 1881.

The peculiarities of place, founded in settlement patterns, the resource endowments of hinterlands, the weight of commercially driven growth, and the mixed legacy of boosterism contributed to the uneven progress of industrial capitalism from region to region, from community to community, and from industry to industry within communities, through the late 1860s and 1870s. For example, the regional differences in the social origins of the Canadian industrial elite of the 1880s that William Acheson has noted presumably reflected different social structures and processes associated with different regions. The most significant variation was in the relative importance of inherited advantage in upward social mobility. From Acheson, opportunity would appear to have been more open to immigrants and artisans the farther west one went, from the Maritimes through Quebec to Ontario.[24] Within regions, contradictions in the historical literature possibly imply some qualitative difference from place to place. On the basis of impressionistic evidence admittedly, John McCallum and Jacob Spelt have argued that many manufacturers in small and medium-sized Ontario urban centres had started out as artisans.[25] Katz, Doucet, and Stern, in their study of Hamilton from 1851 to 1871, have dismissed such prospects for advancement as "mythical," concluding that class position was transmitted from generation to generation. However, this and their contention that "journeyman often was a permanent status, not a phase in the life cycle" are belied by their casual admission of "the inability to distinguish master artisans from those they employed" except in 1871.[26] Even were their conclusion not subject to qualification, one would know only that in Hamilton it was so; elsewhere the pattern of social mobility may well have been different.

Several factors combined in the 1840s and 1850s to create a large number of business opportunities in Brantford and to provide men with limited assets their best chance between 1830 and 1880 to accumulate wealth. As in other urban centres, poor transportation and high freight charges, which only luxury items or essentials could

bear, created a decentralized trading system of imperfectly integrated local urban economies. General merchandising businesses
might grow fairly large by catering to the many needs of a relatively
small population, but more specialized factory production was clearly
constrained by dependence on the local market, the difficulty in
mobilizing capital through partnerships, and the attraction of surplus
capital to commodity speculations. In consequence, the small enterprises of those who produced goods and services for local consumption were protected from outside competition.

Within this context, small-scale enterprise was also supported by
the value placed upon independence and the responsibility felt by
many to encourage it. A community of immigrants shared the experience of mobility in search of opportunity. A sense of mutual
responsibility was expressed in the help that employers, countrymen,
co-religionists, kin, and friends gave the deserving, like Cowherd,
who needed some support to achieve and sustain self-employment.
Character and the recognition of commonality, as much as, if not at
times more than, pecuniary backing, could secure credit. Still the
ideology of independence did not spring unfettered from generous
hearts. The advancement of place, and the realization of individual
ambitions within it, required that the collective credit of the community be pledged. Ultimately, the promise of townspeople to tax
themselves secured the borrowing which built the navigation works
and the railroad, and the various other artifacts of urban ambition.
Brantford's boosters, its wealthy merchants and speculators, recognized and accepted the desire of the town's shopkeepers and artisans
for independence as the price of their political support. Thus, the
ideology of independence, nonetheless sincerely held, also negotiated
social relations in the commercial economy.

Through the late 1840s and 1850s, self-employment grew in pace
with the town. Increasing demand for goods and service from prosperous Brant County farmers and a growing town population were
met by roughly proportionate increases in the number of men who
were self-employed. The same proportion of the adult male work force,
one in four men, conducted business on their own account in 1852
as in 1861. Moreover, small-scale enterprise produced success more
frequently in the 1850s than either of the two subsequent decades.
To a degree, their limited assets insulated small shopkeepers and artisans from the speculations in grain, lumber, and land which entrapped
and ruined many of Brantford's wealthiest following the crash of 1857.
At the same time the failure of the elite undermined established
interests, created opportunities for those who could replace them, and
reinforced the openness of the social structure to small businessmen.

Small- and moderate-scale businessmen may have avoided the immediate consequences of the depression of 1857, but that turn in the business cycle coincided with the beginnings of longer-term structural change in the urban and rural economies. Depressed commodity prices, soil depletion, and demographic pressure upon the land reduced the farm incomes which had supported Brantford's economy. Between 1861 and 1866 more men were driven out of business, especially from small enterprise, than during any other five-year period in the mid-nineteenth century. Economic recovery and renewed urban population growth in the last half of the 1860s did not restore the old patterns of business organization, however. By the mid-1860s the rail system was breaking down the protective isolation of the province's many local economies. The Buffalo, Brantford and Goderich Railway was taken over by and merged into the Grand Trunk in 1863. Ambitious local manufacturers and wholesalers could as a consequence serve a wider market. But traffic flowed both ways, and craft producers had to compete now with retailers selling factory goods made elsewhere. Larger, rather than more, businesses met growing consumer demand in the late 1860s and through the 1870s.

The business population was reduced by approximately 40 per cent in relative size between 1860 and 1880. Only about one in seven adult males in the work force was self-employed at the end of the period of this study. Principally affected were the independent tradesmen and master artisans who had been the backbone of the business community in the 1850s. Fewer and fewer craft producers took the place of those who went out of business in the 1860s and 1870s. Opportunities were presented instead in commerce, and the retailer had replaced the self-employed artisan as the most common businessman by 1880.

The retail merchant of the 1870s, more than the artisan of the 1850s, depended upon sources of supply and credit from outside the community, from wholesalers and financial institutions. The terms of credit changed too, as lenders, reacting against the previous long credit system, wanted to know more about borrowers and sought to secure their advances with assets more tangible than good character. The resulting contraction of credit contributed to the increasing value of business debt secured by mortgage in the 1860s and 1870s.

Although commercial mortgage debt grew more rapidly, industry always bore a disproportionately large share of business debt because of the large amounts of capital needed to finance plant expansion. Manufacturers found considerable sums of mortgage money at home for this purpose. A number of the successful merchants, who had accumulated wealth and had survived the 1860s, invested in mortgages on factories in the 1870s. The flow of capital from commerce to industry contributed in part to the redistribution of wealth in Brantford in the 1870s. At the beginning of the period under review, men in commerce held a disproportionately large share of wealth in the town, as indicated by the municipal tax assessment rolls; by 1880 men in industry, especially in metal fabricating, flour milling, and carriage manufacturing, held the larger share.

Capital formation in Brantford's industrial sector not only derived from the attraction of mortgage investment. Despite the restructuring of the economy, some tradesmen and small-scale producers did gradually accumulate wealth. Prominent among the industrial elite, and among the leading merchants as well, were men who had started in business with little and had slowly worked their way to the top. In most cases their rise was not spectacular, but resulted from a long association with the community which had firmly established their credit and reputations. Yet, the very success of small businessmen from the 1850s and 1860s reduced the prospects of new and small businessmen in the 1870s. Success perpetuated itself and entrenched interests, as those already in business for ten years in 1871 were more likely than men recently self-employed to continue in business for another ten years and to accumulate wealth over the decade. At any time, about half of all businesses lasted less than ten years. Nevertheless, by the 1870s the prospects of new businessmen were considerably less appealing than those of established businessmen. Two-thirds of the former, but only a quarter of the latter, went out of business between 1871 and 1880. Significantly, business discontinuation was not synonymous with the proletarianization of the petite bourgeoisie, at least not in Brantford. Men who went out of business left, rather than accept wage labour locally. The stigma of failure and the greater social distance between employer and employee in an industrializing economy made it uncomfortable for a man and his family to stay. Probably, too, the hope of finding a better place to try self-employment once again drove men on in pursuit of more promising fields of fortune.

In such demanding circumstances, a man needed some advantage or connection to embark in business. By 1881 business had ceased to an activity of newcomers, as Canadians outnumbered immigrants. As well, in the 1870s, more so than at any other time, new businessmen already had some lengthy association with the town, having been born there or at least resided there ten years prior to becoming self-employed. A growing number were sons of men who had been in business, suggesting that by the end of the period a generational transition was occurring which closed off opportunities to outsiders.

Business by the 1870s was a different activity from what it had been in the 1850s, and businessmen were different sorts of men. The shrinkage of the business population, the diminishing probability of advancement for those starting out with limited assets, and the importance of connection and advantage distinguished the self-employed from the employed. These changes also qualified a major way in which masculine independence had been expressed, and frustrated ambitions for independence and dignity contributed to a reassessment of cultural values. In the 1850s independence in self-employment did not need to be personified; observers did not need to point to any individual's success to affirm the virtues of hard work, initiative, respectability, and responsibility. They were self-evident. By the 1870s examples of success, as offered by Cowherd, Shenston, or Cochrane, served not only to remind the community of the efficacy of individual effort but also to legitimize the positions of the successful.

Challenged by an increasingly assertive working class in the 1870s, most notably during the Nine Hours movement, Brantford's business elite struggled desperately to retain control of the apparatus of municipal government and to sustain the social consensus which had supported a political economy of local development for two decades. From the late 1840s the town's leading businessmen had argued that booster policies designed to enhance Brantford's commercial position would benefit the entire community. The support of small property owners, shopkeepers, master artisans, and independent tradesmen, so numerous in pre-industrial Brantford, was essential if municipal finances were to be pledged to the canal and railroad schemes promoted by Brantford's merchants and manufacturers. So long as this petit bourgeois stratum remained convinced of the merits of the politics of community particularism, it accepted elite political leadership. By the 1870s, however, it was becoming only too apparent that forces beyond Brantford were undermining the peculiar opportunities of place and the ability of community to help a deserving man exploit them. In consequence, the patronage of a national state and the protection of a national political economy increasingly appealed to those whose interests seemed poorly served by the urban community and by those who had controlled it.

The social basis of the National Policy is not the topic of this study. Yet, late-century changes in social mobility and the implications which these had for the cultural values associated with independence did contribute to the political climate which produced that policy. Thus, the investigation of the transformation of self-employment as a social activity which follows explores one more dimension of "The Critical Years" in Canada.

1 Business Enterprise and Social Relations in a Mid-Victorian Town

Brantford's factories – the machine works, foundries, farm implement factories, and railroad repair shops – were the most visible evidence of mid-Victorian social change. As John McCallum has explained, early industrialization was widely dispersed throughout Ontario,[1] and Brantford, like other small cities in southwestern Ontario in the 1870s, already possessed a significant industrial sector. Beyond the bricks and mortar of new factories – or just as often, the wood and nails – were very basic changes in social relations and ways of earning a living. More and more men and women went to work for wages in the factories. Raphael Samuel has cautioned against interpreting the advance of industrial capitalism as a relentless process of proletarianization, however. In Britain the industrial revolution spawned "alternate forms of capitalist enterprise," small units of production alongside factories, human skill and hand technology employed alongside steam-powered machinery. Ian McKay, in a study of the baking and confectionery industry in Halifax, Nova Scotia, accepted the "uneven and combined" development, as Samuel termed the coexistence of various forms and scales of enterprise, but, perhaps more than Samuel, McKay has recognized the effects on social relationships. "The permeability of the line between small master and journeyman created an ambivalent sense of class consciousness in both groups." Samuel and McKay have provided significant qualifications to our conceptualization of industrialization.[2] The questions remain now, however, how many new opportunities were created, what sorts they were, and whether or not artisans whose crafts were displaced could seize them.

As Brantford's economy industrialized, the number of people in business did rise substantially, from 238 in 1852 to 372 in 1880.[3] But numerical increase masked what surely has been one of the most important findings of this study – namely, the relative decline, by about 40 per cent, in the level of self-employment within the adult male population over this period, from one in four to one in seven. Larger-scale businesses in the late 1860s and the 1870s, rather than more businesses, as had been the case before, met increases in demand. At the same time, local production satisfied less of local demand as specialized mercantile businesses began to retail a wider range of consumer goods. Retailing was the growth area in Brantford's economy from the mid-1860s, and new retail outlets compensated for the ever-dwindling number of independent tradesmen and craft producers. Attrition among this latter group, then, contributed significantly to the declining relative size of the business population. New opportunities there may have been by the 1870s, but they were too few to support as large a proportion of the population in self-employment as in the 1850s, and the larger scale of industrial and wholesaling enterprise necessarily meant that relatively more people sold their labour power than employed their own labour.

Accompanying declining independence in work were changes in social relations. The organization of workers in the foundries, machine works, and car shops, and their first strike in 1860, introduced industrial discord into community life. In the disputes that continued thereafter, not only did workers and employers bargain over wages and conditions of work, but implicitly they negotiated the social meaning of wage labour in a community previously characterized by pervasive self-employment.

The argument advanced here, and the evidence supporting it, contradict Gordon Darroch's recent assertion that historians have exaggerated the crisis of the petite bourgeoisie in late nineteenth century Ontario and that proletarianization was a fate more feared than suffered. What follows casts no light on the fate of farmers, the stronger dimension of his thesis; rather it addresses the fate of independent artisans. Direct comparisons, however, are frustrated immediately by Darroch's failure to distinguish between masters and journeymen. He has attached little significance to this distinction, since his sample is predominantly rural and he assumes that artisans in rural society were generally self-employed. Thus, the mark of proletarianization for the artisan is not journeyman status, since that is not identified, but a change to a labourer's occupation.[4] This is not good enough.

This study has endeavoured to identify as many of the self-employed as possible, about 1,100 individuals in all at six cross-section years: 1830, 1842, 1851–2, 1861, 1871, and 1880–1. Only half of their 190 occupations explicitly denoted self-employment.[5] The sources for this study reported a number of the other attributes of self-employment. The 1842 census listed the number of workers employed. The 1852 census schedule noted places of business, making it possible to identify those who combined residence and workplace or who lived beside their place of business. The 1851 assessment rolls recorded the value of stock in trade if it exceeded £50.[6] The 1861 census, scrupulously enumerated in Brantford, required the value of capital invested in business, value of raw materials and kind of motive power used in production, number of employees and wages paid, and value of business conducted.[7] The industrial schedule of 1871 listed those manufacturers and artisans engaged in production. The 1871 and 1880 assessment rolls distinguished between householders and tenants, the latter renting business accommodation. An 1880 business directory compensated for the lack of any criterion of self-employment but occupation in the 1881 census, as did the R.G. Dun and Co. credit reports, in manuscript from about 1848 and published quarterly from 1864. Newspaper advertisements and articles named the most visible businessmen, while the Brantford *Expositor*'s year-end building reports for 1870 and 1877–81 listed everyone who took a construction contract in those years. No doubt some businessmen have been missed, but there seems no reason to believe that self-employment was more difficult to identify in any specific cross-section year.

SELF-EMPLOYMENT BEFORE INDUSTRIALIZATION

More pervasive self-employment in the late 1840s and 1850s should not necessarily be taken as evidence of some pre-industrial "golden age" of petty enterprise. The "good old days" lasted two decades at most, the mid-1840s to the mid-1860s. Brantford's economy from the late 1820s through the early 1840s supported very few businesses of any sort. The lack of competition in the village did attract ambitious shopkeepers and artisans anticipating the imminence of a frontier boom,[8] and perhaps three in four men were self-employed. But once set up, most found little demand for their services. Besides factors which affected Upper Canada generally, such as the erratic performance of commercial agriculture and the social dislocation arising from depression and rebellion in 1837–8, Brantford suffered from local peculiarities. Much of its proximate hinterland in Brantford Township had not been ceded to the Crown by the Six Nations Indians and remained part of the Grand River Reserve until 1841. By that date only about 40 per cent of the township's farmland had been brought under cultivation. Notwithstanding Thomas F. McIlwraith's caveat that Upper Canadian roads were not so bad as observers reported, the Brantford to Hamilton road did pass through some difficult swamp, and the frequent disrepair and collapse of the bridge over the Grand River led the travelling public, farmers, and the shippers of staple commodities to avoid the village. Most traffic passed to the north along the Governor's Road through the village of Paris. Business grew slowly: in 1830 taxes were assessed against fourteen merchant stores in Brantford Township; ten years later there were only four more, despite the increase in the township's population from 1,400 to 4,900.[9]

Whether or not Brantford was less hospitable to shopkeepers and artisans than other places is impossible to say. Darrell Norris's study of Adolphustown has revealed high levels of transiency, approximating 20 per cent every two years in the 1810s and 1820s.[10] Outward migration was probably as high in Brantford. Tradesmen especially were out of place and marginal. A number of the disenchanted complained to the commissioner of Crown lands in 1830 that "the advantages which this place possesses for commercial business are over-rated." Their departure troubled those who remained. Jedidiah Jackson, a leading merchant, reported that "our village remains in the same inactive state ... and some of our best Mechanicks [sic] and Merchants are moving to Nithsdale [Paris] our rival Village."[11]

Of the twenty-six businessmen resident in Brantford in 1830, fourteen were self-employed artisans plying a variety of trades. Few had resided long in Brantford, 75 per cent for less than two years. The gunsmith, baker, watchmaker, tailor, and hatter simply could not make a go of it. Two-thirds of the artisans left before 1836. Only by diversifying were businesses viable. The two shoemakers took on additional ventures: William Mathews, an Irish Methodist, acted as an auctioneer; Arunah Huntington, a pushing Yankee from Vermont, traded in leather and later general merchandise when not occupied at his bench. The tanner and the miller also farmed. Perhaps only the blacksmiths and carpenters could occupy themselves, since of all trades theirs were most needed on the settlement frontier.

The ten merchants and two innkeepers in 1830 fared better. Seventy per cent of them had been there more than three years and 30 per cent more than five years. By 1842 only three merchants and one innkeeper were still in business, but the eight others were all farming in the township. Some had started to farm even while in business. Douglas McCalla has questioned whether the Upper Canadian merchant intentionally used favourable terms of credit to expropriate farmland from indebted customers; "he could not farm it himself," he concluded.[12] But, if the Brantford case is representative, agriculture may well have appeared an alternative to frontier commerce for the small-time operator. For the major merchants, farming held little attraction, since their metropolitan connections gave them access to credit and capital to diversify their interests. John A. Wilkes and James Cockshutt had been well established as merchants in York before opening stores in Brantford. Others, like James Muirhead, who was associated with Colin C. Ferrie and Co. of Hamilton, were up-country junior partners in branches of metropolitan firms.[13] Besides running their businesses, they speculated in land, and owned grist and saw mills, carding and fulling mills, asheries, and distilleries, as well as contracting for mail transport and construction projects. Their general entrepreneurship likely connoted the limited local opportunities.

Brantford's leading merchants nonetheless were ambitious for their community and collaborated with businessmen in other Grand River Valley villages in hopes, largely unrealized, of developing the district. The damming of the Grand River at Dunnville to divert water into the Welland Canal raised the river's level sufficiently to permit navigation. With improvement, the Grand might become a major commercial artery. At a public meeting held in December 1827 at Lovejoy's Inn in Brantford, valley boosters decided to petition "the Legislature ... for a charter to incorporate a Company with sufficient Capital to make the Grand River navigable from Lake Erie to Brantford." Opposition from Hamilton and Dundas commercial interests stalled the assembly's consideration of the petition until 1832 when the Grand River Navigation Company finally was incorporated.[14] In 1836 Grand River Valley promoters, led by John A. Wilkes, again bested Head of Lake interests by obtaining the charter for the Gore District Mutual Fire Insurance Company.[15]

But Brantford's gains stimulated little growth. Not until 1842 did navigation reach Bunnell's Landing (now Cainsville), three miles below Brantford, and the final section, a cut across country, was not completed to the town until 1848.[16] Though artisans and manufacturers sought leases to the company's water power sites, the navigation itself never filled its promoters' ambitions, especially with the advent of railroads. Conditions in the early 1840s, then, were similar to the previous decade. The wealthiest merchants in the 1830s continued to dominate, but, for those with more meagre business assets, selling out to new arrivals seemed the surest way of realizing a profit. Forty-three per cent of those listed in the 1842 manuscript census as property owners but only 17 per cent of tenants left town before 1852. As Brian Osborne has explained, frontier urban centres did not easily exert commercial dominance over even their immediate hinterlands, and pedlars and artisans tramping the countryside might reduce business in even a prospering area.[17]

A few merchants could not control business opportunities in the late 1840s and 1850s. The urban economy grew too quickly, feeding on the prosperity of the wheat boom. And wheat put money in farmers' pockets and the tills of Brantford's businessmen. For example, Alexander Bunnell, the leading merchant miller, dealt exclusively in Brant County wheat and conducted nearly a half million dollars in business in 1856.[18]

Brantford's imperfect integration into a larger trading system protected small-scale producers and diminished the economies of scale that might have been achieved had it been easier to service wider markets. As late as 1862, even after rail trunk line construction was fairly well advanced, Alexander Galt, then minister of finance, estimated that transportation costs doubled the price of British manufactured goods in the Canadian market.[19] In consequence, as Ben Forster, among others, has noted, local production, either household or commercial, tended to satisfy much of local consumption,[20] and increases in demand were satisfied by roughly proportionate increases in the size of the business population. From 1852 to 1861 the town's population grew at an average annual rate of 5.4 per cent, while the number of businessmen increased from 238 to 356, an average growth rate which was only slightly slower at 4.6 per cent per year. Put another way, in 1852 there was one businessman for every 16.3 residents of the town and in 1861 one for every 17.6 residents. The rate of self-employment remained constant at one in four males over the age of sixteen who gave an occupation to the census enumerator in 1852 and 1861 (table 1.1).[21]

The rate of self-employment in Brantford the 1850s was relatively high. Paul Johnson has estimated that in Rochester, New York, in the 1820s about 20 per cent of men were self-employed.[22] The forces which were transforming social organization in that American city were only just beginning in Brantford in the 1860s.

Table 1.1
Self-Employment by Occupational Group, 1852–81

Occupational Group	1852			1861			1871			1881		
	N	% of All	Rate (%)	N	% of All	Rate (%)	N	% of All	Rate (%)	Rate	% of All	Rate (%)
Construction	33	14	18	61	17	27	59	16	16	58	14	14
Manufacturing:												
Food products	14	6	37	23	6	48	28	7	47	23	6	14
Apparel	33	14	25	35	10	19	31	8	23	14	4	12
Metalworking	17	7	19	27	8	13	18	5	7	23	6	5
Woodworking	17	7	28	23	6	30	19	5	24	14	4	14
Other	10	4	28	16	5	33	26	6	20	25	6	17
Commerce/ Service	114	48	67	171	48	78	204	53	59	243	60	44
All	238	100	25	356	100	25	385	100	19	400	100	14

Note: The numbers of men holding occupations which did not support self-employment in business were included in the calculation of the overall rate of self-employment, but not in the rate for specific occupational groups. These occupations are: the various railroad running trades and maintenance of way workers; labourers; farmers; professionals, including doctors, lawyers, dentists, teachers; government employees.

See "Appendix: Occupational Categories" for a list of the occupations assigned to each group.

STRATEGY AND STRUCTURE IN THE
METAL-FABRICATING INDUSTRY

The rather complicated history of the partnerships which organized Brantford's foundries in the 1850s through the mid-1860s demonstrated the difficulties in achieving large-scale operations. Not large by current standards, or even in comparison to some American factories of the day, they nonetheless demanded organizational complexity and financial commitments that were qualitatively different from craft shops. Differences of personality and business skills, market limitations, the attraction of alternate investments, and unforeseen disasters resulted in frequent organizational changes. At the same time, the ongoing efforts to consolidate foundries, tinshops, and retail outlets suggest an awareness of the benefits of scale and integration.

Philip C. VanBrocklin, a New Yorker who in 1820 had been a junior partner in the Long Point Furnace of Van Norman and Co. and in 1838 a partner with Elijah Leonard in a foundry in St Thomas, started Brantford's first foundry in 1841.[23] He received financial backing from one of the town's original businessmen, Arunah Huntington. The firm reported ten employees to the census enumerator in 1842. Though Huntington withdrew in 1844, the 1847 assessment roll indicates that he retained ownership of the business's tinshop and warerooms. Franklin P. Goold, a former Rochester, New York, grain merchant, replaced Huntington.[24] The firm of Goold, VanBrocklin and Co. did not last much longer than its predecessor and dissolved in 1848 when the senior partner turned down Goold's offer of $16,000 for his interest.[25] Then VanBrocklin struck an agreement with Thomas Winter, an English immigrant to Brantford by way of the West Indies, and Charles H. Waterous, a native of Vermont who had failed in several machine shop businesses in New York and Ohio. Waterous's contribution to VanBrocklin, Winter and Co. was crucial; his technical expertise and innovative ability transformed the country foundry into a factory producing steam engines. He probably brought little capital to the business, but nonetheless was made a partner, receiving a salary and a quarter share in the profits. In 1851 Ignatius Cockshutt, a general merchant, advanced VanBrocklin funds to expand the machine shop, although he did not become a partner.[26] VanBrocklin, Winter and Co.'s plant was large by the day's standards, with capital of $32,000: a three-storey brick machine shop, 77 by 40 feet in dimension; a one-storey foundry, 60 by 50 feet; a two-storey planing shop, 37 by 30 feet; and a one-storey blacksmith shop, 30 by 24 feet. Forty-five men were employed in 1851 and produced steam engines, ploughs, threshing machines, and mill gearing of approximately $50,000 in value.[27]

VanBrocklin was a "boomer," and as mayor in 1850, he promoted and invested heavily in the Buffalo, Brantford and Goderich Railway. In return he received the contract to operate the car shops, the construction of which was financed with municipal bonds. To this end, he struck a partnership with James Miller Williams, the Hamilton carriage manufacturer and car builder for the Great Western, and Matthew Butler, an English Methodist who had worked for Williams. Since VanBrocklin withdrew from the firm in 1853, just about the time that the shops were completed, it seems possible that he might have been Williams's front man all along. In any case, Van-Brocklin's withdrawal proved prescient. The Buffalo, Brantford and Goderich's failure put Williams, Butler and Co. out of business in December 1855. After the takeover of the road by its English bond-holders as the Buffalo and Lake Huron, the new Buffalo and Lake Huron Railway ran the shops itself.[28]

Butler returned to Hamilton in early 1856 to settle accounts with Williams, but later that year, with his former employer's financial assistance once again and with a new partner, Royal G. Jackson, an American machinist in his late twenties, Butler started a new foundry in Brantford. At first they produced tinware in premises rented from William Mellish, a builder and railroad contractor, while their Depot Foundry was under construction near the railroad station. The partners estimated that the two-storey 140-by-40-foot foundry and the smith shop, 60 by 30 feet, could employ eighty men and turn out castings and machinery worth $125,000 a year. In its first year, production reached only a third of this projection, and only thirty-five men were employed. With the depression, Butler and Jackson's position worsened so that in August 1858, to protect themselves from their creditors, they assigned their assets to Williams. In hopes of recovery, Butler and Jackson cut prices and held wages below those paid to foundrymen elsewhere. Their retrenchment and hard-dealing worked, and by 1861 they were free of the claims against them. That year they reported to the census enumerator yearly sales of $70,000, twice their 1857 level.[29]

Other foundries experienced difficulties in the late 1850s. In 1854 VanBrocklin began winding up his business and settling with his partners. Winter withdrew to devote his time to being treasurer of the Buffalo, Brantford and Goderich Railroad and to backing a grocery business. The store and warerooms used by VanBrocklin, Winter and Co., but which VanBrocklin alone had owned, were sold in 1855 to B.G. Tisdale, a stove and tinware merchant who had previously rented commercial space elsewhere. Waterous attempted to purchase what remained of the business.[30] To do so, he negotiated a deal with the second largest foundry in Brantford, Goold, Bennett and Co.

After VanBrocklin's refusal to sell in 1848, Goold and another New Yorker, Adolphus Bogardus Bennett, had started a new foundry, with backing from Joseph Ganson, Holester Lathrop, and Ralph W. Goold, who, as Ganson and Co., were iron founders in Brockport, New York. By 1851 the Brantford branch was doing well, employing thirty-six men and producing $32,000 annually with capital of $10,000. That year Goold, Bennett and Co. bought an interest in the retail stove outlet and tinshop of Bradford G. Tisdale, a Canadian of Loyalist extraction in business since 1846. The arrangement with Tisdale probably lasted no more than two or three years. Tisdale was ambitious to expand and in 1856 opened his own foundry. In full operation by mid-1857, it employed twenty men and produced stoves and agricultural implements valued at $30,000. The sale of his own tin and copper ware and goods obtained from other manufacturers added another $20,000 to Tisdale's business.[31]

Meanwhile, a fire in their foundry in 1852, for which they were underinsured, forced Goold, Bennett to reorganize their business and to find additional financial backing. Ignatius Cockshutt and another general merchant, John Steele, rebuilt the foundry. They then leased the new plant – including a foundry and machine shop, 132 by 60 feet in size, plus detached offices, blacksmith and tin shops – to Goold, Bennett and Co. for $625 a year, according to the 1854 assessment roll. After Steele's death in 1853, his widow retained only a small interest in the foundry, selling most of her husband's interest to Abram Bradley, a livery keeper, and to Cockshutt and his father James. Together the Cockshutts owned 80 per cent of the plant. Their new financing permitted Goold and Bennett in 1853 to buy a one-third interest in another tinsmithing business, that of W.E. Landon and William Buck, who had become partners the previous year. Landon, an American, had been a master tinsmith for some time, while Buck, from a Loyalist family, had apprenticed and been a journeyman in Brantford for ten years. Whatever Landon and Buck had on their own or received from Goold and Bennett, it was not sufficient to purchase a shop; instead they leased premises from Arunah Huntington, paying $200 rent in 1854 and $250 in 1855, according to the assessment rolls.[32]

The 1855 takeover of the VanBrocklin foundry involved Waterous, the various partners in Goold, Bennett, and, behind the scenes, Cockshutt. Waterous entered a partnership with the members of Goold, Bennett under the style Ganson, Waterous and Co. to buy the business and half of VanBrocklin's plant, the other half being taken by Ignatius Cockshutt. Goold, Bennett continued to operate their foundry until 1857, though the balance of interests in it was reorganized. By 1856 Cockshutt had sold two-thirds of his investment in their foundry to Abram Bradley, while James Cockshutt disposed of all of his interest to the same party. When Goold, Bennett moved out the following year, Bradley bought the foundry outright and rented it to Landon and Buck, who also continued in their tinshop. Goold, Bennett retained an indirect interest in the foundry, since they had transferred their holding in Landon and Buck to Ganson, Waterous and Co. when the new company was formed.[33] Out of the foundry *per se*, Goold, Bennett in partnership with Ignatius Cockshutt opened a storeroom in 1857, presumably to handle the wares of the various firms with whom they were associated. Goold, Bennett owned a third and Cockshutt two-thirds of this property.

The Brantford Foundry and Steam Engine Works, as it was called, was considerably larger than any of the other foundries in town. The machine shop was about doubled in size and a boiler shop was added to the blacksmith shop. The foundry melted less iron than either Goold, Bennett or Butler and Jackson, but its product far exceeded the value of their production. On average in the mid-1850s, a hundred men were employed, though in 1857 prior to the crash of that year, employment reached 130 workers.[34]

Despite the elaborate manoeuvres attending its birth, Ganson, Waterous and Co. did not emerge unscathed from the commercial crisis of 1857. The partners were generally considered wealthy, but their operating capital was tied up in overdue accounts. In 1859 they informed their creditors that they could not meet obligations and would wind up the company. They reported liabilities of $27,000 and assets of $71,000, with only $2,000 in cash. The ledger accounts of $18,000 and court judgments of $8,000 were of dubious value, while the balance of assets, composed of plant and inventory, might have been depreciable as well. In early 1860 their creditors granted a four-year extension in return for assigning their assets.[35] Around the same time, H. Lathrop and R.W. Goold withdrew. In 1857 Bennett, who had other ventures – including a partnership in the Brantford Pottery – sold out. He continued to support Landon and Buck's foundry, which dissolved its formal connection with Goold, Bennett and Co. at the same time; as well, he helped finance another tinsmithing business, J. and W. Potts.[36]

William Mellish, Bennett's replacement in Ganson, Waterous, brought little strength. He had been a contractor for the Buffalo, Brantford and Goderich Railway, and the railroad's failure and his continuing speculations complicated his affairs. In 1859 he found it convenient to leave town to escape embarrassment. In 1862 Ganson dissolved his connection, although to maintain public confidence the name remained the same until 1864 when F.P. Goold withdrew. Goold may have felt that the business lacked a future. In 1854 he provided capital for the expansion of a shoemaking business, Hayden and Goold. He even had some interest in oil refining, and from 1859 to 1867 he and Waterous operated the Brantford Pottery under the name F.P. Goold and Co.[37]

Confronted with financial and partnership problems, Waterous sought a new associate. Ignatius Cockshutt, the wealthiest man in town, might well have provided capital sufficient to bail the business out. But over time, his stake in the foundry declined. From half ownership in the plant in 1855, it shrank to 44 per cent of the assessed value of the firm's real estate in 1859 and 37 per cent in 1867. His share, assessed in 1867 at $2,000, was just 10 per cent of the value of all his rental properties in that year's assessment. He did, however, help William Buck. Buck and Landon dissolved their partnership in 1858 and each continued on his own. Landon plied his old trade for a few months before fleeing to the United States in early 1859 to escape debts. Bennett still supported Buck's Union Foundry, while Cockshutt built a tinshop, which in 1859 he rented to Buck. Fire destroyed the shop not long after its construction, and it was not rebuilt. Clearly Cockshutt wanted to limit his commitment to the foundry business, whether Buck's or Ganson, Waterous's. The prospects did not impress him.

Waterous found a new partner in George H. Wilkes. The latter had been an accountant in the Brantford Iron Works started by his uncle, George S. Wilkes, in 1856, and when that foundry failed in 1859, its creditors hired George H. as manager. In 1861 the Brantford Iron Works merged its operations, though not its ownership, with the Brantford Engine Works, and Wilkes became a partner in Ganson, Waterous. Wilkes brought little capital with him, just $3,600 in lathes, planers, patterns, and other foundry equipment, but he did have accounting ability.[38] Wilkes severed his connection with the Brantford Iron Works in 1864 when it was sold to William Buck, who then moved from his old rented plant. C.H. Waterous and Co. proved a successful partnership and lasted until Wilkes's retirement from active business in 1880.

In 1861 there were more foundries than the two in 1852, six in all, plus a number of small mould and machine shops. But none employed as many workers as the largest in 1852. Ganson, Waterous and Co. and William Buck reported in the 1861 census employment of forty men each, while Tisdale employed just sixteen and Wilkes fifteen. The organizational limits to large-scale production in the 1850s, demonstrated in the shifting and shuffling partnerships of iron founders, allowed men with small amounts of capital to establish craft workshops, even in metal working, particularly if fixed capital investment was kept low by renting premises. The 1861 census identified eight new trades supporting self-employment; five of these – machinist, mechanical engineer, moulder, millwright, wireworker – were in metal fabricating. Of the eleven independent metal tradesmen, including machinists, moulders, stove fitters, tinsmiths, and blacksmiths, who gave information about their businesses to the census enumerator in 1861, only two had more than $1,000 invested in their operations. Only one owned his shop, while the other, Thomas W. Hall, a machinist, contracted work from Ganson, Waterous. Born in Leeds, England, Hall had worked in Toronto, Niagara, and Buffalo before Waterous invited him to locate in Brantford. While Hall had $4,000 invested in his business, smaller shops operated with less than $400 in equipment, consisting perhaps of a short lathe and grinder, with miscellaneous small tools.[39]

The almost perpetual restructuring of iron-founding partnerships from the 1840s through the 1860s may well have evidenced lesser returns to capital invested in industry. However, the horizontal and vertical extension of partnerships among artisans and manufacturers, merchants and retailers also demonstrated a decided unwillingness to compete with other members of the community and a desire to distribute risk through the community. Though it would be tempting to conclude, as Paul Johnson has about the businessmen of Rochester, that Brantford was "a remarkably orderly and closed community of entrepreneurs" tied together in a social network, it must be remembered that these partnerships were transitory and contingent. Without doubt, the brevity of partnerships was symptomatic of trade prospects and profits, but we can only speculate about the interpersonal dynamics among many men each ostensibly the other's equal. In daily or strategic decision making, mutual self-help and individual independence may have become contradictory.[40]

CRAFT INDEPENDENCE AND SELF-EMPLOYMENT IN CARRIAGE MAKING

The craftsman's tenacious commitment to independence made consolidation difficult in carriage making in the 1850s and 1860s. The making of a carriage required several complementary trades, the carriage builder, the trimmer, the wheelwright, the blacksmith. On occasion, masters of different crafts entered partnerships or located beside or near one another to work on each other's jobs. But such commitments were inevitably of short duration, and frequently artisans left one collaborative arrangement to enter another.

Carriage making actually became a smaller-scale industry between 1852 and 1861. In 1852 the largest carriage works – John M. Colver and Co. and John M. Tupper – employed twenty-two and twelve men respectively. Rather than factories, these were complexes of several craft workshops, in which journeymen plied their trades; production remained skill- rather than capital-intensive. The largest carriage maker, Colver and Co. had capital of only $2,000, half in its shops; the balance was insufficient to carry the business through the mid-1850s. Colver's partner, Arthur Smith, bought him out in 1854, though Colver stayed on as manager. The next year Smith took a new partner, John McNaught, former manager of Mellish and Russell's planing mill. Smith and McNaught failed in 1857. Its successor, William Muirhead and Co. lasted no more than a year. John Tupper had located in Brantford in the 1830s, for a time in partnership with Thomas Heeney. Arriving early, Tupper had acquired land cheaply which he subsequently mortgaged to finance exclusive ownership of his large workshop and separate blacksmith shop and paint shop. Tupper, like Colver, encountered difficulties in the 1850s. Though both were self-employed in 1861, neither hired any help, and Tupper was reduced to one workshop.[41] The problems of the larger shops made it possible, or necessary, for artisans to set up on their own account.

Assessment records contain numerous examples of the shifting collaboration among men with different trades. In 1854 Pat Dunn, a thirty-one-year-old Irish Catholic wagonmaker, and William Fletcher, a thirty-six-year-old carriage painter from England, owned adjoining shops. Fletcher bought new premises the next year beside John Rackham, a fifty-eight-year-old English wheelwright. Fletcher died in 1856, and Rackham in 1857 rented part of his premises to William Stubbs, a blacksmith. The next year Stubbs bought his own shop and moved. After Fletcher's death, one of his journeymen, Woods Lyons, an Irish Methodist born about 1831, set up his own business in rented premises. In 1858 George Roy, a twenty-three-year-old carriage maker from Lower Canada, leased a shop beside Lyons. Two other carriage makers, Colver and the partnership of Jerome Wadleigh and James Payne, also moved into rented shops nearby. Wadleigh, a Canadian Baptist born about 1832, had been one of Colver's journeymen in 1852. Wadleigh and Payne parted company quickly, Wadleigh moving to rented premises elsewhere in 1860. Both were still self-employed in 1861. In 1859 Lyons moved and went into partnership with William Monter, a blacksmith, who earlier had been a partner of Joseph R. Craig, a wagonmaker. Monter and Craig had been journeymen for and boarded with Tupper in 1852. Craig in 1861 was a journeyman, while Lyons and Monter continued in partnership until 1863. Though they separated that year, they continued to do each other's work.[42]

In another act of collaboration, Thomas Hext, in drafting his will, appointed another carriage maker, Adam Spence, executor of his estate. He requested that Spence wind up his partnership with his brother, John Hext, or, if he thought it more profitable, continue the partnership for the benefit of his widow and children. Presumably neither testator nor executor perceived any conflict of interest in such an arrangement. Who better to know what to do about a carriage-making business than a brother carriage maker?

All of these carriage-making concerns in the late 1850s and early 1860s were small. Eight of nine rented their premises in 1861, Lyons being the only one owning a shop. The capital reported to the census enumerator that year varied from Wadleigh's $300 to the $1,200 investment of Robert Jackson, a thirty-nine-year-old Irish Anglican wagonmaker. Only Lyons and Adam Spence, a thirty-year-old Orkney blacksmith who had worked for Smith and McNaught, hired any workers, two men each.[43] The carriage-making trade in the 1850s demonstrated one limitation to large-scale operations under craft production. Ownership of several workshops, as achieved by Tupper and Colver Co., might consolidate the stages of production, but did not change the means of production *per se*. When the economy tumbled after 1857, the proprietors of the large shops no longer could finance the inventories of seasoned lumber, iron, hardware, and paints that integrated operations required. Nor could they attract additional capital. In consequence, the organization of production reverted to what probably typified the craft earlier.

THE REPLACEMENT OF CRAFT PRODUCERS IN THE 1850S

The importance of craft production in meeting local demand in the 1850s meant that the independent artisans who went out of business were generally replaced. Throughout the period under study, less than half of all businessmen remained self-employed for ten years. Unlike what had happened in either of the two subsequent decades, the vast majority, 80 per cent, of the business functions or occupations in the industrial sector that were vacated after 1852 were refilled by 1861.

All who provided the basic necessities of food, clothing, and shelter were replaced. Indeed, construction tradesmen and food and beverage producers increased in number, accounting for nearly two-thirds of the expansion of existing business functions. However, two occupational groupings, metal fabricating and woodworking, already revealed stress as vacancies left by the smallest-scale producers – blacksmiths and gunsmiths – went unfilled in 1861. More specialized metal-fabricating businesses eliminated much of the demand for goods formerly produced by blacksmiths, such as ploughs and stoves. Rather than the jacks of all trades they had been, blacksmiths increasingly concentrated on farriery. Horseshoeing had always been the most important work of blacksmiths, especially in rural areas, where William Wylie has calculated it accounted for roughly 40 per cent of operations. In the 1860s it became even more important, though the presence of too many smiths compromised their ability to make a living. When in 1869 the blacksmiths combined to set prices for shoeing horses, the stable keepers hired their own farriers.[44] Coopers and sash makers also declined in self-employment during the 1850s as their trades were integrated into the operations of other businesses. Two flour mills, Bunnell's and Wilkes's, set up their own barrel-making departments, while workers in the Brantford Steam Planing Mill of William Watt and Hoyt Brothers' Steam Planing Mill machined the stock and assembled windows and doors in the factory. Reporting on Watt's operation in 1857, the *Expositor* marvelled that manual labour and skill appeared to have been almost entirely superseded by machinery in the production of nearly every description of woodwork.[45] As well, fewer cabinetmakers were in business in 1861 than in 1851. In 1858 the credit reporter for the Dun Co. warned potential lenders about one, saying that "like most of his craft just now, he is lightly pushed for money."[46]

The substantial turnover in business personnel in the 1850s did not create vacuums for existing firms to expand into. Expansion required more capital, and so long as partnerships remained the most common vehicle for mobilizing capital, distinct organizational limits were imposed upon the scale of operations.[47] The foundries demonstrated that capital accumulated in commerce could be attracted to industrial production, though most frequently those who invested preferred the role of landlord to that of partner. The complicated, though more or less stable, arrangements which characterized metropolitan and transatlantic partnerships, such as those revealed by Douglas McCalla in his study of the Buchanans' businesses,[48] were uncommon in Brantford. There partnerships were brief and in most cases, especially among artisans and shopkeepers in the 1850s, evidenced not the attraction of capital, but its absence: men with individually inadequate means sought strength in company. That partnerships were relatively fewer in number after 1860, and more common in commerce than in industry, indicated that the strategy did not work.

THE OPPORTUNITIES FOR LARGER SCALE PRODUCTION IN THE 1870S

The construction of rail branch lines throughout Canada, the dramatic reduction of freight rates, and the improvement of postal facilities broke down the protective isolation of localized urban economies.[49] Brantford's businessmen in the 1870s no longer promoted railroads as a way to capture staple commerce for their town; rather they sought, with some success, integration in a national transport system. Connections were made with the three main trunk lines in

Ontario: the Grand Trunk took over the Buffalo and Lake Huron Railway; local promoters built the Brantford and Harrisburgh Railway and leased it to the Great Western for operation; under a similar arrangement the Canada Southern ran trains on the Brantford, Norfolk and Port Burwell Railway's track. In 1881 plans were under way to build a branch line to the Credit Valley Railway at Milton, where connections could be made with the Canadian Pacific.[50] With such rail service, manufacturers and wholesalers might serve consumers far beyond their own community.

The Waterous company's 1875 catalogue identified buyers for its grist mills, sawmills, and steam engines, and its lighter stave, shingle, and lath mills, from Manitoba to Nova Scotia, and even in foreign countries. About one-third of its customers were outside the province, mainly in the Maritimes. In Ontario the main market was concentrated in Brantford's traditional hinterland of Brant, Norfolk, and Oxford counties and along the line of the Buffalo and Lake Huron Railway from Fort Erie to Goderich. Beyond, few sales were made near to Toronto, Hamilton, and London. Rather, customers were found in the interstices of the metropolitan network, on the fringes of the hinterlands of other urban centres: in Essex County and along the Erie shore; in Ontario and Grey counties; and east of a line drawn from Kingston to Ottawa.[51]

Factories in Brantford helped each other to penetrate more distant markets. In the late 1870s James Smith and Edward Brophey, saddlers and harnessmakers, filled contracts for the North West Mounted Police and made shipments to British Columbia. They also received orders from Winnipeg through implement manufacturers Alanson Harris, Son and Co., and from New Zealand through carriage manufacturer John Hext. J.O. Wisner Son and Co. also benefited from the Winnipeg sales branch of Harris, which marketed their fanning mills and seed drills. Businesses just expanding their sales territory needed to fill out their offerings, and it was in the Harris company's interest, for example, to handle orders for harness and farm equipment they did not manufacture.[52]

The number of major industrial employers increased sharply in the late 1860s. In 1861 only three firms employed more than twenty workers; ten years later fourteen did so; by 1875, eight employed twenty to fifty hands, three employed fifty to a hundred and four more than a hundred; by 1881 twenty-five factories exceeded twenty employees. The value of industrial production doubled from 1861 to 1871 and more firms conducted $100,000 or more of business annually. Only the Holmedale Flour Mills of Adam Ker and James Coleman transacted this volume of business in 1861. By 1871, as well as the Holmedale Mills, now owned by David Plewes, the Grand Trunk Railway Shops, Alfred Watts's Brant Flour Mills, the Dominion Starch Works of Imlach and Morton, and the Waterous Engine Works reached this level of sales. Three more firms, the Ontario Planing Mills of M.A. Burns, the Victoria Foundry of William Buck, and John Builder's furniture factory, passed the $100,000 benchmark by 1875.[53]

In the 1870s, outside firms could also sell in Brantford. Economies of scale, which compensated for transportation costs, made goods produced at some distance competitive in price with those previously made by craft producers locally. Through the 1860s and 1870s, increases in the demand for goods and services in Brantford, as elsewhere, were met by larger rather than by more enterprises and frequently by retail commerce. In consequence the business population shrank relatively by attrition as fewer and fewer craft producers were replaced. Only 42 per cent of those engaged in industrial production who quit business after 1861 had been replaced by 1871, and just 47 per cent of those who quit after 1871 had been replaced by 1880.

The business community grew more slowly than Brantford's population, which increased by 2.6 per cent per year in the 1860s, about half of the rate of the previous decade, and by 3.3 per cent per year in the 1870s. The number of self-employed increased only 0.8 per cent annually from 1861 to 385 businessmen in 1871. Thereafter the number actually declined to 372 in 1880. Relatively fewer men were in business, one for every 21.1 residents in 1871 and one for every 29.2 in 1880. The rate of self-employment dropped to one in 5.4 adult males in 1871 and to one in 7 in 1880. New organizational forms and new relations of production and distribution reduced the size of the business population by roughly 40 per cent.

The expansion of factories in the metal-fabricating industry produced the most profound reorganization. By 1881 the rate of self-employment was about one-quarter of what it had been in 1852. The largest single number of metal workers were employed in the Grand Trunk Car Shops, in 1871 the nation's largest such facility, the province's largest industrial plant in terms of fixed capital investment ($435,000) and total annual wage bill ($182,000) and the third largest in terms of men employed (300).[54] Brantford's foundries also were larger in the 1870s. Among Ontario and Quebec engine works not engaged in making locomotives, C.H. Waterous and Co. ranked third in number of employees (118) and annual wages ($40,573), but tied for second in value of product ($120,00).[55] The average Brantford foundry employed nearly four times as many workers in 1871 as in 1861. The total amount of capital invested in iron foundries remained constant from 1861 to 1871, but because the number of foundries fell to three in number, the average capital invested rose by 250 per cent. More significantly, as a group foundry owners had at their command operating capital far greater than that of other producer groups. The three foundries, those of Waterous and Wilkes, William Buck, and B.G. Tisdale, had operating capital equal to about two-thirds of their annual wage bill plus raw material purchases, making them less dependent on cash flow for financing. The expanding scale of operations made it possible for foundries to push the average value of production to more than triple its 1861 level. Although this approximated the average value of production of the town's flour mills, the foundries exceeded the average value added per mill by three and a half times (table 1.2).[56]

Four of six businesses incorporated in Brantford the 1870s were in metal fabricating, one machine works and three agricultural implement factories. The Waterous Engine Works Co. Ltd. was chartered in 1874 with capital of $250,000. The former partners continued the management, Waterous as mechanical engineer and Wilkes as secretary-treasurer, but mercantile interests were conspicuous among the officers. Henry W. Brethour, the town's major dry goods merchant, was a director, while James G. Cockshutt, Ignatius's son, was the president.[57] Though his son left Waterous in 1877 to start his own company, the Cockshutt Plough Co. Ltd., the senior Cockshutt decided to put more money in. George H. Wilkes wanted to retire and in preparation for that sold his interest in the plant, half to Waterous and half to Cockshutt who then became half owner of the works. His holding, assessed in 1878 at $15,000, accounted for 30 per cent of his rental property investment.

The incorporation of Alanson Harris, Son and Co. in 1881 eased the inevitable intergenerational transition and accommodated non-family management. Alanson Harris, aged sixty-five years in 1881, passed more and more responsibility to his son, John, who became president of the corporation. James K. Osborne joined the firm in 1872 as secretary-treasurer. Lyman Melvin Jones, also made a partner in 1872, opened the Winnipeg agency of the firm in 1879. Joseph N. Shenston, Thomas's son and brother-in-law of Alanson's son Elmore, rose to a partnership from being a clerk.[58] Another agricultural implement manufacturer, J.O. Wisner, Son and Co., also incorporated in 1881 to make way for a new partner, Edward L. Goold, son of Franklin. He was himself a manufacturer, of refrigerators and caskets, and in partnership with James Agnew operated a hardware store.[59]

Table 1.2
Capital, Employment, and Production of Industrial Firms, 1861–71

Industrial Group	Capital per Firm			Workers per Firm		Value of Production			
	Fixed ($00s) 1861	Fixed ($00s) 1871	Operating ($00s) 1871	1861	1871	Average ($00s) 1861	Average ($00s) 1871	Total ($000s) 1861	Total ($000s) 1871
Metalworking:									
Foundries	147	373	300	22.2	84.0	303	964	151	253
Other	13	11	10	1.2	2.9	21	12	27	36
All	50	95	77	7.0	21.7	99	222	178	289
Food Products:									
Bakeries	2	13	56	1.7	5.8	33	152	10	76
Mills	102	72	72	4.8	5.8	505	974	202	487
Other	20	29	46	0.9	6.0	18	250	13	126
All	42	43	57	2.3	5.9	160	459	225	689
Apparel making:									
Shoemaking	20	7	10	4.9	3.7	29	22	41	26
Tailoring	6	36	79	1.0	13.8	3	116	1	186
Hat making	20	20	17	3.7	3.0	29	28	9	34
Harness making	29	47	33	5.0	7.0	61	85	25	14
All	20	25	41	4.4	8.3	32	70	76	260
Woodworking									
Carriage making	6	28	63	0.4	12.8	6	97	6	39
Cabinet making	19	6	10	2.6	5.2	22	26	11	13
Cooperages	9	10	26	3.5	5.7	22	47	4	14
Other	13	10	40	4.0	4.0	25	7	3	5
All	10	14	30	1.6	7.5	13	21	24	67
Construction									
Materials	16	24	22	1.6	2.9	17	64	7	70
Other	68	54	62	3.6	8.8	66	192	86	173
All	25	38	41	3.7	8.4	66	158	593	1548
Number of firms	93	98	98	93	98	90	98	90	98

Note: Operating capital was not a category in the 1861 census. The assumption is that "capital invested in business" in 1861 meant fixed capital. The category "Bakeries" also includes confectioneries. The category "Construction Materials" includes planing mills in 1871 only, since the 1861 census did not distinguish between the capital of a planing mill and construction business when a builder engaged in both enterprises.

The fourth manufacturing corporation in Brantford was the Craven Cotton Co. City council attracted the cotton mill in 1880 when it offered a $5,000 bonus to Clayton Slater, a Yorkshire manufacturer. Local investment came principally from Ignatius Cockshutt, who, after a reorganization in 1882, became president of the company. About 140 employees worked in the mill, which contained

180 spindles and 250 looms.[60] (The cotton mill was the second factory in Brantford's textile industry. In 1872 William Slingsby, previously the manager of a mill in Dundas, established the Holmedale woollen mill, and by the end of the decade he employed twenty-two men and ten women.)[61] Incorporation, then, afforded a way to attract new men and capital, while avoiding the complications and disruptions of partnerships. The termination of a partnership had legally ended the business; the sale or transfer of stock had no such effect.

Woodworking presented a mixed picture of expansion and displacement. In carriage making, two firms in 1871 hired more than twenty workers, and all six hired at least one, averaging 12.8 workers per establishment. Five of the six concerns each transacted business in 1871 equal to or in excess of the total for the whole industry in 1861. Craft shops, like Robert Jackson's employing three journeymen, still operated, but three factories significantly changed production. After his old shop burned in 1864, Woods Lyons built his Brant Carriage Factory, a two-and-a-half-storey frame building, 44 feet by 77 feet in dimension, with adjacent blacksmith shop and lumber sheds. For a year or two he operated it in partnership with a Mr Tinling, though from 1867 he was sole proprietor. About 1864 Adam Spence opened his Provincial Carriage Factory in a new two-storey brick plant with separate blacksmith shop. In 1866 Thomas and John Hext, the latter a journeyman blacksmith with Lyons from 1863, rented a three-storey brick factory, with blacksmith shop and wood sheds, for their Brantford Carriage Works. After operating the business for a year, they presumably had demonstrated to potential mortgage lenders that they could make a go of it; local merchant Robert Sproule and druggist Frederick Brendon loaned them the money to buy the works.[62] Each of these three businesses operated mainly in one large building, rather than as a series of workshops, and performed within it the various woodworking, painting, and assembly operations. Production techniques may not have changed from earlier craft practices, since none reported having steam power in the 1871 census, and certainly in comparison with, say, the Studebaker brothers' carriage factory in South Bend, Indiana, which employed over three hundred men at about the same time, none of Brantford's plants was very impressive.[63] But what had been achieved was control of the stages of production under one roof. Physically production could not again devolve into the collaboration of separate craft shops.

The changes in cabinetmaking were of the same sort. Joy Parr has explained, "Into the twentieth century furniture factories were craftshops serially replicated rather than workplaces fundamentally transformed by their increase in scale."[64] Though factory-made furniture took business from Brantford cabinetmakers from the 1860s, most of the competition came from outside the community. The average value of goods produced in 1871 was but a third of the 1861 output, even though more labour was being employed per firm. To shave expenses, more cabinetmakers rented than owned their shops, but the lower investment also suggested that these hard-pressed artisans were consuming capital to provide a living. When a furniture factory opened in 1872, the situation worsened. John Builder and Co.'s factory, powered by a water wheel rather than steam engine, was a three-storey brick building, 100 feet by 50 feet in dimensions, with a two-storey wing, 140 feet long, and a separate frame paint and varnish shop. Builder estimated in 1873 that he had invested slightly in excess of $20,000 in the fixed capital of the business, while his partner, H.C. Allen, a physician and insurance agent, agreed to contribute an equal amount for operating expenses. In 1876, 113 workers were employed. That Builder owned eight dwellings including a boarding house in 1872 to accommodate eighty of his workers suggests that he recruited from outside the town. [65] Perhaps, like the workers hired by Daniel Knechtel, a furniture manufacturer in Hanover, Builder's were the younger sons of large farming families who had recently left the land, either permanently or temporarily, in search of better prospects. Brantford sales, almost all retail, and especially to hotels, constituted 90 per cent of the business. Builder could not crack the hold that the Toronto firm Robert Hay and Co. had on the provincial market, and he went bankrupt in 1878. But his local sales must have hurt Brantford's master cabinetmakers, who had to rely more heavily on repair work, retailing factory goods, or undertaking, and even taking contract work from Builder.[66]

The higher than average rate of self-employment among apparel producers in 1871 masked the decline of these trades. In 1852 apparel production, principally shoemaking and tailoring, had been the largest occupational group in the manufacturing sector and had even attracted capital. In the mid-1850s three master cordwainers entered partnerships with businessmen who had no previous experience with the trade but were willing to invest. But competition from shoe dealers proved too much. The credit reporter for R.G. Dun and Co. communicated that "I don't believe that half of the shoemakers are paying expenses ... . [The boot and shoe business] is overdone in this town; ... some must go shortly."[67] The average shoemaker hired fewer workers (5.2 in 1861; 3.7 in 1871), paid them lower wages ($24.84 a month in 1861; $21.26 in 1871), had less capital invested in his business ($2,268 in 1861; $667 in 1871), and conducted less business ($3,763 in 1861; $2,202 in 1871). The decline in shoemaking arose from the withdrawal of capital from the largest concerns. Of the six businesses that reported between $2,000 and $6,000 capital investment in 1861, only two continued in 1871. Both suffered a severe reduction in capital, in one case a drop from $2,000 to $300, in the other from $2,500 to $600; their employment and value of production declined as well. The fate of the other four large shoemaking businesses indicated the flight of capital. Two of the four had involved masons who had backed independent tradesmen in the late 1850s; one mason went back to contracting, while the other left town. Two former shoemakers remained in the area. James Weyms gave up his trade after thirty years to become the police magistrate.[68] William Long sold his business of twenty years to purchase a farm in Brantford Township. The difficulties faced by the larger businesses left some business for smaller operators who might repair factory-made shoes and do a little custom work. Four of the five shoemakers with less than $1,000 in their businesses in 1861 not only were still in business in 1871 but had expanded their operations by investing a little more capital or hiring more journeymen; one shop with just $800 invested in it in 1871 gave work to ten shoemakers. These shops were still smaller than the largest had been in 1861, but they did indicate that some shoemakers could eke out a living by picking up the bits and pieces of a declining trade.

Dun's reporter correctly predicted the failure of a number of shoemakers, but not their replacement. Five of sixteen did quit in the 1860s, but by 1871 four of their positions had been taken up by new men. Twelve of the fifteen in 1871 gave up and only three new shoemakers were in business in 1880. But the next-year, thirteen shoemakers were self-employed, twice as many as in the previous year. The year-to-year fluctuations made evident the insecurity which forced self-employment on some shoemakers. What else was there for them to do?

Tailors had to compete with clothing produced in the tailoring departments of Brantford's dry goods establishments by female and child labour. Dun's reporter judged the tailoring trade "overdone" in the 1860s.[69] Only one of four tailors who left in the 1860s and none of the three who left during the 1870s were replaced. The growth of merchant-sponsored tailoring cannot be easily measured because of the lack of comparable figures, though grow it did. The 1861 census did not distinguish employment in the sales and tailoring branches of dry goods businesses. The total figures for the largest firms, nonetheless, were considerably lower than those given in 1871 just for tailoring. In 1861 Thomas McLean, a Scots Presbyterian born in 1831, employed nine men and sixteen women in both branches of his business, while Henry Brethour, an Irish Methodist born about 1832, gave work to six men and ten women. John Taylor and William Grant, two Scots Presbyterians born about 1825, were the largest employers with twelve men and twenty-five women. Their cutter, the most important asset of any tailoring department, was paid the considerable salary of $1,000. Even at that wage, they found that the best men wanted to work on their own account. John Jenkins had saved $800 to $1,000 while in their employ and in 1861 quit to set up as a merchant tailor. His replacement, Robert Grant, had learned his trade in Aberdeen, Scotland, and in 1853, two years after immigrating, had taken a job in Brantford as cutter in J.H. Moore's general merchandising business. Only a year later he began tailoring on his own account, until illness forced him to work for Taylor and Grant. He remained ambitious and tried self-employment in Dundas in 1864 and later in Guelph. He returned in 1871 to work for William Grant, by then no longer in with Taylor. Nine years later he started another tailoring business in Brantford. The wages earned by his skill, it seems, repeatedly subsidized Grant's desire for independence.[70]

Through the 1860s and 1870s, the employment of large numbers of women in apparel production gave dry goods merchants the flexible and cheap labour needed to control custom tailoring and dressmaking. Whereas twenty-seven women had been so employed in 1852 and eighty-one in 1861, female employment rose to 110 in 1871 and 257 in 1881. Merchants could now break down the stages of production, hiring a large number of seamstresses during peak seasons and laying them off during the slack months; a smaller number of skilled male cutters and tailors were retained all year. In 1871 Henry Brethour and Thomas McLean were the largest employers, the former with nineteen men, thirty-seven women, and four boys and eight girls under the age of sixteen and the latter ten men, thirty women, and four girls under the age of sixteen. In all its departments in 1871, Brethour's establishment gave work to a hundred employees. Three other merchants gave employment to a total of fifty-six people in their tailoring departments, while the town's eight tailor shops employed only forty-nine workers. Dry goods merchants commanded the capital to invest in large operations. Brethour and McLean together had $40,000 in fixed capital and $80,000 in operating capital invested in their tailoring departments. The decline in the average amount of capital invested in tailoring businesses from 1861 to 1871 reflects the meagre assets of self-employed tailors.[71]

Flour mills excepted, the food and beverage producers ran small operations for local consumption. The butcher stalls were most often one- or two-man concerns. Even the two pork-packing and meat-curing plants operated by German grocers John Weinaug and Bernard Heyd, though more ambitious, employed only two or three men on a seasonal basis in the 1870s. The bakeries and confectioneries, despite a fourfold increase in average capital investment, still averaged under $1,500. Yet, as the two largest establishments indicated, a little could go a long way. John Taylor, with $2,000 in fixed capital, $1,000 in operating capital, and four workers, did $20,000 in business. In 1863 H.L. Leeming and William Paterson purchased the confectionery shop of the late William Winter, and in 1871 they took over the cigarmaking business of J. Kirchner, who stayed on to manage it for them. That year the industrial census valued both departments of their plant at only $3,000, but reported operating capital of $30,000. Leeming and Paterson employed nineteen workers and produced 8,000 pounds of confectionery, 15,500 pounds of biscuits, and 250,000 cigars, for a total value of production of $31,704. Probably their operations resembled those of the "manufactories" Ian McKay has identified in Halifax, still dependent more on labour than machinery. Leeming and Paterson made the transition to factory production after a fire in early 1875. Insurance money helped buy new machinery for baking confections, cakes, biscuits, and crackers. The business continued to expand, despite Leeming's retirement in the late 1870s, and Paterson was employing seventy-seven workers by 1880.[72] The firm's growth helped put smaller bake shops out of business: only one of the six bakers and confectioners who quit business after 1871 was replaced.

Self-employment dropped abruptly in the construction industry in the 1860s, from 27 per cent of all those so occupied at the beginning of the decade to 15 per cent at its end. Carpenters, joiners, painters, and plasterers accounted for about 40 per cent of all the tradesmen who went out of business and whose places were not refilled. Through the 1870s, despite much construction at the beginning and end of the decade, the number of builders remained the same in 1880 as 1871. Moreover, the demand for accommodation in the 1870s changed in ways that the larger firms were best able to exploit. The Brantford *Expositor*'s year-end reviews of construction in 1870, 1877, 1878, 1880, and 1881 revealed a progressive decline in residential construction and renovation, the sorts of projects that an individual tradesman might most easily take on his own account. In 1870 only a third of building activity by value was for purposes other than housing; non-residential construction accounted for three-quarters in 1881.[73]

WHOLESALE AND RETAIL COMMERCE

Commercial enterprise was restructured in two directions. As in industry, larger-scale operations developed in the late 1860s and 1870s; but new opportunities for smaller ventures were presented at the same time. In the 1850s those merchants who could operate extensively did so in a geographically small market by expanding into general merchandising. Only four firms in the 1850s and six in the 1860s engaged in wholesaling, and then their distribution was largely local, within the town and to neighbouring villages. Even these larger firms, like the keepers of smaller shops, were closely tied to metropolitan sources for their inventories and credit.

Many of the merchants of the 1850s and 1860s were support houses buying exclusively from a metropolitan wholesaler. Some were relatives or had been employees of their suppliers. About two-thirds of the wholesalers supplying Brantford were Hamilton firms, especially for groceries and general merchandise. Samuel Morphey, who ran a jewellery store in the 1850s and 1860s, was aided by his brothers in the same business in Toronto. Similarly a relative in the Hamilton firm of Whan, McLean and Co. helped Thomas McLean get his dry goods business going in 1854, shortly after he had immigrated to Canada. Andrew Muirhead, a general merchant in 1855, was "sustained *in toto*" by D. McInnis and Co. of Hamilton. When Muirhead failed, McInnis became the assignee of his remaining assets and sold them to Russell Hardy, who agreed to purchase solely from the Hamilton firm. Francis H. Ellis opened a drug business in 1858 with the support of his old employers, J. Winer and Co. of Hamilton. At first Charles Duncan was controlled by William McMaster, the Toronto dry goods wholesaler. In 1846 David A. MacNab of Hamilton set up Allen Cleghorn in the hardware business. By the late 1850s, Cleghorn, in partnership with brother James, dealt almost exclusively with Rogers and Sons of Wolverhampton, England.[74]

Few, however, bought directly from England. Most did not need such arrangements. Those who did were in partnerships, like the Cleghorns, since someone had to mind the store during buying trips. Another example, John Taylor and William Grant, went into partnership in 1856. After the failure of their Toronto wholesaler, Ross, Mitchell and Co., in 1857, they bought nearly all their inventory from an English supplier, Taylor crossing the Atlantic twice yearly to buy. Direct importing must have been only a stopgap until a new Canadian supplier could be found, since in the early 1860s Taylor and Grant dealt with Gordon, McKay and Co. of Toronto.[75]

By the 1870s, the beginning of what George Glazebrook has termed "the golden age of wholesaling," the most prominent Brantford merchants began to assert their independence from Toronto and Montreal mercantile houses.[76] Improved transportation allowed local wholesalers to concentrate on limited product lines and serve a wider area. As well, the failure of major firms, like the Buchanan businesses, left a vacuum for smaller, regional wholesalers to fill.

Twenty-three wholesalers – seven in groceries, four in liquor, one in cured meats, one in fruit, four in hardware, three in dry goods, two in cigars, one in boots and shoes, one in harness and saddlery, and one in glassware and crockery – operated out of Brantford in the 1870s. Joy Santink, in her recent study of Timothy Eaton, has noted that by the late 1870s the Toronto department store operator had substantially reduced his purchases from Toronto wholesalers and dealt instead with a Glasgow supplier or directly with English manufacturers. Despite a vigorous campaign by Toronto wholesalers to retain their accounts, other Ontario merchants bypassed this traditional commercial link.[77]

One needs care in reading the advertisements describing merchants as importers, since some added their own smaller orders to the larger orders of metropolitan buyers, but the claims of the largest Brantford merchants and wholesalers – Ignatius Cockshutt in general merchandise, Henry Brethour and Co. in dry goods, W.H. Stratford and Sons in drugs, Alfred Watts and Co. in groceries and liquor, and George Watts and Son and Alex Fair and Bro. in groceries – to direct imports were probably truthful. The *Monetary Times* in 1876 acknowledged that "the town ... has several wholesale warehouses, doing a thriving business with the rich country around it. Two or three of these are of a magnitude which would do no discredit to any of our cities."[78]

Despite the depression of mid-decade, the 1870s were good years for wholesaling, if one looks at the value of goods imported through the port of Brantford. Imports increased in value from $255,037 in 1871 to $589,902 in 1881. But values fluctuated year to year provincially and at Brantford, and perhaps a more informative measure is the share of imports entering the province through Brantford. From this perspective, Brantford became much more important as a distribution centre, accounting for 0.8 per cent of the Ontario total in 1871 and 1.7 per cent in 1881. Since the shares of the largest cities, Toronto, Hamilton, and London, remained stable or increased over the same period, Brantford's gains came at the expense of the trade through smaller ports of entry. Thus, to the extent that imports reveal anything about wholesaling, Brantford operators seemed to be displacing businessmen in other non-metropolitan centres, rather than taking trade away from those in the province's metropolises.

Of course not all goods imported were for wholesale purposes. Nor were all wholesale goods imported; some were of Canadian manufacture and some local. Several of the city's manufacturers, in order to concentrate on expanding their production, turned over the distribution of their wares to wholesalers and commission merchants. E.L. Goold's stove store acted as William Buck's agent, while John Edgar and Son's Staffordshire House wholesaled the stoneware and fancier crockery manufactured by the Brantford Pottery of William E. Welding.[79] On the other hand, some of the more successful wholesalers operated factories themselves. Joshua Hamilton, a liquor wholesaler who imported Hennesey Brandy, Guinness Porter, and Bass Ale and marketed the whisky of Alfred Watts of Brantford, set up the Vin Villa Vineyards on Point Pelee Island. Jackson Forde, a wholesale grocer, made brooms. About 1875 Alex Fair and Bro., wholesale grocery and liquor merchants, bought the cigarmaking business of James Spratt. The former owner continued as manager of the operation, which in 1875 employed about fifteen hands, three times its employment in 1870. The Fair Brothers no doubt provided cigars to the hotels which were their major liquor customers. By 1883 Alex Fair claimed that he was exporting more cigars to England than any other Canadian manufacturer.[80]

Transportation integration permitted goods to move both ways, out of and into Brantford. British, American, and Canadian manufacturers employed a growing number of commercial travellers to distribute their products. Travellers possessed considerable discretion in advancing credit on generous, if shorter, terms to favoured customers. As well, their frequent circuits made it easier for retailers to keep their stock low. The new wholesaling presented a new risk to the expanding retail sector it spawned, however. No longer did metropolitan wholesalers like the Buchanans meet personally with customers when they visited the big city to buy, and no longer did they regularly tour the country to scrutinize their accounts, evaluate for themselves their clients' businesses, and offer advice. The retailer was on his own. If travellers oversold the market and their customers failed, then so be it. At least their careful study of credit-worthiness would assure partial settlement.[81] The risk devolved even more to the merchandiser.

The passing of the supply-account system, too slowly for the *Monetary Times*, meant that the merchandiser was pressed more quickly for remittances.[82] Men who paid cash were particularly valued accounts and wanted their practice to be known. A drug-wholesaling firm wrote to the Mercantile Agency's reporter in 1870 that "we now pay cash for all our purchases either in England or in this country which mode of payment we shall in the future carry out."[83]

Businessmen paying cash in turn were less willing to tolerate their customers' requests for credit. Thomas A. Noble, who ran a paint and wallpaper store in the 1870s, described the earlier system: "Long term credit was the vogue in merchandising, with much dickering and exchanging and above all a great deal of bartering. Often work was paid for in orders on some store, and this had to be used as a means of exchange. Collections were slow and, if a man paid cash, he looked to the merchant to give a ten per cent discount. Accounts were rendered by twice a year, January 1 and July 1."[84] The interest charges on long accounts could be considerable and contributed to failure, as bad times made credit extended in goods times hard to collect. In 1876 the *Monetary Times* rebuked Brantford's oldest hardware firm, A. and J. Cleghorn, for its "antiquated methods and extensive crediting." Their 1876 failure was not hard for the Toronto paper to understand, given that "the amount they paid in interest and lost by bad debts, during their time, must be enormous." Increasingly, merchants adopted a cash sales policy. Thomas McLean announced that as of 1 September 1878 he would sell dry goods only for cash, believing as he did that the credit system was ruinous to both merchant and customer. Customers could be difficult to persuade, however, and one grocer found it convenient to put his brother-in-law's name over the door so that his firm requests for cash could be attributed to his putative partner's unrelenting policy.[85]

Brantford retailers eagerly informed customers about their stock from outside suppliers. Not only did they hope that readers of their advertisements would recognize the manufacturers' names, but it almost seemed as though goods made elsewhere had a certain cachet, being somehow exotic or at least special by virtue of their distance from source. Thus Joshua Street advertised in 1871 that his stock of boots and shoes were purchased in Montreal. In 1878 Farley and Oliver's Brantford Branch Boot and Shoe Business sold footwear obtained directly from "an immense factory in Toronto." They proudly announced that theirs was one branch in a chain with other outlets in Port Hope, St Catharines, Chatham, Peterborough, Barrie, and Belleville. Sellers of women's clothing enhanced the appeal of their offerings by emphasizing the cosmopolitan styling. Clothing need not have been made in one of the centres of fashion, but only look as though it had been. Dry goods merchant Charles Duncan informed the public that one of his dressmakers, Miss Mathieson, had just returned from the spring shows of Lord and Taylor's, A.T.

Stewart, and other New York department stores and would fashion dresses in the latest styles. Similarly Mrs Bowers advertised in September 1875 that her Emporium of Fashion had just received a new stock of women's ready-made clothing in the finest New York, Paris, and Berlin styles.[86]

Brand names, long touted by druggists selling patent nostrums, figured more prominently in notices to the public in the 1870s. Jackson Forde sold Cross and Blackwell's Pickles and Sauces. James Griffith, "a practical watchmaker," was agent for the Russell Watch and Royal Sewing Machines. J.W. Lethbridge, a former accountant, sold Nordheimer pianos; George F. Sproule, a druggist and stationery dealer, offered Barnett's Zinc and Patina Pens for sale; Erastus Kester distributed Butterick Patterns and Singer Sewing Machines; C.A. Buck and Co., stationers, held the agency for Lazarus, Moses and Co.'s eyeglasses. In a city noted for its stove works, in 1880 Thomas Potts proudly offered the stoves of Edward and Charles Gurney of Toronto and Hamilton, Dennis Moore and Co. of Hamilton, James Stewart and Co. of Hamilton, the St Catharines Stove Co., the Oshawa Stove Co., the McClary Stove Co. of London, and James Smart of Brockville.[87]

Advertising brand names shifted the attention of the consumer from the seller to the commodity, and an interest and confidence in the item, as much as a reliance on the character of the seller, drew customers to a store. Keith Walden's recent study of grocery windows has argued that brand name products de-skilled the neighbourhood merchant: the vendor's expertise in selecting, mixing, and blending food items was irrelevant to the consumer who already knew the product from its label. Instead the grocer proved his effectiveness through advertising and attracting people to his store; the presentation was all. Whether or not they believed that they were catering, as Rosalind H. Williams has argued about Paris department stores, to "the needs of the imagination," Brantford merchants adopted new merchandising methods.[88] They began rebuilding their store fronts and installing plate glass windows, at a cost of roughly $300 a store, so that the public might easily view their wares – "window shopping." When C.A. Buck's stationery store front window featured an animated Christmas display of miniature dancing figures powered by a "ten-mouse power" steam engine, the *Expositor* thought the attraction worthy of note in its columns. One should not read too much into any single display, but Buck's window, which had little to do with his particular trade, advertised his own flair for spectacle and demonstrated the merchant's awareness of selling as theatre.[89]

Changes in the marketing of goods increased the scale of commercial enterprise from 1852 to 1881. Brantford's commercial sector was less developed in the 1850s and 1860s than that of larger urban centres. For example, in 1851 commercial activity engaged 26.8 per cent of the male work force of Hamilton, but only 15.9 per cent in Brantford.[90] Over the next three decades, this gap closed, and by 1881 20.6 per cent found commercial employment. Until 1871 more than half of all businessmen engaged in some form of industrial production. Thereafter the service sector attracted the efforts of more and more until almost 60 per cent were so occupied in 1880. Between 1852 and 1861 self-employment in commerce grew at a slower rate, 2.9 per cent per annum, than the town's population. The increase in the rate of commercial self-employment over the same period indicates that on the average the mercantile enterprises became smaller in the 1850s. That relatively fewer bookkeepers and clerks were employed in 1861 than in 1852 might be attributed either to the desire of former employees to set up shop on their own or the need of employers to pare their expenses to the minimum by letting help go during a downturn in the business cycle. In the 1860s and 1870s, however, the commercial sector grew more rapidly than the town's population. The number of businessmen increased at a rate of 4.8 per cent per year in the 1860s and 3.9 per cent per year in the 1870s. Accompanying this was an abrupt decline in the rate of self-employment from 78 per cent in 1861 to 60 per cent in 1871 and to just 40 per cent in 1880.[91] Greater employment of women facilitated commercial expansion. In 1861 only two women were employed as sales clerks, but by 1881 twenty-seven women held positions in Brantford shops.

The rate of replacement was more stable in the commercial sector than in the industrial sector. Sixty-three per cent of those who went out of business in the 1850s and 66 per cent of those in the 1860s and 1870s were replaced. However, replacements made up a smaller proportion of new businessmen in 1861 than at subsequent cross-sections, since the trend to more specialized commerce from general merchandising had already started. In larger urban centres merchants could satisfy relatively fewer needs for a larger clientele rather than the many needs of fewer customers. Few general merchants had the capital necessary to maintain the extensive inventories in competition with more specialized traders. Half of the thirty general merchants in 1852 were gone in ten years and half of those who remained specialized in fewer retail lines. By 1881 the only general merchant was Ignatius Cockshutt, though one might now better describe his business as a small department store (table 1.3).

Thirty per cent of the new businessmen in the commercial sector in 1861 were engaged in some new business. There were twelve new varieties of retail merchants in 1861. Occasionally an ambitious

Table 1.3
Classification of New Businesses by Economic Sector, 1861–81

	1861		1871		1881	
Types of New Businesses	Industry (%)	Commerce (%)	Industry (%)	Commerce (%)	Industry (%)	Commerce (%)
Those filling vacancies left by out-migration	46	25	32	44	49	38
Those adding to number of existing businesses	37	45	41	44	38	37
Those starting new kinds of businesses	17	30	27	12	13	25
Total	100	100	100	100	100	100
Number	120	119	81	131	61	135

employee took over a particular department of a general merchant who wished to concentrate on fewer product lines.[92] The smaller scale of commerce in 1861 created opportunities for independent bookkeepers and accountants to provide services for small stores that desired professionally kept records. As well, about half of those business functions which expanded in number were already specialized – hardware, books and stationery, and groceries. Services closely related to population growth – hotel, inn, tavern, saloon, and livery keeping – expanded throughout the period under study.

Most of the specialized lines of commercial activity had been defined by 1861. Over the next two decades, but especially in the 1870s, a few more particularities were introduced: fancy goods and millinery separated from dry goods, restaurants and billiard parlours from hotels, tobacco shops from grocery or general stores. Customers could now purchase sheet music and instruments from a music dealer, and flowers from a florist. Undertaking, complete with brand new body freezers and elaborate hearses, grew from cabinetmaking. But these were niches and did not create in total a large number of opportunities. As a result, 88 per cent of all new businessmen in commercial pursuits in 1871 embarked in well-established areas, like hardware, glass and crockery, auctioneering, and boots and shoes. The increase in the number of clothiers from three in 1871 to five in 1880 and shoe dealers from two in 1871 to eight in 1880 made apparel retailers more numerous than apparel producers.

Nevertheless, some areas, groceries for one, in the opinion of Dun's credit rater, were "overdone."[93] Only two-thirds of the grocers who went out of business in the 1860s had been replaced by 1871. Though dry goods, the most prestigious business in Brantford, was similarly judged "overdone," new dry goods merchants filled four of the five vacancies by 1871.[94] In 1861 only two insurance agents were in business, most policies being written by merchants or brokers who sold insurance as a sideline. By 1871 six agents dealt exclusively in insurance. Insurance companies, in an attempt to provide better service, began in the 1870s to promote more training and supervision for their agents. The presence of independent agents reflected not only the demand for a service and new products for sale, but also more effective organizational direction at the level of the firm and the industry. At a more general level, the proliferation of insurance agencies displayed another dimension of the abstraction of commercial commodities: salesmanship challenged the customer to imagine his worst fears and to find in a company's reputation, its brand name, security against the future. What was the real product, some future insurance pay-out or present peace of mind?[95]

Business enterprise in Brantford was restructured in two ways in the 1860s and 1870s. First was the relative decline in self-employment and the concomitant increase in the scale of enterprise. Second, commercial activity provided relatively more opportunities for self-employment than did industrial production.

CLASS RELATIONS AND SOCIAL CONFLICT

The restructuring of business enterprise explicitly involved the restructuring of social relationships: if fewer men were self-employed, more men sold their labour power to earn their livings. Wage labour, of course, was not a product of industrial capitalism alone; the large-scale public works and the construction of canals and railroads engaged vast amounts of brute physical labour. But wage labour as part of an urban-based economy, in Brantford at least, did result from the establishment of rail car shops and factories from the mid-to late 1850s. In consequence, the nature of class conflict also changed. Previously, transient workers on canal and rail projects had struck and rioted against the contractors and companies which were constructing the infrastructure that Brantford boosters deemed essential to advance their town's commercial imperium. From about 1860, when skilled craftsmen, especially in the metal trades, organized unions and struck against the town's major employers, conflict became a part of the fabric of community life and could no longer be easily dismissed as the acts of outside conspirators.

The digging of the canal between Brantford and the village of Cainsville between 1842 and 1848 and the construction of the Buffalo, Brantford and Goderich rail line during the 1850s brought hundreds of migrant labourers into and through the community. The numbers are beyond easy estimation, but several hundred worked on the canal. As well, William Mellish and John Russell, contractors on the Buffalo and Brantford line, employed ninety men in 1851, and Henry Yates, the mechanical superintendent of the Buffalo and Lake Huron Railway and construction contractor on his own account for the road, reported in the 1861 census that he employed 560 men and paid a monthly payroll of $5,500. Labourers struck on the canal in 1843 and on the railroad in 1854–5, not just against the contractors and the companies but against the town and its ambitions as well. Their drunken and boisterously exaggerated comportment in Brantford's streets and their violent defiance of civil authority offered as pointed an affront to the townspeople depending upon these facilities as did their threats and assaults against contractors and strikebreakers. But Brantford's citizens could in the end say that these were not townsfolk and, if they were forced to keep from the streets sometimes, they knew that the disorder would pass with the completion of construction in their neighbourhood.[96]

No doubt countless instances of conflict occurred between master artisans and journeymen in Brantford's craft workshops in the 1840s and 1850s. Brantford mechanics apparently resented the lack of discretion they enjoyed in disposing of their wages and in 1852–3, along with their fellows in Hamilton and London, they petitioned the legislative assembly, unsuccessfully, to "prohibit the payment to mechanics ... of wages in goods or way of truck."[97] Yet, few of such hints of tensions are extant in the sources for the period, and one might conclude that contemporaries would not necessarily have been any better informed than we are about the quality of social relationships. To the extent that they became aware of troubles in any shops, it must have seemed dispersed, diffuse, and occasional. No such impressions could be derived from the strikes and union organization which affected Brantford's factories from about 1860.

Machinists working in the Buffalo and Lake Huron's car shops organized Brantford's first union in 1858, a branch of the Amalgamated Society of Engineers. Despite assistance from Britain, the union seems to have had organizational problems, lapsing in 1863, reopening in 1868 only to close again for good in 1874.[98] The iron moulders organized shortly after the machinists, in affiliation with the Iron Molders' Union of North America, and in July 1860 struck against William Buck and Butler and Jackson. Gregory Kealey and Bryan Palmer have argued that Toronto and Hamilton moulders regularly struck over issues of shop-floor control.[99] Their Brantford brothers demanded wage parity with Hamilton and Toronto. The foundries were effectively closed for about a month, as a combination of solidarity and intimidation prevented employers from hiring replacements. "Good workman have a horror of being called 'scabs'," the *Expositor* explained. In August Butler and Jackson had conspiracy charges laid against the five strike leaders, William F. Beck, A. Helper, Michael Cline, George Middlemass, and John McLaughlin.[100] The accused do not appear to have been brought to trial, or at least reports of the proceedings have not been found in the press. Perhaps the exceptional circumstances of the arraignment, an *in camera* session of the police court to which anonymous witnesses gave testimony, convinced the Crown not to proceed. Or, perhaps following Paul Craven's argument, the Crown recognized that the courts were unlikely to return convictions for conspiracy.[101] In any case, the charges and refusal to negotiate had the desired effect of weakening worker solidarity. Both foundries were able to hire sufficient labour by about September to resume operations, though on a reduced scale it would seem, and Buck settled with his workers by January 1861.[102] Workers at Butler and Jackson, supported by financial assistance from the IMU central fund, stayed out. Despite statements to the contrary, their resolve must have affected the foundry's ability to hire scabs. When William Sylvis, the American president of the IMU, took an organizing trip through Canada in 1863, the partners fulminated that they would ultimately "break up" the union. They did not. In 1864 Butler and Jackson settled with their workers.[103]

Employers also used the courts to impede the cigarmakers' efforts at organization. A small trade of just fifteen men in 1871, cigarmaking had nonetheless been reorganized in the past ten years. Only two cigarmakers, both self-employed and working in their own residences, were in Brantford 1861. Ten years later there were still two shops, but each employed eight workers. Brantford cigarmakers had helped found a short-lived provincial Journeymen Cigarmakers' Union in 1865. By 1871 the six journeymen and two apprentices in John Whitroff's shop had formed a union, Local 59 of the Cigarmakers' International. That year they sought to organize their brothers at H.B. Leeming and William Paterson's establishment. No doubt in response to pressure from their employers, the non-union cigarmakers filed charges against those who pressed them to join. One organizer was fined $20, while another was ordered to place a bond to keep the peace. Nonetheless, the Cigarmakers' Union remained active in Brantford through the decade. In January 1878 the cigarmakers held a charity ball to raise money for their brothers on strike in New York City; later that year, they went out on strike themselves. Just who their targets were went unreported, though three shops were in operation at the time.[104]

Other workingmen organized in the 1860s and early 1870s as well. Carpenters formed a union in June 1864.[105] The Grand Trunk engine drivers belonged to the Brotherhood of Locomotive Engineers, and they too participated in the 1876–7 strike, though the events do not appear to have been as dramatic as in Stratford, Belleville, and Brockville, perhaps because Brantford was not on the main line and the disruption of traffic was less severe.[106] Coopers walked out of one shop in 1871 until the proprietor fired a journeyman who opposed their union. Another "boss cooper," Henry Reid, was less accommodating to his workers the following year. When three men put down their tools to protest changes in the traditional division of labour in barrel making, Reid fired them.[107] Shoemakers organized Lodge 13 of the Knights of St Crispin in 1873, and Eugene Forsey has suggested that the carriage makers may too have been organized by that year, though his evidence, a craft picnic, is hardly conclusive.[108] In 1873 printers struck against E.A. Percy, publisher of the Brantford *Daily News*. Wages were at issue, but workers were equally offended by the abusive attitude of their employer. S.M.L. Luke, a jour printer, informed readers of the *Ontario Workman* that the men had held back taking action hoping that Percy would improve after he joined a "teetotal organization," but that was not to be.[109] That white collar workers did not always identify with their employers became apparent when dry goods clerks formed an association in 1875 to protest their working conditions and drum up public support for early closing.[110]

Hours of work of course were the major issue in the mid-1870s.[111] Brantford workers were aware of their counterparts' efforts in Hamilton, where in January 1872 the Nine Hour Movement was born. On the evening of 7 February, Mayor William Paterson convened a meeting of about five hundred people in the town hall to discuss the question. Shorter hours, argued machinist Fred Bromwich and Donald Buchanan, a shoemaker, would give workingmen more time for social, moral, and intellectual improvement. Alfred Watts, merchant miller, distiller, and soap manufacturer, and Arthur S. Hardy, ambitious lawyer and future provincial premier, suggested that businessmen could support the reduction, if it were universal so as not to disadvantage those accepting shorter hours. The Rev. T. Lowry suggested that a "conference between workmen and the employers" should be called to negotiate the issue. The assembly resolved: "We, the working men of Brantford ... in mass meeting assembled affirm that we heartily concur with the spirit of the resolutions adopted by the working men of the City of Hamilton, on the evening of Jan. 27th, 1872, and we unanimously affirm that the nine hours labour movement has become a social necessity, and we are determined to co-operate with them in securing for ourselves its speedy adoption by every legitimate means in our power."[112] This first nine-hour meeting differed slightly from meetings in Hamilton and Toronto. In the larger cities, they were much more clearly gatherings of workingmen, despite addresses from officials and businessmen. In Brantford, it was a town meeting chaired by the mayor, a major employer.[113]

At a second meeting later that month, the Brantford Nine Hour Workingman's League was formed, with Edwin Davies, a millwright in the Grand Trunk shops, as president; carpenter King Vann, also employed by the railroad, as vice-president; blacksmith George Campbell, a Grand Trunk worker, as treasurer; and Alex Shaw, an engine fitter at Waterous and Wilkes, as secretary. Donald Buchanan was corresponding secretary and at a Nine Hour convention in Hamilton in May was elected vice-president of the Canadian Labor Protective and Mutual Improvement Association. One hundred and twenty-five men joined the league at its first Brantford meeting.[114] Initially the moderate tone of the workers convinced the *Expositor* that "if ... it will embarrass the employers to grant what is asked, we do not think the workingmen will persist in asking it."[115]

The paper was wrong. Negotiations with employers through March and April went unreported. The iron founders and engine manufacturers, who appear to have been the main target of the league, dug in their heels. The *Ontario Workman* judged that, because of the strong combination among Brantford employers, workers there confronted firmer resistance than in Hamilton and Toronto.[116] Like other founders across the province, Brantford's presented their workers with a document to sign disavowing support for any association agitating for a reduction in hours of labour. On 10 May Waterous and Wilkes, committing themselves to meet "reasonable" requests, including shorter hours, locked out eighty-nine men who refused to sign the pledge. The lock-out continued for at least two weeks, until William Cowherd, a machinist, led the men back to work.[117]

The Brantford correspondent of the *Ontario Workman* roundly denounced Cowherd's action, and Buchanan lamented that Brantford's workers were not ready for the "conflict with capital."[118] Perhaps not. Cowherd was the son of Thomas, the Tinsmith Rhymer, and had two brothers self-employed as tinsmiths. William Cowherd was not the only worker whose family background placed him in an ambiguous position. During the nine-hour campaign, Fred Bromwich urged his co-workers to seek change "not by combination of trades union in getting up strikes, but by discussing the matter fairly and squarely with employers." His father, John Bromwich, was a builder. A resident of Brantford since at least 1852, Bromwich Sr had immigrated from England with his wife in about 1841 and had worked at his trade as a carpenter, until some time in the 1860s when he became self-employed. As he had done for his eldest son Fred, John found trades for his other boys, William as a moulder, Ed and John as cigarmakers. William Cowherd and Fred Bromwich were just the sort of young men whom Charles Waterous wanted to work for him, Brantford lads with deep roots in the artisan culture of the community. All Waterous's foremen had served in the factory from boyhood. William Walkinshaw, Jr, in charge of one of the finishing shops, for example, was the son of a self-employed Scottish Presbyterian tailor.[119] The contradictions which emerged in the commitment of workers to the nine-hour cause may have disappointed Buchanan, but they arose honestly from the social origins of many of the men.

Brantford's employers may have been firm in their resolve not to deal with unions, but their origins also produced contradictory attitudes, for they too shared the craft culture of their workers and appreciated independence as a character trait. They were prepared to encourage even those schemes, such as co-operatives, which Steven Langdon for one has taken as evidence of a "radical perspective."[120] In late 1864 a number of workingmen in Brantford, impressed by similar ventures in Toronto and Hamilton, proposed forming a co-operative society which would sell shares to raise sufficient capital to undertake a grocery business. The society, with Henry Carlton, a fifty-year-old English iron fitter at Waterous and Wilkes, as president and John Harper, a thirty-four-year-old Irish blacksmith, as chairman of the board of directors, held a public meeting in March 1865 to drum up support. Whether or not, like their Toronto counterparts, they saw co-ops as a way "to take us from under the hand of our employers"[121] is not known. But they did solicit advice from local businessmen and asked Thomas Shenston, county registrar, moneylender, and former harnessmaker, to chair the meeting. Robert Sproule, a general merchant and one of the town's wealthiest men, offered practical suggestions on purchasing stock. Others discussed how co-operatives in England operated. Finally, the Rev. William Cochrane, formerly a bookstore manager, moved, seconded by A.B. Bennett, a private banker: "Taking into consideration the difficulties and disadvantages under which workingmen labour, in procuring for themselves and their families the necessaries of life and being fully persuaded that 'Union is Strength,' in this as in many other undertakings; therefore this meeting, composed of the workingmen of Brantford and having considered the principles of Co-operative Societies, as worked in Great Britain, – resolve to adopt the principle of said Co-operative Societies." The resolution carried.[122] A co-op store was opened, and though its history remains obscure, one still functioned in the late 1870s.

That businessmen should participate in this workingman's enterprise, and that workingmen should have been open to such participation, may seem strange. Yet, both understood collaboration as a form of mutual self-help. On another occasion, business involvement was sought for a producers' co-op. In 1869 one shoemaker, proposing the establishment of a co-op boot and shoe factory with two to three hundred hands, called on Arunah Huntington to back the scheme.[123] Huntington, the frontier cordwainer grown rich, seemed an archetype of the successful artisan. Though nothing came of it, the proposal revealed a feeling that those who had succeeded were in some sense obligated to help those who were as they had been.

Paternalism, of this and other kinds, and workers' reactions to it have been debated with some vigour. Patrick Joyce has maintained that in the last half of the nineteenth century the paternalism of Lancashire millowners imparted a moral authority to their relations with their workers, and, in communities where paternalism permeated the full range of institutional life, it transformed employees' dependence upon wage labour into a deference which contributed to class quiescence. H.I. Dutton and J.E. King, however, have disagreed. They conclude that the influence of paternalism was limited by millhands' ability to see "factory society in a pluralistic, not unitary, light."[124] In their examination of Canadian railway operations in the 1850s, Paul Craven and Tom Traves concluded that employers adopted paternalism not merely because of some rational calculation of the limits of market forces in disciplining labour, but also because of "ideological and broadly cultural wellsprings." Employers believed it was proper to treat wage labour relationships as personal relationships.[125] Conclusions about the effectiveness and sincerity of paternalism are of course useful, yet more needs to be known about the meaning attached to such relations.

Craven and Traves relate an incident of interest for this study. When in 1856 Henry Yates left his job as the Great Western's locomotive superintendent to take up the position of mechanical superintendent for the Buffalo and Lake Huron Railway in Brantford, a number of employees held a dinner in his honour. The master of ceremonies informed those in attendance that "Mr. Yates is one of our own class, having graduated amongst us." The testimonial not only "honoured upward mobility and workplace harmony," as Craven and Traves concluded,[126] it also was a ritual of recognition which implicitly placed expectations of proper behaviour upon the one who was recognized: you are one of us and should act as one of us; to act otherwise is a betrayal of your origins and identity. It was also a ritual for the benefit of the company and Yates's replacement: this man was one of us and acted as such, thereby contributing to amicable relations and the efficient operations of the plant; you who take his place should learn from his example. If this was paternalism, it was conditional, contingent, and contractual. It also embodied an effort at fraternalism, though because of the obvious differences in status it took a ritualized form.[127]

Numerous instances of ritualized discourse witnessed the attempts of businessmen to restore intimacy to employment relations. Most common was the company party, usually scheduled to coincide with some other festive occasion or during the summer. Robert Storey, a cigar manufacturer, gave a supper at Ben Foster's restaurant for about twenty of his workers and their guests at New Year's in 1878.[128] More common as the venue was the businessman's home, and more often his wife had supervised the preparations, while his children, especially daughters, might offer musical entertainment. Mr and Mrs John Taylor opened their house to the former's dry goods staff as the new year 1881 began.[129] Employees themselves often took the initiative in planning such events. New Year's 1869 provided the occasion for the employees of dry goods merchant Thomas McLean to entertain him and a number of former employees, while the clerks and other staff of another dry goods merchant, Hugh Jones, met at his residence to congratulate him on his marriage in March 1881 and to present him with a gift. Jones was pleased "the cordial feeling that existed between employer and employees," and promised that "if the bond were ever broken, it would not be through any fault of his."[130] Occasions like this were not necessarily evidence of the workplace as family and the employer as paterfamilias, in the mould identified by Patrick Joyce.[131] If seen as negotiation, this was an occasion on which Jones's workers had sought and won a statement of good faith from their boss at a singularly important time in his life and in a place where he was most vulnerable.[132] Was it not at home, that sphere of life separate from the tumult of the business world, where the Victorian man might reveal his true character free from the assault of hostile forces?

The social gathering provided an opportunity to affirm a contract of good intent, which, ultimately no better than the paper it was written on, nonetheless pledged the businessman to good relations.

That the pledge often followed the presentation of a gift from the employees was consistent with a ritual of exchange. The boss paid wages for good service; the workers gave some token of appreciation for the consideration that the businessman gave their interests. Conflict initiated by either party meant that the other had transgressed the non-monetary aspects of their relationship.

The fullest report of this ritual exchange described an evening gathering in early December 1877 at the house of Adam Spence, carriage manufacturer. Presenting a chain and locket to Spence for his wife, Levi Fisher spoke on behalf of his workmates when he thanked their employer for "the generous regard and thoughtful care you have at all times displayed towards those under you." He went on to explain that relations at Spence's plant were somewhat extraordinary. "Between capital and labor perplexing difficulties will frequently occur where the opposing interests appear to clash, but happily with us no serious disputes have arisen, all minor difficulties have been amicably arranged, and our relations have always been of the most intimate and cordial nature." Significantly Fisher accepted that capital and labour do conflict and that matters of contention had occurred in the carriage factory. That no major confrontation or strike had resulted he attributed to Spence's "sound business capacity, mature judgment and desire to do that which is fair and right between man and man." By complimenting his boss, Fisher in effect denied that any of the issues previously implied had involved unreasonable demands from the workers. Deferential the speech was indeed, but it was edged to cut both ways.

Spence accepted the gift; how could he do otherwise when it was intended for his wife? He replied, "I am not unmindful of the good estimation of my fellow men, and have through life endeavored so to live as to merit the esteem of my fellows, but there is no class whose good opinion I would sooner have than of my own employees, for two reasons – first, because I was once an employee myself, and therefore kindly appreciate the feelings and aspirations of an employee; secondly, I am sensible that the mechanical employees are an intelligent class, fully capable of forming correct judgments." Spence expressed an ambiguous understanding of his relationship to his workers; he welcomed the esteem of his fellows, but he also noted that they were a class distinct from him. He had once been of their class, but he was no longer, though his history made him appreciate their intelligence. The ambiguity of status was resolved in Spence's closing benediction, "hoping that each of you will so prosper, that by and by you will all be employers instead of employees."[133] Did Adam Spence really believe it was a possibility, and did his workers take him seriously? Of course, we cannot know. But, if we accept an element of negotiation in the ritualized exchange, then perhaps it is sufficient to conclude that each side was trying to define some ground rules. The workers attributed responsibility for good relations to Spence, while the latter argued that in the past he had been like them and the future they would be like him, his past as their future.[134]

Spence was not alone in assuming that wage labour should be a temporary condition for the ambitious individual. The obverse was that those unable to transcend it were deficient in some way. One cynic, signing "Old Style" in a letter to the newspaper, dismissed the proposed boot and shoe co-operative as chimerical: "Any one who knows the laws of trade understands that the mass of men, particularly mechanics, will only work for their weekly pay, and have no thought of anything further than how to make out their weekly expenses. They are unfitted for any intelligent appreciation of the future, and are made only to be servants of the men of business and capitalists."[135]

The slander met with as blunt a rejoinder: "he is one of those 'bloated aristocrats', who having made money out of trade or the law, in which his father the blacksmith started him, cannot say a good word of the honest, intelligent, working mechanic." Significantly the workingman's defender chose to explain the insult as a consequence of someone forgetting his social origins, his own history; in attacking the mechanic, "Old Style" had attacked the source of his own good fortune.[136]

The editor of the *Expositor* was somewhat more sympathetic to the workingman in an article entitled "Strikes and their Remedies," though he too doubted the character of men who worked for wages. "The status of hired labour will gradually tend to confine itself to the description of work-people whose low moral qualities render them unfit for anything more independent." But this latter comment might be read, not specifically as a criticism of workers, but of the factory. A man keen for independence would not choose wage labour, and therefore the factory could not satisfy and hold the men who possessed the finest qualities of character because it denied the property that labour created in its product. "Everyone who contributes to the work, either by work or pecuniary resources, has a partner's interest in it proportionate to the value of his contribution." Thus, factories – or dry goods stores for that matter, one assumes – should distribute profit shares, rather than wages, much as had been the case on sailing vessels or whaling expeditions or in the Cornish mines.[137] Profit sharing understood in this sense was no mere bonus for good behaviour. While an employer like H.B. Leeming, the confectionery and cigar manufacturer, might tell his workers that "the interests of employers and employees are identical," no one seriously considered introducing the *Expositor*'s proposal.[138]

CONCLUSION

Industrialization spawned new businesses and new social relationships in Brantford. The expansion of retail commerce may have offset the reduction in the number of self-employed occasioned by the increasing redundancy of craft production in the 1860s and 1870s, but it did little to diminish the effect upon craft producers. Self-employment declined as fewer and fewer of the discontinued businesses of independent tradesmen and master artisans were replaced, and more and more tradesmen found employment in the growing factories.

Despite the need of more men to take wage labour, many of those who hired them viewed the condition of employment with some ambivalence and, because of their own histories, were unwilling to acknowledge that it might be a permanent experience. At the same time, many of those who earned wages, because of their backgrounds, could not easily or for long accept social conflict and class identity as an inherent part of their work life. Workingmen and their employers shifted between two poles of interaction, class confrontation as evidenced most dramatically in the unionization of the metal trades and the Nine Hour Strike on the one side, and renegotiated paternalism as articulated by Adam Spence and his carriage makers on the other. Greater recourse to one or the other was probably related to the progress and extent of changes in production in particular industries, but each evidenced a consciousness of social change.

2 Who Was Self-Employed?

The mid-Victorian decline in self-employment called into question widely held personal aspirations. No longer could a mature man realistically expect to demonstrate his independence by working for himself, even if only in a small way. Greater difficulties in embarking upon a business career gave more importance to advantage and connections and altered the social meaning of self-employment. In consequence, the demographic profile of Brantford's business community changed, so that business in 1881 was not the accessible activity that it had been in 1852.

In the 1840s and 1850s the absence of entrenched business interests attracted immigrants intent on independence to Brantford. Their presence, numerically and relatively larger than that of the Canadian-born, made business very much an affair of newcomers. The persistence of the successful among them and the contracting opportunities for self-employment in the 1870s set higher entry qualifications for the next generation. Advantage went to those who not only understood their trade and custom thoroughly but also knew the community and were known in it, men whose fathers or brothers or in-laws might pledge capital, credit, and reputation to get them set up. Few immigrants enjoyed connections of this sort, and more frequently new businessmen by the end of the period under review were Canadians by birth, who in many instances possessed a lengthy association with the community. The need to form connections and accumulate advantage delayed self-employment, and by 1881 the self-employed were not just a smaller group but an older one as well.

Business had ceased to be what it had been earlier, a stage in a man's life, to be embarked upon at full maturity along with other responsibilities.

IMMIGRATION FOR SELF-EMPLOYMENT

Immigrants were attracted to Brantford at a time when self-employment was receding as a possibility in the more industrialized societies of Britain and the American northeast. Brantford and Ontario, then, were on a particular sort of frontier, the cutting edge of which afforded chances to reprise social processes passed elsewhere. Land and farming no doubt held the greatest attraction for immigrants to British North America. But despite the continuing accessibility of farming in Ontario even in the 1860s, as Darroch and Ornstein maintain, agriculture was not the only "promise of Canadian life."[1] The urban businessman, whether merchant or manufacturer, artisan or shopkeeper, was not merely the frustrated farmer, forced from the land or waiting to take it up – though examples of both were surely common. Bruce Elliott's meticulous genealogical research on chain migration has suggested that immigrants tried to reproduce their former lifestyles. Few among the North Tipperary Irish farmers and rural tradesmen sought urban self-employment, or even urban employment, and few Irish town dwellers settled in the transplanted communities he studied.[2] The converse – that all urban immigrants chose the city over the country – is of course not necessarily true.

H.C. Pentland's contention that the immigrant English artisan had already accepted wage labour and factory employment exaggerated the progress of British industrialization. Contemporary reporters, such as George Dodd or Henry Mayhew, documented the continuing pressure on traditional crafts well into mid-century.[3] The immigrant might well have chosen to take up farmland in British North America. Yet, to find an alternative to capitalist wage labour he need not farm or bring his sons up to be farmers, since crafts depreciated at home were valued in British North America.

The opportunity for independence in British North America at a time when it seemed less possible elsewhere became a major theme of immigration literature.[4] Joseph Pickering in 1832 pinpointed "the chief of evils complained of" in Britain as being "the accumulating of immense wealth into large masses, virtually monopolizing (since the introduction of steam power and other modern machinery) the means and sources of the middle and lower classes, like large globules of quicksilver swallowing up small ones within their sphere of attraction."[5] An anonymous English publicist, claiming a long experience in commerce, concluded: "Commerce is doubling itself with men of bulk, to the great privation of the middle order of trades, and I have no doubt that the time is fast approaching when they will be as mere tools or engines, in the hands of grand monopolies. ... Commerce [in reaction] is winging its flight, and is rapidly transporting itself to the shores of the Atlantic."[6] Men with modest funds were warned about their futures in England and advised of the greater remuneration given to small business in Canada.[7] Joseph M. Cobbett wrote in 1832 that Canada "is a country for an industrious person; he may live well and be more independent than in England."[8] In the absence of competition in Canada, an 1857 pamphlet explained, "the opportunity for taking job-work and setting up on his own account is much greater."[9] Moreover, the shortage of skilled labour made it possible for even those whose command of their trade was incomplete to be self-employed.[10]

The greatest opportunities were offered in the small towns and villages. As one author observed after visiting Brantford in 1828, "villages in this country are mostly embryos of towns, full of trade and business, and some of them increasing fast."[11] Another in the 1830s recommended Guelph, where there "are no long-established interests to contend with."[12] The immigrant was advised that "he would get paid more regularly in cash in large towns, but he will not get the same opportunities of accumulating capital" as in "a rising village."[13] But, small places were not without their own peculiar risks. Because of lack of development, capital once invested was not easily liquidated. Nor were enterprises "on too large a scale for the resources of the country to compensate" recommended.[14] While these last caveats may have given pause to wealthy prospective immigrants, they afforded the small businessman a certain protection and a chance to prosper as the country developed.

James Cockshutt, founder of Brantford's most successful business family, appears to have followed this sort of advice. In later life he explained that the sight of a Luddite mob smashing several wagonloads of machinery in the streets of Colne, Lancashire, had convinced him to seek a more hospitable place in which to invest the small inheritance he had received from his grandfather, a manufacturer and landowner. Cockshutt had engaged in business for some time before he decided to emigrate. His first venture, a partnership in a Bradford cotton factory, failed in 1816 in the commercial depression following the Napoleonic Wars. He then managed his grandfather's farm at Warsaw Hill near Clitheroe, Lancashire, until 1822, when he again went into business, this time in Colne. Five years later, in July, Cockshutt and his family sailed from Liverpool.

Initially destined for Pittsburgh, Pennsylvania, Cockshutt was persuaded on board ship by a friend, James Laycock, to go into business with him in York, Upper Canada. Their partnership lasted only a year before Cockshutt started a general merchandising business on his own. In 1829 he formed another partnership, this time with Christopher Batty, who went to Brantford, with Cockshutt's son Ignatius as clerk, to open a branch store. Though this up-country venture folded in less than a year, the younger Cockshutt convinced his father that business conditions would be more favourable once the village and surrounding township were ceded by the Six Nations to the Crown and opened for settlement. In 1832 Ignatius reopened the Brantford branch, and it proved so profitable that two years later his father closed the York operation to concentrate on Brantford. When James Cockshutt sold the business to his son, Ignatius, and daughter, Jane, in 1840, he was a wealthy man. He returned briefly to England and paid in full his old creditors with whom he had compromised following his 1816 failure.[15]

James Cockshutt's example illustrated much that was expressed in nineteenth-century immigration literature. It also demonstrated that more was at stake than merely a way of earning a living. A whole set of social values, of ways of organizing lives, and most important a conception of self was at risk: a man had to be independent, yet responsible; his financial obligations were moral commitments that must be fulfilled, even if the law granted remission. Self-employment marked most clearly and completely that goal which, according to John Vincent, men in the nineteenth-century coveted most deeply – independence, to call no man master.[16] Being one's own master distinguished the mature and manly individual who knew his trade thoroughly and could maintain his family decently through his own endeavours. Self-employment, the ability to partake of the fruits of one's labour, to hold the property that was the product of one's labour, was considered a right and a legitimate aspiration. Respectable businessmen did not infringe on each other's rights by cutthroat competition or unfair advertising. Instead, they favoured the stability of modest livings for all over large profits for a few and failure for many.[17]

The desire for self-employment was founded in a shop culture that was familiar to both British and North American artisans. The whole process of learning skills and traditions of a trade had as its logical conclusion for the initiate the possibility of becoming a master, and in close contact employer and journeyman came to accept many of the same values of success through hard work and self-improvement.[18] Susan E. Hersch has argued that, rather than barriers, the different statuses of apprentice, journeyman, and master were the stages of individual advancement leading to maturity and independence. For this reason, she argues that artisans constituted a single class. Hersch may, however, assume too much from the artisanal work and life cycle. Perhaps the journeyman's prospects for and past experiences of self-employment, along with his craft skill and ownership of his tools, are better conceived as factors at play in negotiating the wage labour relationship with a master. Craft unity, based at least at the level of ideology upon the mutual acceptance of the artisanal work and life cycle, cemented the wage labour relationship between men more nearly equal in bargaining power than later under industrial capitalist relations.[19]

Among masters, acceptance of upward mobility through a trade acted as a check upon unbridled competition and led those already established in business to encourage worthy protégés and associates.[20] As Paul E. Johnson has reminded us in his study of Rochester, "it is the ... assumption that the entrepreneurial world was filled with freely competing individuals that must be set aside." Business was a social activity, entry into which was often achieved through the co-operation and patronage from others who had already attained that status.[21] Similarly, nineteenth-century artisans seemed to express a generosity in conveying information about their craft to others. Machinists and mechanical engineers, for example, as Anthony Wallace and Monte Calvert have both noted, considered the expansion of knowledge a responsibility of their craft and therefore willingly publicized their own innovative practices and processes.[22] Not only did this attitude reveal a sense of brotherhood in a trade, but it also reflected the attitude common in the early stages of industrial capitalism that the principal threat to business longevity was not competition but a "capricious environment" of natural disasters, unforeseen panics, and individual conspiracy.[23]

In the first half of the nineteenth century in Britain and in the American northeast, men increasingly found that their conviction that a man should partake of the fruits of his own labour confronted the reality of ever more pervasive wage labour.[24] To achieve the manly independence which they believed was their due, many immigrated, seeking new places free from the complexities of emergent industrial capitalist relations.

BIRTHPLACE, RELIGION, AND SELF-EMPLOYMENT

Recent scholarship has challenged the association between immigration and occupational structure that once characterized much of the historiography on mid-Victorian social change and which may seem implicit from the foregoing discussion of immigration literature. Pentland's early theory of the segmentation of the labour force along lines of ethnic cleavage, of an Irish Catholic proletariat and English and Scottish skilled labour, is simply not consistent with the evidence presented in Donald Akenson's study of the Irish in the combined townships of Leeds and Landsdowne, or in Darroch and Ornstein's analysis of south-central Ontario in 1861 and 1871. Akenson has concluded that the Irish, whether Protestant or Catholic, were "a rural people in Ontario," drawn to farming, and just as likely to be successful at it as any other ethnic group. His admission that Ontario social structure varied, from gritty urban Hamilton to the rugged Shield frontier, has not restrained him from arguing for the typicality of the locus of his own micro-study and rejecting Michael Katz's portrayal of the Irish Catholics, on the basis of the Hamilton example, as the Canadian lumpenproletariat.[25] The reiteration of Ontario as a predominantly rural society in the nineteenth century is a needed corrective to the urban focus of much social history and the lingering influence of the metropolitan theory. On the other hand, without wishing to make a virtue of inconsistency and disagreement, one might argue that the unevenness and local variation which characterized the social experience and economic development of Ontario might well be distorted by either the search for the representative micro-study or the general regional analysis. The peculiarities of settlement patterns, the particular locales which drew chain migration, the commercial and transportation ties that arose from boosterism, all contributed to differing patterns of stratification and structure. The homogeneity of processes and structure from place to place should not be assumed, but rather be seen as developing more slowly over time.

Darroch and Ornstein have found in their regional data "no single, dramatic difference in the occupational distributions of the people with different birthplaces or between Catholics and others." While they accept some indication of ethnic specialization, especially with Irish Catholics as urban labourers, the pattern does not convince them of any "deep splits" in the occupational structure. Rather they argue that the major ethnic groups were "institutionally complete," that is each contained a full range of occupational possibilities. This they interpret to indicate the ability of immigrants to draw upon various resources and opportunities, such as employment, lodging, credit, and other aid, from within their own group.[26] Darroch and Ornstein's work suggests the need for more detailed study of the institutional completeness and complexity of various groups. But it also requires some refinement. The thesis of ethnic segmentation cannot be sustained, but there is sufficient variation in the occupational structure of groups to conclude that all groups were not equally complete or complex in all communities. Further, one might speculate about the social strategies inherent in intra-group assistance. Why should one with advantage help a countryman in need? What mutual benefits were involved? Building custom and establishing political influence among one's countrymen surely were as important as memories of home in the mind of the established businessman when he offered credit, work, or advice.

The evidence from Brantford, where immigrants predominated in business and where different groups concentrated in different lines of business, provides some variations on the interpretation of the relationship between birthplace and occupational structure. The "splits" may not have been "deep" or "dramatic," but there was a discernible pattern. An evaluation of the significance of birthplace in explaining patterns of self-employment requires a consideration of two related variables, religious affiliation and age. Religion reinforced birthplace, providing an institutional structure within which national affinities might be expressed. As well, because immigration was not a constant source of population increase through the period under study, immigrant groups over time tended to be older than Canadians. In a review of recent studies of working-class history, Chad Gaffield has suggested that the possible influence of demographic transitions ought to be taken into account when discussing workers' responses to industrial change.[27] Such a coincidence affected self-employment in mid-nineteenth-century Brantford.

The immigrant presence in Brantford increased in the 1840s, and though it declined after 1852, immigrants still accounted for 55 per cent of the self-employed in 1881. In the four cross-section years from 1852 to 1881, the English were the largest immigrant group, followed by the Irish, the Scots, and the Americans. The English might well have been expected to be the most numerous immigrant group among businessmen, since they were most numerous among the adult male work force, defined for the purposes of this study as those men sixteen years of age and over who reported an occupation in the census. But only to a degree was the representation of national groups in business a function of their representation in the larger workforce. In 1852 and 1871 different levels of self-employment were associated with different groups. In particular, the Canadians had a significantly lower rate of self-employment and the Americans a higher rate in both years, while the Scots were over-represented in the latter year. The 1881 structure revealed a more specific pattern: although birthplace and self-employment were not associated in any statistically significant way when national groups were considered separately, the two largest groups did differ from each other and the rest of the population, the Canadians being less likely and the English more likely to be in business (table 2.1).

The over-representation of immigrants in business might be expected. Having left home in pursuit of independence, they probably were highly motivated to attain their goal. Charlotte Erickson, in her collection of letters written by English and Scottish immigrants, concluded that the immigrant felt compelled to set up on his own account and guilty if he failed to do so. Alan Wilson has emphasized the power that the need to succeed had upon John Northway, a Devon tailor who immigrated in 1869. Perhaps too, deprived of opportunities at home, the immigrant was more eager than the native to seize the initiative in his adopted country.[28]

Instinctively the immigrant sought out his countrymen, hoping for the advantage of custom and support rooted in national affinities. That some immigrant groups should be over-represented at one time and not another suggests that those advantages were not a constant and that the success or failure of particular individuals might affect the prospects of their countrymen. Immigration and adjustment to a new society, as Bruce Elliott demonstrated, followed networks of connections; the failure of a link in that chain might compromise the fortunes of others.

Brantford's immigrants were well aware of the significance of contacts. In 1852 John Wilson, a journeyman tinsmith from Westmoreland, sought out Thomas Cowherd, who gave him employment and board in 1852. Ignatius Cockshutt hired and boarded one servant, a labourer, and four clerks who attended Farringdon Independentist church with him. Two clerks were from Yorkshire, while the servant and the labourer had been born in Lancashire, both counties in the district from which the Cockshutts had emigrated. Organizational as well as personal connections facilitated chain migration. In 1844 several of the English residents of Brantford formed Brant Lodge of the Independent Order of Oddfellows and affiliated with the Manchester Unity. A lodge associated with the English body gave men from the old country an entry into Brantford society, providing them with introductions and help in adapting to a new society. But the Brantford lodge was less useful in facilitating mobility within North America. In 1849 Gore Lodge split from the Brant Lodge and, though initially linked to Manchester, it switched its affiliation to the American IOOF in 1854. A Brantford Oddfellow later explained that "such of the members as found it necessary to travel were very much isolated, and without that aid and comfort resulting from being able

Table 2.1
Birthplace of the Self-Employed and Wage-Labouring Adult Male Population,
1852–81

Birthplace	1852		1861		1871		1881	
	Self-employed (%)	Wage labour (%)	Self-employed (%)	Wage labour (%)	Self-employed (%)	Wage labour (%)	Self-employed (%)	Wage labour (%)
Canada	**14**	22	15	19	**26**	38	**44**	56
United States	**16**	8	9	10	**9**	5	6	4
England	33	26	36	31	30	30	**27**	20
Scotland	11	12	11	11	**14**	9	8	7
Ireland, Protestant	19	16	16	12	**16**	7	**9**	5
Ireland, Catholic	**7**	15	10	13	**2**	10	**3**	6
Other		1	3	4	3	1	3	2
Total	100	100	100	100	100	100	100	100
Number	238	710	356	1,069	375	1,585	400	2,012
Chi square	21.423		4.251		25.545		6.186	
Probability	0.001		0.373		0.001		0.186	
DF	4		4		4		4	

Note: Because of the small numbers in the category "Other," it was not included in the calculation of the chi square statistic for each cross-section. For this reason there are only four degrees of freedom.

Figures in bold type indicate that self-employment among members of a national group were significantly higher or lower than average. To calculate this, the population at each cross-section was divided into a series of dichotomies for each group and all others. Chi-square, significant at <0.05 probability, identified those groups whose level of self-employment differed significantly from the rest of the population. In 1852 the English narrowly missed meeting this criterion.

to visit sister lodges." By 1860 the Gore claimed 140 members. Its growth perhaps persuaded the Brant Lodge to join American Odd-fellowship in 1868 and encouraged the establishment of another lodge, Harmony, in 1873. After 1870 fraternal organizations of various kinds – Foresters, Shepherds, United Workmen, and the Royal Arcanum, among others – proliferated in Brantford, with twelve forming in as many years.

As Joan Jacobs Brumberg and Faye E. Dudden have remarked about fraternal organizations in the United States, "if they had not been useful for cultivating business contacts and sources of credit, securing insurance in an unpredictable marketplace, and maintaining transferable networks of sociability in an era of great geographical mobility, they would not have survived and thrived." Brumberg and Dudden levelled their comments in a review of Mark Carnes's recent study of the role of fraternalism in defining masculinity in the mid-nineteenth-century. While they accept his thesis that secret rituals affirmed male identity at a time of crisis when the participation of men in organized religion, child-rearing, and family organization was being reduced, they contend that practical benefits also accrued to the brothers in such orders. The psychological and economic rewards of fraternalism were not necessarily separate, however, since the material support of one's lodge brothers might contribute to the achievement of that independence which for so long was at the heart of mature masculinity. The Grand Secretary of the Grand Lodge of the United States, James Nicholson of Philadelphia, said as much when he explained to Brantford Oddfellows that secrecy protected them from public humiliation when they needed their lodge's help and charity. By concealing what some might take as masculine inadequacy, the lodge promoted moral improvement, mental recreation, and good citizenship; thus, "the tendency of the institution is to make men true men."[29]

At first glance, the Irish appear to have enjoyed little comparative advantage in gaining their independence through immigration. However, the absence of a significant association between an Irish birth and self-employment at any cross-section is a consequence of considering Catholics and Protestants as a group. Protestants born in Ireland were by far the most likely group to be self-employed in 1871 and 1881. Though they were only the third most numerous group in these two years, they did attain the highest rate of self-employment: 35 per cent of them in the first year and 28 per cent in the second were in business, compared with 28 per cent of Americans and 26 per cent of Scots in 1871 and 21 per cent of the English in 1881, the groups next most likely to be self-employed.

Irish Catholics, on the other hand, were significantly under-represented among businessmen in 1852, 1871, and 1881. That they should not have been so in 1861 is puzzling and might be attributed to two possible factors. First, self-employment was not associated with birthplace at all in that year. Depressed conditions limited the aid or custom that any group might give its members, and no doubt some individuals chose self-employment in 1861 in the absence of any employment alternative. Second, the manuscript census of that year was the only source in which it was possible to identify self-employed labourers, eighteen in number, fifteen of whom were Irish Catholics.[30] Labourers accounted for about 40 per cent of Irish Catholic businessmen in 1861. They were in some ways a remarkable lot. They were older, fifty being the median age, one-third being in their sixties. They had modest amounts of money at work: their median capital investment was just $250, but a third reported between $400 and $700. Representative was James McQuillan, who was born about 1798 and immigrated sometime in the early to mid-1830s and settled in Brantford before 1852. In 1861 he had $600 in his business and was helped out by his thirty-four-year-old son, Richard. His three unmarried daughters, Betsey, aged twenty-eight, Ellen, aged twenty-six, and Anna, aged twenty-three, also contributed to the family income by working as a dressmaker, milliner, and vestmaker respectively. Richard built upon his father's achievements. By 1871 he was working in one of the local tanneries and by 1881, though illiterate, had set up a small grocery store. Men like the McQuillans were jacks of all trade, hauling things, cleaning away debris, engaging in rough construction; few probably required credit, and in all likelihood, most would not have received much had they asked. Still their self-employment later in life marked one margin of possibilities for unskilled labour. The under-representation of Irish Catholics, then, was in some undetermined way a partial consequence of the inability to identify consistently the most marginal of the self-employed, men whose investment in business consisted of initiative, a horse and cart, a strong back, and a healthy son or two. This in itself is worthy of note.

But equally important is that Irish Catholics were not a sufficiently prosperous population to support a complex business community. Also the Catholic population in Brantford was declining in size, from 19 per cent of the adult male work force in 1861 to only 14 per cent in 1871 and 16 per cent in 1881. One wonders too whether St Basil's, the Catholic church in Brantford, was the most hospitable place for the successful, at least in the 1850s when its priest, Father Ryan, expressed decidedly levelling opinions. John Comerford, a general merchant and one of the two or three wealthiest Catholics in town, drew Ryan's wrath in particular. Comerford's young wife, Eliza, just twenty-one years of age, died suddenly in 1855, probably from complications arising after giving birth to her second daughter in two years. Her distraught husband wanted to place an elaborate monument over her grave. But Father Ryan objected to the display of wealth before his humble parish and forbade such a tombstone. The money, he counselled Comerford, would offer a better memorial to his wife if put to good works within the parish. Not to be denied the display of his grief, Comerford waited and, while Ryan was for a time absent from Brantford, had the stone installed. On his return, Ryan was furious. He denounced Comerford before the whole town, saying to the press that "Comerford would not raise a monument to the glory of God, but had raised one to the glory of the devil."[31] In and of itself, an incident like this probably did less to restrain Catholic entrepreneurship than did the lack of resources and the prejudice they may have suffered from Protestant lenders. Still the assertion of the Church's claim to share in the fruits of a man's labour was a sanction against the free exercise of individual choice.[32] For whatever reasons, as a group Roman Catholics were by far the least likely religious denomination to be self-employed, and their birthplace did not distinguish the Irish from others of the same faith.

Among Protestant businessmen, religious affiliation, to a degree, reinforced immigrant identities, most groups being at some time or other associated with one or two denominations and being under-represented in others. The Scots of course were overwhelmingly Presbyterians and only infrequently Anglicans or Methodists. Congregationalism was strongly associated with Americans. The English were significantly over-represented among communicants of the Church of England in 1852, 1871, and 1881, and nearly so in 1861. A disproportionately large number of them in 1861 and 1871 were Baptists. Very few were Presbyterians. Irish Protestants divided among Anglicans, Presbyterians, and Methodists, although in 1861 they were over-represented among the first and in 1881 among the last denominations. They were always conspicuously absent among the Baptists (table 2.2).

To relate differences in business behaviour to religious factors is inherently controversial and, in the end, not very satisfying. Yet, some puzzling relationships do emerge from the data. Congregationalists in 1861, 1871, and 1881 were more likely than members of any other denomination to be self-employed, and American Congregationalists were more likely than other Congregationalists or Americans of other faiths to be in business. Presbyterians in 1861, and Presbyterians more than other Scots that year, were over-represented in business. Similarly, among Englishmen in 1861 Baptists were most likely to be in business, and Baptists had significantly higher than average self-employment. These are not many instances, but they do suggest that, in those years in which certain national groups were over-represented in particular denominations, those denominations had significantly higher self-employment. One form of identity seemed to reinforce another in a way which helped to sustain self-employment (table 2.3).

Those denominations with greater self-employment among their members generally were ones with strong congregational structures and Calvinist theological tendencies – Congregationalists, Baptists, and Presbyterians. T.W. Acheson has maintained that "there is considerable evidence to suggest that a strong commitment to the Calvinist tradition can contribute to kinds of behaviour which promote

Table 2.2
Religion (Major Protestant Denominations Only) by Birthplace, 1852–81

Year	Religion	Canada (%)	United States (%)	England (%)	Scotland (%)	Ireland (%)	All (%)
1852	Church of England	45	**21**	**57**	8	55	43
	Presbyterian	7	3	**1**	**81**	15	15
	Methodist	14	27	20	11	28	21
	Baptist	**27**	15	16			12
	Congregationalist	7	**34**	6		2	9
	Total	100	100	100	100	100	100
	Number	29	33	76	26	46	210
1861	Church of England	37	21	42	**2**	**49**	35
	Presbyterian	**8**	14	**2**	**88**	20	19
	Methodist	24	25	29	8	27	25
	Baptist	**29**	18	**22**		**2**	16
	Congregationalist	2	**21**	5	2	2	5
	Total	100	100	100	100	100	100
	Number	49	28	120	41	55	293
1871	Church of England	19	27	**33**	**2**	31	23
	Presbyterian	**9**	10	**3**	**74**	22	20
	Methodist	**45**	17	33	**16**	36	33
	Baptist	21	17	**24**	6	**7**	17
	Congregationalist	6	**30**	7	2	4	7
	Total	100	100	100	100	100	100
	Number	86	30	108	51	58	333
1881	Church of England	**22**	29	**39**	3	37	27
	Presbyterian	19	25	**3**	**81**	16	20
	Methodist	28	17	23		**47**	25
	Baptist	27	8	29	16		23
	Congregationalist	4	**21**	6			5
	Total	100	100	100	100	100	100
	Number	168	24	105	31	38	366

Note: Figures in bold type indicate a statistically significant positive or negative association between birthplace and religious affiliation when these two variables are dichotomized. Significance is reported only when the expected cell size exceeds five cases.

high levels of accomplishment in the business world."[33] One wishes that such "considerable evidence" were more readily available. In her study of middle class formation in nineteenth-century Oneida County, New York, Mary P. Ryan has elaborated upon the significance

Table 2.3
Rates of Self-Employment by Religion (Major Protestant Denominations Only) by
Birthplace, 1852–81

Year	Religion	Canada (Rate %)	United States (Rate %)	England (Rate %)	Scotland (Rate %)	Ireland (Rate %)	All (Rate %)
1852	Church of England	21	78	32	25	27	29
	Presbyterian	10	14	17	29	21	23
	Methodist	9	39	22	75	**48**	26
	Baptist	25	28	31			26
	Congregationalist	17	**79**	28		33	32
	Total	17	46	29	28	29	28
	Number	29	33	76	26	46	210
1861	Church of England	20	19	**39**	6	30	23
	Presbyterian	21	31	17	**34**	38	32
	Methodist	14	9	28	27	29	21
	Baptist	**47**	10	**61**		14	32
	Congregationalist	13	**54**	38	20	33	36
	Total	21	15	29	27	31	25
	Number	49	28	120	41	55	293
1871	Church of England	9	42	12	9	30	14
	Presbyterian	10	20	13	26	33	21
	Methodist	16	14	**25**	89	36	22
	Baptist	18	28	**29**	50	80	25
	Congregationalist	14	**56**	30	33	40	28
	Total	13	29	18	29	35	20
	Number	86	30	108	51	58	333
1881	Church of England	13	100	14	25	17	15
	Presbyterian	13	20	18	17	24	16
	Methodist	**22**	11	23	50	34	23
	Baptist	14	29	21	14	75	17
	Congregationalist	20	78	36	100	20	31
	Total	17	30	19	20	25	19
	Number	168	24	105	31	38	366

Note: Figures in bold type indicate that men with this religious affiliation are significantly more likely to be self-employed than men with the same birthplace adhering to another denomination.

of evangelical religion, in that community primarily the faith of small businessmen. To "farmers, artisans, and shopkeepers ... struggling to maintain and improve themselves as small-scale independent businessmen ... evangelical churches and reform crusades ... were often

... an exercise in self-control."[34] Still, even if the question of the theological impact upon business behaviour is set aside, such denominations, by encouraging self-denial and congregational unity, did provide useful supports for business.

Adherence to such religious beliefs made easier that reinvestment of profits which promoted business expansion, but which denied a family the full measure of comfort possible in the short term. Religious conviction removed the burden of worry from the businessman who feared his family might suffer materially from his entrepreneurial commitments. As well, the congregation stood behind its members in business in a number of ways. A deserving young man might receive encouragement or even financial backing from his co-religionists to start his own business.[35] Once in business, he could reasonably hope to enjoy the patronage and confidence of the members of his church. Drawing upon her experiences as the daughter of a Brantford Presbyterian Scot dry goods merchant, Sara Jeanette Duncan in *The Imperialist* related the decision of Dr Drummond, the Presbyterian minister, to purchase a new stove from John Murchison, a member of his church: "it was not likely that Dr Drummond was going 'outside the congregation' for anything he required. It would have been on a par with a wandering tendency in his flock, upon which he systematically frowned."[36]

Should a businessman not live up to his moral responsibilities as a church member, be discovered to be dishonest in business, or not fulfil his partnership obligations to a co-religionist, he risked expulsion from his church or the loss of its custom. Moreover, he too was expected to help his church and co-religionists by hiring deserving young members recommended by the minister. The Rev. William Cochrane of Zion Presbyterian Church, the likely model for Dr Drummond, on occasion found clerking positions for young men in the dry goods establishments run by members of his congregation, Charles Duncan, William Grant, and Thomas McLean.[37]

A shared religious affiliation also cemented some partnerships. Not only did partnership inhibit the independence of a businessman, prior to limited liability it made him responsible for his partner's affairs. Business behaviour and honourable fulfilment of partnership obligations could become a matter of discussion, group criticism, and even arbitration.[38] Table 2.4 does suggest that factors other than religion weighed heavily in determining with whom a man might combine. Fourteen per cent found associates within their religious denomination, while about a third took relatives as partners, a proportion similar to that discovered by Mary Ryan in her study of Utica and by Melanie Archer in Detroit.[39] Approximately 50 per cent of

Table 2.4
Categories of Partnership by Religion, 1842–81

Religion	Relatives (%)	Co-religionists (%)	Others (%)	All (%)
Church of England	29	24	19	23
Presbyterian	13	17	22	18
Methodist	25	19	24	24
Baptist	16	9	17	16
Congregationalist	13	31	14	16
Roman Catholic	4		4	3
Total	100	100	100	100
Number of partners	132	54	193	379

all men chose partners with a different religious affiliation and to whom they were not related. Perhaps one should not be surprised that the resources of capital, connections, and experience that one might bring to business outweighed considerations of faith or blood in making a match. Yet, other studies have made observations that are somewhat different. Bernard Farber, studying a rather more exclusive population, Salem, Massachusetts, merchants in the early nineteenth-century, found that over 40 per cent of partnerships included family members. For an elite, partnerships frequently provided a way of satisfying inter- and intragenerational claims upon family capital without fragmenting a collective resource.[40] Paul Johnson in his study of Rochester, New York, has concluded that religion and family were interrelated factors in determining partnership choices in the 1820s. Businessmen who attended church or who were revival converts were significantly more likely to enter family partnerships than "non-religious" men, though the two groups were nearly equal in numbers and did not differ significantly in their propensity to collaborate. Though the Rochester data are not strictly comparable to those for Brantford, they do imply that partnerships were less common in the Canadian town. Though Johnson did not provide information on the birthplace of his subjects, the impression is that Rochester's business community was more native-born, and hence less uprooted than Brantford's in the 1850s and 1860s at least. The latter may have possessed fewer of family resources to draw upon (table 2.4).[41]

One association is notable, however, in Brantford. Congregationalists, never more than 8 per cent of the business population, accounted for 16 per cent of all those entering partnerships, largely because of their significantly greater propensity to collaborate with other Congregationalists. In this case, religion does seem to have afforded a useful sanction and guarantee of good behaviour.   /

ETHNICITY AND OCCUPATION

Even before the contraction in self-employment from the late 1860s, ethnic groups were not found equally in different occupations. Canadian and immigrant businessmen differed in the types of businesses in which they engaged and the amount of capital with which they could engage in them. Craft production was an activity of immigrants, in particular the English, who were significantly over-represented among tradesmen in 1861 and 1881, and the Scots, who also were significantly over-represented in 1861. English tradesmen differed from the Scots, however, in their apparent lack of adaptability. The impression gained, admittedly from a rather small number of examples, is that the English were committed to plying their crafts on a small scale in the face of the reorganization of the economy. While Americans and Canadians in the 1870s set up various metal-fabricating plants, foundries, and farm implement factories, the English remained blacksmiths and tinsmiths. On construction projects, they were the subcontractors, the carpenters, joiners, masons, bricklayers, and painters, seldom the builders. The Scots, who in 1861 had been independent tradesmen, carpenters especially, were mainly builders by 1871 and 1881. The tailoring trade in Brantford was divided between the Scots and the English. The Scots, however, expanded in the 1860s into dry goods retailing and included tailoring as just one more service along with dressmaking, millinery, and ready-made clothing. Unlike the English, then, the Scots used their trades as the basis for new businesses in the industrializing city (table 2.5).

As well, more than the average, Americans were manufacturers and tradesmen. Brantford's largest factories in the 1850s – four of six iron founders in 1852 and three of seven in 1861, a paper mill, a carriage factory, and a pottery – were American operations.[42] A unique willingness on the part of Americans to enter into partnerships with men to whom they were not related facilitated their leading position in large-scale enterprises. Only about one in six Americans taking partners chose family members, while one in 2.5 of the rest of the business population did so. Americans never made up more than 16 per cent of the business population, and their numbers were in decline from 1852, but they accounted for 18 per cent of men entering partnerships. Though they seemed eager to get and to share

Table 2.5
Occupational Groups by Birthplace, 1852–81

Year	Occupational Group	Canada (%)	United States (%)	England (%)	Scotland (%)	Ireland (%)	All (%)
1852	Manufacturers	6	13	13	8	3	9
	Tradesmen	**9**	45	45	46	44	40
	Merchants	**58**	18	22	27	18	26
	Grocers	3	8	10	15	**29**	14
	Accommodation/ Service	**24**	16	10	4	6	11
	Total	100	100	100	100	100	100
	Number	33	38	78	26	62	237
1861	Manufacturers	17	13	11	15	4	11
	Tradesmen	24	43	**44**	**51**	**21**	36
	Merchants	20	6	11	24	12	14
	Grocers	11	13	**9**	7	**31**	15
	Accommodation/ Service	28	22	21	**3**	15	18
	Labourers		3	4		**15**	6
	Total	100	100	100	100	100	100
	Number	54	32	127	41	91	345
1871	Manufacturers	**23**	9	17	13	**6**	15
	Tradesmen	25	38	38	29	29	31
	Merchants	29	22	**16**	**46**	25	26
	Grocers	**2**	9	12	6	**25**	11
	Accommodation/ Service	21	22	17	**6**	15	17
	Total	100	100	100	100	100	100
	Number	97	32	114	52	68	363
1881	Manufacturers	13	24	14	15	11	14
	Tradesmen	**19**	16	**36**	38	30	26
	Merchants	39	36	27	44	26	35
	Grocers	13	4	6	3	**26**	11
	Accommodation/ Service	16	20	17		7	14
	Total	100	100	100	100	100	100
	Number	185	25	104	24	46	394

Note: Figures in bold type indicate a statistically significant positive or negative association between birthplace and occupational group when these variables are dichotomized. Significance is only reported when the expected cell size exceeds five cases.

a piece of the action in manufacturing, Americans generally kept out of commerce, especially the grocery trade.

Groceries always attracted a disproportionately large number of the Irish. Immigrants found it an easy branch of commerce to enter, since its capital and credit requirements were modest. Moreover, since the grocery trade was one of the first in Brantford to support whole-saling, credit could be obtained locally on a face-to-face basis, thus minimizing the need for external connections.[43] It was a business of infinite gradations of status and scale, from the most respectable to the boldly illegal. In the 1850s groceries were also a department of the general merchandising firms and often those who called them-selves grocers were merely minor shopkeepers. In some case, neigh-bours and former co-workers might patronize the shop of a widow or an otherwise unemployed or disabled worker as a matter of com-munity obligation or in recognition of its proprietor's desire for self-sufficiency. Gradation made the trade one of the few avenues along which a man might progress from rough to respectable over his career, at the same time as credit relationships made it one of the few doors through which respectable society might interact with rough society.[44] The "low groceries," as they were disparagingly labelled, frequently covered illegal activities, such as unlicensed liquor sales or the receipt of stolen goods.[45] But the low grocers performed an important social function in working-class community life. Their shops provided a focus for neighbourhood activities, a place to meet and relax after work and on Sundays. The low grocer was a source of credit and, if successful, might become a landlord. These communal and financial roles gave the grocer influence within his neighbourhood and, for the ambitious, laid the foundation for political activity of various sorts. The most prominent grocer in pol-itics was John J. Hawkins, the Canadian-born son of a successful Irish Catholic carpenter who settled in Brantford the 1830s. The younger Hawkins worked first in construction, like his father, before opening "a small grocery and groggery in the back part of the town."[46] This provided the base for his entry into municipal politics, first as alderman and then as reeve, as well as into the provincial and federal arena as chief local organizer for the Conservative party in the 1870s. The Irish were involved throughout the whole spectrum of the grocery trade. Irish Catholics constituted the core of the low grocers, while the major wholesalers of the 1870s, Alex Fair, Jackson Forde, and George Watt, were Irish Protestants.

The Irish, though less so than the Canadians, were under-repre-sented in the industrial sector and, like the English, generally were independent tradesmen who did business on a small scale. The only trade in which they were consistently over-represented was shoe-making. The Irish provided seven of seventeen shoemakers in 1852, six of fifteen in 1861, five of fourteen in 1871, and three of four in 1881. Moreover, Irish masters gave preference in employment to their countrymen, especially in the early part of the period under review. For example, in 1852 eight of the eleven shoemakers hired and boarded by Andrew Wilson, a thirty-five-year-old Irish Anglican, were from Ireland.

There seemed some truth to the observation made in 1855 by the editor of the Brantford *Expositor* that Canadian youths were averse to learning trades and preferred commerce or the professions instead.[47] Canadians were always under-represented among self-employed tradesmen, significantly so in 1852 and 1881. Perhaps in the 1840s and 1850s they lacked the skills to compete with immigrant tradesmen and artisans; by the 1870s they may have perceived that skills were depreciated too easily by industrialization. Though they were not tradesmen, Canadians ran some of the largest industrial enterprises in Brantford. Five of six iron founders and farm imple-ment dealers in 1871 and six of nine in 1881 were Canadian. About 40 per cent of the builders and contractors in 1871 had been born in Canada. Significant as the participation of native-born busi-nessmen was in the construction and metal-fabricating industries, Canadians did not generally possess the funds needed to participate in the largest enterprises. Information on "pecuniary strength," busi-ness assets presumably, provided in the Mercantile Agency's credit manuals revealed that Canadians were over-represented among those with the least capital. Seventy-nine per cent of Canadians but only 59 per cent of immigrants in 1871 had less than $2,000 in their operations; in 1881 the respective figures were 67 per cent and 54 per cent. Perhaps because of their more limited capital and their aversion to trades, Canadians in the 1870s increasingly concentrated in retail merchandising, selling such consumer items as apparel, drugs, hardware, glassware, and crockery, but seldom groceries or provisions. Specializing in one line, a merchant might simplify his overhead and, if able to turn his capital over quickly, conduct a volume of business much larger than might be assumed from his "pecuniary strength." Canadians may have been under-represented in business generally, but by 1881 they were notable in those sectors, metal fabricating, construction, and retail commerce, which were transforming the urban economy.

Afro-Americans and Jews were out of place in Brantford and, to the extent that they were in business, they engaged in stereotypical endeavours. Often blacks were local characters: Francis Bond, the septuagenarian street vendor, and old Doc Johnson, a cloth cleaner and "old beaver rejuvenator" – a dry cleaner and hat blocker, in other words. Isaac Foreman, the most successful black, saved enough money as a hotel porter to buy a small farm and a few cows and to become a milk dealer. He was not, however, included in 1870 and 1871 when other milk dealers organized to fix prices and eliminate Sunday deliveries.[48] As barbers, blacks enjoyed the patronage and kind solicitations of whites. For example, when Hugo Tedball announced his intention to open a restaurant, his customers protested so earnestly that he relented and continued as a "tonsorial artist." Another barber, John Henry Inglis, was able to borrow money from several sympathetic white citizens willing to help a polite and deserving black man open his own shop. After he fled on the night train to Buffalo, it was discovered that Inglis was really Joe Ringo, a criminal of minor notoriety.[49] Ringo, like Tedball and Bond, confirmed the prejudices of Brantford's citizens about blacks: dependable in some instances, criminal in others, but never equal.

Like Afro-Americans, Jews, of German origin in the 1850s and of Polish and Russian origin in the 1870s, wandered through but did not stay in Brantford. Though historians have debated the impact of anti-Semitism upon Jewish businessmen in large North American cities – David Gerber contending that Buffalo Jews suffered significantly from discrimination; Gerry Tulchinsky concluding that, despite anti-Semitism, Jews were judged by the same standards of credit-worthiness as others – consideration has not been directed to the experiences of Jews in smaller communities like Brantford.[50] There they lacked the resources of family and congregation which not only supported Jewish enterprise elsewhere but were important more generally in the success of any businessman. One wonders, for example, about the fate of the twenty-seven-year-old Russian Jew who was a broker in Brantford in 1881. Arriving in the United States more than a decade before, he gave up his name to become Andrew Merican, and as A. Merican came to Canada in the mid-1870s. Uprooted several times already, did he ever fulfil the optimism of his new identity? Was he like the other ten Jewish businessmen, stereotypically self-employed in the rag-picking, second-hand clothing, tailoring, cigarmaking, and pawnbrokering trades? None lasted ten years in business. Or was he like the only Jews who remained in business for ten or more years, three brothers in the construction business in the 1870s? They were, however, completely assimilated, Canadian by birth, belonging to the Baptist church, and ultimately claiming English ancestry.

The under-representation of the native-born population in business distinguished Brantford from several other communities recently examined by social historians. In Hamilton, according to Katz, Doucet, and Stern, Canadians were over-represented among the business class in 1851–2, and, although "native Canadians slipped from a particularly favoured to a more or less representative position" among industrial capitalists in 1871, they still were the group most likely to belong to the business class as a whole. In explanation the authors have contended that "most probably these young people who moved upward were disproportionately sons of men already in the business class."[51] T.W. Acheson has determined that half of the merchants in Saint John in 1851 were native New Brunswickers, twice the proportion of natives among heads of household. Ethnic stratification characterized the trades of that port city, and, although the majority of artisans were immigrants, New Brunswickers dominated the more lucrative crafts.[52] Similarly, in Halifax David Sutherland has found that wholesale merchants became a more closed business group as the proportion born in Nova Scotia rose from half early in the nineteenth century to nearly three-quarters in the 1840s.[53] In other words, Hamilton, Saint John, and Halifax differed from Brantford in that as early as the 1850s inherited positions restricted opportunities in business. Similar disadvantages confronted newcomers to Poughkeepsie, New York; they too were under-represented among that city's proprietors in the 1850s and 1860s. In the opinion of Clyde and Sally Griffen, the longer term of residence bestowed a number of advantages upon natives, including the chance of a clerkship as training for business, easier access to credit, and the opportunity to accumulate capital.[54] Unlike Poughkeepsie, San Francisco in 1852 was a city with an immigrant majority. But, even in this booming, instant city, where the very rapidity of growth precluded significant entrenched business interests, Peter Decker's study has revealed that immigrants were under-represented among the city's merchants.[55] A simple comparison of small-town Brantford and the larger cities of Hamilton, Poughkeepsie, and San Francisco ignores the vast difference in the sorts of business opportunities and rewards offered by each place. To state the obvious, Brantford, despite its pretensions, was a much smaller community with much more limited horizons. Yet, the comparison reveals something about the locale in which immigrants could best exploit the opportunities for self-employment. Small but growing places like Brantford were sources of self-employment for immigrants because business in large centres was locked up by earlier arrivals and newcomers could not break in.[56]

That Canadians remained under-represented in business through the period of this study should not distract attention from the absolute increase in their numbers from 33 to 179 between 1852 and

1881. Rather, the increase should be seen as part of a larger demographic transformation. Decade by decade Canadian participation in business grew steadily at a slowly increasing rate, while immigrants declined in number after 1861. Changes in the wage labour force, however, were more dramatic. The number of workers born in Canada tripled between 1861 and 1871 and increased by 86 per cent in the next ten years. Over the same twenty years the immigrant wage labour force was roughly constant in size. The rapid "Canadianization" of business and labour distinguished Brantford from the south-central Ontario region studied by Darroch and Ornstein. Whereas the Canadian group in Brantford doubled in size from 18 to 36 per cent of the adult male work force between 1861 and 1871, in the larger context it grew from 34 to 43 per cent. Put another way, the number of male Canadians reporting occupations in the census increased 3.4 per cent annually at the regional level and 11.6 per cent annually in Brantford. Men, a lot of men it seems, were moving off the farms to urban centres in search of business opportunities or more often wage labour.[57]

On the other hand, greater competition for jobs and business opportunities made central Canada less attractive to immigrants in the 1860s and 1870s. The tone of immigration literature communicated the change. "The workshop system," advised one author in 1870, "is fully as bad as in England."[58] Another warned that Canadian cities and towns were glutted with tradesmen.[59] In an 1873 pamphlet outlining the labour needs of the country, the Canadian Department of Agriculture stated that "the chief demand is for agricultural and other labourers and female domestic servants." In Brant County over eight hundred labourers were required, but only fifty skilled workers. Professional men, clerks, bookkeepers, and tradesmen were discouraged in general from immigrating, although it was thought that "small capitalists may in many cases do well."[60] By the 1860s, however, small capitalists may have been less interested in coming to Canada, especially given this rather ambivalent evaluation of their prospects. British emigration in general dropped as the British economy improved markedly through the 1860s and 1870s, and immigrants constituted a declining percentage of the Canadian population.[61]

Fewer immigrants were self-employed in Brantford as roots in Ontario society in general, and the local community in particular, became a valuable asset in business. The proportion of new businessmen drawn from Canadians doubled in the 1860s, and by 1881 60 per cent of those in business less than ten years were Canadians by birth. As well, new businessmen increasingly had a lengthy association with the community. By 1871, 37 per cent had resided in Brantford or Brantford Township ten years earlier. Among Canadians, too, local or regional connections became increasingly important. Unlike the situation in 1852, when one of every four Canadians had been born outside of the province, in 1881 only one in fourteen came from another province. Internal migration had either declined – which seems unlikely – or it had been redirected, westward or southward perhaps.[62]

LIFE CYCLE AND GENERATIONAL TRANSITION

That more new businessmen in the 1870s were Canadians than immigrants was a symptom of a generational transition in business. The first generation, immigrants in the main, had found in Brantford, as in other growing towns in the 1840s and 1850s, a particular frontier. New men in new places confronted little entrenched competition in satisfying the demands for goods and services from the surrounding agricultural hinterland. Larger metropolitan centres, like Hamilton, possessed well-established commercial interests, but in smaller places the field was freer. The persistence of the first generation in business naturally left progressively fewer places for the newcomers who might have followed, and anyone who did consider self-employment in Brantford had to compete with a second generation spawned by the successful among the first. In consequence the social values associated with being in business, values that had been asserted in migration, became more difficult to realize in the Brantford of the 1870s.

Self-employment was more than a mere way of earning a living; it was also an assertion of independence and a statement of personal identity. In pre-industrial society, embarking on a business career was one aspect of a man's full maturity, along with marriage, raising a family, and heading a household. To some degree, then, transitions in class situation, from wage labour to self-employment and/or the employment of others, conformed roughly to stages in the male life cycle. The demographic dimension of class was undermined, however, by the shrinkage in the relative size of the business population in the industrializing economy of the 1870s and the entrenchment of the first generation. Most affected were men in their prime, between thirty and fifty years of age. Young men who in the 1840s and 1850s might have reasonably expected to be their own bosses by their mid-thirties found in the 1860s and 1870s fewer opportunities for self-employment. Those who did achieve self-employment took longer to do so. Narrowed horizons must have had some psychological impact upon the ways in which men looked at themselves and explained their fates.

It is tempting to interpret the concern for "manly" behaviour expressed by workers in the 1870s as a defence of masculinity by men less easily able to enjoy that form of livelihood, self-employment, previously associated with maturity. Indeed Gregory Kealey has argued that assertions of manhood were workers' ways of claiming equality with their employers. Peter Bischoff has reported that William Saffin, president of the Iron Molders' International Union, upbraided Montreal moulders for being scabs, rather than cultivating that "spirit of manhood and independence, only gained through the Union." Yet, as Steven Maynard has rightly commented, historians have not questioned why a defence of gender identity should be mixed with an evolving consciousness of class. He argues that industrial capitalism, by altering relations between men and women, precipitated a crisis of masculinity. The nature of these changes in gender relations is not explained beyond the contention, grounded in theory rather than sustained by historical evidence, that manly posturing responded to the de-skilling which threatened to reduce man's work to the less esteemed and less remunerative level of female labour.[63]

Important as Maynard's observations are, his interpretation of the crisis of masculinity remains rooted statically in the production process and the identity arising from it at a single moment in time. But the meaning of work at any time should be interpreted in terms of a man's understanding of its significance for his life prospects. Industrial capitalism altered not only the relations of production but also the significance of wage labour in the work and life cycle of a large number of men who confronted vastly different circumstances, opportunities for advancement, and standards by which achievement had to be measured.[64]

The mature, manly, and ambitious individual in Victorian Canada sought, even craved responsibility, the responsibilities of his own business, his own capital, and his own family. Charles Clarke, the Elora merchant and Clear Grit politician, argued the social and individual necessity of achievement when he wrote in 1850: "A man must have an interest in his property: he must be brought to regard it as sacred. By such means only can industrious habits, proper pride, and manly independence secured."[65] John Steele, a general merchant in Brantford, confided his life's ambitions in his will: "How often, oh! how often has ... [a father] endured the greatest privations that possibly could prey upon his mind with the anxious desire to provide

... [his family] with all the comforts of life and elevate them in the scale of existence. ... The attainment of this – the comfort and independence of my kind and sweet wife and children – has been the strong incentive to no ordinary exertions and denial of comforts – this with the determination so peculiar to a Scotchman to achieve an eminent position to his children and wife."[66] To be responsible and to have responsibilities like these was part of the self-image of the independent man.

The single businessman was thought to have too little responsibility and, therefore, raised questions in the minds of customers and creditors about his reliability. Self-employment was exceptional at any time for those under twenty years of age and was dictated by exceptional circumstances. For example, in 1852 Joseph Donovan, a seventeen-year-old Irish Catholic, ran the shop of his deceased father in order to support his mother and sister. Another youthful grocer, still living with his parents in 1881, was the eighteen-year-old Albert E. Cutterson, Jr. Albert Sr. was a carpenter, who probably provided the funds to set up the shop and put his son in it in order to supplement the family income. But most teenaged businessmen were sons in partnership with their fathers. Generally a young businessman, even in his early twenties, was suspected of being "rather too young to be his own master."[67]

Throughout the mid-nineteenth century, the majority of businessmen were in their thirties and forties, although the average age of men in business less than ten years did increase over time. Immigrants starting in business always tended to be older than Canadians. Migration and adjustment took time: just how long, however, is difficult to estimate. Identifying immigrant businessmen by their birthplace does not reveal the age at which they settled in British North America; they may have arrived as infants. The manuscript census does provide a partial answer. Fathers of children born outside of Canada did immigrate as mature men. About one-quarter of all foreign-born businessmen are in this category. While some variation existed in the percentage of each group which immigrated in family units – the Americans and the English more often, and the Irish and Scots less often – the differences are not statistically significant. Probably some immigrated to Canada shortly after marriage but prior to having children, although it is impossible from the sources examined to conclude how many. Charlotte Erickson, however, has postulated in her study of English and Scottish artisan immigrants that most were young, single men for whom immigration was one step in the artisan's "tramp," an extension of the journeyman's search for work, experience, adventure, and a future.[68] Indeed, proponents of

immigration to Canada informed the artisan that he "may peram-
bulate the country and find work in almost every part, and may thus
become acquainted with the manners and habits of the people."[69]

Numerous Brantford examples of immigrant perambulators could
be cited, especially since the successful immigrant mechanic became
a literary stereotype in the 1870s and 1880s. Adam Spence, the son
of an Orkney Island farmer, served three years as an apprentice
blacksmith before immigrating to Canada in 1849 at age nineteen.
Immigration may well have been his way of shortening an apprenticeship. He worked as a journeyman for two years in Quebec and
then Belleville, cw, and another two years for the Hamilton carriage-
building firm of Williams and Cooper. In 1854 he took employment
as a carriage blacksmith in Brantford; in 1857, a year after his
marriage, he started his own small carriage-building business.
Another farmer's son, John Elliott, born in Huck, Yorkshire, in 1822,
immigrated in 1842 after completing a seven-year stonecutter's
apprenticeship. His first year was spent working on jobs in Montreal,
Kingston, and Toronto, and his second in tramping the United States.
He returned to Toronto in 1844 and worked as a journeyman for
two years before setting up as a contractor with two partners. In
1848 he struck out on his own as a master stonecutter in Toronto.
Elliott moved again in 1850 when he and his brother William set up
shop in Brantford. Briefly in 1853 they tried business in London;
William stayed, but John returned to Brantford, which remained his
base of operations throughout the period of this study.[70] That this
was a common career pattern in Brantford is suggested by the age
difference between immigrants and natives starting in business.
Immigrants were on the average older than their Canadian counterparts. If the immigrant had arrived in infancy or early childhood,
one would expect little difference in the age at which he became self-
employed; growing up in Canada, he had already been naturalized.

In 1852 immigrants recently self-employed, the Americans and
English especially, were significantly older than Canadians in business for less than ten years, although there were no significant differences among immigrants groups themselves. Yet, young
immigrants in their twenties were not under-represented among businessmen as were Canadians in the same age cohort. Immigration
may have delayed the age at which a man started on his own account,
but at this cross-section at least it did not disadvantage him. The
pattern of Canadian self-employment reinforces this impression: it
differed from that of immigrants in 1852 and 1861 by peaking
among those in their thirties and declining in older age groups.
Immigrant self-employment reached its height in older age cohorts.

The most likely to be self-employed were the English in their forties and Americans in their forties or fifties in 1852 and the English in their forties or fifties and the Irish in their forties in 1861. Ambitious, mature Canadians may not have perceived much to attract them from the countryside to small-town employment; certainly their numbers were relatively low, just 7 per cent of men forty years and older in 1852 and 9 per cent in 1861 (table 2.6).

From 1861 immigrants still started in business later in life than Canadians. The average age of Canadians and immigrants in business less than ten years increased from 1852 to 1881 by roughly the same amount, five to six years. But age interacted with birthplace in a different way. Newcomers in their twenties, albeit certain national groups at different times, were, like Canadians of comparable age, under-represented in business. Birthplace did not distinguish the opportunities of the youngest men in the community. Older groups continued to be the most likely to be self-employed, but rather than representing a cycle of wage labour to self-employment and back to wage labour again as implied by the age structure in 1852, the distribution of rates of self-employment by national groups suggests the entrenchment of various groups. Whereas men in their thirties and forties had been over-represented in business in 1852 and 1861, men in their forties and fifties were so in 1871 and 1881. This upward shift in the incidence of self-employment is consistent with the aging of a particular age coeval, roughly those born from the 1810s to the 1830s.[71] That Canadians born in the 1820s stand out for their high self-employment in 1861, 1871, and 1881 suggests a coincidence of individual maturity and economic opportunity which distinguished them from other Canadians. They were perhaps the last group to be in the right place at the right time to achieve high levels of self-employment.

BUSINESS FAMILIES AND FAMILY BUSINESSES

The greater difficulties associated with achieving self-employment in the 1870s demanded greater discipline from the ambitious young man. The dedicated and self-sacrificing ascetic businessman who postponed marriage and the expenses of his own household was rare in the 1850s. Few repeated the experience of Toronto dry goods merchant John Macdonald, who opened his store in 1849. His biographer explained that Macdonald decided to marry only after stock taking and "as soon as possible after his books had been balanced. ... He had been looking forward to the prospect of having his own

Table 2.6
Rates of Self-Employment by Birthplace and Age Group, 1852–81

		Years of Age				
Year	Birthplace	20–9 (Rate %)	30–9 (Rate %)	40–9 (Rate %)	50 plus (Rate %)	All (Rate %)
1852	Canada	**15**	**47**	29	9	22
	United States	17	**50**	**63**	**64**	42
	England	22	28	**43**	39	32
	Scotland	15	30	35	15	24
	Ireland	21	19	28	**9**	21
	Total	18	29	38	27	27
	Number	60	82	65	26	233
1861	Canada	**17**	**47**	42	19	26
	United States	**11**	28	33	33	20
	England	**8**	32	**42**	**38**	29
	Scotland	10	35	33	33	29
	Ireland	**18**	27	**39**	30	27
	Total	14	33	36	33	27
	Number	57	122	102	65	346
1871	Canada	**8**	26	**38**	22	14
	United States	15	33	9	**55**	29
	England	**4**	18	24	**36**	20
	Scotland	7	33	**41**	24	26
	Ireland	14	26	23	22	19
	Total	8	24	27	31	21
	Number	44	105	113	99	361
1881	Canada	**7**	**29**	23	**37**	14
	United States	7	24	**63**	**26**	22
	England	**6**	14	24	**36**	21
	Scotland	11	11	11	**34**	20
	Ireland	4	18	29	24	18
	Total	7	23	22	32	19
	Number	51	115	89	136	391

Note: Figures in bold type indicate a rate of self-employement that was significantly higher or lower than the average when the population was dichotomized into the national-age group and all others.

home. But he had determined that until his means would warrant the maintenance of a wife he would remain unmarried."[72] Nevertheless, there is evidence that aspiring businessmen did sacrifice domestic life and that sacrifice became more necessary over time. At a time when contraception was difficult, delayed marriages were indicated by differentials between the number of children residing in the households of new and persistent business personnel in the same age group. In 1852 new businessmen in their thirties had on the average fewer children than men in business for ten years. But, the reluctance to marry did not last long after the beginning of a business career. The two decisions – to marry and to open up shop on one's own account – were clearly related, since only 12 per cent of new businessmen remained single in 1852. The near doubling of the relative number of single new businessmen to 22 per cent in 1881 reflected the new and more restrictive conditions. Greater discipline was required to get into business, and in every age group in 1881 the family size of new businessmen was smaller than that of persistent businessmen and that of new businessmen in the same age groups at previous cross-sections. As well, the decline in the family size of persistent businessmen in their thirties in 1881 demonstrated the effect of delayed marriage throughout the business population (table 2.7).[73]

For a man in business, a family could be an important resource providing capital and labour. A wife's connections or savings – and they need not be large savings – often provided the wherewithal to start an enterprise. In the relatively open economy of Upper Canada in the 1840s and 1850s, the labour of wives and children was particularly important. Immigrants were warned, for example, that often employees worked only as long as it took to learn the business and then established themselves in business as competitors.[74]

Ira Mayhew, the American author of a widely distributed mid-nineteenth-century business manual, suggested that a wife or daughter could provide useful assistance with bookkeeping. It was an activity which did not bring women into frequent contact with customers. At the same time as it saved the expense of hiring help, it educated the female members of the family about the nature of the business and more generally about the need for just as disciplined an accounting of domestic expenditures. Mayhew recommended that "Women, when not otherwise employed, may also properly enter the counting-room, and engage with father and brother in its quiet duties, for the discharge of which she is as well fitted by nature as they. She thus acquires a knowledge of business, and if bereft of husband or father, upon whom too many females are entirely dependent for support, she may be enabled herself to conduct the business advantageously, or to close it without a loss."[75]

A survey of the wills of sixty-eight Brantford businessmen who died before 1890 suggests that husbands were favourably impressed with their wives' business acumen. Twenty-eight of the fifty wills

Table 2.7
Average Number of Children by Length of Time in Business (Married Couples Only), 1852–81

Years of Age	1852		1861		1871		1881	
	Less than 10 years	More than 10 years	Less than 10 years	More than 10 years	Less than 10 years	More than 10 years	Less than 10 years	More than 10 years
20–9	1.1		1.3		1.1	3.0	0.9	1.6
30–9	2.2	3.8	2.6	3.7	2.8	3.2	1.9	2.4
40–9	3.6	3.9	4.1	4.0	4.0	4.1	3.2	4.1
50–9	1.8	2.3	3.5	3.7	4.0	4.2	2.6	3.6
60 and up	1.6	1.0	2.7	2.7	2.0	2.0	1.8	3.0
All	2.3	3.9	2.8	3.7	3.1	3.8	2.2	3.4
Number	167	26	210	86	177	127	158	187

which specifically mentioned wives named the wife as an executrix of the estate, and twenty-five left the entire estate to her.[76] Even a small business could require considerable business sense to settle to advantage. Although John Jenkins, a clothier, advised his wife that she might benefit from consultations with several of his business associates about his affairs, he appointed her alone to administer his estate.[77] Limited as this evidence may seem, it does contradict Leo Johnson's contention that "as wealth and property accumulated in the hands of their husbands," wives were disadvantaged because of "the greater emphasis placed upon the necessity of its safe transmission to the inheriting male."[78] Still, while a businessman lived, although they might help out in the family business, his wife, and children, were clearly subordinate. Too creative a role, like employment of wives outside the household, necessarily diminished the status of the head of the family and called into question his ability to provide for his family. Thus, those men whose wives played too significant a role in the family business were at times rebuked by Dun's credit reporter. He commented about one husband and wife bakery that "Mrs. W. is superior woman and his capacity is fair." More condescending was his remark about the contribution of a particular dry goods merchant's wife to the business: his "wife [is the] best man of the two."[79] For the Victorian seeking to proclaim his independence, then, there was a close connection between his family and his business.

This connection was also manifested in the association of workplace with residence in the commercial economy. One half of all businessmen in 1851 combined their residences and place of business. As well, at least 14 per cent provided lodging for their employees, on the average 2.7 employees each. That fewer provided accommodation for employees in Brantford than in some larger places, like Rochester, New York, for example, should not necessarily be taken as evidence of greater privatism in living arrangements.[80] Enterprise probably operated on a smaller scale in Brantford and so demand for board may have been somewhat below that in larger centres. But still, even Ignatius Cockshutt, the leading merchant, lived over his store in 1852 and boarded seven of his clerks.

Businessmen sought more private domestic arrangements with the progress of industrialization. Katz, Doucet, and Stern found little change in the pattern of the separation of workplace and residence from 1853 to 1871 in Hamilton. The reasons for this difference between Hamilton and Brantford are difficult to pin down, although perhaps the disparity in the size of the two communities has some bearing. Separation might have entailed greater distance in Hamilton than the smaller city of Brantford in 1881. Real estate value in Hamilton may have been higher and therefore residential separation may have involved a greater drain on capital available for business purposes.[81] In Brantford, residences separate and at some distance from places of business were deemed preferable, and by 1880 only 29 per cent of the city's businessmen lived at their place of business. Relatively fewer businessmen, less than 6 per cent, took employees into their homes as boarders and those who did lodged fewer, an average of 1.8 in 1881. Other forms of household extensions, relatives and boarders, were similarly reduced from 1852 to 1881. Even the employment of domestic servants became more private. In 1881 only 60 per cent of domestic servants resided in their employers' households, whereas almost all did in 1852. With greater difficulty that arose from the mid-1860s in translating independence into self-employment, the equation of domestic and business life was strained, and a man's family life became more private, more of a refuge from the stress of business.

There were not many family businesses in Brantford, though there were with time a growing number of families in business. The second generation, the sons of businessmen, remained small in the 1850s, just 8 per cent of the business population in 1852 and 6 per cent in 1861. Thereafter their numbers doubled in relative size each decade, to 13 per cent in 1871 and 22 per cent in 1881. But the number of family firms grew less slowly. Father and son partnerships engaged no larger a proportion of the business population in 1872 than in 1852, just 5 per cent, and only 8 per cent in 1881.

Not many enterprises were sufficiently large to support a new partner who brought no capital or connections to the firm. Thus, intergenerational partnerships emerged most commonly in particular circumstances. Businesses already as large as Bradford G. Tisdale's Britannia Stove Foundry could easily support his son Arthur too. If sons were capable, a large concern could grow even larger. George Watt expanded his grocery business into a substantial regional wholesaling operation after taking his four sons into the firm in the 1870s. Occasionally fathers dissolved existing partnerships to make room for their sons. Probably dissolution of existing arrangements was necessary, since a man's original partner would not likely share a father's concern for a son and might resent giving a share of the profits to a young man who brought little more than filial obligation to the business. In 1877 Francis P. Adams ended his three-year partnership with Michael Brophey so that son George could share in his retail shoe store. Also in 1877 Jackson and Robert Forde ended their grocery wholesaling partnership of sixteen years so that the former could go into business in the same line with his son, William. The majority of fathers taking sons as partners, however, were sole proprietors, and the partnership rewarded sons for years of working in the shop for wages that were probably lower than hired help would demand. As well, as a man grew older he could hand more and more of the daily toil to a son whose energy might better sustain a viable business.

But the majority of the second generation were proprietors of their own businesses and increasingly different kinds of businesses than those run by their fathers. About three-quarters of sons in business in 1852, fourteen of nineteen, were in the same businesses as their fathers. Thirty years later, less than half, forty-two of eighty-five, were following in their fathers' footsteps. Tradesmen's sons especially chose different careers, perhaps acknowledging that many of the old ways of production no longer offered dependable futures. Whereas 75 per cent of tradesmen's sons in 1852 operated the same sorts of businesses as their fathers, only 41 per cent did so in 1881. Prior to the 1870s, if a son of a tradesman chose a different business, he was likely to pick a different trade. In 1871 60 per cent of those not following their fathers were engaged in another trade. But by 1881 almost two-thirds had decided on some branch of commerce. There were some notable exceptions, however. The sons of English tradesmen were far more likely than any other group to be self-employed tradesmen in 1881.[82] The sons of merchants, shopkeepers, and agents had always preferred commercial activity, which after all was the growing sector of self-employment. Two-thirds of those with different occupations from their fathers nonetheless engaged in commerce in 1881, just as in 1852.

Successful fathers could go to considerable lengths to get their sons established in business. In 1873 Robert Sproule, a general merchant and one of the wealthiest businessmen of the 1860s, purchased a drug business for his son George.[83] A.B. Bennett, a former iron founder engaged in private banking, helped his son A.B., Jr., even more to set up. The senior Bennett in 1873 struck a deal with Francis Ellis to buy from the latter Brantford's major retail drug store, with assets of $10,000. Ellis, who intended to enter the wholesale petroleum business, further agreed not to engage in the drug business in Brantford for ten years. However, Ellis had second thoughts and tried to renege on the agreement, arguing that he had acted "rashly and imprudently." Further, he claimed that the lease to his rented store did not permit him to assign the premises to another party. Bennett would not be trifled with. He immediately sued Ellis in chancery to force compliance and purchased the store, valued at $5,000, to make moot any restrictions in the lease. With his wealth, Bennett forced Ellis out of business in order to provide Bennett, Jr., with a proven concern.[84] Few fathers could go so far, but a small loan, a co-signature on a note, or just a good name around town could help.

A father might help a son to become self-employed, but gifts were not free and in most cases were recorded as charges against future inheritances. Unlike farmers, in matters of inheritance businessmen tried to provide for their sons during their lifetime, and wills were more likely to be a balancing of accounts than strategic instruments in themselves for intergenerational mobility.[85] To record money given to his sons, Reuben and Joseph, Thomas Shenston, the county registrar and president of the Royal Loan and Savings Co., explained that "during my life, I have made at least a dozen wills as circumstances altered." In his wills, Shenston stipulated that these sums plus interest on them be deducted from the shares of each son in the estate.[86] Thomas Glassco, who had already given his hatter and furrier business to his son George, left him nothing "save my best wishes for his personal and material prosperity." To each of his three other sons, he gave $1,000, and to his unmarried daughter, Elizabeth, who had stayed at home to help her aging parents, he left $10,000.[87] Robert Sproule, having bought the drug business for his son, paid more attention in his will to providing for his wife. He left his entire estate of $32,000 to her and instructed that, if she felt their children were deserving, she might give them something from the estate, although under no circumstances was she to become dependent upon them.[88] Likewise Fred Walsh, a hotelkeeper, did not want his wife to be dependent upon their children. When he had earlier given sons William and Percival capital to start a tobacconist business, he had required them to give him a mortgage against their store. In his will, Walsh ordered his wife to foreclose the mortgage if the boys failed to pay her $800 a year for the rest of her life.[89]

Providing for sons during their lifetime strengthened the patriarchal force of businessmen fathers. William Gilkison, a land speculator in Brantford and developer of the village of Elora in the 1830s, feared that his son Jasper had acted irresponsibly and foolishly in quitting his job as a clerk in Brockville. When Jasper failed to find a new position in Montreal, New York, Albany, Schenectady, or Niagara, William reproached him formally in writing: "Again I urge thee forward, my dear child, to provide for thyself. Thou art in a world which judges harshly and it will not spare thee or me, so it is our interest to become independent of its frowns, by steady and correct attention to whatever we shall undertake: we are not at liberty to chose for ourselves in such a manner."[90] To a man concerned about his own reputation, it would seem that the sins of the son might be seen as those of the father.

James Wilkes, a general merchant, used the promise of business capital to deal with a prodigal son, George H. Wilkes. Born in 1836, George received a very good education, first at the Carradoc Academy and the American College in Buffalo and then as a clerk in a Brantford dry goods store. Although only sixteen, by 1852 he was under considerable pressure from his family to decide upon some sort of career. His cousin Henry, a clerk in a New York commission house, suggested that he and George speculate in apples, George acquiring them in Ontario and Henry selling them in New York. Later Henry wondered if George might like to go into partnership with him in a grocery business, either in Port Burwell, Upper Canada, or Texas. George's uncle, "California Charlie" Wilkes, back from the American West and recovered from his gold fever, wanted his nephew to assist him in a store he intended to set up in the family's fiefdom of Wilkesport in Sombra Township. Uncle William, a Buffalo merchant and forwarder, used George to handle some of his Brantford transactions and offered him a job on his steamboat. George accepted the offer, and for several years he travelled the lake and river between Buffalo and Brantford. As well, he dabbled in some minor business schemes: when a lake steamer sank, drowning a number of passengers, George capitalized on the public's new awareness of water safety by renting life preservers to travellers as they departed from Buffalo. George's apparent wanderlust drove his father to distraction. James Wilkes upbraided George for not going to Wilkesport with Charlie, since he soon could have been a partner in the business. "My opinion," James offered in 1854, "is that if you can get a good situation in a hardware or dry goods store it will be the best thing you can do and at once and forever give up the roving kind of business you have been following." He even held out the promise of some money if George wanted to set up his own business, although "I have not yet seen that you could use it to advantage." Should he behave better, James assured him that the money would be available and that he would himself consider going into partnership with him. Parental pressure had the desired effect, for George decided to take a clerking position in the Montreal firm of Hooper, Jacques and Co. He returned to Brantford around 1856 to work as bookkeeper in the foundry of his uncle, George S. Wilkes. After its bankruptcy, George H. was employed by his uncle's creditors to manage the business. While acting in this capacity, he probably used his father's money to purchase the foundry's machinery and tools.[91] George H. Wilkes turned out well, but he enjoyed the benefit of a well-established family prepared to indulge, if not always with the best of humour, his youthful enthusiasms and indecision. His father's advice, nonetheless, betrayed a decided worry about the future that awaited his son, if he did not choose his occupations wisely.[92]

Not all sons could become self-employed, especially in the 1870s. Still, a father could help by finding his sons a good first job, a placement which best reflected a father's influence and status. The occupations of 424 sons, under the age of twenty-five and living at home or on their own, of 157 businessmen have been identified. Michael Katz's Hamilton project attempted one of the few historical studies of occupational inheritance. However, Katz chose to study the inheritance of occupational rank, rather than the inheritance of occupation itself. From this perspective, a baker's son who became a blacksmith and a baker's son who became a baker were both examples of inheritance, since each held occupations with a ranking equivalent to that of their fathers.[93] This study takes a much more limited definition of inheritance, restricting it to identical or functionally equivalent occupations. A narrower definition is more difficult to interpret, since the prospects of trades varied. For the son of a shoemaker to remain a shoemaker was not the same or as advantageous as the son of a builder who worked as a carpenter.

Applying this definition of occupational inheritance produced considerably lower rates than those determined by Katz. The trend to lower rates of inheritance over time, however, is the same in this and the Hamilton study. In 1852 nearly one-half of the second generation had the same occupations as their fathers. Ten years later just 30 per cent took the same occupation, a rate which remained nearly constant in 1871 and 1881. The decline was almost entirely due to changes in the commercial sector, in particular the growing importance of clerking as a first occupation. In 1852, 42 per cent of the sons of fathers in commerce had the same occupation; in 1881 none did. Employment as a clerk occupied only 9 per cent of the sons of businessmen in 1852, and all of these clerks were sons of tradesmen or manufacturers. The sons of merchants quickly set up on their own account without this period of initiation. By 1881 nearly 36 per cent of sons of businessmen were clerks and nearly all of these clerks were the sons of men in commerce. Not only did commercial enterprise by the 1870s require more infrastructure and more clerks, but self-employment in this sector demanded the preparation and education derived from clerking.

The industrialization of Brantford's economy opened employment opportunities for businessmen's sons. Not surprisingly, more sons of men in commerce took jobs in industry than sons of men in industry took jobs in commerce. Nonetheless, those men whose sons went into the factories did not occupy very prominent positions in commerce and probably had themselves risen from wage labour not too long in the past. Thirty-one of the fifty-three sons in this category – 59 per cent – had fathers who were tavern or saloon keepers, market vendors, pedlars, low grocers, or teamsters; ten of the thirty-one were Irish Catholics.

Occupational inheritance declined only slightly in the industrial sector. A man's mastery of his trade was an important part of his self-image, and with pride he passed his knowledge of his craft to his son. Still, the number of sons whose first occupation was the same as their father's varied from trade to trade. Between 1852 and 1881 only three of eighteen tailors' sons became tailors, whereas nineteen of thirty-one shoemakers' sons followed their fathers' trade. One wonders whether fathers in each trade responded differently to the problems of their craft. Shoemakers, hard pressed by competition from factory-made goods, relied upon the cheap labour of their sons, offering in return instruction in a redundant trade. Tailors may have responded to competition from ready-made clothing by hiring seamstresses, freeing their sons to pursue more promising trades. The largest number of tailors' sons, six in all, chose metal-working trades, which might not have afforded the best chance for self-employment, but did offer regular factory wages.

Unlike the experience of sons of apparel makers, occupational inheritance increased among the sons of men in the construction industry. In 1852 only three of ten worked in the building trades;

thirty years later nine of nineteen were in construction. As larger firms displaced smaller contractors, their proprietors could provide good jobs within their own firms for their sons or could help them set up as subcontractors on their own. By 1881 those sons of builders and contractors who decided not to follow their fathers' footsteps found good positions in commerce, five as clerks and three as merchants. The construction boom of the late 1860s and early and late 1870s aided businessmen in that industry in helping their sons find jobs with good prospects.

At all times occupational inheritance was generally associated with the wealthiest members of the business population. Sons naturally were more willing to follow, and fathers more eager to encourage them, when the fathers' success demonstrated the rewards of a particular line of endeavour. As the likelihood of success of the least wealthy declined through the 1870s, only one in eight sons of fathers among the poorest 40 per cent of businessmen in 1881 followed the paternal calling. Almost one in three of the sons of fathers in the wealthiest 60 per cent inherited their occupation.

The growing number of business families along with the decline in occupational inheritance and the development of clerking as a first occupation revealed the greater complexity of business life in an industrializing economy. It was also symptomatic of fewer opportunities for self-employment and of the necessity of some advantage in seizing the chances that remained.

ENTERPRISING WOMEN

Nearly but not all those who ran businesses were men. Women made up a small minority, about 4 per cent, of the business community of Brantford.[94] Perhaps there were more, but only fifty-two have been positively identified. Like men, women sought independence in business. But, for them independence was compelling for more than a positive self-image.

The overwhelming majority, over 80 per cent, were widowed or separated from their husbands. Most opened shop on or shortly after widowhood or separation; about half were in business within five years of being left on their own, judging by the dates of husbands' wills and by the age of their youngest children. Half definitely, and probably nearly all, were residents of Brantford at the time of their husbands' death or flight. As in Montreal, few of Brantford's self-employed widows inherited businesses. That only five took over their husbands' enterprises suggests that those who did set up small shops constituted a fortunate segment of the working class, that with

Table 2.8
Characteristics of Women in Business, 1852–81

	(%)		(%)
Marital Status:		Religion:	
Married	10	Church of England	16
Single	10	Presbyterian	19
Separated	15	Methodist	40
Widowed	65	Baptist	12
		Congregationalist	4
Total	100	Roman Catholic	7
All	43	Other	2
Years of Age:		Total	100
20–29	21	All	43
30–39	33		
40–49	28	Occupation:	
50–59	14	Milliner	4
60 and up	4	Weaver	2
		Seamstress	19
Total	100	Grocer	20
All	43	Second-hand dealer	2
		Bookseller	2
Birthplace:		Storekeeper	4
Canada	26	Fancy goods dealer	6
United States	2	Market pedlar	4
England	21	Merchant	2
Scotland	9	Confectioner	2
Ireland	40	Boarding-house keeper	25
Other	2	Hotelkeeper	6
		Restaurant keeper	2
Total	100		
All	43	Total	100
		All	52

savings, borrowings, or insurance sufficient to secure premises and inventories (table 2.8).[95]

As Michael Katz concluded about widows in Hamilton, they "apparently strove ... to maintain their independence by retaining their own home as long as possible."[96] For Brantford's self-employed widows, keeping their homes was necessary to hold their families together, since with only two exceptions all had dependent children. But it was a hard struggle, since to a considerable degree their businesses, like those of the infirm and decrepit, depended upon their customers' sense of pity and moral obligation. Not surprisingly, nearly 70 per cent of the self-employed widows belonged to Protestant denominations with a strong sense of congregational unity, the

Methodist, the Presbyterian, and the Baptist churches. Nevertheless, only three widows lasted for ten years in business.

Most successful, exceptionally so, was Margaret Smith, an Irish Anglican grocer. A mother of five children, she was left penniless at age thirty when her husband John died about 1850. Described by Dun's reporter as "a steady prudent industrious little woman," who was "much respected" for her "integrity and shrewdness," the widow Smith enjoyed "a good support" locally and was judged safe for small loans. She obtained a small stock of groceries on credit, about $200 worth, after her husband died. By 1862, through scrimping, saving, and hard work, she built her stock to about $800 and had purchased free and clear of debt real estate worth $2,000. More important, she had kept her family together and her children in school. Her eldest son, Benjamin, had obtained a job as salesman by 1861. Her other son, Robert, a law student in 1861, had been called to the bar ten years later. By 1881 Margaret Smith, now in her sixties, had given up her store and lived upon her savings and real estate investments, the board paid by one lodger, and, one hopes, remittances from her children whose futures in life she struggled so hard to secure.[97]

The alternatives to self-employment varied in attractiveness. The Brantford Widows' Home was a last resort, though more and different opportunities for female employment were present in 1881 than in 1852, and, in the industrializing city, a widow might keep her family together by doing sewing at home. Erastus Kester, a sewing machine agent, advertised in 1868 that he would arrange credit so that "widow women and working women can purchase sewing machines and pay for them in small sums monthly."[98] Most likely, self-employment proved a stopgap until one of the children reached maturity and could assume responsibility for his or her mother and siblings.

Single and married women were less frequently self-employed than widows. Single women commonly worked as servants or in shops as clerks or as seamstresses. Those in business can be classified in two ways: first, young women who operated a small shop to supplement the family income; and, second, women like Henrietta Duncan, who ran a millinery shop from the mid-1850s through the mid-1870s, who would have been unkindly called old maids. Married women similarly can be divided into two categories. Some were in business to supplement their husbands' incomes, while others were partners with their husbands, like Eliza and "Second Hand" Smith who ran Brantford's largest pawnbroking business in the 1870s.

Women most frequently ran small stores, mostly "low groceries," but also a number of specialty shops selling stationery, millinery and fancy goods, and confectionery and fruit. A few engaged in the most marginal of businesses, market vending. Pedlars of sweets, soda pop and fruit on market days, like "old Mother Beggarlegs" of Sara Jeanette Duncan's *The Imperialist*, were subject to taunts and abuse, even assault from young local "roughs."[99] In other areas of endeavour, women drew upon their domestic skills for support. In number, boarding-house keepers constituted the single largest business occupation, followed closely by seamstresses and dressmakers.

Women in business, women in a man's world, were an anomaly, and, because they were out of place, they were not independent in the same terms as were men. For widows and "old maids", self-employment was a means of survival with dignity. Yet, their independence was a matter of form and appearance only, since it often depended upon the patronage of people touched by their plight and their efforts. Married women and self-employed daughters were in a more ambiguous situation, since their endeavours could be construed as demonstrations of the inadequacies of their husbands and fathers in performing their roles as heads of the family.

CONCLUSION

For a time in the 1840s and 1850s Brantford had offered a second chance for immigrants with frustrated ambitions for independence through self-employment. But the reduction in the size of the business population that began in the 1860s meant that business was no longer an activity associated with a stage of life, with being a fully mature man. Self-employment required that a man have some sort of advantage and, as a result, immigrants could less frequently establish themselves in business. More often new businessmen were men of Canadian birth or men who had resided in the community for some time. Though they may have been the children of immigrants, they had a chance from their youth in this country to make their reputations, establish connections, and draw upon the resources and support of their families.

To the extent that there was a mid-century crisis of masculinity, as some scholars have claimed, it was a crisis arising not just from changes in relations of production and work, or from new standards of domestic organization. Men embarking upon life confronted in the 1870s far different prospects for the achievement of independence and had to find new standards by which to demonstrate maturity than their fathers before.

3 Credit and Debt

The new social meaning of self-employment could be revealed no more clearly than in the credit reports compiled on Brantford businessmen by the Mercantile Agency. With industrialization, and the necessary decline in self-employment associated with larger units of production and exchange, to be in business connoted new and different qualities of personality, values, and social role. Rather than the representation of full maturity and independence, as in the culture of the British North American commercial economy, a business career came to identify the exceptional man. In this transition, the credit system exercised a significant influence. Not only did the allocation of credit affect the scale and opportunities for business, but the criteria of credit-worthiness expressed an ideology which imposed positive and negative sanctions on behaviour. This chapter examines the changes in the credit system as they affected the ratings and mortgage-secured indebtedness of the businessmen of Brantford.

The credit reports on Brantford businessmen assembled by the Mercantile Agency of R.G. Dun and Co.[1] from the late 1840s through the early 1860s expressed an appreciation of the ideal of independence through self-employment as the central tenet of the social role of the businessman. Men whose self-employment bespoke independence often received recommendations for credit by virtue of their character despite their limited wealth or trade prospects. The financial collapse of 1857, however, and the ensuing difficulties experienced by private and public lenders in recovering loans granted on this kind of intangible security promoted a contraction of credit.[2] Indicative of this change was Dun's more extensive reporting on the credit-worthiness of a larger proportion of the businessmen in Brantford. From 1864 the firm issued to its subscribers credit manuals which stressed the primacy of only one variable, "pecuniary strength," as the appropriate basis for lending decisions. Besides relying on this service, the chartered banks at least from the 1870s employed their own credit raters to evaluate assets and liabilities and pursue the business of major industrial and commercial borrowers. In essence, then, as more businessmen came under the scrutiny of external agencies, self-employment became more narrowly sanctioned by reference to wealth, making character a less acceptable criterion. This redefinition affected most adversely the independent commodity producers and the self-employed tradesmen who had relied upon skill, maturity, and community support for collateral.

This contraction of credit and the insistence of creditors on more tangible security contributed to the increasing value of mortgage debt that accompanied industrialization in Brantford the late 1860s and 1870s. The demand for greater credit or security forced businessmen to indenture their real estate, and the assumption of debt, though often necessary for business purposes, represented a qualification to the independence sought in self-employment.

Studies of the role of credit in early Canadian industrialization have generally adopted a functionalist approach, concentrating upon the institutions and mechanisms which have linked production and consumption and the implications that these have had for the flow of merchant capital into industrial investment. Such concerns have been most evident in the debate provoked by Tom Naylor's contention that Canadian merchants and the financial institutions they spawned preferred short-term and relatively safe ventures and thus from the 1850s hesitated to invest in longer-term, more risky manufacturing enterprises.[3] Gerald Tulchinsky has explained the separation of commerce and industry in Montreal from 1837 to 1853 in similar terms, although he has added that the proprietorial form of industrial organization may also have deterred mercantile participation.[4] On the other hand, noting that this theory of the nature of merchant capital contradicts what has been discovered about capital formation in England, Douglas McCalla has maintained that credit from merchants provided the very sort of capital – operating capital – most needed by early industrialists to bridge the time lag between their purchase of inputs and the sale of their products.[5]

McCalla's own work has astutely noted the ways in which one of the largest mid-nineteenth-century wholesaling firms in Canada, that of the Buchanan family, performed this function. The partners selected their clients on the basis of their evaluation of personal character and ability, informed by a prejudice for Scottish or at least British background and sustained by occasional meetings and inspections. If at times there seemed caprice in the termination of backing – as Michael B. Katz has too quickly concluded in explanation of the failure of Hamilton's entrepreneurs[6] – it arose from a creditor's recognition that his trust had been misplaced or that he was himself overextended. Mercantile credit may have been easily obtained, but it was held with difficulty, as the high turnover in the Buchanans' accounts indicated and as the cyclical collapse of the commercial economy revealed.[7]

The resolution of this contradiction in the credit system periodically involved the destruction of capital – for example, in 1837, in 1847, and, of interest here, in 1857 – along with those institutions which acted as intermediaries in its circulation. The demise of the two main Ontario banks in the late 1860s, the Commercial Bank and the Bank of Upper Canada, discussed by Max Magill and Peter Baskerville respectively, demonstrated the risks to capital at the margin of the commercial system where information concerning clients' financial positions was obtained with difficulty and was often hypothecated upon values inflated with the optimism attending early development.[8] The reduction of capital arising from the collapse of 1857, as Breckenridge's and McIvor's classic surveys of Canadian financial development suggested, provoked a restructuring of the credit system: not only did institutional lending policy become tighter and more directly tied to security, but also the legal definition of what could be demanded as collateral security was broadened to include bills of lading and warehouse and other commercial receipts.[9] More recently, attention has focused upon the ways in which the court system interpreted the law pertaining to the nature of contract, the allocation of losses, and the procedures of bankruptcy. R.C.B. Risk has concluded that in Ontario the judiciary's reluctance to break with existing precedents under English common law qualified the significance of legal initiative in economic development.[10] Peter George and Philip Sworden have admitted this, but have also contended that any body of case law in and of itself clarified the legal framework of business. Simple knowledge of how the commercial system was to be interpreted reduced transaction costs and thereby improved allocative efficiency.[11]

Concerned with credit as a function, Canadian historians have not directly considered the other implication of Naylor's thesis; that is that granting credit was discretionary. It necessitated choices and those choices influenced economic structures. Study of the grounds upon which choices were made and the implications of these choices involves a study of relative access to credit, a social problem, perhaps best approached through a community case-study.

THE QUALITIES OF THE CREDIT-WORTHY MAN

Credit made the economy run and businessmen were dependent upon it. A businessman held much of his wealth in trust, which, in turn, depended on the good opinion, confidence, and esteem of his associates. Should a man lose that confidence and be pressed to settle his affairs, his wealth might quickly collapse, since only with time could he realize the full value of the accounts of customers to whom he himself had extended credit. The credit system of the commercial economy, as described by T.G. Ridout, the cashier of the Bank of Upper Canada, recognized the right of "every farmer or person in trade or in respectable circumstances, who can give unexceptional personal security, to secure from the public banks reasonable accommodation."[12] Credit was the prerogative of the respectable and responsible man, and a lender felt assured that an honourable borrower would fulfil his obligations. The ideal of this code of honour was well stated in 1857 in the *Canadian Merchants' Magazine and Commercial Review*, no doubt as a reminder to debtors tempted to abscond:[13]

The true merchant is but the true man, illustrating a particular condition in life. ... The ethics and moralities, prevailing in, and governing all other relations, should be those which suggest his mercantile life and conduct. He should have no rule of right and wrong for the social circle and drawing room, and another for the counting house and busy marts of trade. ... His promises ring out like true gold – contracts are never violated – his drafts are never dishonoured – he needs no endorser. ... His bank is integrity and his bank book shows always a large credit side to his account He values equities above legalities, and moralities above advantages. He looks the sheriff and the constable full in the face, like an honest man; and lawyers and agencies he never invokes.

Credit, then, depended upon the businessman's conformity to a role model that stressed qualities of character and personality.

The agents, both local and itinerant, retained by the Mercantile Agency to report on Brantford business expressed this personal approach to credit in the 1840s and 1850s. A man's wealth determined the amount of credit he might receive. But his character determined whether or not he would receive any credit. Though wealthy, a man lacking in character was a poor risk. For example, potential creditors of one of Brantford's wealthiest general merchants, a "rather sharp and unscrupulous[man] ... who will make money by hook or by crook," were forewarned in 1854 that "his word is of no moment or importance to him, if the observance of it stood between him and gain." Consequently lenders were advised to have little to do with this poor risk.[14] On the other hand, a bookseller, "honest as the day is long," but who, the reporter admitted, would "never make more than a living ... [since he] unfortunately can't get on in business," was considered deserving of a good credit rating as encouragement.[15]

Those who conformed to the image of the ideal businessmen – an independent, respectable, responsible family man who was determined to succeed – impressed creditors. The independent businessman did not seek credit lightly, since to assume indebtedness, even for trade purposes, compromised his freedom and independence of action. Thus, it was a compliment for a businessman's credit rating to declare that "he would ask no credit he may not be entitled to" or that he "always pays up like a man" or that he is "good for all he would ask."[16] Of course, a man had to be respectable and of good character to be credited, or rather, if of bad character a man found great difficulty in obtaining credit. Comments on the honesty, industry, and decency of businessmen were so frequent in the credit reports that they became clichés. One simply expected a businessman to deal fairly; thus, it was not honourable actions that impressed, but dishonourable ones. A man taking advantage of his partner, breaking a business contract, betting on horses, speculating, gambling, cutting prices ruinously, or simply having "not much heart" received a qualified credit rating.[17] So did a man "too fond of the glass," even if he took the pledge.[18] Yet, ethnic stereotypes might mitigate the stigma. Thus, for an Irish Catholic or a German the consumption of intoxicants was considered part of his life style. The German grocer who "eats, drinks and sleeps at a great rate" was just a colourful local character, as was the Irish Catholic grocer "who gets on a spree once in a long while which sharpens his wits."[19]

A businessman might be independent and his character above suspicion, but if he had "no responsibility," then he was a poor risk.[20] Responsibility was for the mid-Victorian more than mere accountability for one's actions and behaviour. It was something quite tangible and included those things to which the mid-Victorian man was most passionately committed, his property and his family. Real estate holdings demonstrated to creditors that a businessman had made a commitment to a town. He was not "in a position so that he could take up his traps and leave at five minutes notice."[21]

A family and a wholesome family life were probably the most important factors in establishing a man's responsibility and his worthiness of credit. A single man, it was felt, lacked the order in his life of a married man and father and had less reason to be ambitious.[22] A family man who did not live up to his obligations was morally reprehensible. The Dun credit reporter was shocked and disgusted by a general merchant who "has left for British Columbia and left nothing here but his wife and three children."[23] If a man would not fulfil his responsibilities as a family man, he was certainly not to be trusted with credit.

A man's family, were it not organized and disciplined properly, could prove a disadvantage in establishing good credit. Failure to maintain family discipline raised doubts concerning a man's ability as head of the household and might occasion gossip that an extravagant wife or wild sons were a drain on the profits of the business.[24] Creditors were even wary of a man with a family too large, which might gobble up all the fruits of his endeavours. Noting similar comments from Dun's reporters concerning Utica businessmen, Mary P. Ryan has concluded that large families seemed too obviously a waste of resources and evidenced a lack of self-control.[25] Preferable was a man with a small family, such as the "Scotch, stingy, close, hardworking" saddler whose "whole family expenses cannot possibly be over $35 or $40 per annum, unless oatmeal should rise and his cow die."[26] These, then, were the characteristics which influenced the decisions of potential creditors. A businessman ought to be honest, moral, hard-working, committed to independence, and vested with responsibilities. Such a man had too much to lose should he fail to meet his obligations.

The frequent contemporary complaints against the favouritism of bank accommodation policy, and historical studies like that by Baskerville on the Bank of Upper Canada, would seem to controvert the even-handedness of a credit system based on evaluations of character.[27] Easy access to credit for the self-employed artisan and small businessman was not necessarily incompatible with bitter infighting and discrimination among major merchants and financiers. Rather, this contradiction was symptomatic of the bifurcation of the economy of the commercial city and the overlapping dualities of the inward/outward perspectives and engagements of merchants and of the at times divergent interests of artisans and merchants. Different though these two components were, mercantile enterprise and petty enterprise did impinge one upon the other. As T.W. Acheson has noted in his study of Saint John, New Brunswick, the acceptance of mercantilism by artisans depended upon their perception of benefits in the promotion of mercantile enterprise.[28] It was in the interests of merchants to promote this artisanal acquiescence to their leadership of the commercial economy. The implementation by merchants of what essentially was a credit standard of petty enterprise ought to be seen in this light.

The petty enterprise of artisans and shopkeepers who obtained most of their stock and credit locally constituted the largest part of Brantford's business community from the 1830s to the mid-1860s. To them, being in business asserted their social maturity, their independence, rather than revealed any commercial acumen.[29] Their operations were small in most instances, but still such businesses satisfied much of local consumption by producing basic commodities and retailing what could not produced. Some did venture the twenty-five or so miles to Hamilton and a few did go as far as Toronto or Buffalo to procure some items. But these excursions were limited, and at times suspicions were provoked by the small-timer wandering too far from home.[30]

In crediting petty enterprises, merchants and even bank managers in the 1840s and 1850s demonstrated a generosity within their community that they themselves might not have enjoyed. General merchants and purveyors of alcohol willingly supported "low grocers" with no security. Some employers helped set up employees in business, at times as competitors.[31] The local banks too could act favourably to tradesmen of laudable character. About two German tanners, Dun's agent remarked in 1861: "although their capital is small, [they] are treated liberally on account of their character and industry [and they] are well thought of by the local banks." In another act of generosity, the Bank of Montreal's agent backed a former labourer in opening a general store.[32]

To have friends was important, but connections did not necessarily distinguish a man. Many, if not most, small operators appear to have been so favoured. If they did not have a sympathetic employer or acquaintance in business, co-religionists might offer encouragement.[33] Valuable friends in deed to members of Farringdon Church, an Independent Methodist sect, were James and Ignatius Cockshutt, from the 1840s the wealthiest merchants in Brantford. One beneficiary, Thomas Cowherd, the Tinsmith Rhymer, expressed his gratitude in his own peculiar verse:[34]

TO MR. JAMES C——T.
NOVEMBER, 1853.
"A friend in need's a friend indeed"

O, can I look back to the time of my need,
When thou, under God, prov'dst a kind friend indeed,
And feel no emotion my bosom to swell?
'Twere baseness of conduct too shocking to tell.

Time was when chill penury stared in my face,
And I was made feel it almost a disgrace.
As a fruit of thy kindness that time has gone by,
So I to be thankful would constantly try.

O, well I remember how often I thought
My business endeavours would all come to naught;
That I, 'midst my toiling should surely stick fast,
And most sad disappointment meet me at last.

The Lord sent thee to me at such time of trial,
When exercised well with the grace of Self-denial.
Thy kind way of speaking took from me my sadness,
And left in its place a rich increase in gladness.

And oft since that time through a much checkered life
Amidst this world's bustle, its turmoil and strife,
My mind has been solaced with thoughts of thy love,
Which does thy relation to Christ clearly prove.
...
May thy good example to those that remain,
Be useful in showing Religion is gain.

Though Cowherd's poetic genius may not have done justice to his
sincerity, his verse does eloquently attest to his self-denial, and the
burden he felt from not getting ahead. But more significantly he
explained Cockshutt's help not as a favour but as the act of true
Christian friendship. His example also affirmed a central tenet of
the moral economy of petty enterprise: as Dun's agent put it about
another, "By the assistance of Friends, [he has] got a small stock."[35]
Knowledge of someone's good character conferred an obligation
upon a creditor to respect and, if possible, to advance his client's
independence. Even Timothy Eaton, hardly the most open-handed
of Victorian businessmen, accepted responsibility as part of the cred-

itor's role. "I like best to deal personally man to man," he wrote; "know your man and help him all you can."[36] To the Victorian artisan, as Geoffrey Crossick has observed, "independence, self-government and self-reliance were theoretically attainable by all" within a society of one's equals.[37]

Fraternalism distinguished petty enterprise from the moral economy of eighteenth-century paternalism that E.P. Thompson has examined. In fact, patronage and the appearance of being patronized were deeply resented by those who interpreted the acceptance of patronage as a compromise of their independence.[38] A reluctance to be beholden to another imposed a limit upon the line of credit a small proprietor might seek. Dun's reporter took this into account when recommending two tanners for "any amount they would ask for as I don't think they like being in debt." Similarly, although one cabinetmaker was deemed a good risk for $600 in 1858, the investigator doubted whether the "close-fisted Scotchman ... will ever have courage to ask for more than $50 credit or buy more than that amount of goods at one time."[39] The debts assumed and the credits extended in this moral economy often amounted to little individually: less than $500 generally was suggested by Dun for the lowest category of subjects. Yet a few dollars or a few days more could mean the difference between continuing business and closing shop.

ACCESS TO CREDIT

A rating from Dun tended to affect such men only if their horizons broadened. By definition, unless they stood in low local opinion, they would have been unlikely to seek much credit from the sorts of American firms that used Dun's service in the 1850s. Brantford's transportation links with Buffalo did, however, present the temptation to touch American lenders. Dun's representatives often received requests to check certain names, presumably men who had approached one of their clients. Numerous entries simply give the name and occupation of a subject followed by such lone comments as: "Can't find out about them"; "No such firm here"; "Questionable!!" Or, when the reporter became suspicious, he communicated his concern: for example, in 1858 about two tavern keepers, "fearing they might trouble some of the NY merchants, we advise you of their position."[40] For the artisan and shopkeeper, a rating probably had more effect when it recommended against credit.

In this role, Dun's advice seems to have been fairly reliable. Studying the evaluation of fifty-one of Hamilton's elite, however, Michael Katz was impressed by the sudden turn of fortune and by the lack of warning of failure in their credit ratings.[41] The Brantford ledger reveals a similar predictive weakness for the town's largest merchants, but had Katz studied all the ratings, he might have found that, as in Brantford, sounder counsel was available concerning self-employed artisans. In the ninety-three instances of failure explicitly mentioned between 1850 and 1870, warning of impending difficulties in the form of a recommendation against credit or exposure of serious business problems was provided one year in advance in about 50 per cent of the cases (table 3.1).[42]

Unexpected failure proved that character was less effective in allocating credit within mercantile enterprise because of more entangling credit relationships beyond the community. Three groups of merchants can be defined in accordance with the role of character in these relations. First, those support houses which received the stock from a single wholesaler generally possessed slight capital and depended entirely upon their supplier. In selecting men to support, wholesalers undoubtedly preferred those whom they knew at first hand and might therefore trust at a distance. For this reason, a number picked their clerks, deeming knowledge of ability and character more important than capital. While acknowledging their character, Dun's representative tied their ratings to the reputation of their backers – "unsafe alone." Support houses, even when conducting a profitable business, failed suddenly, should their suppliers encounter trouble. Anticipating such a problem, a retailer might approach some new wholesaler on the basis of the health of his operation without indicating the extent of his obligations to his original backer.[43] Dun warned against this, when possible.

A second and probably the largest category of mercantile enterprise included those merchants whose capital was sufficient to allow them either to pay cash or to offer security. Their metropolitan connections were limited to specific transactions, and, though they might deal with only one or two wholesalers, they could shop around for the best terms. Risk arose from dealing with a firm prepared to oversell the market by supplying whoever wished to buy. The grocery trade, in which margins were small and profits depended upon volume, suffered from this and accounted for the largest number of failures (nineteen) noted by Dun in a single trade. Knowledge of character helped a creditor anticipate debtor behaviour. Merchants did seek protection by contriving the priority of claims of friends to whom they could then assign their assets should difficulties arise.[44] Both wealth and character then interested potential lenders: the former assured that a man in this category could pay, the latter that he would.

Table 3.1
Reliability of the Mercantile Agency's Credit Reports, 1850–70

| | Warning Given of Failure | | | |
	1 Year in Advance N	Less than 1 Year N	None N	All N
Merchants	11	4	19	34
Petty shopkeepers	10	5	5	20
Manufacturers	6		2	8
Artisans	20	2	9	31
Total	47	11	35	93

Note: The category "Merchants" includes hotelkeepers. "Petty shopkeepers" includes tavern and saloon keepers. "Manufacturers" includes millers, builders, and planing mill owners.

Most of the unanticipated failures in the 1850s and 1860s fell among the ranks of the third group, the wealthiest merchants who possessed extensive interests and connections. They relied upon multiple metropolitan suppliers and brokers, the chartered banks, and each other for credit, and they complained when it was not forthcoming to the extent they sought.[45] Nevertheless the wealthiest were credited most extensively and unwisely in the halcyon years before 1857. Somewhat different standards measured their character than were applied to more plodding businessmen. Boosters might have seemed "rather sanguine and speculative," but their vision and enthusiasm, as well as their extensive participation in the town's economy, blinded Dun's reporter as thoroughly as the chartered banks to the susceptibility of their interests and assets to cyclical devaluation.

Unrivalled in ambition and in the confidence of lenders was George Samuel Wilkes. From the late 1840s through the 1850s, Wilkes immersed himself in nearly every opportunity presented by the commercial economy: wholesaling and forwarding, flour milling and grain speculating, rail promotion, iron founding, newspaper publishing, and real estate speculating. His reputation as a "good man of business" and his and his family's extensive landholdings stood him in good stead with lenders, Dun's opinion being that he was "entitled to any credit he may require."[46] At one time able to pass and repay an unendorsed promissory note for $48,000, in 1857 he defaulted on notes and endorsements to the sum of $238,674 – about 10 per cent due the banks – and mortgages for $83,380. The 141 court judgments registered against him for non-payment of notes demonstrate that, while endorsements may have been provided somewhat too freely, a degree of reciprocity was expected. The endorsee, in exchange for having his note co-signed, either co-signed a note for his endorser or gave a note indebting himself to his endorser. Neither offered much protection to someone mixed up with Wilkes, but the choice of protection revealed something about credit/debt relations in the bifurcated commercial economy. P.C. VanBrocklin, railroad promoter and steam engine and car manufacturer – a "fast man" in his own right – typified the strategy of other prominent businessmen in demanding security for co-signing. Notes from Wilkes for $27,000 offset VanBrocklin's obligations of $44,500 as an endorser. On the other hand, William Lines, a former labourer assisted as general merchant by the Bank of Montreal, took no notes from Wilkes in return for backing $6,100 of the latter's debts. Wilkes did, however, co-sign $1,657 of Lines's notes. Similarly John M. Tupper, a successful carriage maker, endorsed for $14,500, while Wilkes reciprocated with $2,100 in endorsements. Lines and Tupper, men who had risen from petty enterprise, acted in a way appropriate to that moral economy. They could trust Wilkes, just as he could trust them to make good on their paper. Those engaged in mercantile enterprise wanted more security. In hindsight, to hold a Wilkes note was to hold little, but it still seemed before the crash to be an asset.

One last pattern was evident in the debt of George S. Wilkes. Among his liabilities were a number of notes which he had endorsed for men with whom he had no business or personal connection: $120 for a self-employed painter; $116 for a bookseller; $508 for a small grocer to buy stock locally; $528 for a tavern keeper for liquor from a Brantford distiller.[47] To him such transactions were insignificant. But Wilkes's action implicitly accepted the moral economy and recognized that his own ventures, like those of other boosters, rested in part upon the political confidence that small proprietors had in men of his sort to run the affairs of the town. The ability of Mayor Wilkes to pledge municipal credit to promote railroads, navigation improvements, or the gas company depended upon the perception, by artisans and shopkeepers as voters, that mercantile enterprise promoted petty enterprise.

The collapse of the commercial economy in 1857 bankrupted many of the town's merchants who were overextended by speculations in the grain, lumber, and land markets. In the autumn of 1857 creditors rushed into the Brant County Court in attempts to recover their losses. Three hundred and sixty-seven judgments for overdue debts, more than twice as many as in all of 1856, were registered in county court against Brantford businessmen. The biggest loser was the Toronto private banker E.F. Whittemore, who registered judgments of over $100,000 against local businessmen, while the chartered banks suffered losses totalling $125,000 on Brantford business paper. On 3 March 1858 alone, the court issued 130 summons against people unable to satisfy judgments against them.[48] Suits from creditors seeking attachments of goods and mortgage foreclosures clogged the County Court of Chancery and local newspapers regularly noted sheriff's sales of property seized by court order.

With the collapse of the commercial economy, acceptance of a credit system founded on intangibles was a luxury. Some suppliers despaired of ever determining the credit-worthiness of their clients. James Austin, a Toronto grocery wholesaler, for example, decided to give up the trade for that very reason.[49] In an effort to secure more accurate commercial information, a group of Toronto businessmen founded the Canada Trade Protection Society, a credit-reporting and debt-collecting agency.[50] As well, greater use was made of the credit-rating service provided by the R.G. Dun and Co. From 1864 the agency published a quarterly register of credit ratings of businessmen in British North America for the use of their subscribers, who included Canadian wholesalers and the chartered banks.[51] This sped up credit investigations, since no longer did potential creditors have to telegraph for an evaluation. Furthermore, the chartered banks themselves hired credit reporters to investigate and recruit major accounts.[52]

More intense scrutiny by the Mercantile Agency presented a moral dilemma to the *Monetary Times* of Toronto: "On the one hand, to legalize these institutions ... is placing one portion of the mercantile community under an organized system of espionage and inquisition for the benefit of the other; and, on the other, to refuse to legalize them may be restricting injuriously the right of enquiring into the character and standing of the customer asking for credit in his business transactions." [53] In the journal's opinion, the issue opposed two conceptions of the proper relationship between creditor and debtor: an older one in which the lender himself judged "character and standing" and a new and impersonal one mediated by spies who separated the business community. In the end, the *Monetary Times* concluded that new conditions making it impossible for a lender to obtain knowledge independently justified the use of some intermediary.

The Dun ledger does reveal an improvement in the quality of information available to the firm's clients, in particular precise accounts of business assets and liabilities. Recognizing the importance of their rating, Brantford businessmen appear to have provided the reporter with financial statements from the late 1860s and to have protested when they believed they had been unfairly evaluated. Such

Table 3.2
Percentage of Businessmen Receiving Credit Ratings by Percentile Rank in
Distribution of Assessed Wealth, 1851–81

Percentile Rank	1851–2 (%)	1861 (%)	1871 (%)	1880–1 (%)
0–39	12	40	53	65
40–79	13	47	57	67
80–89	42	69	88	87
90–100	65	84	86	87
All	21	50	62	92
Number	40	155	214	343

Note: Businessmen were grouped into economic ranks on the basis of the total of real and personal property recorded for them in the municipal tax assessment rolls. More detail about methodology is provided in chapter 4.

complaints were met with requests for detailed statements, and reluctance to comply raised suspicions.[54] The subjects themselves changed the role of the credit reporter from spy to agent: whereas the first raters were cautioned to remain anonymous, potential borrowers who wanted to be known would not allow later ones to remain so.[55]

In consequence, Dun's credit reporting on Brantford's businessmen became more detailed following the depression of 1857. Whereas only forty businessmen (17 per cent of all) had established ratings in 1851–2, 155 (44 per cent of all) had done so by 1861. During this decade, coverage was extended beyond the major businessmen – loosely defined as the wealthiest 20 per cent of the business population – who had previously attracted the most attention. Included were more of those in the lower percentile ranges of the distribution of wealth (table 3.2). As well, greater attention was paid to independent commodity producers in all trades. For example, only one shoemaker received a rating in 1851; ten of sixteen did in 1861. No tailors or cabinetmakers were reported in 1851; four of each were in 1861. The concentration on these groups suggested a re-evaluation of the locus of risk in the economy. Over the ensuing twenty years this pattern persisted as coverage became more complete, reporting on 250 businessmen (67 per cent of all) in 1871 and 371 (93 per cent of all) in 1881. Moreover, by 1881 credit ratings had become more clearly related to wealth. Since Dun's reporter pronounced a judgment which was not merely positive or negative but graded, the ratings can be quantified and treated as a ranked order: no good or poor, fair, and good. The meaning of the middle rank remained constant through this period. It indicated one of two things: either a man's business was respectable but modest in scale and he was

Table 3.3
Credit Ratings by Percentile Rank in Distribution of Assessed Wealth, 1851–81

Year	Percentile Rank	No Good or Poor (%)	Fair (%)	Good (%)
1851–2	0–39	56	11	33
	40–79	70		30
	80–89	25	12	63
	90–100	15	23	62
	All	40	12	48
	Number	16	5	19
1861	0–39	78	6	16
	40–79	59	18	23
	80–89	32	50	18
	90–100	19	19	62
	All	54	19	27
	Number	83	30	42
1871	0–39	61	39	
	40–79	26	56	18
	80–89	10	31	59
	90–100		26	74
	All	34	42	24
	Number	72	91	51
1880–1	0–39	54	45	1
	40–79	13	70	17
	80–89	12	34	54
	90–100	11	11	78
	All	31	49	20
	Number	108	167	68

entitled to only "reasonable" credit, or he was experiencing difficulties which could be resolved with the careful forbearance of creditors.

Redefinition altered the meaning of the other two ratings. In the 1850s a "no good" or "poor" rating identified those whose character was suspect even if they were wealthy, who possessed no responsibility, or who were newcomers and relatively unknown. None the less, it was not unknown for the poorest of Brantford's businessmen to receive a "good" rating. In 1851 one-third of the ratings given to those in the poorest 40 per cent were "good," an approval rate that exceeded that of the next wealthiest 40 per cent (table 3.3). A small businessman's self-control, self-knowledge, and realistic evaluation of his prospects might inspire the same confidence and credit rating as that given to a more wealthy man. Time, however, diminished the likelihood of a favourable report for the least wealthy.

The expansion of reporting in the 1860s acted to the detriment of the least wealthy rank of businessmen and was probably, in part, an effort to warn potential creditors about men who in time of economic adversity might attempt to search farther afield for credit support. Only half as many in the poorest rank received a "good" rating in 1861 as in 1851 and nearly 80 per cent were considered a poor risk. The message was clear: doing business with a man possessing little capital was dangerous in 1861. For that matter, the credit reporter did not think highly of business prospects in general in Brantford the aftermath of the crash of 1857. More than half of the business community were given "poor" ratings in 1861. "Good" ratings dropped from 47 per cent in 1851 to 27 per cent in 1861. Even a sizeable proportion of the wealthiest 20 per cent were considered questionable. Nearly a third of businessmen in the 80–89th percentile received a "poor" rating, while fewer, under 20 per cent, were judged "good" in 1861, compared with more than 60 per cent ten years before.

Overall, Brantford business was more favourably evaluated in 1871. Nevertheless, the wealthy were clearly divided from those men of limited means. In fact the revival of lender confidence in Brantford did not extend to the latter businessmen: between 50 and 60 per cent of the least wealthy 40 per cent were deemed unworthy of a positive report; none in 1871 and less than 1 per cent in 1881 of that rank were recommended as good risks in 1881. On the other hand, about three-quarters of the wealthiest 10 per cent of the business community were rated "good."

Another feature of the re-evaluation of risk involved more frequent comments about trade prospects, especially the poor outlook for artisans. The shoemaking trade, for example, was overdone, according to the reports in the 1860s: "Some must go shortly. ... I don't believe that half the shoemakers are paying expenses," wrote Dun's reporter.[56] The more intensive credit reporting through the 1850s resulted in a dramatic increase in the number of tradesmen who were deemed unworthy of credit: whereas less than one-quarter of those self-employed in industrial production received a "poor" rating in 1851, more than one-half suffered this evaluation in 1861, an opinion that did not improve in 1871 or 1881. On the other hand, the risk associated with craft production, with such traditional occupations as blacksmithing, harnessmaking, shoemaking, and tinsmithing, was clearly distinguished from that of factory production, especially the

Table 3.4
Number of Businessmen Receiving Negative Credit Ratings, Selected Occupations,
1851–81

Sector	Occupation	1850–1	1861	1871	1880–1
Industry	Blacksmiths	1 of 1	2 of 2	2 of 4	7 of 11
	Founders	0 of 2	1 of 5	0 of 3	0 of 3
	Jewellers	0 of 1	2 of 5	0 of 3	0 of 3
	Millers	1 of 2		0 of 4	0 of 5
	Saddlers	0 of 2	1 of 4	3 of 5	4 of 7
	Shoemakers	0 of 1	6 of 10	8 of 12	7 of 13
	Bakers/Confectioners		1 of 3	1 of 5	3 of 10
	Brewers/Distillers		0 of 3	0 of 1	0 of 1
	Builders/Contractors		1 of 1	3 of 8	7 of 21
	Cabinetmakers		4 of 4	0 of 3	0 of 1
	Carriage makers		2 of 3	0 of 4	1 of 5
	Hatters		1 of 2	0 of 2	0 of 2
	Tailors		2 of 4	2 of 3	3 of 5
	Tanners		0 of 3	1 of 4	0 of 2
	Farm implement makers			0 of 2	0 of 3
	Tinsmiths			3 of 5	3 of 6
	Painters			0 of 1	2 of 7
Commerce	Druggists	2 of 2	0 of 3	0 of 4	4 of 10
	Forwarders	1 of 2			
	General merchants	7 of 17	2 of 6	0 of 1	0 of 1
	Grocers	3 of 4	15 of 26	22 of 47	20 of 58
	Hardware merchants	0 of 1	0 of 3	0 of 3	0 of 3
	Booksellers		3 of 3	2 of 2	2 of 4
	Dry goods merchants		3 of 12	1 of 10	2 of 8
	Grain merchants		2 of 2	1 of 3	1 of 2
	Hotel/Innkeepers		3 of 4	4 of 16	7 of 23
	Tavern/Saloon keepers		3 of 4	4 of 9	1 of 5
	Liquor merchants		2 of 2	2 of 2	1 of 2
	Clothiers			2 of 3	1 of 2
	Produce merchants			0 of 3	0 of 1
	Coal/Wood merchants			0 of 3	3 of 8
	Barbers			0 of 1	3 of 5
	Furniture merchants			0 of 1	3 of 5
	Insurance agents			1 of 1	1 of 5

large foundries, carriage factories, and agricultural implement factories, and even from that of retail merchandising, a new and growing
sector of the business community in the 1870s (table 3.4).

The credit system in Brantford rested on a firm evaluation of
wealth and business prospects in 1870s. No longer was good character a significant variable in obtaining credit. Like the Dun reporter,
the Bank of Commerce's agent in Brantford, Thomas S. Shenston,

investigated those criteria of importance to lenders. As Brant County registrar, able to conduct title searches and consult court judgment registries, Shenston could provide the most complete financial information available at the time and this he did in detail with, he admitted, "plodding caution."[57] His favourable ratings addressed finances in the main.[58] Only negative reports raised character,or life style as decisive factors. One man was dismissed curtly as a "former farmer with some of the worst habits of the city."[59] James Tutt, a builder and planing mill owner, was thought to lack forcefulness and was judged weak because he "appear[ed] to have little control over his workmen."[60] Personal qualities, then, could be liabilities, but seldom assets. By establishing a harder line in determining credit-worthiness, both Dun's reporters and Shenston were acting implicitly on the assumption that individual effort and good intentions did not guarantee success in business.

MORTGAGE INDEBTEDNESS

The contraction of credit and accompanying demands for tangible security rendered the management and finance of debt more difficult. Mortgages registered in the land records comprise the only complete set of data available for a systematic examination of debt over time, and while these data cannot be related to other forms of debt, it is clear that mortgages did become a fact of business life with the transition to industrial capitalism. They formalized credit relationships and were a mechanism of fixed capital formation. Mortgages, then, became one strategy to sustain viable enterprises at a time of structural change, and, consequently, more businessmen were indebted, and to a greater extent, in the industrial than in the commercial economy.[61]

Businessmen in the commercial economy were not an overly indebted class. David P. Gagan's study of mortgaging in Toronto Gore Township has indicated that about one-third of rural property owners bore indebtedness. His conclusion that "plainly, this was not a society of chronic debtors" might apply with somewhat more force to urban businessmen, who were even less indebted.[62] The majority in 1851, 52 per cent, owned real estate free from mortgage debt. Less than 20 per cent of all businessmen, only about one-quarter of property owners, had mortgages against their holdings. Similarly, seven of the ten businessmen who became property owners between 1851 and 1861 were able to do so without assuming a mortgage. Few, it would seem, desired or found it necessary to compromise their independence by assuming indebtedness of this form.[63]

Table 3.5
Index of Relative Mortgage Debt by Percentile Rank, 1851–81

Percentile Rank	1851–2	1861	1871	1880–1
0–39	626	694	295	86
40–79	34	73	175	94
80–89	57	62	54	119
90–100	121	102	66	96
All	100	100	100	100
Number	191	307	343	373

Note: Relative mortgage indebtedness was calculated by dividing the percentage of mortgage debt owed by each rank by the percentage of real property wealth held by each group. The product was multiplied by 100 to create an index number which was less than 100 when the group was less indebted than the average and more than 100 when relatively more indebted.

Table 3.6
Index of Relative Mortgage Debt by Age Group, 1851–81

Years of Age	1851–2	1861	1871	1880–1
20–9	401	72	129	526
30–9	110	185	249	99
40–9	29	61	74	107
50–9	30	46	45	54
60 plus	0	19	75	93
All	100	100	100	100
Number	190	307	331	351

Debt in the commercial economy was relatively concentrated at the extremes of the business population, among the wealthiest and the poorest, and among the youngest members (tables 3.5 and 3.6). Among the wealthiest 10 per cent of the business class were Brantford's "boomers" and speculators. In most cases this indebtedness – amounting to 60 per cent of the mortgage obligations of all businessmen in 1851 – encumbered vacant land and often supported speculative activities that were tangential to primary business concerns.

For the poorest businessmen, as for those under the age of thirty, the combination of self-employment and property ownership was a strain and debt a mark of their marginality and recent embarkation in business. Yet, relative indebtedness in 1851 and 1861 diminished steadily from age cohort to age cohort, especially after the age of

Table 3.7
Economic Mobility and Mortgage Debt, 1851–81

	Per Cent Increasing Mortgage Debt		
Mobility	1851–61	1861–71	1871–81
Up	36	44	49
Stable	55	42	30
Down	89	37	45
All	46	42	42

Note: This study has defined mobility in relative terms: those businessmen who rose to a higher decile in the distribution of wealth within the business population were defined as being upwardly mobile. Conversely, those who fell to a lower decile were considered downwardly mobile.

forty years, and in the middle range of the distribution of wealth. Nor did the assumption of indebtedness play a permanent role in the strategy of those pursuing success in the 1850s: greater indebtedness was associated with declining fortunes. Of those who grew wealthier between 1851 and 1861, only one-third became more indebted, whereas 54 per cent of those who maintained their wealth and nearly 90 per cent of those who lost wealth owed greater mortgage debt (table 3.7). The greater indebtedness of those who maintained or lost wealth reflected the lengths to which they had to go in order to stay in business. For some businessmen, land was a savings bank and mortgages were withdrawals from their accounts. With time and business longevity, then, a man could hope to reduce his obligations and the qualifications to his independence.

This situation changed after the crash of 1857. The rate of property ownership fell, and mortgage indebtedness grew so that half of landowners in 1861 and three-fifths in 1871 carried mortgages against their property. The total value of their mortgages tripled from $80,000 to $250,000. Significantly, more men were obligated for smaller sums, suggesting that the threshold of creditor tolerance had been lowered and that the strain of sustaining self-employment forced men to utilize all their assets (table 3.8). Moreover, the concentration of indebtedness shifted. Most affected were men who earlier had avoided indebtedness, those in the middle range of the distribution of wealth, men in their thirties and forties, and craft producers. Absolutely and in relation to the value of their real estate, the indebtedness of men in the middle range of the distribution of wealth – in the 40–79th percentile – rose dramatically. In 1851 they had been responsible for just 10 per cent of all debt and 18 per cent

Table 3.8
Mortgage Indebtedness of Businessmen, 1851–81

	1851–2	1861	1871	1880–1
Average mortgage debt ($)	2,253	2,724	2,132	3,830
Median mortgage debt ($)	1,020	860	1,000	2,000
Debt of industrial sector ($)	50,640	163,630	150,560	206,440
Debt of commercial sector ($)	30,480	87,010	91,840	191,940
Total mortgage debt ($)	81,120	250,640	253,800	398,380
Property owners in debt (%)	27	51	59	48
Businessmen in debt (%)	19	30	35	29
Number	36	92	119	104

in 1861, but by 1871 they owed 50 per cent. Similarly, debt entangled more and more tradesmen as the rate of indebtedness in the industrial sector rose from 22 per cent of real property owners in 1851 to 59 per cent in 1861. Moreover, on the average this indebtedness was for small amounts. These were the men who had typified the ideal of the independent men, married with a family and self-employed in a small but solid way.

For them, no longer was mortgage debt a temporary condition associated with entrance to and early years in business. Rather it became a necessity for staying in business. Indeed, the relationship between debt and business longevity – defined as persistent self-employment for more than ten years – changed with industrialization. In the 1860s and 1870s mortgage debtors had higher rates of persistence in business than in the 1850s and were more likely to remain in business for ten years than were the owners of unencumbered real estate (table 3.9). Moreover, for advancement all of a man's assets had to be in play and at risk. By 1880 nearly half of the self-employed property owners who grew wealthier fell deeper in debt. On the other hand, those property owners who lost money in business were less likely than they had been in the 1850s to go deeper into debt and more likely to give up their real estate. Thus, land was increasingly another form of business capital rather than a repository for business profits.

Mortgages appeared more important as instruments of capital formation in the 1870s. Despite a decline of 10 per cent in the relative size of the indebted business population to just under half of all property owners, total indebtedness grew by 57 per cent from 1871

Table 3.9
Rates of Persistence in Business for Mortgage-Indebted and Unindebted
Property Owners, 1851–81

	1851–61 (%)	1861–71 (%)	1871–81 (%)
Debtors	44	60	61
Non-debtors	49	43	52
All	48	50	56
Number	136	180	207

to 1881 to nearly $400,000. Two factors produced this: first, the use of mortgages to finance factory expansion; and second, the doubling of commercial debt. Both resulted from larger mortgages being carried by the wealthiest businessmen. More than half of the total mortgage debt was owed by the wealthiest 10 per cent. This was not a return to the pattern of the 1850s, however, since borrowing does not appear to have accompanied significant speculation.

The industrial sector always bore most of the mortgage debt of the business population. Yet, in the commercial economy the increase in the amount of mortgage debt did not finance the growth of existing industries; rather, it supported more industries. Businessmen in the largest industrial enterprises bore less average debt in 1861 than in 1851 (table 3.10). The total debt of the iron-founding industry increased from $44,000 to $68,000 over these ten years, while the average debt of iron founders declined from $2,200 to $1,400. In the industrial economy, debt financed the expansion of productive capacity. The average debt of carriage makers rose from only $400 in 1861 to nearly $14,000 in 1871 and $5,000 in 1881. Their ability to carry this amount of debt and to retire nearly two-thirds of it suggested the profits that could be realized by increasing the scale of production. Likewise, the mortgage debt of the average iron founder increased from $1,400 in 1861 to $6,000 in 1871 to $12,000 in 1881. In total, the mortgage debt of those engaged in production in Brantford 1881 equalled about 20 per cent of all capital invested in manufacturing.

Mortgages were similarly a mechanism of capital formation in the commercial sector. They financed the expansion of distributive capacity and office space and secured the consignment of inventories.[64] The very rapid increase in commercial debt, which doubled from 1871 to 1881, ought to be interpreted in conjunction with the enhanced credit ratings of men in commercial enterprises as an

Table 3.10
Average Value of Mortgage Debt by Selected Occupations, 1851–81

Occupation	1851–2 ($)	1861 ($)	1871 ($)	1880–1 ($)
Builder/contractor	680	730	1,464	2,031
Carpenter	600	554	590	760
Miller	8,280	140	3,063	9,970
Iron founder	2,200	1,352	6,388	11,940
Shoemaker	350	600	630	450
Carriage maker	1,080	405	13,888	4,950
Blacksmith	1,200			890
Tinsmith		900		1,467
Tanner		3,000	2,480	2,550
Hatter		870	1,150	
Painter		1,800	445	3,324
Jeweller/watchmaker		1,563	5,700	
Grocer	904	3,221	1,831	3,480
Druggist	160	140	1,975	
Hotel keeper	96	2,588	783	6,876
Tavern keeper	160	250	3,090	
Boarding-house keeper		700	1,633	
Dry goods merchant		3,621	2,174	6,517
Insurance agent			775	3,400
Auctioneer			950	3,280
Grain merchant			450	3,010
Milk dealer			985	490

indication of the structural change in business. As has already been explained, commerce was, in terms of numbers of new businesses at least, the new growth area of business opportunity. During the 1870s – at the same time as industrial enterprises were declining in number by attrition – the commercial sector was growing at a more rapid rate than the city's population. The result was that by 1881 the retail merchant had displaced the craft producer as the typical Brantford small businessman.

By the 1870s, then, mortgage indebtedness was a fact of business life. It not only provided the security that was essential for credit but also mobilized capital for investment in the expansion of both industrial and commercial enterprises. Moreover, debt ceased to be associated as in the commercial economy with a temporarily compromised independence to be reduced with business longevity. In consequence, land, a mark of social respectability a short decade or so before, was rendered merely another commodity to be figured into the calculation of economic collateral.

CONCLUSION

Increasing mortgage indebtedness in the 1870s marked the decline of the role model of the businessman that had typified the commercial economy. Self-employment and independence were not equivalent because of the necessity of indebtedness for a business career. With the transition to industrial capitalism, no longer was the businessman "the true man illustrating a particular condition in life" and no longer was character consistent with that condition a significant criterion in obtaining credit. That such should ever have been the case may seem somewhat romantic. But, as E.P. Thompson has cautioned, "it is difficult to imagine the moral assumptions of another social configuration." It is too easy to impute calculations of business rationality in the strictest of economic terms we now expect of entrepreneurs to men whose moral assumptions rested on a different foundation. Not only did "the new political economy of the free market," as Thompson has argued, "break down the old moral economy of provision,"[65] it also supplanted the values of petty enterprise. These values comprised another moral economy, a system of socialized individualism, in which character, responsibility, and independence could be sustained and translated into self-employment through mutual self-help.

Acceptance of this morality by merchants and credit agencies when dealing with petty enterprise and to varying degrees with mercantile enterprise demonstrated one side of what Elizabeth Fox-Genovese and Eugene Genovese have termed the "Janus face of merchant capital": its tendency to accommodate to existing social relations. Its other side, "the transformative abilities of exchange relations," appeared in the contraction of credit through the 1860s and 1870s.[66] The inability of the petty proprietor to stay in business was a condition necessary for the transition to industrial capitalism. It may of course be attributed to a number of factors, but not the least was the reluctance to credit him. That he had not been so disadvantaged in the past reveals that change involved an element of discretion. The irony, of course, was that the collapse of the commercial economy after 1857 could be attributed more to the unexpected failure of the major merchants and their various promotions than to the misfortunes of the self-employed artisan and small shopkeeper. Yet, the latter far more than the former suffered from the re-evaluation of risk in terms of pecuniary strength not character.

4 The Structure of Wealth

Access to credit and the ability to borrow inflated a businessman's capital and increased his wealth. Data on the distribution of wealth are not easily obtained, although municipal tax assessment rolls do provide one component: each year municipal assessors valued the worth of real estate and taxable personal property owned within the municipality. With credit more closely tied to tangible assets like real estate, landholdings constituted an important indication of the scale of business a man could conduct. As well, the assessment records revealed the conditions under which a businessman possessed the means of transacting business. Did he rent or own his premises? Did certain types of businesses at different times hold their premises under different tenures? Capital formation in business facilities, in the plant and in operating capital, can also be examined. The strategies adopted in assembling capital were evident in the choices men made in owning residential accommodation and rental property. Each of these two forms of real property holding offered a form of security at the same time as it diverted assets from actual business operations.

The transition to industrial capitalism altered the way in which wealth, as revealed in municipal tax records, was structured in Brantford. The self-employed were still wealthier in the 1870s than those working for wages, though by a narrower margin than in the 1850s. Within the business population itself, by the 1870s, men engaged in industry had become relatively wealthier than men engaged in commerce. But capital formation in iron founding and farm implement manufacturing especially, and to a lesser degree in carriage manufacturing and flour milling, masked the declining wealth of independent tradesmen and artisans. Commercial enterprise experienced the reverse of this trend. The large-scale merchants of the 1850s whose general merchandising operations had required and generated considerable wealth were being replaced by men with more limited capital, running more specialized retailing operations. But, if industrialists were growing wealthier than men in commerce, they did so in part because their ventures attracted mortgage investment from Brantford's successful merchants.

MUNICIPAL TAX ASSESSMENT: LEGISLATION AND METHODOLOGY

Financial data gleaned from assessment rolls present several challenges when used to study socioeconomic trends. Because of changes in municipal tax law, the sums recorded for assessed real and personal property cannot simply be added together to calculate total wealth. Even if they could, inflation or deflation in currency values would make comparisons across time difficult. Finally, the undervaluation of the assets of the wealthy seems a real possibility. Therefore, some transformation is needed to combine real and personal wealth and to allow some degree of comparison from one to another cross-section.

The municipal taxation system in Canada West changed in 1866 from one which, like the English system, was essentially a tax on income from property to one which was a tax on wealth, as in the United States.[1] As well, legislation clarified the definitions of the types of real and personal property subject to taxation. The earliest assessment rolls used here were compiled under legislation enacted in 1846, 1850, and 1853. Prior to 1846, nominal categories of real and personal property were assessed at fixed values, so much for each acre of cultivated and uncultivated land, type of building, species of livestock, and so on.[2] William Henry Draper introduced legislation requiring *ad valorem*, or market value, assessment in 1846, arguing that categorical assessment "was becoming more and more obnoxious as the country was rapidly improving."[3] Some districts developed more quickly than others, and land values varied with location. Draper's act provided for local assessors appointed by municipal authorities to appraise real property each year at its actual value. Taxes, however, were to be levied on the income generated by real property, its annual value, rather than its actual value. The distinction between actual and annual values of property derived from a fear that the real estate market might not return the true value of property were it sold and, thus, a property owner might be taxed on a value which he could never realize. The exchange value of real property, in other words, did not translate directly into its use value. Henry John Boulton maintained in 1849 that taxing actual values might be fair in England where "property of all kinds had a well-regulated value, and everyone having property for sale ... could get the fair value for his property. Not so in this country, where there are masses of property of real intrinsic value for which, under present circumstances, absolutely nothing could be got."[4] Boulton's concern revealed that the market had not yet been taken as the sole standard of values. As well, a tax on annual values declared that the proper incidence of taxation was upon the income derived from wealth, rather than upon wealth itself. In the case of rental properties, the annual value equalled the rent. For owner-occupied real estate, the assessor recorded an imputed rent which would have been earned had the property been put to rent. The assessment act of 1850 set 6 per cent, the figure considered a "just return" in earlier usury legislation, as the minimum rent for vacant land and lawns larger than a quarter acre.[5]

The assessment acts of 1866 and 1869 prescribed that the actual value of real property be taxed. Whether "intrinsic value" was now considered to be a market value or whether a market value was believed now to approximate "intrinsic value" more closely remains unknown, since, in the absence of an official Hansard, debates on the assessment bill introduced in August 1866 were lost in reports of the death of E.P. Tache, the formation of the new Belleau ministry, and the progress of the Confederation proposal. The effect of the new legislation on assessed wealth and the burden of taxation is difficult to judge. However, an examination of the relationship between actual and assessed values reported for 1,066 commercial and residential properties owned or occupied by businessmen between 1847 and 1854 suggests that properties with low actual values returned a higher percentage of their value annually in real or imputed rent than properties with higher values. Thus, taxation of actual values shifted the tax burden upwards.

To the extent that it has been possible to reconstruct the debates over assessment, it is apparent that greater contention arose over the taxation of personal property than real property. From 1841 Francis Hincks led the efforts of Reformers to extend *ad valorem* taxation to personal property and income.[6] Without changes, he argued, farmers and owners of improved real estate would bear the greatest burden of taxation. David Thompson criticized the system of categorical assessment in 1846 for being "oppressive to the poor ... [because] it taxed what was the possession of every poor man, *viz.*, a cow, where many articles that the rich usually possess are exempt."[7] Commercial and professional interests succeeded in their opposition to the extension of *ad valorem* taxation to personal property in Draper's act. In 1850, however, Hincks introduced legislation to tax the annual value, set at 6 per cent of the actual value, of cows, horses, carriages for pleasure or hire, and the shares held in commercial water vessels. The inventories of tradesmen and merchants were assessed for their average value through the year, rather than for their value at the time of the assessment. Individuals whose incomes in the previous year exceeded the value of their personal property at the time of the assessment were taxed on 6 per cent of their incomes. The rationale for taking income as a surrogate for personal property was never stated, although one might speculate that this reflected a conviction that property was accumulated from labour. The income one received was a measure of the value of one's labour as property and, since the return on property rather than property itself was taxed, the legislation assumed that the rent paid to labour was the same as the rent received by other forms of capital, that is, 6 per cent. That mortgage income was exempt from assessment reinforces the impression that income was treated as a surrogate for personal property. The 1853 act exempted the income received by farmers from the sale of farm produce. Since rent was considered to be a payment for the productivity of the land, a tax on real property and farm income would have been double taxation. In 1869 others were granted this privilege through an amendment to the Assessment Act which exempted "income of mechanics, merchants, or other income derived from capital liable to taxation." While capital not its return was taxed after 1866, the amendment revealed an effort to avoid double taxation. Income derived from rental property was never assessed for taxes.[8]

Complaints from businessmen that the incidence of taxation under the 1850 Assessment Act fell too heavily on their shoulders persuaded the government to set up a committee of inquiry in 1852. It reported that the "complaints ... are well-founded. ... A very large and evidently unjust proportion of the taxes in the cities ... fall on particular classes of the community, and ... the unjust and unequal bearing of the law is mainly attributed to the fact that merchants and manufacturers holding stocks of goods on hand are liable under its provisions, to taxation on the interest of their average stock in trade, (which interest is found in many cases to exceed their actual incomes)." Those on fixed incomes were taxed only on the imputed interest on their earnings. Thus, a man in this category might well remit less tax than a merchant, for example, whose income was the same, but whose shop carried a large stock.[9] Rather than reducing the tax on business, however, legislation in 1853 subjected additional categories of personal property to taxation and noted exemptions explicitly: "all goods, chattels, shares in chartered banks and railroad companies, money, notes, accounts and their full value and all other property except land" and imperial and government pensions, farm income, debts unsecured by mortgages, clergymen's salaries, personal property invested outside of the province, household and personal effects, income from land transactions, total personal property under £25 and total income under £50.[10]

Despite changes in the definition, many critics continued to believe that much personal property escaped taxation because of its easy concealment and difficulty in appraisal. The Ontario Select Committee on Exemptions from Taxation in 1878 reported the opinion of the Toronto assessor that, while the total personal property assessment in that city was one-quarter of the value of the real property assessment, in reality the two categories were probably equal.[11] Gordon Darroch's caveat should be remembered: the assessment of personal property "reflects the values of tangible and probably readily visible personal property and of relatively substantial incomes, but not of major capital holdings."[12] Not until 1904 was municipal taxation of personal property abandoned.[13]

Mortgages and income derived from mortgages were not taxed as personal property. Despite arguments from the defenders of indebted farmers, parliament concluded that their assessment would encourage indebtedness as a means of transferring the burden of taxation from the mortgagor to the mortgagee. Henry Sherwood argued in 1846 that "if mortgages were to be taxed, and the nominal owner only to pay according to the actual amount he owned of the property, then the mortgagee would be compelled to pay all the taxes; it would be an inducement to mortgage: the mortgagee would be paying all the taxes, the actual owner would be enjoying all the benefits."[14] Mortgagors were given some relief in the 1853 Assessment Act. Mortgages were interpreted as a way of converting real to personal property, and personal property equal to the value of the mortgage on the land was granted an exemption.[15] The exemption benefited businessmen the most, since they were likely to have secured their inventories with mortgages and have personal property equal to or greater than the value of the mortgage. Of course, if one did not have personal property equal to the value of mortgages owed, the exemption could be meaningless. Prior to 1866 the exemption did not remove the entire burden of paying tax on mortgaged wealth, since the annual value of developed real estate was greater than the imputed annual value of personal property. Once actual values were taxed, the exemption did compensate fully for debt. For the social historian, the exemption of mortgage debt, in effect the subtraction of one form of liability, renders assessment data a more accurate measure of the wealth.

Businessmen were afforded relief from the taxation of personal property in another way by the act of 1853. Personal property was assessed as a ranked category rather than at a true figure. Property worth between £25 and £50 was entered in the rolls at the lower figure; similarly higher categories, 50–100, 100–250, 250–500, 500–1,000, 1,000–2,500, 2,500–5,000, 5,000–10,000, and so on at in £5,000 units, were assessed at the lower value.[16] From 1869 actual values were assessed. Though not clearly stipulated in the assessment legislation, the Ontario Select Committee on Exemptions from Taxation revealed in the 1878 that in practice only inventories which were paid for were assessed, while those held on credit were exempt.[17] Again a liability is thereby deducted from the wealth figures.

The changes in assessment legislation and changes in the value of currency make comparisons of assessed wealth over time difficult. To overcome the problem, a very simple transformation has been employed. At each cross-section the assessed real and personal wealth of each individual was converted to a percentage of total real wealth and total personal wealth. The total wealth of an individual was calculated by adding these two percentages together. The assumption supporting this method is that while currency values, forms of taxable property, and undervaluation may have changed over time, these would not necessarily affect the place or ranking of an individual in the distribution of wealth. For the purpose of generalization, businessmen were then ordered from poorest to richest and ranked in percentile groups. Those in the bottom 40 per cent were arbitrarily labelled the poorest, those in the 40–79th percentile mostly well-off, those from the 80–90th percentile the well-to-do, and those in the top ten percentiles the rich. Michael Katz adopted similar ranks in his Hamilton study. However, his method of "measuring an individual's wealth" adopts an unacceptable double accounting. Katz determined his "economic rankings" for each individual by adding together the value of real property owned, the value of annual rental payments received, the value of rent paid annually, the value of personal property owned, and the value of annual income. Adding rental payments to the value of real property counts the same variable twice in a different way. It would be just as logical to create a figure for the annual return upon personal property and add it into the calculation. Similarly, since rent was paid from income, Katz's formula inflates income by the amount of the rent paid.[18]

The transformation employed creates a relative, not an absolute figure for total wealth. An individual's or a group's wealth is measured in relation to the total and consequently is affected by the number of individuals included in the population, since there is no way to measure the absolute growth or decline of the business population. To compensate for this when examining changes in the distribution of wealth among groups, the relative concentration of wealth in the hands of the members of a particular group can be described by dividing the percentage of total wealth held by the group by the percentage of that group among the assessed business population. Multiplying the result of this calculation by one hundred produces an index number which is greater than one hundred if the group holds a disproportionately large share of the total wealth and is less than one hundred if a disproportionately small share is held. The index of relative wealth then can be compared from one cross-section to another to determine whether any group improved or lost ground in relation to the rest of the business population.

The following analysis of the distribution of wealth deals with populations identified in the manuscript census and linked to the most appropriate assessment roll. Because the 1852 assessment has not survived, the census taken that year was linked to the 1851 assessment. The 1861 and 1871 censuses have been linked to the assessments of those years. Because the 1881 census lacked as detailed internal evidence of self-employment as earlier census manuscripts, an 1880 directory was used to increase the identification of the self-employed. Linkage to the 1880 assessment, therefore, seemed most appropriate. The interval between the compilation of the two sources necessarily precluded the linkage of some cases to the assessment; either they had not arrived or they had left, depending on the cross-section years.

EARLY INDUSTRIALIZATION AND THE SOCIAL REDISTRIBUTION OF WEALTH

The benefits imparted by early industrialization to working people have been heatedly debated by scholars of the Canadian experience and those of other national economies. Most would admit that factory production, railroad operations, and wholesaling demanded skilled labour and created new opportunities for wage labour with the possibility of steady employment. And, for the long term at least, one can accept Ian Drummond's reminder that any thesis of the immiserization must confront the reality of the improving material conditions of the Ontario working class.[19] Though he would have us remember the winners in industrial change, the poverty which blighted late-nineteenth-century industrial cities only too visibly reminds us that there were losers.

Gordon Darroch, in a study of Toronto from 1861 to 1899 that uses similar sources to the ones employed here, has tried to sort out the balance of losers and winners. More important, he has pointed out that the patterns in the distribution of wealth in one period might not necessarily persist in subsequent periods. Though inequalities increased through the 1860s, disparities in wealthholding diminished after 1871 and until 1899. Darroch's findings in general are consistent with the discovery by Lee Soltow among others that there was a certain levelling, in the short term at least, in the "startling" inequalities which accompanied early industrialization.[20] Reasons for lesser inequality are difficult to advance, though Darroch's hunch that lower commodity prices might have left workers with a larger part of their incomes to invest in housing is consistent with the trends apparent in the various series of standard-of-living indicators assembled more recently by David and Rosemary Gagan. The latter scholars, however, have qualified Darroch's intuition by demonstrating that enjoyment of lower prices remained contingent upon the availability of steady work.[21]

In Brantford the distribution of real property changed in the period under review, but not in a way that would necessarily suggest a levelling or deepening of inequality. Rather, real estate holdings appear to have fluctuated with the business cycle. At higher points in the cycle, in 1851 and 1871, businessmen held a share of real wealth that was larger than at lower points in the cycle. That wealth of this kind was less disproportionately concentrated in 1861 and 1881 may support Michael Doucet's contention that downturns in the economy benefited workingmen by offering them better housing at lower prices. But it may also mean that recession deflated the values of commercial and industrial properties more than the values of residential property. Unfortunately the data collected for this study do not permit one to determine whether Brantford workers, like their Hamilton counterparts, increased their rates of home ownership.[22] That men working for wages held a larger relative share of real estate in 1880 than in 1851 may indicate an improvement in living conditions, but that betterment cannot be easily attributed to structural change (table 4.1).

On the other hand, the redistribution of personal property and income is less ambiguous in its implications. One hundred and ninety-

Table 4.1
Real and Personal Property/Income Assessments of Business Population as Per Cent of Total, 1851–80

	1851	1861	1871	1880
Business assessment as per cent of:				
Total real property assessment	46	37	45	36
Total personal property + income assessment	93	83	72	73
Assessed businessmen as per cent of adult male population	20	19	18	20

one businessmen, comprising about 20 per cent of men over twenty years of age in 1852, accounted for 93 per cent of the assessed value of personal property plus income in 1851. In 1880, 375 businessmen, again roughly 20 per cent of the men over twenty years old in 1881, were assessed for 73 per cent of the value of wealth in this category. Put another way, the share of personal property plus income assessed against businessmen declined from 4.6 times the size of their representation in the male population over age twenty in 1851 to 3.6 times in 1881. It seems unlikely that a change of this magnitude could result solely from changes in assessment legislation or undervaluation, and, since the largest constituent part of this category related to business – inventories and accounts owing, mainly – the increase in the assessment of the employed population probably reflected a real increase in the incomes of working people.

The period studied here is probably too brief to support any firm contributions to the standard-of-living problem. However, it does suggest that the increased share of real property owned by workingmen in 1880 may have been a consequence of cyclical, not structural, change. On the other hand, the relatively higher personal property/income assessment of workingmen that year, may have been translated into greater real property ownership later. As one might expect, relative gains in income preceded the accumulation of wealth.

GENERAL TRENDS IN THE DISTRIBUTION OF WEALTH AMONG BUSINESSMEN

Within the business population itself, the distribution of wealth remained stable and unequal despite the transition to industrial capitalism. Gini indexes measuring the inequality in the distribution of wealth remained almost constant from cross-section to cross-section.[23] Only 1861 differed, as depression reduced overall inequality slightly. The wealth held by those in the 60–94th percentile range declined from 51 per cent of the total in 1851 to 45 per cent in 1861. Balancing this was the gain of an additional 3 per cent of the total by the least and most wealthy groups, the poorest 40 per cent and the richest 5 per cent. The shift of wealth upward, at the expense of those in the 60–94th percentile range, continued through the 1870s. The wealthiest 5 per cent of businessmen by 1880 had increased their share of total assessed wealth to 45 from 36 per cent in 1851. Redistribution of wealth, to the extent that there was any among businessmen, occurred among the wealthiest 40 per cent (table 4.2).

More evident were changes in the distribution of real property. Ownership of real estate declined from the frontier era. When the village was first opened to settlement in 1830, twenty-two of twenty-six businessmen, or 85 per cent, held land, though the value of holdings was not equally distributed. Tradesmen made up one-half of all business property owners, but accounted for only one-tenth of the valuation placed on the village's real estate. Two merchants, John Aston Wilkes and Jedidiah Jackson, possessed 75 per cent of the total valuation.[24] The 1842 census indicated that only 50 per cent of businessmen were property owners, fewer than in any other year examined. Presumably those who had been on the spot when the village plot had been subdivided and auctioned in the early 1830s retained control of urban space into the next decade. Businessmen arriving in the late 1830s and early 1840s either possessed insufficient capital on arrival to purchase their premises or could not accumulate enough to do so over time. In the 1840s Brantford real estate must not have seemed a wise investment. Property owners in 1842 were much more likely to leave town over the next ten years than were renters: 17 per cent of the former, but 43 per cent of the latter, remained in business in 1852.

Over the 1842 to 1851 interval, real property ownership rose substantially, whether because of deflated values in the recession following 1847 or because of the immigration of men with some capital. In 1851, 71 per cent of businessmen owned some land in Brantford. The depressed economy of the late 1850s and early 1860s reduced this level of ownership to 58 per cent of businessmen. The depression of 1857 may well have created a buyer's market for land in Brantford, as Doucet has claimed it did in Hamilton,[25] but few could buy. The wealthiest 5 per cent of real estate owners in business, sixteen men, increased the share of landed wealth held by that percentile group from 39 per cent of the business total in 1851 to 50 per cent in 1861.

Table 4.2
Distribution of Assessed Wealth by Percentile Rank, 1851–80

Percentile Rank	1851 Type of Property (% of Total Held)			1861 Type of Property (% of Total Held)			1871 Type of Property (% of Total Held)			1880 Type of Property (% of Total Held)		
	Real	Personal	Total	Real	Personal	Total	Real	Personal	Total	Real	Personal	Total
0–19	0	2	1	0	5	3	0	4	2	0	4	2
20–39	2	3	4	0	6	5	0	4	4	0	4	2
40–59	8	6	8	4	6	8	6	5	8	11	4	8
60–79	18	13	20	14	12	15	20	18	17	18	11	14
80–89	16	10	15	19	15	16	19	11	16	15	11	14
90–94	17	16	16	13	10	14	17	12	14	15	11	13
95–98	19	26	15	27	20	14	22	19	18	22	24	21
99–100	20	24	21	23	26	25	16	27	21	19	31	24
Total	100	100	100	100	100	100	100	100	100	100	100	100
Number	191	191	191	307	307	307	343	343	343	373	373	373
Gini index	0.69	0.7	0.64	0.76	0.63	0.62	0.69	0.64	0.65	0.65	0.7	0.65

It seems likely, however, that the property-owning elite acquired their considerable holdings during the boom period of the early 1850s, rather than picking up bargains in the later 1850s. The real estate portfolio – if it might be termed that – of Ignatius Cockshutt, the wealthiest man in town from at least 1850 to his death in 1901, exemplified this trend. Cockshutt invested heavily in rental properties, for both residential and commercial accommodation, between 1847 and 1857, and in the latter year had fifty-four units paying rent. The depression and the decline in Brantford's population from 1857 reduced the demand for accommodation. Thereafter Cockshutt began unloading his investments. Though he still had tenants in nineteen of his properties in 1860, eleven houses, one store, and a warehouse stood vacant. By the 1861 assessment, even though two more stores had become vacant, he had found tenants for eight of his empty houses and had bought two more houses. In general, it would appear that through the 1850s Ignatius Cockshutt played the housing market much as later investors would play the stock and bond markets. Certainly he did not look at rental housing as a permanent investment, but he was prepared to buy and sell as conditions seemed to warrant. In 1861 Cockshutt was prepared to start buying again: even though the annual value, presumably the rent, per property remained 80 per cent of that in 1857, his return per property was still higher than in 1851 (table 4.3).

After 1861 the level of inequality in real property wealth fell, even though the proportion of the business population owning no real estate remained nearly the same in 1871 and 1880 as in 1861. Within the property-owning group, wealth shifted downward so that the share held by the top 5 per cent dropped to 40 per cent of the total. The beneficiaries of the modest redistribution were businessmen approximately in the middle, those in the 40–79th percentile group. Their share of the total rose from 18 to 28 per cent between 1861 and 1880. This shift suggests that businessmen of the middling sort were improving their fortunes, while the elite either had little more to invest in real estate or, more likely, had placements other than land for their surplus wealth.

Again, reference to Ignatius Cockshutt's holdings might shed some light on the strategic decisions of the wealthiest. From 1860 Cockshutt steadily increased the number to rental properties that he owned, until 1867 when he held fifty-nine. The next year he had only thirty-four rented, and thereafter the numbers fluctuated from year to year, from a high of forty-five in 1877 to a low of thirty-two in 1879. What was he doing? Cockshutt seems to have followed two strategies which combined the way in which he could profit from

Table 4.3
Real Estate Holdings of Ignatius Cockshutt, 1847–80

		Rental Property Owned		Other Property		Total Property	
Year	N	Actual Value ($)	Annual Value ($)	Actual Value ($)	Annual Value ($)	Actual Value ($)	Annual Value ($)
1847	4	2,360	192	7,600	600	9,960	792
1851	13	5,320	494	7,100	666	12,420	1,160
1854	29		1,796	9,400	1,404		3,200
1855	38		2,858		2,806		5,664
1856	37		2,976		2,086		5,062
1857	54		4,680		1,720		6,400
1858	41		3,486		1,366		4,852
1859	45		3,574		1,587		5,161
1860	19		2,139		1,602		3,741
1861	27		1,869		1,540		3,409
1862	26		1,850		1,536		3,386
1863	33		1,977		1,554		3,531
1866	42		2,083		1,380		3,463
1867	59	22,470		19,400		41,870	
1868	34	18,810		13,000		31,810	
1869	41	22,220		21,600		43,820	
1870	35	20,890		16,920		37,810	
1871	36	20,870		17,720		38,590	
1872	34	23,920		21,600		45,520	
1873	42	40,250		18,900		59,150	
1874	44	35,400		17,750		53,150	
1876	35	45,580		22,700		68,550	
1877	45	51,150		26,720		77,870	
1878	36	51,900		24,550		76,450	
1879	32	59,150		27,000		86,150	
1880	41	56,100		20,750		76,850	

Note: Assessment figures prior to 1859 were converted to dollars at the rate of 1 pound = 4 dollars. Not all of Cockshutt's rental properties brought him income. Included in the rental category from 1876 was the Orphans' Home and from 1877 the Widows' Home, both of which he supported as charities. Cockshutt also owned considerable property outside Brantford. In 1871 he reported to the census enumerator that he owned 50 dwellings, 6 stores, factories, or warehouses, and 30 barns.

real estate investment. Not only did he earn rent from his properties, but he pursued capital gain by selling the properties to advantage when he could. Probably he kept alert for sales, bought those he thought would appreciate in value and rented them until a purchaser

Table 4.4
Economic Rank of Rental Property Owners 1851–80

Percentile Rank	1851	1861	1871	1880
0–39	22	6	3	7
40–79	32	52	51	43
80–89	22	11	17	23
90–100	24	31	28	26
Total	100	100	100	100
Number	37	71	88	95

could be found. But significantly, Cockshutt had proportionately more of his real property wealth invested in rental accommodation in 1880 than he ever had before. Rental units accounted for 43 per cent of his real estate assessment in 1851 and 55 per cent in 1861 and 1871, but 73 per cent in 1880. At the same time Cockshutt's personal property assessment dropped by nearly 30 per cent, from $70,000 in 1871 to $50,000 in 1880. Perhaps the result of under-assessment, the lesser figure may also have demonstrated that his mercantile enterprise had reached some threshold in the amount of capital which it could absorb profitably; real estate holdings provided a vent for his surplus.

The number of businessmen who were landlords rose from thirty-seven, or 16 per cent of all, in 1851 to ninety-five, or 26 per cent, in 1880. As one would expect, the wealthiest always owned the most rental units and the poorest, the fewest, and over time the association grew considerably stronger. But why should businessmen invest more heavily in rental properties in the industrializing city? Presumably, had they so chosen, the capital which they diverted to the accom-modation market might have been reinvested to expand their busi-ness operations (table 4.4).

Perhaps not all felt that their businesses warranted such an infusion of new capital. Businessmen in the middle stratum of the distribution of wealth, in the 40–79 percentile group, increased their participa-tion in the rental market the most: they owned about a third of all rental units in 1851 and about a half in 1861 and 1871. For the middling sort of businessmen, rental units represented savings which might be cashed in at the appropriate moment or a source of income for old age. Some, especially grocers and shopkeepers, probably could not reabsorb profits in their businesses, or thought it undesir-able to do so. For tradesmen, rental properties may have helped cushion the loss of income as their crafts were devalued.

William Dalrymple, an English Baptist cabinetmaker born about 1822 and self-employed through the period, demonstrated one survival strategy of the artisan. In 1851 Dalrymple owned his two-storey brick house and his adjacent detached workshop in King's Ward. Over the next ten years, his business grew, and with his profits he purchased one vacant lot in 1854 and another the following year. The purchase had required a small mortgage of $70 in 1855, but this was paid off on time in three years. On one lot he had a house erected in 1859, which was reported the following year to be rented for $108 annually. It stood vacant in 1861, but Dalrymple found a tenant the next year, though at the reduced rent of $96. In 1861 he reported to the census enumerator that he had $7,000 invested in his business, employed four workers, and made furniture worth $5,000. Ten years later his business was quite different. Dalrymple employed more labour, but less capital in 1871. Four men, including his sons John, aged twenty-three, and William, aged nineteen, worked for him, as did one woman, and one girl and two boys under the age of sixteen. Given his employment of family, female, and child labour, Dalrymple probably lowered his labour costs and may thereby have compensated for his reduced capital, $1,500 in fixed capital and $1,000 in operating, and lower value of production, $4,400. But he accumulated no wealth through the 1870s. By 1880 his property assessment was essentially the same as in 1871, but with two exceptions. First, whereas he had been free of mortgage debt in 1871, he had mortgaged his holdings for $1,100 in 1874 and again for $1,000 in 1875. He had reduced his indebtedness by 1880, but he still owed $1,300.[26] Second, in 1877 he had leased part, and in 1878 all, of the shop to his two sons. As he approached his sixtieth year, Dalrymple and his wife Mary lived on whatever he could earn from undertaking, plus the rent from their one rented house and the shop. William Dalrymple had survived the decline of his trade, gaining some security from his early rental investment, from mortgaging, and from bequeathing his trade and his shop to his sons. They were unlikely to be as lucky as their father. William Jr departed Brantford in 1880, while John remained at home in 1881, single at an age when his father already had six children.

John Stapleton and Thomas Strong, both self-employed shoemakers, invested in rental accommodation and then withdrew capital to invest in their businesses. Stapleton, an Irish Methodist born about 1823, expanded his business considerably in the 1850s. He gave work to two journeymen and two apprentices under the age of sixteen in 1852 and eight journeymen and two women in 1861. In the later year he had $2,000 in his business. By 1871, however, he employed only six men, including his twenty-four-year-old son William. Though he made shoes worth only half the total value produced in 1861, his capital remained intact, with $300 in fixed capital and $2,400 in operating. Stapleton used the latter to finance an inventory of ready-made shoes which he appears to have sold out of his workshop, detached but adjacent to his residence. Reorganizing his business, he still had sufficient funds to purchase one house to rent out. Before 1880, however, he sold his rental property, using the proceeds to help purchase a proper store for his and his son's retail shoe business.

Thomas Strong, an Irish Anglican about the same age as Stapleton, worked as a journeyman shoemaker from the early 1850s to the early 1860s and earned wages reported as $200 in the 1851 assessment and $210 in the 1861 census. He rented his residence in 1851, one unit in a two-storey frame triplex. Though he still rented in 1861 and provided room and board for his younger brother Robert, he had been able in ten years to save enough to purchase two houses, which he rented out for $280. Sometime between 1863 and 1866 Strong sold one of the houses and with $200 in personal property went into business, working in his own rented residence. By 1871 he was able to lease a separate workshop. That year the census enumerator recorded that Thomas Strong had $600 fixed capital, presumably in the form of machines, tools, benches, and other shop fixtures, and $400 operating capital, and employed three shoemakers, including his brother and his nineteen-year-old son, John. Strong, an exception in his trade, did well through the 1870s. By 1880 he had bought a house and acquired again a second rental property, but he was not so sanguine about his trade as to own, rather than rent his shop.

Dalrymple, Stapleton, and Strong may not have had the same amount of money to place in rental properties that Cockshutt did, but they too displayed a sense of strategy. In all likelihood, businessmen in the wealthiest two deciles exercised similar discretion in their rental holdings. The percentage of rental units owned by each did not differ greatly in 1880 from 1851, though through the thirty year interval businessmen in each stratum had followed different courses. The share of the 80–89 percentile group fell sharply in 1861 and then rose slowly thereafter. The reverse trend was present in the rental holdings of those in the wealthiest decile. The former group had probably strained their resources in the 1850s and could not spare capital from their business operations in the 1860s. The latter, possessing some surplus, found nothing more attractive than rental properties in the 1860s, though in the next decade industrial and commercial expansion drew their investment.

Large-scale operations demanded large inventories, and Ignatius Cockshutt's falling personal property assessment, from $70,000 in 1871 to $50,000 in 1880, was not typical of the trend. The greater inequality in the distribution of personal property in 1880 – the largest component of which was business inventory – does indicate the investment of relatively more operating capital in the largest businesses. Brantford's major businessmen had more tied up in their stock. The largest dry goods operation in 1871, that of Henry W. Brethour, reported personal property of $8,200; the largest in 1880, that of Hugh Jones, reported $10,000. The wholesale drug business of William H. Stratford was assessed personal property of $10,000 in 1871; under his son Joseph in 1880, the business's assessment was $14,000 in personal property. Alfred Watts's wholesale grocery business had personal property of $12,000 in 1871; in 1880 Watts, now in partnership with Robert Henry, paid taxes on $30,000 of personal property in the business. The personal property assessment of another of Watts's ventures, his merchant milling business, rose from $10,000 in 1871 to $20,000 in 1880. Even the assessment on the humble store of hatter and furrier Thomas Glassco increased from $1,000 to $3,200 over the same interval. The Gini index for inequality in 1880 was the same as that for 1851. While inequality may have been of the same magnitude, its incidence was different, so that three strata of businessmen can be distinguished in 1880. The share of the wealthiest 5 per cent increased over the thirty-year period, but so did the share of the bottom 40 per cent. The increase in the personal wealth of the latter group was small, from 5 to 8 per cent, but it does highlight the greater importance of assets for self-employment in the industrializing economy. Gains at each pole of the distribution of personal wealth came at the expense of businessmen in the 60–94th percentile group whose share dropped from 39 per cent of the total in 1851 and 41 per cent in 1871 to 33 per cent in 1880.

The need to free capital to finance inventories and accounts probably contributed to the declining rate of real property ownership. Whereas 71 per cent of businessmen had owned real estate of some form in 1851, slightly less than 60 per cent did so in the three subsequent cross-sections. In 1861 and later, capital which earlier might have been invested in real estate probably went instead into business operations. Despite the decline, Brantford businessmen still achieved a rate of property ownership higher than the provincial average.[27]

Another factor of significance in explaining declining real property ownership was the desire of businessmen to separate their residence and place of business. The levels of home and business premises

Table 4.5
Tenure of Business and Residential Accommodation, 1851–60

		Percentage of All			
Category of Property	Tenure	1851	1861	1871	1880
Separate residence	Own both	22	6	11	13
and business	Own res. / Rent bus.	4	13	14	18
	Rent res. / Own bus.	5	2	3	4
	Rent both	8	15	19	28
Combined residence	Own	35	27	23	15
and business	Rent	26	37	30	22
	All	100	100	100	100
	Number	191	307	343	373

Note: The category "Combined residence and business" includes those with an indeterminate or
no fixed business premises.

ownership cannot be stated easily or simply, because at different cross-section years different proportions of the population combined the two. As well, some occupations – for example, construction tradesmen and teamsters – had no fixed place of business. Nonetheless, businessmen increasingly desired to live away from their workplace. Thirty-nine per cent in 1851 and 36 per cent in 1861 maintained separate residences, while 47 per cent did so in 1871 and 63 per cent in 1880. At the same time the self-employed found it more difficult to own either or both kinds of accommodation. In 1851 about the same percentage of businessmen, a little more than 60 per cent, owned their places of business and residence, whether or not the two were combined. Ownership dropped abruptly in the 1850s, so that only about a third owned business premises and slightly less than a half owned their homes; these ownership rates remained more or less constant from 1861 to 1880. Looking just at separate places of business, and setting aside combined accommodation, the pattern is slightly different. Ownership fell more steeply in the 1850s, by two-thirds from 69 per cent in 1851 to 21 per cent ten years later, but it increased to 32 per cent by 1880. Recovery connoted the judgment of businessmen that ownership of premises was more desirable, and profitable, than tenancy (table 4.5).

Katz, Doucet, and Stern in their study of mid-nineteenth-century Hamilton have argued that real property held a different significance for the business class than for the working class. It appealed to the latter for its use value as shelter and security. The former were interested in the exchange value of property, as an investment and a speculation, and its acquisition depended upon an evaluation of its potential for liquidation and appreciation in value. Status considerations, they suggest, persuaded businessmen to rent rather than purchase residential accommodation; more could be obtained for less.[28] The distinction between the use value and exchange value of real estate is helpful, and Katz, Doucet, and Stern are probably correct, as far as they go, in attributing different class motivation. Yet, for some categories of real estate, business property in particular, the distinction between use and exchange values cannot be so easily drawn, and for all categories, the payment of exchange values, either through rent or purchase, is necessary to obtain ownership of the use values. The use value of a store, workshop, or factory was derived from its ability to generate other exchange values through the production and/or distribution of various commodities. The businessman needed to decide whether the use value of a property, its ability to produce exchange values, was sufficient to justify its acquisition either on a long-term basis, through its purchase, or on a short-term basis, through renting. The purchase of business property established a finite exchange value, one which could be paid off at a fixed rate. Rental rendered the exchange value infinite, an ongoing payment and possibly inflating charge against business profits. Thus, it made good sense to own rather than rent premises. The ability to do so, however, depended upon either one's ability to build one's own premises or the willingness of landlords to sell.

The strategies of Cockshutt, Dalrymple, and others were efforts to adapt to and seek advantage or protection from structural change in the social organization of enterprise. The decline in real estate ownership, growing landlordism and the separation of residence and workplace, and the increasing personal property assessment of the largest businesses demonstrated how totally an individual's wealth had to be committed to his undertakings.

OCCUPATIONAL AND SECTORAL VARIATIONS IN WEALTHHOLDING

Inequality in the overall distribution of total wealth may have remained of the same general magnitude through mid-century, but the wealthholding of economic sectors, occupational groupings and various occupations did change with industrialization. In the 1850s and 1860s wealth was concentrated in commerce. The relative wealth of men self-employed in production was only about 60 per cent that of men in commerce. The difference between the two sectors

narrowed in 1871, and by 1880 industry accounted for a disproportionately large share of relative wealth. Of total wealth, rather than
relative wealth, men in industry held only 2 per cent more in 1880
than 1851, but because the sector was shrinking in relative size, a
small change was sufficient to shift the concentration.

A growing component of commercial wealth, that is mortgage
investment, escaped municipal assessment. Local mortgage holdings
of Brantford businessmen increased more than tenfold, from $18,000
in 1851 to $231,000 in 1880. Between 1851 and 1871 the average
value of mortgages held by businessmen on town property increased
little, though more businessmen did invest in the market. Through
the 1870s average mortgage investment grew substantially, so that
the 1880 figure was two and a half times that of 1871 – all this
despite the depression of mid-decade. With the exception of 1861,
men in commerce contributed a disproportionately large share of
these mortgage funds, 80 per cent of the total in 1871 and 70 per
cent in 1880 (table 4.6).

One might posit that funds which could not be profitably absorbed
in business operations might be transferred to the mortgage market.
The source of surplus funds changed through the period, however.
In 1851 most money came from businessmen of middling wealth,
those in the 40–79th percentile range of assessed wealth. Presumably
they did not require more capital in their businesses, and mortgages
offered a secure investment. Mortgages failed to interest those with
more resources at their command. Only two of the wealthiest twenty
businessmen invested in mortgages, and Ignatius Cockshutt did not
hold a mortgage on a single town property in 1851 or 1861. More
lucrative, if speculative, options were available to the town's capitalists. By 1880, however, nearly 80 per cent of mortgage money came
from the wealthiest 10 per cent of the business population. Also
notable in that year was the marked decline of lending by the second
wealthiest decile of businessmen. To remain competitive with larger-
scale business in the 1870s and 1880s, men in this rank had to
expand and borrow, rather than lend.

To the extent that the wealthiest merchants loaned funds to manufacturers, mortgages helped finance the restructuring noted above.
Ignatius Cockshutt was the major commercial lender, investing
$37,000 in the late 1860s and 1870s on terms as long as ten, fifteen,
and even twenty years. He loaned $10,000 to the Waterous Engine
Works, $1,800 to a carriage-manufacturing firm, $1,200 to a builder
and planing-mill owner, $1,500 to the Brantford Pottery, $4,400 to
a brewer, $3,000 to a soap and candle manufacturer, $3,000 to
the lessee of the Brantford Gas Works, $2,300 to one agricultural

Table 4.6
Mortgage Investment: Selected Statistics, 1851–80

		1851	1861	1871	1880
Value of investment ($)	Average	1,406	1,211	1,778	4,533
	Total	18,280	41,200	88,910	231,220
Share of investment: by sector (%)	Industry	35	56	18	29
	Commerce	65	44	82	71
	All	100	100	100	100
by economic rank (%)	0–39 percentile group	4	7	4	3
	40–79	44	8	9	13
	80–89	30	24	23	6
	90–100	22	61	64	78
	All	100	100	100	100
Sector of self-employment of lender (%)	Industry	46	41	48	43
	Commerce	54	59	52	57
	All	100	100	100	100
Economic rank of lender (%)	0–39 percentile group	25	18	10	14
	40–79	33	26	24	37
	80–89	25	18	26	23
	90–100	17	38	40	26
	All	100	100	100	100
Number		13	34	50	51
Per cent of all in business		5	10	13	14

implement manufacturer, $3,000 to another, and $6,500 to a third.[29] Other merchants invested on a smaller scale. George Foster, a wholesale grocer, held a $4,900 mortgage on a starch factory which he later took over. Michael Brophey, a retail shoe merchant, loaned $1,000 to a soap and candle manufacturer. Bernard Heyd, a Swiss grocer and pork packer, loaned a carriage manufacturer $2,500.[30] In the 1870s more businessmen, especially from the commercial sector, were prepared to lend more money on mortgage security, and those with the most to lend were particularly attracted to industrial placements. Thus, men who had retained profits from the commercial prosperity of the 1850s directed their wealth to new industrial opportunities in the 1870s.

To some degree, variations in the relative concentration of assessed wealth among various occupations and occupational groupings derived from idiosyncratic factors, as individuals with different backgrounds, resources, and abilities filled the limited number of positions in each category. Examining ranks of wealth – defined by ranking the relative wealth indices of occupations and dividing them into quartiles – reduces some of the wide swings in wealthholding and makes changes associated with the vagaries of cyclical fluctuations and structural reorganization more apparent. In each decade the two elements of change coincided differently. The 1850s demonstrated the insecurity of wealth accumulated in and through large enterprises and the relative stability of the holdings of small proprietors. Thereafter wealth formed in large operations and was accumulated by the men who ran such businesses. The wealth of tradesmen, shopkeepers, and other small businessmen, on the other hand, offered a more mixed picture depending upon the erosion of skills and the displacement of function (table 4.7).

The collapse of the wheat boom and the bankruptcy of the railroad hurt those businesses and businessmen with a stake in Brantford's pursuit of commercial imperium. Most notable among the fortunes of the town's biggest boosters was the steep drop in the wealth of participants in the grain trade – buyers, agents, merchants, millers, and forwarders. Their wealth declined as local entrepreneurs lost ownership of the trade's infrastructure, the mills, storehouses, and offices, after the crash of 1857. The grain trade engaged two sorts of businessmen in Brantford in the 1850s: those who owned mills and traded in the commodity and those who bought grain for milling elsewhere.

First, and hit the hardest, were those families – the Wilkeses, Kerbys, and Bunnells – who owned the town's milling facilities, besides participating in the grain trade. Early arrival had given John A. Wilkes in the mid-1820s and William Kerby in the early 1830s first pick of milling sites. By 1850 they each had transferred their milling and trading operations to their sons, James and George S. Wilkes, and John and Abraham T. Kerby. Alex Bunnell, born of a pioneer farming family which had settled in the area before the War of 1812, engaged in forwarding from about 1847, built his own mill in 1857, and subsequently took his younger brother, Enos, into the business. The three businesses, though not formal partnerships, were family concerns. Members of these families, especially the Wilkeses, so complicated their financial dealings with intra-family borrowing, endorsing, and securing that the affairs of one could not be easily disentangled from those of parents, children, or siblings. The Wilkes family's interests were the most complex, and their reconstruction brings into relief what happened on a smaller scale to the other families. Their entanglements differed from those of the Kerbys or Bunnells, or other business families, in scale, though not in kind.

John Wilkes was Brantford's wealthiest landowner in 1851, being assessed for approximately $32,000 worth of property, about a third of which was rental accommodation and the balance vacant land assembled at the time of the cession of the village plot by the Six Nations to the Crown in 1830. Though he still owned his mill, valued at $10,000 in the 1852 census, he rented it to his son, James, who also managed his father's real estate holdings.[31] James co-ordinated the mortgaging and encumbering of the Wilkes patrimony, and the not inconsiderable holdings of other family members.[32] No doubt contending claims upon family assets were thereby satisfied: a son embarking on business might draw upon future inheritance and, in return, mortgage property to his father. The intent probably was less to assure repayment than an accounting procedure to facilitate the ultimate settlement of the estate. But less-than-arm's-length transactions afforded a degree of protection in the event of business reversal. Relatives were assured prior claims to assets, and the time taken to draw up and balance accounts for demanding creditors might provide sufficient breathing space to wait out market downturns and collect unpaid accounts. But, if conditions did not improve and if payments due remained unremitted or were insufficient to cover obligations, the failure of one family member could in the fullness of time seriously compromise the resources of relatives.

The strategy involved granting several mortages to family and creditors for amounts less than the full value of the property concerned, thereby creating a multiplicity of interests in any one holding. As land appreciated in value through the early 1850s, additional mortgages tapped newly created wealth. To further muddy the water, mortgages within the family were not always registered.[33] In this way James helped finance his own milling operations and the forwarding business of his younger brother, George S. Wilkes. The latter's own real estate holdings, assessed at $13,500 in 1851, exceeded those of Ignatius Cockshutt, though they were composed differently. George was a commodity speculator – land, grain, it mattered little. Slightly more than half of his landed wealth was in owner-occupied business and residential property; the balance, with the exception of one small rental unit, was vacant land, some of which his father had conveyed to him and some of which had come from his wife's family in a marriage settlement.[34]

In the fall of 1853 fire destroyed the old Wilkes mill, and the site was sold to Alex Bunnell, whose new mill, distillery, and feeder lot was completed there in 1856. The Wilkes family shifted its interest to George's Holmedale subdivision, on the town's western edge, where with family backing he constructed the Holmedale Merchant Mills

Table 4-7
Relative Wealth for Economic Sector, Occupational Groups, and Selected Occupations, 1851–80

	1851			1861			1871			1880		
	Index	Rank	N	Index	Rank	N	Index	Rank	N	Index	Rank	N
Builders/Contractors	215	4	4	103	3	12	101	3	29	134	4	21
Carpenters	55	3	8	46	2	20	26	1	6	30	1	9
Bricklayers	39	2	5	44	1	7	49	2	5	18	1	5
Painters	47	3	5	14	1	4	34	2	3	50	2	6
All construction	80		24	60		46	84		51	81		53
Millers	211	4	2	52	2	6	100	3	7	809	4	4
Brewers/Distillers	53	3	6	147	4	4	9	1	1	59	3	1
Bakers/Confectioners	226	4	2	91	3	5	81	3	10	84	3	4
Butchers	11	1	4	39	1	1	54	2	6	28	1	12
All food processing	65		14	90		16	96		28	169		23
Founders/Implement mfrs.	299	4	4	175	4	6	457	4	5	485	4	7
Blacksmiths	38	2	2	53	2	4	34	2	4	70	3	4
Tinsmiths	34	1	2	43	1	3	46	2	4	48	2	5
All metal fabricating	119		10	79		23	152		15	200		21
Tailors	38	2	8	44	1	8	34	2	5	17	1	2
Shoemakers	105	4	14	61	2	14	28	1	15	32	1	6
Saddlers	86	4	4	223	4	4	64	3	5	72	3	2
All apparel making	80		29	84		28	36		30	58		13
Carriage makers	55	3	4	112	3	7	137	4	6	136	4	4
Cabinetmakers	20	1	8	79	3	5	55	2	6	32	1	8
All woodworking	39		16	80		16	81		17	63		15

Tanners	81	3	1	190	4	4	120	4	6	85	3	3
Jewellers	34	1	4	125	3	4	77	3	4	38	1	5
All other production	60		7	73		14	78		25	61		32
All industry	75		100	75		143	85		166	103		157
Grain merchants	141	4	6	68	3	4	33	1	3	50	2	9
All staple commerce	129		10	112		7	69		13	62		26
Grocers	36	3	22	97	3	46	108	4	38	84	3	59
Fruit dealers				28	1	1	113	4	2	45	2	4
All food sales	38		23	93		50	97		43	82		67
Hardware merchants	48	3	1	614	4	3	152	4	5	127	4	4
Dry goods merchants				184	4	12	264	4	9	255	4	8
Clothiers				56	2	1	34	2	9	83	3	5
Shoe dealers				50	2	1	56	2	2	44	2	8
Druggists	74	3	4	209	4	3	230	4	6	143	4	11
Booksellers	4	1	2	57	2	5	32	1	2	58	2	5
All other merchandising	228		37	275		35	187		67	185		63
Auctioneers	36	2	1	73	3	2	77	3	3	97	4	3
Barbers	5	1	2	14	1	2	18	1	4	16	1	6
Insurance agents				21	1	2	22	1	6	39	2	8
Hotelkeepers	46	3	11	148	4	13	57	2	22	66	2	22
Tavern keepers	63	3	2	29	1	20	41	2	7	42		
Livery keepers	31	1	2	60	2	4	86	3	3	49		6
All service and accommodation	53		21	63		72	51		54		2	60
All commerce	129		91	127		164	115		177	98		216

at an estimated cost of $30,000. The mill was ready for operation in August 1857, just in time for the collapse of the boom.[35] The ensuing devaluation of real estate, the mortgage of which had in part secured the construction of the mill, as well as George's forwarding business, iron foundry, and railroad speculations, left the Wilkes family grossly overextended. Between 1858 and 1866 their creditors pursued the Wilkeses through various lower courts and Chancery, forcing sales or negotiating quit claims to their holdings. At one sale on 23 Nov. 1858, twenty-one lots in Brantford and 958 acres in Holmedale owned by George S. Wilkes were auctioned.[36] That court proceedings dragged so long attested to the complexity of their affairs. In the end, ownership of the mill, warehouses, and offices, and nearly all of the rental properties owned by John Wilkes, passed into the hands of non-resident owners, among whom the banks of Montreal and Upper Canada figured prominently.

Similar fates befell the Kerbys and Bunnells. Ownership of their mills passed to their creditors, the former taken by the Bank of British North America and the latter by that bank in partnership with the Bank of Montreal.[37] The new owners of the three facilities could not sell the properties in the depressed market of the late 1850s and early 1860s and so leased them. Holmedale Mills, for example, was leased to Adam Ker and his partner, James Coleman of Dundas, for $2,000 a year. Though they were reported in the 1861 census as having capital of $70,000, they also rented their office and storehouse, and Ker rented his residence. Even a large concern like Coleman and Ker, who also had a mill in Galt, was not prepared to stake much on Brantford's place in the staple trade. Three of Brantford's four mills in 1861 were run by tenants. The fourth, the relatively small Brantford New Grist Mill, was built in 1860 by John Tobin and James Spence on land leased from the Grand River Navigation Co. for $139 a year; its ownership then was shared. The partners' capital, listed as $8,000 in the 1861 census, was severely impaired when the mill burned the next year. A mortgage for $3,000 financed rebuilding, but the business never earned enough to make payments on the debt, and in 1867 the mortgagor foreclosed. Tobin, the junior partner, left the business, while Spence continued as a tenant for about a year.[38]

The lower wealth of businessmen engaged in various aspects of staple commerce between 1851 and 1861 reflected, then, the bankruptcy of the three milling and grain-trading families. A second group of businessmen in staple commodities, about five in number in 1851 and 1861, were buyers and dealers in grain, working in their own interest and/or as agents for merchant millers elsewhere. Most owned little real estate, even if they had in some cases a fair amount of capital with which to work. They generally rented their offices, storehouses, and homes, if their residences were separate, not just to keep their wealth in play, but also to allow them to pull up stakes if market conditions changed. Of the five present in 1851–2, only one, Thomas Cooke, a Lower Canadian born about 1815, remained in business in 1861. He owned neither his residence nor his storehouse, though he reported transacting $20,000 in business with $15,000 capital in 1860. The grain buyers who replaced those who left also rented business and residential accommodation and turned their capital over even more rapidly than Cooke: with $4,000 William Smith traded $90,000 worth of grain; William Poe conducted business of $50,000 with $2,000. The assessed wealth of this sort of grain merchant changed little from 1851 to 1861, even if the individuals themselves were different. The wealth of merchants trading commodities declined through the 1860s and 1870s, that of grain dealers falling more than that of others in the occupational group such as coal and wood dealers, hop dealers, and produce dealers. As the commerce focused more on the domestic market, less capital and less elaborate facilities were required. The Mercantile Agency's *Reference Book* for 1871 estimated that only four of nine traders in this group had assets greater than $2,000; ten years later a smaller proportion met this benchmark.

The restoration of local ownership to the milling industry and the attraction of men with capital to it left a smaller field for those who just bought and sold grain. The relative wealth of millers increased substantially, although the 1880 index number is inflated by the diversified holdings of Alfred Watts, who owned a complex of industrial and commercial property besides his mill. A figure half that reported would be a more likely measure of the millers' wealth. New capital, about half of which had been accumulated locally, was invested in Brantford milling in the late 1860s.[39] Outside investment came from David Plewes, an English Methodist born about 1823, who made the largest single investment, purchasing the Holmedale Mills in 1866 and the Kerby Mills in 1868. With the two mills and a storehouse and office, Plewes calculated his investment in milling at $20,000 fixed and $20,000 floating capital in 1871. That year he also owned two rental properties, but he still rented his house, assessed at $3,000. By 1880 he had so prospered that he now owned, besides his mills and other business properties, a house assessed for $5,500. Other investment in milling from the mid-1860s through the mid-1870s came from within the town. The second most important miller was Alfred Watts, who about 1865 purchased Bunnell's Mills.

In 1871 he set his investment at $10,000 in fixed capital and $4,000 in operating. The mill was but a part of his stake in Brantford's industrial capacity. Watts also owned a soap and candle factory and a distillery, interests which he had acquired from his father, Charles. Watts senior had settled in Brantford about 1835, engaging in a general merchandising business and expanding into grist milling, distilling, and soap and candle making. Some time in the 1850s he turned the operation of the distillery, grist mill, and stock feeding lot, located outside of the town, over to Alfred. The census of 1861 listed the distillery and mill's capital at $20,000 and its yearly output as 90,000 gallons of whisky worth $18,000. Charles Watts was the fourth wealthiest businessman in 1861 and on his death in November 1868, besides his considerable real estate holdings, left personal property and effects worth $58,000.[40] Alfred took over and expanded the remaining elements of his father's business, going into partnership to do so with Robert Henry, formerly his father's clerk and the son of a local self-employed carpenter. Alfred Watts was the second wealthiest businessman in Brantford in 1871 and 1880, and the growth in the value of his business holdings between these two years raised his total municipal assessment from 39 per cent of that of Ignatius Cockshutt to 65 per cent – a fair measure of the acceleration of industrial accumulation.

The two smaller grist mills in Brantford, also run by their owners in 1871 and 1880, demonstrated another facet of local capital accumulation. In 1871 the Brant New Mills were owned and run by Thomas Robson, an English Baptist born about 1825. Robson had leased the Kerby Mills, prior to their purchase by Plewes. He managed the mill for the new owner for a year, but then purchased James Spence's operation in December 1869. From 1870 to 1880 Robson's property assessment doubled from $5,500 to $11,000. The mill was valued the same, $5,000, and his residence was worth slightly more, $800 rather than $500. The balance comprised two rental properties and vacant land. Robson assembled this property during the mid-decade depression, financing the acquisition in part with mortgages for $925 taken out in 1874, but paid off by 1877.[41] The second grist mill, smaller than the Brant New Mills and assesed at $1,600 in 1871 and $2,000 in 1880, was built about 1867 by David Spence, who ran it in partnership with Moore Hill in 1871. Between the 1872 and 1873 assessments, Spence and Hill were bought out by Thomas Draper, an English Baptist born about 1831. Draper had worked in the Kerby Mills since about 1857 and managed the mill for Plewes after Robson left. When he purchased the mill, Draper also owned the house for which he had paid $240 in 1871 and which was mortgaged for $192.[42] He did not own his home for long, since in 1876 he and his family were living in a rented house assessed at $750. By 1880 the house's assessment had risen to $950. The move to rental accommodation was a considerable step up in terms of housing quality; it also demonstrated that Draper preferred renting a residence to encumbering the ownership either of a house or his mill with a mortgage. Draper, like Robson, had accumulated capital within the milling industry, the former by wage labour, the latter by leasing premises. Both experiences, however, attest to the profitability of the industry despite the depressed years of mid-decade.

Patterns similar to that in milling and staple commerce emerged in the relative wealth of other occupational groups. The relative wealth of men self-employed in construction, the builders and contractors as well as the independent tradesmen, declined from 1851 to 1861 as the demand for building slumped and rail construction halted. The large operators recovered in the 1870s: William Watt's construction, lumber yard, and planing-mill business captured the largest share of residential and business construction, while Henry Yates and John H. Stratford obtained lucrative contracts for railroad construction. All three ranked among the wealthiest 10 per cent of businessmen in both 1871 and 1880. Independent construction tradesmen suffered a decline in relative wealth over the same period. Of the three main trades – carpenters/joiners, bricklayers/masons, painters – only painters, the least numerous of the three trades, improved in wealthholding. Unlike other construction tradesmen, painters moved into retailing. John Noble, who emigrated from Enniskellen, Ireland, in 1831, apprenticed in Toronto before starting on his own account in Brantford in 1848. He provided his son, Thomas, with a similar training, finding an apprenticeship for him in London in 1862. Father and son went into business in 1866, and as well as house and sign painting and paperhanging, they sold wallpaper and stained glass windows.[43] John Noble belonged to the second rank, the 40–79th percentile group in 1851 and 1880; Thomas rose from among the least wealthy 40 per cent to the second rank from 1871 to 1880. Diversification no doubt helped the business to survive and support two generations; more important in sustaining the independent tradesmen, however, was their deepening indebtedness. John Noble owned his house and adjacent paint shop in 1851 free from debt. Over the next five years, not only did he borrow to finance the purchase of a small vacant lot, but he heavily encumbered his other property, so that in 1856 outstanding mortgages totalling over $1,000 were registered against his holdings. No doubt in the optimistic early 1850s, Noble felt obligations to this extent could be easily met. In 1856 he rented out his house and moved his family to a higher-priced house which they rented. The depression caught Noble short. By 1858 his mortgage debt had risen to $1,450, and to meet his creditors he sold his rental unit. Noble recovered through the 1860s, purchased a house again, still owned some vacant land, and in 1871 owed only $400 in mortgage debt. That year he and Thomas rented their shop/store. Through the 1870s father and son borrowed to invest in more real estate. John purchased two rental units, and though he owed $1,050 in 1880, his real estate assessment that year totalled $3,000. Thomas owned his home and one rental unit assessed at $1,800 and mortgaged for $1,200 in 1880.[44] The Nobles willingly assumed mortage debt and on balance did not do badly through mid-century; the reverses experienced by John in the late 1850s were recouped by father and son in the 1870s.

The decline of the relative wealth of metal fabricators in the 1850s reflected problems of undercapitalization affecting iron founders noted by the Dun Co.'s reporter.[45] Metal fabricating doubled its relative wealth in the 1860s and by 1880 regained its place as the wealthiest group. Within the group, significant gains were made by iron founders, who had persisted from the 1850s and weathered the cyclical and structural changes in the economy, and agricultural implement manufacturers, principally Alanson Harris, John Harris, and James K. Osborne, partners in A. Harris, Son and Co. Because of their large fixed capital investments, in 1880 all seven were among the wealthiest twenty-five businessmen.

Independent tradesmen like blacksmiths and tinsmiths benefited from the continuing need for the everyday essentials which they made. Unlike the large manufacturers, both trades remained stable, if not slightly wealthier through the mid-century. Thomas Cowherd remained in the 40–79th percentile group, free from mortgage debt, at all cross-sections, and his assessment changed little throughout the period. His business may have been somewhat smaller in 1871 than in 1861, since his capital investment as reported in the censuses fell from $4,000 to $1,200 fixed and $1,500 floating, but it supported his large family and launched his sons into working life. The business depended to a considerable degree on family labour, and while Cowherd made certain that his eight sons and five of his six daughters attended school, once his sons entered their teens they worked in the shop. During the period examined here, four sons, Thomas Jr, William, James, and Christopher, were in business with their father. The business, albeit the oldest and largest tinsmithing concern in the town, could not support two generations and four families. Perhaps for this reason Thomas Sr found it necessary in the mid-1870s to sell the one rental unit he had owned in 1871. His eldest son, Thomas Jr, ran his own small tinsmith business in 1871; at thirty years of age he had $200 in fixed capital and $500 operating capital and gave work to two journeyman tinsmiths, one of whom boarded with him in his rented house and shop. His experience demonstrated that there was a limit to the number of tinsmiths Brantford could support: while he could afford to rent property assessed at $1,600 in 1871, the following year he was insolvent and out of business.[46] By 1879 he rented property assessed at just $300. That year he left town for greener pastures. In the early 1870s number two son, William, went to work as a machinist in the Waterous Engine Works and in 1880 rented his house which was assessed for $500. James, thirty-two years old in 1880, was still in partnership with his father at the end of this study and doing better than his other brothers. He held the same rank in the distribution of wealth as his father; he owned a workshop adjoining his father's and one rented house, clear of mortgage, but rented the same residence, assessed at $1,100, which he had owned in 1872. Christopher, though a partner in 1880, owned none of the business's real or personal property and probably only claimed a share of the profits. He rented his house, assessed for $800. Cowherd's tinsmith business contrasted with Dalrymple's cabinet-making business in its ability not only to sustain its original proprietor but also to launch, if not sustain entirely, a second generation.

Producers of wearing apparel did not fare as well. The wealth of tailors increased slightly from 1851 to 1861, but in 1880 was the second lowest of occupations listed in table 4.7. That of cordwainers and shoemakers dropped drastically as those who had accumulated land in the early days of settlement lost their holdings in the depression of the late 1850s or left the town. Their replacements in the 1860s and 1870s had fewer resources at their command and fewer chances to accumulate any. In 1871 Peter H.S. Crooks, for example, born in Ontario about 1835, ran a shoemaking business in his rented house and shop. He gave work to two other shoemakers and reported having $600 fixed capital and $1,000 floating. The Mercantile Agency did not think highly of his chances, however, and did not recommend credit.[47] By 1876 he was out of business. He stayed in Brantford through the decade and still lived in a rented house in 1880. Crooks had been the sole income earner in his family in 1871; ten years later, he worked at his trade, though for wages, but his wife and five children all had jobs. Mrs Crooks and daughter Ada, aged twenty years, were shirtmakers; Sirena, aged sixteen, was a mantle-maker. Son George, aged twenty-four, was a printer, and Albert, aged eighteen, was a clerk. At their ages, one would have expected that the children would be working, although the two boys might well have moved out. That his wife worked and provided room and board for two lodgers, however, does attest to the inadequacy of Peter Crooks's wages.

By 1861 woodworkers, particularly carriage makers and cabinet-makers, had grown wealthier, despite the reorganization and uncertainty of their trades. Their accumulation of wealth, like that of the craft producers already mentioned, indicated that they too benefited from local population growth and agricultural prosperity. The higher indices of relative wealth for the grouping in 1871 and 1880 resulted from the accumulation of wealth by the owners of carriage factories and masked the decline of cabinetmakers who continued in their craft workshops. The gains which their trade had made in the 1850s eroded steadily through the 1870s. Dalrymple's fortune was only too typical of his trade and certain others, tailors, shoemakers, carpenters. But even in those independent trades that remained healthy – such as painters, blacksmiths, tinsmiths – there was little significant accumulation of wealth. The redistribution of wealth from the commercial to the industrial sector, then, was not evenly spread among different forms of production, but was concentrated in large-scale operations.

The changes in the pattern of wealthholding among occupations and groups in the commercial sector are more difficult to sort out than those in the industrial sector because of the trend to more specialized retailing. The major trend through mid-century, the decline in the wealth of non-food consumer merchandising and the corresponding increase in the wealth of food sellers, may well be a consequence of that specialization. The general merchants in 1851 offered groceries, dry goods, hardware, drugs, and other articles for sale which later on were retailed by businessmen operating on a smaller scale in the two different groups. Thus, the increasing wealth of food merchandising in general and grocers in particular may have arisen from the reorganization of commerce; groceries by 1880 was no longer the marginal shopkeeping that it had been in 1852 when general merchants offered the best stock in the trade. Similarly, specialization explains the high relative wealth of hardware and dry goods merchants from 1861. Each of these lines was a major component of the general merchant's business in 1851. The other groupings in commerce – staple commerce, already discussed, and service and accommodation – held much smaller shares of wealth and did not figure significantly into the redistribution of wealth between 1851 and 1880.

Too much significance should not be attached to the increase in the wealth of grocers between 1851 and 1861, since the major retailers in the trade were general merchants and not included in the calculation of the 1851 index. A more appropriate period is 1861 to 1880. Over this shorter period their wealth remained more or less stable, rising in 1871 and falling in 1880 to approximately the 1861 level. The fluctuation arose from the changing numbers of grocers; in 1861 and in 1881 there were more small shopkeepers and therefore lower relative wealth than in 1871. Despite this almost cyclical rise and fall in numbers, significant changes in the forms of wealth-holding among grocers did occur in twenty years. Real property ownership increased substantially, as owner occupancy of combined grocery store/residences doubled from 24 per cent of such units in 1861 to 47 per cent in 1880. Separation of residence and workplace changed little: 72 per cent of grocers in 1861 and 68 per cent in 1880 lived above or behind their shops. Moreover, about the same proportion, one in four, owned separate residences in 1861 and 1880. Through the period, the grocery business remained a neighbourhood trade, and the grocer's custom depended upon his knowledge of his neighbours and their trust in him.

Because retail groceries was a localized trade, clear limits existed to the amount of capital that could be invested in the business. Inventories could only be as large as might be consumed by customers in the neighbourhood; consequently there was little incentive to expand the size of shops. Profits might be used to purchase the shop, if the landlord would sell, but after that some other investment had to be found. A large number of grocers were attracted to rental properties; at each of the three cross-sections about 40 per cent of grocers owned at least one house for rent. The average number of rental properties owned by grocer/landlords declined, however, from 4.6 units in 1861 to 3.2 in 1871 and 3.6 in 1880. Perhaps the increase in shop ownership left relatively less for rental investments. The example of Joseph Quinlan, an Irish Catholic born about 1820 who owned more rental properties than any other grocer throughout the period, would seem to confirm this connection. In 1851 Quinlan rented his one-storey frame store and residence. Over the next ten years he acquired, without recourse to mortgages, twelve rental units and a three-storey brick residence separate from his rented store. To buy eight more properties, including one grocery store, Quinlan sold his house and moved into rented accommodation. By 1880, however, he owned his store and a separate residence, but only sixteen rental units. Quinlan's case demonstrated that, despite a desire to separate home and residence, the decisions to own rather than rent, and vice versa, were made within a larger strategy of rental holdings. Presumably he made his choice in response to trade vicissitudes and the relative attraction of rental income.

The declining wealth of the non-food consumer merchandising group can be attributed in part to the dilution of relative group wealth because of the presence of more small-scale operators. But, regardless of the numbers of businessmen in the group, non-food merchandisers held a smaller share of total business wealth in 1880, by about a third, than in 1851. The group embraces such a very wide range of commercial operations, from clothing and fancy goods to hardware and dry goods, that representative examples are difficult to find and generalizations are not easily formed. However, most of the decline occurred between 1851 and 1861 with the drastic reduction in the holdings of general merchants – the exception being Ignatius Cockshutt. The major merchants were deeply involved in nearly all facets of the commercial economy, as creditors of master artisans and shopkeepers, endorsers of associates, speculators in staples and land, promoters of railways, debtors to metropolitan suppliers, and general purveyors to the town's citizens. For example, Richard S. Strobridge and Thomas Botham, partners in the second largest general merchant business in 1851, became greatly overextended and were forced in January 1862 to compromise with their creditors.[48] Others, including William Lines, an English Anglican born about 1815, and John Heaton, an English Methodist born about 1810, experienced similar business reversals which cost them a significant part of their accumulated wealth.

Another factor contributed to the reduced share of business wealth held by non-food consumer merchandisers. By 1880 about 80 per cent of the commercial space by value that businesses in this group occupied was rented. This figure needs qualification, however, since a number of merchants were second-generation businessmen who enjoyed the backing of their fathers, an advantage which mitigated to some degree the apparent lack of wealth suggested by high levels of tenancy. Bill and Percy Walsh rented their tobacco store and house from their father, Fred, a hotelkeeper. George Sproule rented his drug store from his father, Robert, and at age twenty-eight in 1881 still lived with his parents. James A. Wallace, a twenty-two-year-old druggist, also lived with his father, James, a leather merchant. Hugh Jones, a dry goods merchant born about 1840, though married, still lived with his parents and brothers and sisters. George Edgar, a partner in his father John's glass and crockery business, was assessed as his father's tenant, renting half of the store. A variant form of intergenerational support was adopted by William Batchelor, an English Baptist and in 1881 at seventy years of age still a journeyman tailor. Two of his three sons were taught the tailoring trade and one, Tom, was a merchant tailor, who probably employed his father and brother Sam. The senior Batchelor transferred ownership of the family home to his other son, Benjamin, who had recently opened a drug store and could use the property to secure his stock. Despite the variety of intergenerational strategies subsumed in tenancies of various sorts, the largest number of merchants rented to reduce overhead or because they could not find appropriate commercial space to purchase.

Unfortunately the discussion of the wealth of non-food consumer merchandising in particular, and of the commercial and industrial sector in general, must remain in relative rather than in constant dollar terms. One cannot tell for certain whether any or all, or what proportion, of the more specialized retailers in 1880 were wealthier than the general merchants of 1851, or how the latter compared to the industrialists of thirty years later. One suspects that in the 1870s several of the dry goods and a few hardware merchants may have been wealthier, and that most if not all of the iron founders and agricultural implement manufacturers, and a number of other manufacturers, were wealthier than the earlier general merchants, excepting Ignatius Cockshutt. But, though comparable data are lacking, the direction of change is discernible. Wealth became more concentrated in industry, while commerce may have remained somewhat more open to men with limited capital.

THE ESTATES OF BUSINESSMEN

Probate records might be expected to provide actual property values, and thereby to overcome some of the qualifications inherent in analysing relative data. This source is fraught with its own complications, however. Not many of the subjects of this study died during the time period, and not all of the estate files contain wealth declarations: only three before 1860, thirty-three between 1860 and 1880, and forty-four from 1881 to 1890. Moreover, estate valuations do not always distinguish between personal and real property. Prior to 1880 hardly any listed real estate; after 1880 most listed both categories of wealth, although figures for each were not always declared separately. Nor is it clear in some instances after 1880 that the failure to mention real estate connoted the absence of any property of this sort.[49] Despite these qualifications, a comparison of the distribution of wealth by broad occupational categories from 1860–80 to

Table 4.8
Value of Probated Estates by Occupational Group, 1860–90

| | 1860–80 | | | | 1881–90 | | | |
	N	%	$	%	N	%	$	%
Manufacturers	6	18	53,485	14	8	18	501,317	58
Tradesmen	11	34	28,410	7	15	34	57,940	6
Merchants	9	27	290,902	75	7	16	229,989	26
Grocers/Shopkeepers	3	9	901	< 1	9	21	67,472	8
Hotel/Saloon/								
Livery keepers	4	12	13,453	3	5	11	14,884	2
All	33	100	387,151	100	44	100	871,602	100

Note: The 1860–80 data report only personal property. The 1881–90 data report personal plus real property, although in some cases it was uncertain whether the deceased had no real estate or whether such property was simply not declared.
Source: Brant County Surrogate Court Records.

1881–90 confirms some of the general trends noted in the distribution of assessed wealth, if one assumes that the second period is more likely to reflect the effect of industrialization upon accumulation (table 4.8).

The three estates probated before 1860 are best treated separately from the other cases, since they seem exceptional and unrepresentative cases. The source from which they are taken, the records of the Probate Court,[50] responsible until 1859 for granting probate of wills and letters of administration for the property of persons dying intestate, are far from complete. A search of the land records, in which wills involving the transfer of land were registered, uncovered a few more wills, though no estate valuations, of course. A comparison of the documents in the two collections suggested that those from the Probate Court survived because the testators possessed sizeable, complex, and contested estates, not typical of the more modest affairs of those whose wills remain extant only in the land records. The three who died between 1853 and 1857 possessed large holdings, at least until their estates were settled: James Steele, a merchant, left personal property of $38,200 approximately; George Babcock, stage proprietor and partner in a paper mill, left personal property of $6,700; and John Russell, railroad contractor, left real and personal property of $98,200. But much of their wealth, perhaps typical of holdings before the crash of 1857, was in highly depreciable forms. All three possessed unsecured promissory notes and court judgments for the recovery of overdue debts. Babcock and Russell had significant holdings of securities issued by the Buffalo, Brantford and Goderich Railway. Nor were their own business interests likely to yield full value to their heirs. One doubts that Steele's Oxford Road Co. was worth the $32,000 nominal value of his shares. Russell's affairs, with those of his partner, William Mellish, were hopelessly entangled with the bankrupt railroad. As well, Babcock's executors wrote off as worthless his investment of $4,520 for a one-third interest in the Mohawk Paper Mill, just outside of Brantford. Unrepresentative though these three may have been of the estates of businessmen in the 1850s, they are perhaps illustrative of the tenuous hold on property of some of Brantford's wealthiest.

The 1860–80 and 1881–90 data are more representative of business wealth. That the figures are skewed by several exceptionally large estates does not qualify, but only reinforces, the nature of the shifts in wealth distribution. Between 1860 and 1880, merchants' estates make up 27 per cent of all businessmen's estates in the Brant County Surrogate Court records; however, they account for 75 per cent of the value of estates. More than half of the personal property in this occupational category, $180,500, was contributed by one man, Arunah Huntington, a former shoemaker, general merchant and *rentier*. Though one of Brantford's very first residents, on his death in 1877 Huntington had relatively little invested locally: besides his personal effects, he had $30,000 in real estate, $4,500 in mortgages, and $1,500 in shares of Brantford's Royal Loan and Savings Co. The balance of his investments, $165,000, was in American bank and railroad securities.[51] Even if Huntington were excluded from the analysis, merchants would still hold a disproportionately large share of wealth, 53 per cent. Commercial endeavour, then, would seem to have the most profitable avenue for accumulation in this earlier period.

The estates of merchants remained disproportionately wealthy in the 1881–90 period, but by a much lesser extent. Instead, manufacturers, builders, and contractors were the wealthiest group. However, two estates, those of John Harris, the farm implement manufacturer, who died in 1887, and John H. Stratford, a railroad contractor, who died in 1888 – valued at $281,300 and $181,200 respectively – made up 90 per cent of the group figure and more than 50 per cent of the overall total.[52] Also worthy of note is that Harris and Stratford were both second-generation Brantford businessmen: the former the son of implement manufacturer Alanson Harris; the latter the son of a successful wholesale druggist, William H. Stratford. Exceptional though their estates were, they nonetheless attest to the extent of wealth which might be accumulated through a certain category of enterprise.

Two additional trends in the data merit comment. First, the larger estates of grocers in the 1880s seem consistent with the greater concentration of assessed wealth owned by those in this trade, as has been noted previously. For example, Joseph Quinlan, who died in 1887, left $17,200 in real and personal property, while Bernhard Heyd, a Swiss who had been a carpenter and then foreman of the Buffalo, Brantford and Goderich Railway car shops before opening his store, in 1884 left the largest estate of any grocer, $26,890.[53] Second, that the share of wealth held by independent tradesmen and master artisans, roughly 6 to 7 per cent of the total, should remain constant does not necessarily qualify any interpretation of the hard times generally confronted by those self-employed in small craft enterprises. The absence of real estate valuation in the first period makes true comparison impossible. As well, in neither period were there many who died wealthy, and the median value of estates of men in this occupational category was considerably lower than the median for all estates: $450 for tradesmen and $2,700 for all in 1860–80, and $2,040 for tradesmen and $4,400 for all in 1881–90.

WEALTH AND LIFE CYCLE

The inconsistent reporting of real and personal property in the probate records precludes any determination of whether businessmen who died after 1880 were wealthier than those who died before that year. The assessment data, however, do suggest changes in the way in which wealth was distributed by age cohorts in the 1870s. Wealth became concentrated in the hands of the elders of the business community, men who, in the words of Dun's credit reporter, "grew with the town."[54] The lower relative wealth of younger businessmen and those recently self-employed suggested in 1880 a greater difficulty in translating business profits into property ownership.

In 1851 and 1861 the distribution of wealth by age cohort resembled a bell curve with wealth concentrated disproportionately in the hands of men in the middle years of life, men in their forties. The pattern suggests that a period of accumulation of wealth was followed by a period of liquidation of assets, either for consumption needs or to assist children attaining their maturity. A system of small enterprise did not permit the devolution of daily management into the hands of younger and more energetic men – these could instead easily work for themselves – and so, the earning power of aging businessmen was likely to diminish year by year. Wealth then was not necessarily self-perpetuating and the energy and capacity of the businessman himself was essential to sustain an enterprise. After about the age of fifty, a self-employed man had to compensate for his declining earning power by consuming earlier savings, stored in property. The cyclical rise and fall of wealth meant that wealth was not permanently entrenched and that young men starting business did not confront permanently established interests. Men in their twenties in 1851 were wealthier than men in their 1850s and older and, although they were the least wealthy group in 1861, a mark of their vulnerability to depression, the persistence of the bell-shaped distribution of wealth indicated no structural change in the decade (table 4.9).

Structural change was evident at subsequent cross-sections. After 1861 wealth ceased to peak in middle age, and older groups were as wealthy as or wealthier than men in their forties. In 1871 businessmen between the ages of fifty and fifty-nine held the greatest amount of wealth in proportion to their representation among the assessed business population. Men in their sixties, the oldest age group, were tied in 1880 with those in their forties as the wealthiest age group. By the 1870s wealth once accumulated was held and could be invested in enterprises which would not only leave the principal intact, but which were also large enough to permit delegation of authority.

Intergenerational partnerships were the most obvious example of this strategy. The cumulative pattern in the distribution of wealth put younger businessmen at a disadvantage. The wealth of the two youngest age groups decreased year by year and, whereas the relative wealth of twenty- to twenty-nine-year-olds was 54 per cent of the wealthiest in 1851, it was only 31 per cent in 1880. The disparities in wealthholding had increased and were associated with the age polarities of the business population.

Naturally the association of the accumulation of wealth with age involved a change in the age composition of wealth ranks. In 1851 relatively more men in their twenties than in their fifties were in the wealthiest 20 per cent of the business population. Those in their thirties were the most over-represented cohort among the elite in that year and continued to be over-represented in 1861. However, by 1880 the representation of any group in the bottom 40 percentiles decreased with age, while representation in the top 20 percentiles increased with age. More than three-quarters of men in their twenties belonged to the least wealthy 40 per cent, while more than one-third

Table 4.9
Distribution of Wealth by Age Group, 1851–80

Year	Years of Age	Percentile Group				Relative Wealth	N
		0–39 (%)	40–79 (%)	80–89 (%)	90–100 (%)		
1851	20–9	45	41	7	7	71	44
	30–9	40	31	14	15	108	72
	40–9	33	49	9	9	131	53
	50–9	29	64		7	67	14
	60 plus	72	14	14		27	7
1861	20–9	53	40	2	5	53	45
	30–9	31	46	15	8	100	108
	40–9	31	48	9	12	118	94
	50–9	24	44	12	20	114	41
	60 plus	32	58	5	5	89	19
1871	20–9	61	36		3	41	34
	30–9	48	38	3	11	86	93
	40–9	27	43	19	11	104	112
	50–9	38	42	8	12	148	72
	60 plus	33	43	14	10	102	20
1880	20–9	74	18	4	4	38	52
	30–9	39	46	8	7	80	96
	40–9	32	43	10	15	121	99
	50–9	18	49	17	16	104	67
	60 plus	24	40	16	20	121	37

Note: Rows under "Percentile Group" total 100 when added horizontally.

of those sixty years of age or older were among the wealthiest 20 per cent. Wealth and age then were becoming synonymous.

The age polarities of wealth also indicated one of the qualifications to the goal of independence imposed in the industrializing city. Younger men were less likely in 1880 than in 1851 to own real estate, the mark of a stake in the community. The rates of real estate ownership dropped for all men under the age of sixty in the 1850s; however, the rate for men in their twenties suffered the greatest decline in that decade and continued to fall over the next two decades. Young men just starting out on their own account needed to have their wealth at hand, ready to use as their trade required. For that reason men in their twenties always held more of their wealth in personal property, in inventories, customer accounts, and so on, than in real estate. Because the conditions of business were far more demanding in 1880 than in 1851, young men had to forego real estate ownership even longer and the ratio of personal to real wealth among men in their twenties rose from 1851 to 1880, as it also did for men in their thirties. The difficulties that younger men confronted are clearly revealed by a comparison of the relative concentration of personal property plus income in 1851 and 1880. In the first year men under forty held a disproportionately large share of wealth in this category. By 1880 the situation was reversed, and the share of personal wealth held by the oldest groups had risen significantly.

The relative concentration of wealth in the hands of the older businessmen in Brantford was a necessary consequence of the presence of more and more men who had been self-employed longer than ten years. At each consecutive cross-section new businessmen were at a greater disadvantage and entered the business community at a progressively lower level in the distribution of wealth. In 1851 a new businessman started with wealth equal to about three-quarters that of the average businessman. This dropped steadily until 1880, when the wealth of a new man was just about 45 per cent of the average. Consequently new businessmen were increasingly over-represented at the bottom of the distribution of wealth (tables 4.10 and 4.11).

Within this context of declining wealth for new businessmen, a significant and puzzling change took place in the wealth of Canadians and immigrants self-employed for less than ten years. From 1851 to 1871 immigrants possessed the advantage of greater wealth, particularly greater real property, than native-born businessmen. Indeed between 1851 and 1871 the distance between the two groups increased until the immigrants were nearly twice as wealthy as Canadians. This situation dramatically reversed in the 1870s, so that Canadians were nearly twice as wealthy as immigrants. A number of possible explanations can be offered. By the 1870s members of the first generation of businessmen, mainly immigrants, had established themselves firmly in business and were able to supply capital or credit to their children. As well, immigrants with capital may no longer have found Brantford as attractive location. Those who did try self-employment in Brantford in the 1870s may have been drawn from a transient population of earlier immigrants who had been dogged by failure in place after place and in business after business. This could offer one reason for the older age of immigrants starting in business in Brantford in the 1870s. One final and tempting possibility is that self-employment was one response of Canadians to the demographic crisis caused by the scarcity of agricultural land. Previously, successful farmers had rewarded their sons for their labour on the family farm by granting

Table 4.10
Indices of Relative Concentration of Real Property and Personal Property Income by
Age Group, 1851–2 and 1880–1

Years of Age	1851–2		1880–1	
	Real Property	Personal/ Income	Real Property	Personal/ Income
20–9	53	165	9	41
30–9	108	101	87	102
40–9	135	94	128	110
50–9	103	30	136	66
60 plus	38	38	198	210
Number	190	190	351	351

Table 4.11
Rate of Real Property Ownership by Age Group, 1851–80

Years of Age	1851 (%)	1861 (%)	1871 (%)	1880 (%)
20–9	64	27	21	17
30–9	76	62	53	58
40–9	70	64	71	63
50–9	100	58	69	82
60 plus	71	89	80	84
All	71	59	60	61
Number	136	180	207	213

them their own land. Capital insufficient to allow a father to purchase a viable farm for his son in the more expensive land market could be enough to launch a business career. As well, recourse to the so-called "English-Canadian" or preferential system of inheritance by more and more Ontario farmers provided younger sons with capital at the same time as it burdened inheritors with debt; the greater wealth of new Canadian businessmen may have been financed by greater agricultural indebtedness (table 4.12).[55]

CONCLUSION

The reorganization of business activity that was associated with the transition to industrial capitalism redistributed wealth in Brantford. Within the business population, the inequality of wealthholding changed little from 1851 to 1880, but there were signs that working

Table 4.12
Indices of Relative Wealth for Canadian and Immigrant Men in Business Less Than
Ten Years, 1851–80

Year		Real Property	Personal/Income	Total Wealth	N
1851	Canadians	88	85	85	143
	Immigrants	102	102	102	20
1861	Canadians	74	81	79	180
	Immigrants	105	104	103	34
1871	Canadians	30	85	60	133
	Immigrants	134	107	120	65
1880	Canadians	116	130	125	56
	Immigrants	80	61	68	72

Note: the average wealth of men in business less than 10 years equals 100 in each category.

for others was becoming a more attractive alternative to self-employment. Among businessmen the major change was the greater relative wealth of the industrial sector which arose from the increasing investment in manufacturing and obscured the relative impoverishment of independent artisans and tradesmen. As the relative wealth of the industrial sector grew, that of the commercial sector naturally fell, and commerce, particularly consumer merchandising and service and accommodation businesses, became the area of opportunity for those with modest capital at their command. The generational change in the business personnel also restructured wealth, as older men became the wealthiest businessmen. The result was that men starting out in business faced the disadvantage of limited wealth in comparison with those in business for some time. Thus the level of inequality in wealthholding may have changed little from 1851 to 1880, but the wealthiest groups by the latter year were clearly discernible as those in manufacturing and those well established in business.

5 The Making of the Self-Made Man

"I am not rich," disclaimed Thomas Shenston, "and by the grace of God I will never be a rich man."[1] Shenston may not have wished others to consider him rich, but, as president of the Royal Loan and Savings Co., secretary and treasurer of the profitable Brantford Waterworks Co., part owner of the Brantford *Expositor*, real estate speculator, landlord, mortgage broker, and money lender, he was one of the wealthiest men in Brantford, Ontario, in the 1880s. Yet, prominence did not rest easily upon him. Shenston felt compelled on occasion to explain his conduct and intentions and, as the ultimate justification, to offer his own example of self-made success to others. He explained, "As a workingman, I managed to accumulate considerable property and am confident if it became necessary I could and would do so again." He urged the workingman to accept that "he has nothing but his two hands and brains to carve out a position for himself."[2] His prescription for success recapitulated the commonplaces of mid- and late-nineteenth-century self-help – hard work, individualism, clean living, Christian morality, and self-improvement. In itself, his advice warrants little comment. More significant was Shenston's need to bear witness to his own achievements, at the same time as he denied them.

Such contradictory evocations of individualism were rooted in changes in the prospects for social mobility that accompanied early industrial capitalism.[3] The most successful and wealthiest businessmen in Brantford by the 1880s were in the main men who had, like Thomas Shenston, begun in business in a small way, often brushing with failure before achieving their success. Self-help made good history, but it set a poor course for action. The relative absence of entrenched business interests and the failure of the wealthiest because of their speculative entanglements in the 1850s extended the benefits of the prosperity of that decade to a wide range of businessmen. Men with few advantages did in fact succeed. By the 1870s, however, a dichotomy had emerged in the mobility experiences of businessmen, a pattern which was the reverse of the 1850s: the insecurity of men with meagre financial backing and new businessmen in general now contrasted with the stability and the prosperity of the wealthier, established men. Moreover, if success could be attributed to personal character, so might failure, and the personal burden of not getting ahead increasingly tended to drive those who went out of business out of town. Their absence confirmed the universality of the history of those who persisted: those who remained were the successful or those on their way to success.

The presence in the elite of men who started with little and worked their way to the top seemed to confirm the efficacy of individual effort. However, their very advancement and success left little room at the top and few opportunities for others to follow their example. The ideology of success responded to this contradiction. For the capitalist it offered a useful reply to labour, since it argued that with strength of character one could transcend the difference between master and servant. Certainly Shenston had this intent, and such an appeal, as Russell Hann has noted, did not go unheeded.[4] But what has not often been considered is that the ideology of self-made success attempted to bind together the various strata of businessmen. Emphasis upon character and background reduced the significance of material achievements and inherited advantages among businessmen. In effect, the historical record obscured the reality of prevailing business conditions. Thus, the self-made man was made culturally, through the elaboration of ideology, and materially, through the accumulation of wealth.

Any attempt to relate culture to material forces empirically is necessarily tendentious and only as strong as the agency linking the two. The first and longer part of this chapter examines the contradiction that emerged in the pattern of social mobility with the transition to industrial capitalism in Brantford: that is that the reality of self-made success among one generation of businessmen diminished the likelihood of similar experiences among a subsequent generation. The second section explores the ideology of success as expressed by Brantford's leading intellectual – if he might be so called – the Rev. William Cochrane. In his sermons and in a four-volume biographical dictionary published in the early 1890s, he sought to demonstrate "success by example" and thereby to deny the contradiction inherent in the reality of the self-made man.

Allen Smith has argued most persuasively that the contradiction between reality and ideology provoked the qualification of success ideology in late-nineteenth-century English Canada. Increasingly the ambitious were urged to make education a prerequisite for advancement in life and to be satisfied with modest achievements as evidence of success in an increasingly complex society. These modifications attempted social control, "to induce satisfaction with existing forms of social organization and economic activity."[5] Such a judgment seems well-founded in the revised content of the literature. But it also assumes cynicism on the part of the advocates and gullibility on the part of those being addressed. Though he never really questioned its social purpose, Irvin G. Wylie at least clearly delineated the moral strictures that success ideology placed upon the actions of the successful. The argument for a stewardship of wealth might have too easily conferred authority upon the capitalist, but it did also demand explicitly some demonstration of Christian behaviour.[6] The burden of past moral convention was surely not so easily cast off as social control theory might assume. R.J. Morris has contended that for the English petite bourgeoisie the doctrine of self-help described a utopian vision, a moral economy in which personal qualities subject to individual will – character, morality, effort – prevailed over those forces of cyclical and structural economic change to which small capital remained ever vulnerable.[7] Such a vision, as Michael Bliss has explained, was subsumed in the demands of Canadian businessmen for "a living profit."[8] Even with late-nineteenth-century qualifications, a man's fate was still believed to rest in his own hands. From this perspective, the ideology of success constituted a form of self-affirmation calming the anxiety of those in fear of some descent in social station.

Both Smith and Morris have addressed a tension within the nineteenth-century discourse on success and explained it implicitly in terms of the contradiction between reality and ideology. The implication is that ideology could not resolve the discontinuities of social change and was thus itself contradictory. In different ways, John Cawelti and Rex Burns both have tried to explain the strains within the ideology of success by identifying a variety of intellectual traditions contained in it. They have disagreed, however, about the ability of "the yeoman ideal" to adjust to changing circumstances, the former contending that its irrelevance displaced it from late-nineteenth-century popular culture, the latter affirming its accommodation to new social conditions.[9]

Helpful as these interpretations are in untangling the strains of the myth of self-made success, another possibility might be suggested. Success mythology was a form of social contract for those within the bourgeoisie and for those who aspired to membership in that class. Discourse on the theme of self-help constituted bargaining in which modifications and qualifications were negotiating positions requiring compromise from adherents. Thus acceptance of self-help by those whose achievements and prospects were at best modest did indeed imply acquiescence in the *status quo*. For the successful, accepting the myth meant denying that they were greatly different from others and implicitly obligated them to respect the efforts of others in pursuit of success. Consensus remained contingent upon action consistent with ideology.

Much of the scholarship on the social background of the nineteenth-century business elite has utilized biographical dictionaries as convenient sources for both identifying that elite at a national level and compiling data on it. The quibbling over the appropriate biographies and the appropriate elite definitions that occurred in reaction to C. Wright Mills's contention that upward social mobility increased in the nineteenth century and declined thereafter has not affected the Canadian literature, perhaps because the sources and the businessmen are less numerous.[10] In the Canadian context, T.W. Acheson found that the industrial elite of the 1880s demonstrated some moderate upward social mobility on the part of immigrants and men from a farming or artisanal background, if not from the labouring class. Nonetheless, geographical variations suggested that advancement depended upon the length of settlement and the better opportunities of those who succeeded first in one location to provide for the futures of the next in that same place. From this, Acheson concluded that while the elite might exist objectively in historical analysis, its own outlook remained bounded by community rather than class interests.[11] Community-based studies of business as an avenue for advancement have been less frequently undertaken. This has been regrettable, since, as has been argued by Herbert Gutman in his study of Paterson, New Jersey, and by Stephan Thernstrom concerning the labourers of Newburyport, Massachusetts, within the industrializing community frequent examples of the material rewards of hard work must have affected the beliefs of the less successful.[12]

SUCCESS, FAILURE, AND THE DURATION OF SELF-EMPLOYMENT

To examine the incidence of changing opportunities, this study employs two criteria of social mobility: persistence in business and the accumulation of wealth. First, to be self-employed for ten years represented no mean achievement and clearly demonstrated that independence so desired by the mid-Victorian male. Linking the business populations identified from the 1842, 1852, 1861, 1871, and 1881 manuscript census schedules distinguished between those who continued in business roughly for a decade, the successful, and those who did not, the unsuccessful. To date more precisely when men gave up self-employment, additional assessment rolls were examined, thereby providing interdecadal cross-sections for 1847, 1856, 1866, and 1876.

Business discontinuation, though it may blur specific circumstances, does mark failure in relative terms. A businessman may have considered his enterprise, though profitable, a failure if it did not meet opportunity costs; that is, if it did not meet the financial and psychological return upon his assets and energy from wage labour. The alternative of home ownership and dependable employment in some factory or wholesaling house may have led a man with limited means to quit business. Or he may have decided that some new locale might present more favourable opportunities and so he might move on. In either case, his current business failed to meet his expectations, and he did not consider the rewards of self-employment commensurate with the aggravation and sacrifice.

The accumulation of wealth, as revealed through linking the assessment rolls of 1847, 1851, 1856, 1861, 1866, 1871, 1876, and 1880, adds a second dimension in explaining social mobility and reveals certain trends in discontinuation. Changes in wealthholding were examined relatively by establishing whether a man moved from one decile in the distribution of wealth to another. Those men who moved into a higher decile were considered more successful than those who maintained or who lost wealth. This method has proved preferable to that employed by Michael Katz, which measured movement into and out of the four economic ranks: the 1–39th, 40–79th, 80–89th, and 90–100th percentile ranges. While these ranks themselves do conform roughly to some breaks in the distribution of wealth and so are useful units for generalization, Katz's method did not reveal movement within ranks that was equal to or greater than that required in some cases to move into another rank, and in consequence underestimated the instability of wealth in the two lowest ranks.[13]

As Clyde and Sally Griffen have remarked about new businesses in Poughkeepsie, New York, "only a minority were very promising at the outset."[14] It is not surprising that in Brantford the decennial rate of business discontinuations claimed about half of all businesses

Table 5.1
Rates of Business Discontinuations, 1851–80

	1851–61	1861–71	1871–80
New businessmen	52	66	66
Persistors	46	44	25
All	51	53	48
N of discontinuations	91	156	152

Note: In this and subsequent tables rates of discontinuation and persistence were adjusted to exclude the retirements and deaths which occurred in each interval.

(table 5.1). While the relative numbers quitting did not vary significantly, longevity in business did change from decade to decade. Fifty-seven per cent of those who quit in the 1850s were gone by 1856, while 85 per cent of all those who gave up their businesses after 1861 did so in less than five years. The comparable figure for the 1870s was 72 per cent. Cyclical forces may explain some of the change. For whatever particular conjuncture of cyclical and structural factors, the 1850s were much better years to be in business than the following two decades, which were characterized by businesses of shorter duration.

Over time, longevity in business was self-perpetuating. Distinguishing between the persistent business population, those in business for ten years in any cross-section year, and the new business population, those in business for less than ten years in any year, reveals further variations in the pattern of discontinuations. First, the rates for the two subpopulations differed little in the 1850s. Admittedly those in business for a decade were relatively few in number, given the recent arrival of the vast majority. Second, while a substantial rise in the number of newcomers quitting business did produce an increase in the overall rate of discontinuation in the 1860s, the association between quitting and a recent start in business nonetheless remained statistically weak. Third, by the 1870s, new businessmen were significantly more likely to go out of business.[15] The decrease in the rate of discontinuation in that decade was due entirely to the entrenched position of already established businessmen. The depression of the mid-1870s exerted a differential impact, taking most often as its victims men in business a short time. One financial commentator of the day, W.W. Johnson, identified newcomers as the cause of the depression: "The severest stress," he wrote, "was largely caused by the advent among us of many traders for whom there was no possible future insofar as success was concerned."[16] In contrast, those who had been self-employed for at least ten years found the 1870s less perilous than the previous decade; times had improved, so that only one-quarter failed to remain in business from 1871 to 1880.

The equation of success with character and the defence of the equality of opportunity put a great burden upon the failing businessman, since his failure implied some character weakness. "The modern English soul," Thomas Carlyle wrote, "does in very truth dread infinitely, and contemplates with entire despair ... the terror of 'Not Succeeding'; of not making money, fame or some other figure in the world."[17] The fear of failure grew not only from unsatisfied personal ambitions, but also from the meaning placed upon failure by the rest of society. In an article entitled "Failures in 1876," the editor of the *Monetary Times* tried to dissuade those unsuited for business, especially farmers and farmers' sons, from embarking on such a career by detailing the shame awaiting the unsuccessful. "A large number of the unfortunates ... have broken down this year and last ... . We should perhaps recall the word 'unfortunates', for long experience has convinced us that most men fail from some fault of their own. But, be the cause what it may, it may be taken generally as a serious reverse in life for a man to break down in business. He can never be the same man afterwards. ... No man can feel the same after failing as he did when he honestly paid everybody their due. ... He has had the humiliating experience of meeting angry creditors to go through, and heard very unpleasant comments on his folly or bad management."[18] The author expressed a concern for the best interests of men whose ambitions, he believed, presaged only their own ruin, and he no doubt shared Johnson's opinion of the futility of much self-employment in the 1870s.

For some the burden of failure was indeed heavy, perhaps too heavy to bear. Before absconding, J.A.D. Baker, a grocer who was heavily indebted to Brantford wholesalers George Watt and Sons confessed, "I have been fretting over this fizzle-out until I am sick, fretting does no good and won't help us out of this mess."[19] Some fled. Others found temporary solace in drink. A few took more direct action. In April 1868 William Muirhead, a carriage blacksmith, jumped into the cold waters of the Grand River and drowned, rather than face a lawsuit brought against him by a relative.[20] Alex Glass, a baker for more than ten years, hanged himself in 1869. Failing after twenty years in the grocery trade, William B. Hurst moved to Titusville, Pennsylvania, where in 1875 he died from an overdose of laudanum. Thomas Martin, a bookseller who had failed in Paris, moved to Brantford. When his business did not improve there, he

Table 5.2
Business Discontinuations and Transiency: Percentage of Men Quitting Business Who Left Town, by Economic Rank and Sector, 1851–80

		Rank				
		0–39	40–79	80–89	90–100	All
Year	Sector	(%)	(%)	(%)	(%)	(%)
1851–61	Industry	70	53	67	75	64
	Commerce	74	86	67	100	80
	All	71	72	67	86	74
	Number	71	74	17	17	179
1861–71	Industry	70	56	75	0	61
	Commerce	73	76	71	100	75
	All	72	66	73	83	70
	Number	98	139	32	26	295
1871–80	Industry	82	73	50	0	75
	Commerce	83	79	75	75	81
	All	83	76	63	50	78
	Number	134	122	31	31	318

shot himself. Extreme and desperate acts were uncommon; yet, they did evidence the burden of failure and made understandable the decision of most failed businessmen to leave town rather than face friends and acquaintances.[21]

For most feeling such pressure, going out of business generally meant leaving town. "Burst and gone" or "out and gone" were the comments most frequently reported about transients by the credit reporters for R.G. Dun and Co.[22] The transiency rate among those who went out business, always very high, became even higher in the 1870s, as formerly self-employed tradesmen rejected wage labour in Brantford (table 5.2). Whereas two-thirds of those who had been engaged in some form of industrial production left town in the 1850s, fully three-quarters departed in the 1870s. The major reason for this was an increase of 20 percentage points in the transiency rate of those in the middle of the distribution of wealth, the 40–79th percentile rank. They were the master artisans possessed not only of skills but small amounts of capital as well. In the 1850s and 1860s they might have found it easier to accept employment in some craft workshop or other small-scale business where skill and experience would command respect. By the 1870s their skills and experience were less marketable and, depending on their trade, might not have won for them wages higher than those paid any other new worker in a factory or on a construction gang. Rather than accept such an extreme alteration in status, the master artisans left Brantford for more lucrative employment or for a second chance at self-employment. The status distinction between manual and non-manual labour made the descent into the working class even more upsetting for those who had been self-employed in commerce. Transiency rates in the commercial sector remained roughly constant, and overall as many men in the commercial sector in the 1870s as in the 1850s moved away from Brantford after closing their shops.

By 1880 the class line between the self-employed and the employed was more clearly drawn and a step from the former to the latter covered greater social distance. The burden of failure, weighted if a man had been a booster, must have made remaining in town uncomfortable. Accepting wage labour was probably easier elsewhere. Thus, to the extent that industrialization proletarianized the petite bourgeoisie, it encouraged geographic mobility. On the other hand, a man might despair of his chances through self-employment in Brantford but still harbour hopes for a brighter future in some new location. But the peripatetic businessman increasingly confronted the prejudice of creditors who associated transiency with failure and newcomers with mystery. As Dun's representative communicated about one dry goods merchant, he "just opened here, was at Dundas, removed to Berlin, and now here – a rolling stone gathers no moss."[23]

George Hague, general manager of the Merchant's Bank, held a similar opinion and advised ambitious young men to avoid "restlessness." By "restlessness," he meant "exchanging the occupation with which they have been familiar from childhood, and of whose conditions they are perfectly cognisant, for one they know nothing about, and the entering upon which is as pure a venture and speculation, as would be the embarking of a man on an unknown sea who had never manned an oar, or trimmed a sail. It is sometimes boasted of as a virtue by our American cousins, that if a man fails in one pursuit, he can, under the conditions of society prevailing there, easily change it for another and that to another again. ... 'A rolling stone gathers no moss.'"[24]

Some businessmen, it might be argued, chose to liquidate profitable enterprises and with their capital move on to even more lucrative ventures elsewhere: geographic mobility built success upon success. This seems to have been a strategy in the 1830s and early 1840s when Brantford's economic position in the Upper Canadian economy remained uncertain. But with the wheat boom of the 1850s and the extension of railroad connections from that decade and through the 1870s, businessmen vocally proclaimed their town's locational advantages. Going into business, men identified their fortunes with the fate of their community. To sell out in preference for some other locality made hypocrites of formerly committed boosters. "Boosterism presumed," Clyde and Sally Griffen have contended, "that they had settled for life."[25]

Little evidence remains of men willingly selling their businesses. The Mercantile Agency of R.G. Dun and Co. noted just sixteen sales from the late 1840s to the mid-1870s. Inventory sales must have been a reluctant decision for traders, since to prospective buyers the occasion promised cut-rate bargains. C.L. Burton, a president of the Simpson's department store company, remembered the sale and auction of the stock of his father's general store in Green River, Ontario, in 1888 as a great disappointment to his family; goods with a retail value of $12,000 returned only $7,000, a 40 per cent mark-down.[26]

Nor after the 1840s did men often exchange one form of independence for another, selling businesses to buy farms. Only three from the 1852 population and only one from each of the 1861 and 1871 populations were enumerated at subsequent census years as farmers in Brantford Township. Former businessmen may have gone further afield to farm, but Dun's credit reporter listed only two such cases. Richard Barrett, born in England about 1810, closed up his jewellery and watchmaking shop in 1863 when he inherited his father's farm near Port Hope. Though his business, started in 1849, was considered moderately secure and he owned two brick buildings, he had failed previously as a wagonmaker and later as a brewer. Perhaps returning to the land while in his early fifties and still able to farm seemed a prudent and secure move.[27]

Moreover, few businesses were sold because of retirement, because few men retired: only four in the 1850s, seven in the 1860s, and fifteen in the 1870s.[28] The increasing number of retirees over time marked the aging of Brantford's first generation of businessmen. But even in old age, most remained remarkably active. As early as 1857, when he was forty-five years old, Ignatius Cockshutt was judged by the Dun reporter to have "accumulated a fortune ... [so that he] might retire from business any moment he might think proper."[29] Not until 1882 did Cockshutt, at age seventy, turn over the various departments of his general merchandising business to his sons. But even then he remained engaged in business affairs as president of the Brantford Waterworks Co. until 1889 and the Craven Cotton Co. until 1891 and as a careful investor.[30] Seldom, then, did men willingly close their businesses.

Because of their small numbers, it is difficult to generalize about the fates of those who quit business but remained in Brantford. In each decade, however, two activities – labouring and construction – accounted for just about half of the occupations of ex-businessmen. That this should have been the case was not surprising, since construction tradesmen were the most numerous ex-businessmen in Brantford in 1871 and 1880, making up about one-quarter of all. These men appreciated the general good health of the local construction industry and perhaps hoped to pick up work on their own account. Indeed, Bryan Palmer has noted that one contentious issue between bricklayers and Hamilton's master builders in the 1880s was the former group's practice of taking small contracts.[31] The line between labour and self-employment blurred in the construction trades, where journeymen owned their tools and clients might purchase the materials themselves. After construction workers, shoemakers were the most numerous ex-businessmen, 20 per cent of all in 1871 and 12 per cent in 1880. Their persistence in Brantford witnessed the sorry state of their trade and their despair about better opportunities elsewhere.

Real estate ownership held some former businessmen to Brantford. In fact, ex-businessmen's rate of real estate ownership exceeded that of businessmen in 1861, by 68 per cent to 57 per cent, and in 1871, by 81 per cent to 57 per cent. Only in 1880 did approximately the same proportion of each group, about 60 per cent, own some real estate. The considerable difference between the two rates in 1871, taken with the lower transiency rate among men quitting business in the 1860s, raises the interesting speculation that some men perceived their marginal position in business and quit while they could salvage some of their assets (table 5.3). The year 1871 was the only one in which real estate ownership of former businessmen was higher after they had quit business than when they had been self-employed: only 77 per cent had owned land in 1861. The pattern of economic mobility in the 1860s also suggested good timing. Just less than a third of ex-businessmen retained wealth that would have given them the same decile ranking in the distribution of wealth had they still been in business, while nearly 30 per cent were wealthier. It was a more positive experience than that of the 1850s, when more than two thirds of those who went out of business lost money, and certainly much better than the situation suffered later by those who came after them. In the 1870s nearly three-quarters of business discontinuations involved a loss of wealth. By this last decade, there could be little doubt that those who quit business did so because their businesses were not viable.

As might be expected, the least wealthy – those who, in the words of the Dun Co.'s credit reporter, had "no backbone to their business

Table 5.3
Economic Mobility of Persistors, 1851–80

Direction of Mobility	1851–61		1861–71		1871–80	
	Businessmen (%)	Quitters (%)	Businessmen (%)	Quitters (%)	Businessmen (%)	Quitters (%)
Up	64	24	43	30	54	18
Stable	19	8	24	32	34	18
Down	30	68	48	56	25	74
Number	88	25	139	47	166	33

Note: The calculation of upward mobility excludes those in the wealthiest ten percentiles at the first cross-section. Since they are in the top decile, upward mobility is not possible for them by definition. Similarly in the calculation of downward mobility, those in the poorest deciles have been excluded from the calculations. For this reason columns do not total 100. This adjustment is necessary in comparing businessmen and quitters because of the absence of the latter in the wealthiest decile and their over-representation in the poorest decile.

in the shape of capital"[32] – always quit business more frequently than the wealthiest (table 5.4). Nonetheless, in the 1850s the difference in the rates of discontinuation between those in the lowest forty percentiles and those in the top two deciles was not statistically significant. The 1850s were best decade for those in the bottom rank: the rate of upward mobility was higher than in either of the two subsequent decades, and between 1851 and 1856 the rank achieved the highest five-year rate of upward mobility, 45 per cent, of any rank through this study. Their gains were insecure, however. Forty-five per cent of all businessmen who increased their wealth in the five years after 1851 maintained or further increased their standing in the five years after 1856, while only 30 per cent of the bottom rank held or increased their wealth.

Not until the 1860s and 1870s did the lowest forty percentiles confront a greater probability of quitting business. Nearly three-quarters of them quit between 1861 and 1871, roughly two-thirds leaving before 1866.[33] Those who did stay in business until 1866 benefited from the better economic times of the late 1860s, and, though fewer from the lowest rank augmented or sustained their wealth, their experience did not differ in a statistically significant way from that of the higher ranks.

Conversely, not until the 1860s and 1870s were the wealthiest 20 per cent significantly more secure.[34] The chances of survival improved markedly for the wealthiest decile in particular.[35] In the 1850s, 40 per cent of the top rank went out of business. Manufac-

Table 5.4
Direction of Mobility by Economic Rank, 1851–80

		Direction of Mobility				
Rank	Decade	Quit %	Down %	Stable %	Up %	N
0–39 percentile	1851–61	59	7	9	25	71
	1861–71	73	1	8	14	98
	1871–80	65	2	10	23	134
40–79 percentile	1851–61	49	14	5	33	74
	1861–71	48	23	6	22	139
	1871–80	41	15	12	32	122
80–89 percentile	1851–61	35	18	0	47	17
	1861–71	34	25	22	19	32
	1871–80	26	26	29	19	31
90–100 percentile	1851–61	41	18	41	n.a.	17
	1861–71	23	38	39	n.a.	26
	1871–80	19	19	61	n.a.	31
All	1851–61	51	12	10	28	179
	1861–71	53	19	12	17	295
	1871–80	48	11	18	24	318

turers and craft producers generally failed more quickly than men in commerce. All of the wealthiest 10 per cent and two-thirds of those in the ninth decile who were engaged in production lost wealth or quit business.[36] Millers, iron founders, and rail car manufacturers confronted serious difficulties, but so did wealthy craft producers whose participation in the commercial economy remained indirect, one step removed from their main business interests. For example, Matthew Whitham, an English Baptist baker and confectioner since the mid-1830s, had over the years assembled considerable real estate, including in 1851 a two-storey frame house and separate shop, three rental properties and some vacant land, assessed in total for the equivalent of $8,000. This landed wealth he mortgaged and, acting in effect as a private banker, he financed the speculations of others through loans and endorsements. By so doing, he sought a return on capital which could not be productively employed in his own business. In the crash of 1857, he lost all, as he became liable for nearly $35,000 in debts which he had co-signed. In 1858 he assigned his assets to his creditors and vacated his bakery, which was then let to a competitor. Whitham continued in business, but nominally in partnership with Johnson Jex, who signed for purchases, but otherwise did not participate in the bakery and confectionery.[37] Whitham fell from the wealthiest decile in 1851 to the poorest 40 percentile range in 1861. Whitham's experience was not unique, and many other craft producers were tapped, even for relatively small amounts, by Brantford's "fast men," often with results as unfortunate as those besetting Whitham.

The wealthiest men in commerce in many instances persisted longer not from healthier enterprises, but from the greater complexity of their affairs and the interest of metropolitan suppliers in their continuance. Moreover, their assets included accounts due, promissory notes, and inventories which may have depreciated less rapidly than did land. Eleven of the fifteen merchants who were among the wealthiest 20 per cent of the business population in 1851 either maintained or improved their positions. But more than half of them were in serious trouble and deeply indebted. For a time, they were able to absorb the impact of the depression and delay failure – but only for a time.[38] Matthew W. Pruyn, for example, a wholesale and retail grocer, encountered difficulties from endorsing for his brother-in-law, Abraham Kerby, a merchant miller. Liable for about $30,000, he forestalled insolvency by assigned his assets to a friendly trustee. He continued to trade by opening three different shops in the names of others. Pruyn thereby delayed but did not prevent his failure, and in 1862 he was gone.[39]

Similarly Richard Strobridge and Thomas Botham, general merchants, were acknowledged as "superior businessmen ... next to the wealthiest and safest firm in town" and judged in 1857 to be worth $60,000 clear of mortgages or judgment. However, they sold extensively on credit and had endorsed the paper of several grain merchants, principally Alex Bunnell, incurring liabilities of $30,000. After the crash of 1857, the Bank of Montreal carried them for years, to the extent of $8,000 a month credit. By early 1862 Strobridge and Botham had to call a meeting of their creditors to reschedule their payments. Though they met their obligations for two years, in September 1864 they assigned their assets for their creditors' benefit. Their obligations totalled about $20,000, while their assets consisted of stock worth $9,000 and outstanding accounts of $5,000. Their real estate, valued at $37,000 in 1861, had depreciated in value so that by 1864 it was worth far less than the mortgages taken out against it since 1857. After the assignment, Strobridge rented out his house, took six months' rent in advance, and quietly left town.

Botham stayed to face creditors and community. He operated as broker through the rest of the period under study and in 1871 ranked among the least wealthy 40 per cent of businessmen.[40]

In the 1860s the mobility patterns of men in commerce and industry in the upper two deciles did not differ significantly. In the 1870s, however, the incidence of security among the elite marked the implications of the transition to industrial capitalism. For the first time quitting business and losing wealth were associated in the wealthiest decile with merchants not manufacturers.[41] Fifty per cent of merchants, but only 15 per cent of manufacturers, experienced downward mobility. In part this may have been cyclical, as merchants, especially in dry goods and hardware, but also in other lines, suffered from the overselling of the market by manufacturers' agents and wholesalers trying to pass surplus production farther down the chain of distribution.[42] But the stability of the industrial elite was also structural. Manufacturing, the Brantford *Expositor* contended, was "about the only avenue that pays substantial interest on investments."[43]

Similarities, principally in humble origins, existed in the backgrounds of the thirty-eight merchants, manufacturers, and contractors in the wealthiest decile in 1880–1. Only six had fathers who were or had been elite members in Brantford: Joseph Stratford took over his father William's wholesale drug business; his brother, John, left the family business to become a railway contractor. Alfred Watts, miller, distiller, and soap manufacturer, inherited the major components of his business from his father. Ignatius Cockshutt took over his father's general merchandising business in the 1840s. His investment in the Waterous Engine Works won his son, James, the office of president in that company, until he left to start the Cockshutt Plough Co. John Harris was in partnership with his father, Alanson, in the manufacture of farm implements. Seven others may have brought wealth with them to Brantford, although this supposition rests on a complete lack of knowledge of their past. Admittedly only one – Terence Jones, a "note shaver" or, more politely, a private banker – had previously been a labourer, and only two others, like Jones, were Irish Catholics – Joseph Quinlan, a merchant and landlord, and William Clelland, a liquor merchant. But the remaining twenty-five came from backgrounds that seem at best modest, if not impoverished. Of those whose fathers' occupations can be ascertained, five were the sons of farmers and four, sons of artisans. William Paterson, confectioner/cigar manufacturer and member of parliament, was orphaned at age ten and started his working life in his mid-teens as one of Cockshutt's clerks. Likewise, Charles Waterous lost his father while very young. Apprenticeship, journeyman employment, or clerking had been common experiences for the self-made elite: ten had plied trades before starting businesses, while six had been clerks. A number, Waterous, for example, had tried self-employment elsewhere unsuccessfully before locating in Brantford. Finally, the rise of the self-made elite was recent – only five had held the top rank since 1861, – but not rapid – twenty-one of the twenty-five had resided in Brantford since at least 1861.[44]

About 80 per cent of those in the wealthiest decile in 1880 had been self-employed locally in a small way prior to 1861; that is their wealth placed them outside the wealthiest 20 per cent in 1861. They had survived the collapse of 1857 and the stagnation of the early 1860s. Trying as those years were, self-employed tradesmen in the 0–79th percentile range fared slightly better than shopkeepers in the same range[45] and better than wealthier businessmen. Some trades did quite well in the 1850s: three-quarters of the blacksmiths in this range increased or maintained their wealth, as did two-thirds of the shoemakers and half of the tailors.

Further advancement in the industrial sector after the 1850s required tradesmen generally to move beyond their own trades. Carriage making afforded a good example of this, since production combined several crafts – blacksmith, builder, painter, trimmer, and wheelwright. Similar proprietorial mobility appeared in other trades. Carpenters became builders; builders started to manufacture building materials. Some trades demanded more lateral movement for business expansion. An Irish saddler, James Smith, independent at his trade from at least 1861, went into a wholesale saddlery and harness business in partnership with Donald B. McKay, a Scot harnessmaker, in the late 1860s and in the next decade with Edward Brophey, formerly a retail shoe dealer. Several tailors moved into dry goods retailing. John Jenkins, for example, an English immigrant and an Anglican, opened a tailor shop some time in the late 1850s. Postponing marriage until his mid- to late thirties, he did well enough in the 1860s to move into dry goods retailing in the 1870s. But these adaptations were exceptional, and most apparel makers, if they remained in business through the 1860s, had lost wealth by 1871 and moved on in the 1870s.

Men in the two least wealthy ranks in commerce did not enjoy success comparable to that of master artisans in the 1850s. Only four of eighteen grocers in 1851 grew wealthier, and only five were still in business ten years later. Three of the four who were richer had been "low grocers" who rose significantly from the bottom rank, two to the seventh decile and the third, Joseph Quinlan, to the ninth decile. Other merchants in the 0–79th percentile range fared even more poorly than the grocers. Four of thirteen stayed in business, and only two acquired wealth. Merchants of this sort financed their businesses almost entirely on credit, and if economic conditions were favourable, they did well. If not, they failed quickly. The operator of a small general store who received a good credit rating from Dun in May of 1857 had failed and left town by August. A bookseller declared insolvency, owing just $300, while a grocer landed in debtors' prison for unpaid bills of just $120.[46] Creditors quickly cut adrift those with few assets and fewer prospects.

After 1861 a man in the 0–79th percentile range had about as good a chance for success in commerce as in industry, although limited capital was less of an impediment to persistence in craft production. The specialization of retail merchandising after 1861 meant that a merchant might find success in any of a number of lines, although food (groceries, milk, fruit, liquor) retailing was the most stable business for those merchants in the middle range, the 40–79th percentiles. Their rate of persistence was somewhat higher than average in the 1860s (52 per cent) and significantly better in the 1870s (81 per cent).[47] They were, however, no more likely than other merchants to accumulate wealth in either decade. Two whole-sale grocers, George Foster and Jackson Forde – both of whom had run small "one-horse groceries" in the 1850s – and one wholesale liquor merchant, Alex Fair, were among the wealthiest 10 per cent in 1880, but dry goods merchants, four in number, were much more greatly over-represented at the top. Dry goods, the most prestigious commercial line, was also perhaps the most difficult in which to succeed, experiencing generally higher than average rates of failure and downward mobility. However, the two leading merchants in this line, Henry Brethour and Charles Duncan, had been in business from the late 1850s and among the wealthiest decile for some time, Brethour since 1861 and Duncan since 1871.

The most successful in Brantford by the 1880s, on the whole, had advanced steadily from modest origins to prominence. That their experience was not representative – for by definition they were a minority – was obscured by the increasing transiency of those unable to stay in business; examples to the contrary were not long present. Yet their very success and security by the 1870s impeded the advancement of those starting with limited assets. Not only was there little room at the top, but the greater productive and distributive scale of successful businesses in Brantford and elsewhere by this time generated vigorous competition for the newcomer to meet. The past was not being replayed in the present.

COURT ACTION AND BUSINESS FAILURE

Some might argue that more obvious evidence of business success and failure is contained in legal proceedings against those unable to pay their debts. However, an inability to meet obligations did not lead inevitably to discontinuation. Rather than indicating weakness, indebtedness might demonstrate that assets were used to the fullest for trade purposes. Similarly, litigation, whether insolvency or property seizures, indicated that a man's affairs were complicated and not easily settled.

The relationship between debt and persistence changed through the mid-nineteenth century as creditors more frequently demanded security. In the 1860s and 1870s mortgage debtors had higher rates of persistence in business than in the 1850s and were more likely to remain in business for ten years than were the owners of unencumbered real estate. Debt tied a businessman to one place; he could not easily liquidate his assets and in fact could only enjoy their use so long as he remained in one place and did not abscond. This, of course, was what his creditors hoped to achieve.

Debt did not play a major role in the strategy of those pursuing success in the 1850s. Greater indebtedness was associated with declining fortunes. Of those who grew wealthier between 1851 and 1861, only one-third became more indebted, whereas 54 per cent of those who maintained their wealth and nearly 90 per cent who lost wealth owed greater mortgage debt in 1861 than in 1851. Land could be a savings bank, and a mortgage a withdrawal from the accounts. However, since real estate ownership was more restricted in cross-section years subsequent to 1851, this cushion was not available for as many businessmen encountering later difficulties.

By 1880 nearly half of self-employed property owners who grew wealthier fell deeper into debt. For advancement, all of a man's assets had to be in play and at risk, and he needed to borrow to multiply his assets. Thus, land was increasingly another form of business capital rather than a repository for business profits. On the other hand, those property holders who lost money in business in the 1860s and 1870s were less likely than in the 1850s to go deeper into debt and more likely to give up their real estate, either selling or having it seized to settle debts. In the 1860s just 37 per cent of those who lost wealth, 45 per cent in the 1870s, became indebted, while more in the former decade, and as many in the latter decade, lost all of their real estate.

Debt, then, was not a factor necessarily contributing to failure, especially after 1861. In fact, those who became wealthier were also more likely to become more indebted than those who lost wealth. Problems did arise, however, when debt could not be managed or retired. At those times a businessman could find himself in court pleading insolvency or having his property seized.

The pattern of involvement in legal proceedings, declarations of insolvency and property seizure litigation, reflected the pattern of failure previously outlined with two important qualifications. First, not all businessmen who were in difficulty were likely to become involved in court action. Against some, legal proceedings were pointless, since they possessed no assets worth distributing. Second, because legal action was taken by and against businessmen whose assets were still more or less intact, if somewhat compromised, often they were able to continue in business following their day in court. In some cases insolvency was means of avoiding being forced out of business.

Recourse to the legal system became less frequent for businessmen in Brantford as the nineteenth century wore on. Less than one-fifth of the business population in 1851 declared insolvency or had their property seized in the next ten years. In the 1870s, despite the depression of mid-decade, only about two-thirds as many businessmen, in relative terms, as in the 1850s were subject to legal proceedings. In particular, the wealthiest 20 per cent were more secure: accounting for 40 per cent of the insolvents and 41 per cent of the property seizures in the 1850s, they contributed only 18 per cent of the former and 21 per cent of the latter in the 1870s. In contrast, the least wealthy 40 per cent of the business population became the respondents in legal action more frequently. In the 1850s they made up only 10 per cent of all insolvents, but nearly 36 per cent in the 1870s; they accounted for only 12 per cent of all property seizure cases in the 1850s, but 21 per cent in the 1870s (table 5.5).

Neither bankruptcy nor property seizures led inevitably to quitting business. The majority of bankrupts in the 1850s and 1870s did quit business. Yet, about a quarter of those who filed for insolvency were able subsequently either to increase their wealth or to maintain their relative wealth. This good fortune was even more marked in the 1860s. Even though insolvency was then at its highest, more of those who declared insolvency between 1861 and 1871 had maintained or increased their wealth by the later date than had quit business. That insolvency rose in the 1860s and that relatively more insolvents recovered suggest that creditors in those years were taking few chances and did not grant extensions as readily to businessmen whose obligations at other times might have been suffered a while longer. For the debtor, insolvency worked best as a delaying tactic until economic

Table 5.5
Property Seizures and Insolvencies, 1851–81

		1851–61 (%)	1861–71 (%)	1871–81 (%)
A. Property Seizures:				
Rank:	0–39	12	7	36
	40–79	46	34	46
	80–89	12	22	14
	90–100	29	7	4
Mobility:	Up	36	15	11
	Stable	32	15	47
	Down	5	29	
	Quit	27	41	32
	Number	26	30	20
B. Insolvencies:				
Rank:	0–39	10	25	36
	40–79	50	39	46
	80–89	25	17	14
	90–100	15	19	4
Mobility:	Up	10	11	4
	Stable	16	33	19
	Down	16	20	19
	Quit	58	36	58
	Number	21	36	29

conditions took a turn for the better. If they did not, as was the case in the 1850s and 1870s, then insolvency only postponed the inevitable. As one would expect, the poorest insolvents were always most likely to quit business soon after assigning. In both the 1850s and the 1870s the correlations for quitting business weakened with increasing wealth. But, in the 1860s the wealthiest bankrupts failed to recover as in previous and subsequent decades, emphasizing the structural change of that decade.[48]

Except in the 1860s again, having property seized was less likely than insolvency to result in a businessman quitting business or losing wealth. In general, the wealthiest 20 per cent were slightly more vulnerable than other economic ranks if involved in property seizures. A member of the elite must have been in very serious trouble if it became necessary for creditors to sue him for recovery of debts. Thus property seizures were symptomatic of serious difficulties in a wealthy man's affairs. Once more the 1860s were exceptional: the wealthiest were less likely than average to quit business after having property seized. This was another reflection of the crisis of credit. Devalued real estate was no longer able to support previously contracted debt or renewals thereof, and creditors were frantic to force repayment before further devaluation of their clients' assets.

Indebtedness was the natural condition of the businessman, especially as credit contracted in reaction to the crash of 1857 and as creditors demanded more solid security. This demand for security made a businessman's affairs more involved and it was not always possible to meet obligations when they fell due. Court action – insolvency or property seizure – only made sense to creditors if their clients had assets worth taking. Thus, litigation provided a way of resolving difficulties which wiped the slate clean for an embarrassed businessman and which did not necessarily put him out of business.

THE IDEOLOGY OF SUCCESS AND FAILURE

The citizens of Brantford could scarcely remain unaware of the profound changes in the social organization of business in their city. Legal notices peppered the local newspapers announcing insolvencies and property seizures. More poignant were the human tragedies, the suicides and mental breakdowns. On 30 April 1875, for example, the *Expositor* incredulously reported the bizarre flight of Seth Park, twenty years a photographer in town. Seriously in debt, Park quietly emptied what remained in his bank account and borrowed $2,000 from friends. Besides this, he procured six watches and two revolvers on approval from local retailers. He abandoned his wife and, suitably armed, he and his teenaged son, Edward, headed for the American West. The *Expositor* was perplexed: "Mr. Park ... had always maintained ... a character for probity and honorable business dealing, of a high order. Indeed there were few men in the community one would not sooner have suspected of an intention to defraud. ... We could not help believing that some extraordinary business pressure or mental aberration had driven him to an act so mad."

In 1879 another case of business misfortune was brought to public attention. The Hamilton *Spectator* reported that a destitute Brantford tailor named Nettleton had his sewing machine and all his furniture seized and sold because he could not pay his rent. Unable to obtain custom jobs or even put-out work from local merchants and clothiers, Nettleton could not support his family or afford medical attention for his wife, who had died shortly before on a bed of rags. The reporter was convinced that "if Mr. Nettleton had stated his case, no one could have refused him work."[49] But no man found it easy to confess failure and beg custom as charity. The unexpected collapse of solid businessmen like Park or the destitution of others like Nettleton challenged the deep-seated mid-century ideology of self-help that was a critical component of artisan and shopkeeper culture.

The Rev. William Cochrane was troubled by the changes he saw around him. In his sermons and lectures and in the multi-volume biographical dictionary which he edited, he tried to explain what was happening. Cochrane, born in Paisley, Scotland, in 1831, proclaimed himself self-made: "I knew what it was to labor from before dawn of day till long after darkness, at wages which no Canadian apprentice would accept."[50] His father died when the boy was quite young, and at age twelve, because of financial necessity, young William took employment as a message boy for a local bookselling firm. "By business capacity, diligence and fidelity," in the words of his eulogist, "he quite early rose to the onerous and honourable position of manager."[51] Despite his success in business, Cochrane felt drawn to the ministry and began attending classes at the University of Glasgow. An old friend of his family, who had immigrated to Cincinnati, Ohio, and become a successful merchant, recognized Cochrane's abilities and offered to pay for his education in America. Cochrane accepted. He completed his theological training at Princeton University in 1859, and in 1862 received a call to Brantford's Zion Church, where he served until his death in 1898. During these years Cochrane achieved prominence beyond his own congregation, becoming the convenor of home missions of the Presbyterian church from 1872 to his death and the moderator of the church in 1882.[52]

Cochrane was committed to a minister's obligation to address social issues and to provide guidance in their resolution. Themes apparent in his own experiences provided him with critical elements for commentaries upon success. These included not just the virtues of individual effort and self-improvement but also the necessity of presenting a good character in public so that personal virtues might be recognized by those in positions to promote one's further advancement. That the already successful should promote the careers of the deservingly ambitious, for Cochrane, arose naturally from an awareness of commonalty. Too infrequently have historians noted, as Robert Wohl did in his study of Horatio Alger,[53] the theme of the recognition of character as a stage in advancement: success could be the reward bestowed for displaying self-help, rather than the product of self-help. Dedicated hard work, in the pursuit of education or in diligent service to one's employer, manifested the qualities of character which instilled confidence and warranted promotion by others.

Cochrane hoped that his biographical dictionary – *The Canadian Album. Men of Canada or Success by Example*[54] – which reported upon many small and generally undistinguished businessmen as well as the prominent, would facilitate that process of recognition.

"The world knows nothing," he exclaimed, "of its greatest men." Appearances deceived, especially for men whose prominence was recent and whom one had little opportunity to know at first hand. Prominence could itself be misleading, since Cochrane, somewhat cynical in his views of the ways of the world, charged many of the richest and most respected men with being "void alike of character and talent ... . The men whom the world calls prosperous – whose bank account is heavy – whose credit is inexhaustible – who are daily adding to their real estate in houses and land and know not how best to invest their capital ... are miserable beyond conception."[55] Material success imperilled salvation: "Long continuance in worldly prosperity is adverse to spiritual growth."[56] Cochrane argued that appearance was often not reality; what seemed to be success often was failure, and apparent failure might be success. He used this reversal of success and failure as a device to provoke public awareness of character as the true determinant of success. True insight into their character would reduce many of the richest and most respectable men to abject poverty: "from being looked up to as the honorable and exalted of the earth, they would be despised and forgotten in their poverty and obscurity."[57] On the other hand, many truly deserving men did not display the outward and material evidence of success and went unnoted by the public.

The assertion of the public's right to judge was a new feature of success ideology and implied the possibility of scepticism. How ought one to judge success? Are the wealthy really successful? By the 1870s exhortation no longer sufficed to instil the virtues of self-help. Proof – names and histories – was needed in the form of the identification of the truly successful. Cochrane emphasized not just that many of the successful really did conform to the precepts of self-made success but also that those with appropriate qualities of character were successful even if their experiences had not produced material rewards of the magnitude to mark their achievements publicly.

The recognition of self-made success would also shorten the social distance between those who employed labour and capital on a large scale and those who did not, small businessmen and workers. Trade unions, strikes, and socialism troubled Cochrane. He denounced class polarization and attributed it to two factors: the demagogy of outside labour agitators and changes in the business environment. Union leaders, he believed, exaggerated the workingman's legitimate concerns and thereby made agreements with employers difficult. Nonetheless he did recognize that the pressures of business competition might be passed onto workers unfairly: "Merchants and manufacturers, underselling each other, are compelled to reduce wages, until the existence for the workingman becomes a weary struggle."[58] This sort of "reckless competition" had to stop.

Businessmen themselves suffered in such circumstances. Cochrane described their psychic state: "To keep pace with the demands of commerce and the customs of the age, day must be prolonged into night and night turned into day. ... Business men seem to walk from day to day on the verge of a rugged precipice, – their minds tortured and harassed by brooding over expected monetary convulsions, and wide spread panics."[59] To cope demanded great discipline and application of energy. Retreat into himself and into his family offered refuge to the businessman by increasing the social distance between himself and the causes of stress. This stress, masked by self-discipline, at times could lead the unthinking businessman to treat his employees insensitively. The quiet concern that Cochrane believed most employers to have for their workers remained unapparent to the workers because "masters and servants stand apart."[60]

If each party just knew the other, then jealousy and conflict could be eliminated. The first responsibility in effecting this rested with the employer, who ought to take a benevolent interest in his employees. In remedy Cochrane urged a return to what he called "patriarchal times." This should begin with the treatment of workers just entering the job market: "Young men coming from Christian homes to strange cities, lonely and friendless, should be introduced to good companions, invited to the homes of masters and made to feel that they are the objects of interest, beyond civil contract."[61] Cochrane accepted that work in industrial society separated family members. Yet, if the ties within biological families had to weaken, the family's responsibility for sustaining moral behaviour had to continue in some other form. That task should rest with the employer, who ought not to construe his relationship with his employees simply as a wage labour contract, but ought to admit workers to his home and take an interest in their after-work well-being. Moreover such close contact ought to allow each worker the opportunity to demonstrate his abilities fully and to be rewarded accordingly by his employer.[62] The workplace, then, should become a meritocracy organized in recognition of its participants' characters rather than in response to external market factors.

The business system itself had to change, for it too was impersonal and failed to acknowledge character. Cochrane hoped that his biographical dictionary would act as one agent of change. Indeed he presented it as a supplement to more conventional credit manuals reporting only financial details. He argued: "Mercantile reports are good so far as they go, but they give a man's financial 'rating' only, and private reports are often necessary to find out who and what the man is. There is a felt need to know more about men than is indicated by their mercantile standing."[63] Just who felt this need remains unclear; certainly those small businessmen slighted by lenders more interested in manufacturers and large-scale merchants would have shared this conviction. Cochrane's statement does suggest his awareness of the fundamental changes in the Canadian credit system.

The Canadian Album, then, endorsed the credit-worthiness of men whose "mercantile standing" might not recommend them. Cochrane did not hesitate in co-signing on the basis of personal qualities: "Character, capacity and capital are the qualities which tell the story of a man's worth, and, as a rule, the second 'capacity' is a product of the first, while the third 'capital' is generally a result of the second. Still ... capital is only an incident in the life of a man of character and capacity, and not a necessary part of it." The reverend gentleman understood capital and property not as an input factor of enterprise but as a part of a man's identity and a product contingent upon his labour. Character necessarily produced capital because capital was an expression of character. "To say that private property ought not to exist," he protested, "is to say that individuals ought not to be themselves."[64] Though he recognized a man's right to sell his property in himself as wage labour, Cochrane was reluctant to accept that a man of deserving character should be forced to do so unfreely because of business failure.[65] Failure, with its destruction of capital, was alienating: a fragment of self was destroyed.

Yet Cochrane knew failure to occur where it should not. He endeavoured to explain: "Some men of the purest intentions, of the most upright character and honorable name ... never succeed in anything they undertake. ... [T]hey think it hard ... to give up all they have amassed to maintain their credit and honest name – to begin life anew so often, and never make any substantial progress."[66] Their fortune was providential, however, and "in the other sphere" they would find cause to thank God for removing the cause of their worry and strain. Losers would become winners.

The entries in *The Canadian Album* were true to Cochrane's conviction that outward prosperity told little of the true man. Few details were related about a man's material success beyond assurances that "it has assumed gigantic proportions" or that "it may be taken for granted that he is a success."[67] No doubt this was purposeful, since some subjects were men who must be judged respectable, but clearly undistinguished. From Brantford, besides representatives of the elite – William Buck, stove manufacturer; Adam Spence, carriage manufacturer; Alanson Harris, farm implement manufacturer; Charles H. Waterous, engine manufacturer – Cochrane selected Jacob Daniels, self-employed harnessmaker; William G. Raymond, piano tuner; John A. Leitch, insurance agent; Samuel G. Read, real estate agent. Concentrating on their pathways to success blurred the differences between them. Just as Spence's "untiring energy" enabled him to recover after fire consumed his factory, so too Daniels "lost all through fire but with unbounded energy ... started business again."[68] That the former operated a carriage factory and the latter a craft workshop was not the point. Through "enterprise and perseverance," Buck accumulated sufficient savings as a journeyman tinsmith to start his own business. Leitch, "raised under ... severe hardships and privations," "through energy and honest dealing ... soon obtained the confidence of the public, and before long made his way to the top of the ladder." Surely to be a major national manufacturer was to be considerably more successful than to be the leading insurance salesman in Brantford.[69] But each received equal space in *The Canadian Album*. Juxtapositions of this sort were innumerable: W.W. Ogilvie, Montreal miller, with Hugh Falconer, merchant tailor in the country village of Shelburne, Ontario; James H. Ashdown, former tinsmith and Winnipeg's leading hardware wholesaler, with D.C. Taylor, the leading tinsmith and hardware merchant in the village of Lucknow, Ontario.

Incongruities were denied, commonalties were stressed. Public service and good works attested to strength of character and spiritual well-being. The piano tuner was lauded for his work with the blind, the real estate agent for chairing his church's finance committee, the stove manufacturer for being treasurer of the Baptist Church Edifice Society – "earnest Christian workers" all.[70] And those who knew them already recognized them as such. The Shelburne tailor held "the confidence of all his acquaintances," while "all who are intimate with [the Montreal miller], especially his employees, are greatly attached to him."[71]

By today's standards, *The Canadian Album* was not a very good biographical dictionary. Historians do not often consult it, because its entries are short on detail and repetitious with homilies and clichés. It was so for a purpose. Cochrane sought to demonstrate incontrovertibly the commonalty of the bourgeoisie – solid, worthy men all, moral in character and diligent in labour. But should we conclude

that the differences in status which now seem so obvious were unapparent to the dictionary's first readers? Not necessarily. For fiction to
be sustained as fact demanded faith, and faith in individualism was
what Cochrane wished to strengthen. Still he was realist enough to
understand that faith, in this secular realm at least, was contingent
upon the recognition of merit by those in some position to reward
it. Such was the nature of the contract.

CONCLUSION

Discourse on the basis of success in individualism in the late nineteenth century took place within the context of significant changes
in the fortunes of the self-employed. By 1880 the small businessman,
committed though he might have been to independence as a social
and an economic goal in life, confronted a business climate which
offered him little chance of survival, let alone the accumulation of
wealth. Two-thirds of new businessmen and two-thirds of the least
wealthy 40 per cent failed to survive in business from 1871 to 1880.
Of course, the odds have probably seldom favoured small businessmen. However, even though they had earlier experienced high
rates of discontinuation, no statistically significant relationship
existed in the 1850s between quitting business and either recent self-
employment or limited wealth. In fact, it was this absence which had
created pre-industrial opportunities for self-employment. Ironically,
those men whose businesses and accumulated wealth made them
prominent as the captains of industry and merchant princes within
their community were men who had in general embarked upon their
careers in the 1850s with few assets or advantages. The security
which they enjoyed through the 1870s, despite a depression, contributed an obstacle to a similar advancement by men similar in social
origin: as a class, the bourgeoisie had become too successful, too big.
There was no more room at the top and, for that matter, little at the
bottom.

When men like Thomas Shenston and the Rev. William Cochrane
struggled to understand what had been and was happening, they
worked within long-accepted values of individual behaviour. They
could not deny the power of the strenuous individual and the justice
of the culture within which he toiled. To do so would deny their
understanding of their own success. Yet to sustain such convictions
required demonstrable evidence of their truth and their continuing
relevance. The first, truth, could be provided in the form of examples. The myth of the self-made man was myth in the sense that

history seldom repeats itself – faithfully at least – but it did personify the rewards of self-help. Relevance, however, required action from those already successful. Cochrane, for one, believed this would follow from the recognition of a common adherence to the values of self-help.

6 Social Change and Urban Politics

On the evening of Monday, 24 July, when William Paterson mounted the platform in the Brantford Town Hall to deliver his major speech as the Liberal candidate for South Brant in the 1872 Dominion election, he confronted an audience leavened with vocal critics of his party and his class. "What have the Reformers ever done for the workingman?" shouted one. Had George Brown not revealed the true face of liberalism just last month in his reaction to the Toronto printers' strike?[1] For that matter, had not the town's metal trades workers found out for themselves just the previous month in the Nine Hour Strike that Brantford's Reform manufacturers remained unprepared to accept their union and their collective demands for better wages and hours? What indeed had the Reform party ever done?

Paterson did not pander to the workingmen in his audience. "Many of you," he retorted, "would never have had the franchise if it had not been for the efforts of the Reform Party." He welcomed the participation of workingmen and mechanics on his campaign committee, for he believed that "one man is as good as another." But, he admitted that he "did not disapprove of the distinctions that exist in society, but did not believe that an honest man, strong in his inherent manhood, had any occasion to go down on his knees before another who happened to be more wealthy. ... If a man was a cringing sycophant in the presence of his superiors in the social scale, he was sure to adopt the role of despot towards his inferiors."[2] His liberalism was that of a self-made man and a major employer of industrial labour. He had started his working life in his mid-teens as a clerk for Ignatius Cockshutt. In the early 1860s he went into the confectionery business with Henry B. Leeming. Paterson's was the proud and conscious individualism of the master artisans and shopkeepers who had grown successful with their town. It was also a liberalism that was increasingly class specific in its appeal.

By the 1870s partisan politics in Brantford organized discernible class interests. Ben Forster has maintained that by the late 1870s pro-tariff businessmen had formed, albeit incompletely, "an ascending elite, which had both a sense of national mission and a consciousness of class."[3] Paul Craven and Tom Traves have argued that political support for the National Policy from the 1870s through the 1930s drew upon cross-class alliances within "a triadic class structure" of capitalist, labour, and farm interests.[4] The example of Brantford qualifies both of these interpretations. First, coalitional politics pre-dated the National Policy, and indeed existing alliances had to be supplanted prior to the formation of the National Policy coalition. Second, though Brantford's leading businessmen were increasingly conscious of their class, they remained uncommitted to tariff protection in the late 1870s. As Forster does acknowledge, businessmen gravitated to the Conservative party at an uneven pace and there did exist in the Liberal party a protectionist tendency in the mid-1870s.[5] In South Brant the Liberal party voiced the social convictions and community particularism of Brantford's successful industrial and commercial bourgeoisie and the successful farmers of the surrounding townships. It appealed to those for whom the policies and social processes of the past had been good. The Conservative party's espousal of a national political economy drew the support of a broader variety of social fragments, most prominently those of organizing workingmen and corporate capital, that is the Grand Trunk Railroad. By the late 1870s, it also attracted the interest of the increasingly marginalized petite bourgeoisie. For different reasons each group rejected the localism of Brantford's bourgeoisie.[6]

From the 1840s the town's leading businessmen had striven to sustain a community-oriented political agenda. Through the 1860s a conviction that the social benefits of policies designed to enhance the community as a centre of enterprise would be widely distributed held together Reform, Hincksite, and Tory coalitions of several social fragments for varying periods of time. A combination of factors shook that faith. Brantford's dreams of a regional commercial empire collapsed in the depression of 1857. With the Grand Trunk Railroad's take-over of the Buffalo and Lake Huron Railroad in 1864, control of transportation links passed beyond the reach of the community. Industrial capitalism distanced employers from their workers, and the confidence and control that was bred of close social contact in and out of the workplace diminished the deference that workers were prepared to grant their employers. Brantford's rail integration into a regional and national economy presented opportunities for expanded production and distribution, at the same time as it promoted competition from outside suppliers. Most susceptible to the toll of competition were those in the lower strata of the bourgeoisie, the independent tradesmen and small shopkeepers. Increasingly, they retreated into a "protective mentality," as Michael Bliss has termed it,[7] preferring the patronage of a national state to the leadership of the local capitalist elite.

As Herbert Gutman demonstrated, in small cities, more frequently than in larger centres, cross-class alliances could tie together fragments of labour and capital. However, while Gutman documented the formation of community-based common fronts against the intrusive power of large corporations, the example of Brantford reveals that in some political circumstances workers allied with those corporations they opposed over issues of wages and employment conditions.[8] The Conservative party assembled the dissatisfied social elements into a new coalition of interests. The Tory machine was a well-liquored combination of trade unionist sympathizers, vestigial Orange and Irish Catholic roughs, railroad contractors, distillers and liquor merchants, saloon keepers and ward politicians, shopkeepers and small manufacturers, contract seekers, Grand Trunk Railroad workers and especially Grand Trunk management. More than the sum of its parts, the South Brant Liberal-Conservative Association presented political forces that transcended the community particularism to which Brantford's bourgeois elite remained committed. Francis Hincks may have lost the 1872 election to William Paterson, but he carried the city, the farmers' vote giving Paterson a majority. The following year the Conservatives won control of municipal government and held it for nearly a decade.

Privatism, the use of public institutions to promote the private appropriation of capital, characterized, indeed drove, Brantford politics through the entire period under review. But to conclude, as Leo Johnson has concerning Guelph, Ontario, that the business community's use of municipal government evidenced a "clear perception concerning their interests as capitalists,"[9] is to take too broad a view and misses the fact that elections were contested. As an ideology, privatism may explain the lack of social justice in the city, as Alan Artibise has contended,[10] but by definition it also made urban politics an arena for competition among bourgeois fragments, with partisanship as its vehicle. So long as decisions critical to the economic well-being of Brantford's citizens could be made within the city, the local bourgeoisie fractured in efforts to build coalitions to seize the municipal apparatus. Once bourgeois control of local government was lost, and once forces perceived as external to the community came to exercise their influence over the urban economy, the local bourgeoisie itself coalesced and espoused an ideology of liberalism which defended the social processes to which it believed itself heir.

THE POLITICS OF COMMUNITY PARTICULARISM

From the late 1840s through the late 1860s, issues of local development preoccupied politics. Convinced that their community afforded the best location within which to achieve independence, Brantford residents chafed under the burden of obstacles to their progress. Initially town residents accepted and deferred to the leadership of the town's major businessmen and property owners. Who could better attend to local affairs than those with the most to gain from local advancement, argued the Brantford *Expositor*. "Are their interests not identified with those of Brantford? ... Is it not, therefore, ridiculous to suppose they would be obstruc[tive], and [have] their business and property deteriorated in extent and value?"[11] But, once the projects upon which the town's fate rested encountered difficulties, support for elite leadership decayed. By the late 1850s three elements voiced disaffection: an insurgent fragment within the business elite; a socially more varied group of discontented ratepayers from the small-property-holding stratum of shopkeepers, master artisans, and journeymen; and restive elements within the labouring class. Discontent shook elite leadership, briefly dislodging it from municipal office in 1855 and 1856. But the discontent proved too socially diffuse and mutually antagonistic to align for long. By the late 1850s and early 1860s, the elite won back the confidence of the majority of urban electors and regained control of municipal government on a platform of fiscal responsibility and law and order.

Transportation improvements were the major component in a political economy of local particularism. The Grand River Navigation Co., incorporated in 1832, had never lived up to its promise as a major commercial artery, and, by 1848 when it was finally completed to Brantford, its older works already needed repair. Its spotty financial record made the company's debentures difficult to market.[12] The better connections that a railroad might provide were contingent upon the ability of local interests to raise investment capital. But, prior to town incorporation in 1847, just maintaining the Brantford bridge sorely tested community resources. The leading boosters came to believe that district government was too distant and unsympathetic; the "supervisors of Gore & Brock District Council," they complained, are "individuals having different local interests, & [are] comparatively unconcerned in [Brantford's] advancement." Petitions calling for municipal institutions were submitted to the provincial government from the mid-1830s, but not until the incorporation of the town in 1847 and the county in 1853 were matters placed in the hands of "persons wholly chosen from its own residents and personally interested in its prosperity."[13]

Brantford's political and business leaders in the 1850s included the wealthiest men in town: P.C. VanBrocklin, iron founder and car manufacturer; Arunah Huntington, former shoemaker and general merchant, landowner and rentier; Ignatius Cockshutt, general merchant and landowner; Allen Cleghorn, wholesale and retail hardware merchant. Supporting them was a cadre of politicos, with their own more modest business and property interests, most notably J.D. Clement, former innkeeper, post master, and through the 1850s and 1860s frequent alderman, reeve, and mayor. At the provincial level, David Christie, whose extensive farm was not far from town, ably served the elite.

The register of the subscribers for stock in the Buffalo and Brantford Railway in 1850 attested to the elite's support among shopkeepers and artisans (table 6.1).[14] Forty-six of the town's self-employed took shares in the corporation. It is not surprising that 60 per cent of the local business investors were among the wealthiest 20 per cent of the business population. The other 80 per cent were not unrepresented. Their participation, accounting for 40 per cent of business investors, demonstrated a willingness to risk higher taxes to promote the railroad. So long as the elite was successful, it enjoyed wide social support.

Yet, the design was flawed. Most of Brantford's canal and railroad supporters hoped to profit from the facilities as users, clients, suppliers, and speculators. A fascination with the potential social benefits of these projects blinded their sponsors to the operational challenges attending the management of viable private corporations. Moreover, their limited perspective led them to assume that transportation companies should quickly become self-financing.[15]

This assumption was explicit in the town's fiscal policy. In 1851, council approved a loan for the Grand River Navigation Co. of £42,000 in municipal bonds secured by a mortgage upon the company's works and the right to nominate two members to its board.[16] The navigation company in turn assigned the town bonds to the

Table 6.1

Occupation and Economic Rank of Brantford Investors in the Buffalo and Brantford Railway, 1850

Occupation	Economic Rank				
	0–39	40–79	80–89	90–100	All
Iron founder			2	1	3
Builder/Contractor			1	2	3
Miller	1			1	2
Cordwainer			1	1	2
Carriage maker		1			1
Saddler			1		1
Fanning mill maker		1			1
Newspaper publisher		1			1
General merchant	2	2	3	7	14
Hardware merchant		1			1
Forwarder				1	1
Wood and coal merchant		2			2
Grocer		2	3		5
Druggist	1		1		2
Innkeeper	1	2	1		4
Stable keeper	1				1
Stage proprietor				1	1
Auctioneer					1
All	6	12	13	15	45

Bank of Upper Canada as security for its line of credit.[17] The town's recourse to the Consolidated Municipal Loan Fund made possible more extensive financial assistance. The fund pooled the borrowing power of individual municipalities. Provincial debentures, paying 6 per cent annually, were transferred to a municipality for marketing. In return the municipality agreed to pay the fund 8 per cent annually to cover the interest due bondholders, the 2 per cent difference going to a sinking fund to retire the bonds on maturity. Loan fund bonds were secured, in principle at least, first, by the participating municipalities' collective ability to tax their residents and, second, by the provincial government's commitment to impose a property tax on municipalities defaulting on their payments to the fund. The Brantford Town Council in 1852 used loan fund bonds to purchase £25,000 in shares of the Buffalo and Brantford Railway. After the destruction of its Brantford car shops in 1854, council transferred a further £100,000 in bonds to the railroad, taking as security £119,000 in second mortgage bonds upon the road's works.[18] As with the earlier loan to the navigation company, this transaction was intended to allow a painless redemption of the bonds. The interest on railroad bonds and the mortgage payments from the navigation would pay the town's obligations to the loan fund and the municipal bondholders. The greater value of bonds given to the town in security would make possible contributions to the sinking fund without raising municipal taxes. At least that was the theory of municipal finance to which the first town councils subscribed.

Municipal grants gave transportation companies serving Brantford a financial structure which was, in the words of the Baring brothers, "a pyramid – a very excellent pyramid – but one which unfortunately stands the wrong end up."[19] When the pyramid tipped, it fell on the companies and the Town of Brantford. The companies' payments of interest upon their bonded and mortgage debt depended upon their operating revenues. Neither proved sufficient. Moreover, the practice of exchanging company and municipal bonds worsened the companies' financial position, since they remained liable for sums greater than the par value of the bonds conveyed to them. The need to discount municipal and loan fund bonds further increased the spread between the amount owed and what was received from the town. The Grand River Navigation, for example, had to offer a 25 per cent discount on Brantford bonds in 1855.[20]

Operational problems beset both the navigation and the railroad. Even with improvements, the navigation could not compete with railroads and could not even maintain its works. Maintenance problems made the flow of water so undependable that the lessees of the water power sites and wharves were reluctant to pay their rents. For two years, 1851 and 1852, navigation was closed for want of repairs. In 1859 the company could not meet its obligations to the Bank of Upper Canada, which in turn threatened to auction Brantford bonds to cover the overdraft. Nor could it pay interest on its mortgage; it was bankrupt. To protect its own credit, the town bought its bonds from the bank, and two years later foreclosed the mortgage on the navigation and itself became the proprietor of the works.[21]

The Buffalo, Brantford and Goderich Railway was no more successful. By 1855 its liabilities exceeded its assets by $1.9 million. The line remained incomplete past Brantford, although road work had progressed to Goderich. Between Buffalo and Brantford, the track had been laid quickly and still required additional ballast; many of the trestles were temporary and some of those which were not had been poorly designed and constructed. To make matters worse, the company still had not obtained clear title to five-sixths of its right of way. In January 1856 the trains stopped running, and the board of directors sought government approval to sell the company to its

English bondholders, who had formed the Buffalo and Lake Huron Railway to take it over.

Through these difficulties, the Town of Brantford still had to make payments to the Consolidated Municipal Loan Fund. By late 1854 it was readily apparent to all that taxes would have to be increased the following year. Concerned ratepayers held a public meeting in January and struck a citizen's committee to investigate the affairs of the railroad. Their fears seemed only too real when, in early May 1855, the provincial government demanded a payment, and a municipal delegation hurried to Quebec for discussions.[22]

The failure of the Buffalo, Brantford and Goderich Railway broke the unity of the business elite. A group of ambitious businessmen, who, though perhaps not as wealthy as Cockshutt, Huntington, or VanBrocklin, did command significant assets, hoped to develop more effective transportation links for the town. Chief among them was George S. Wilkes, Brantford's own "John Law," as the *Expositor* called him. Supporting him were A.B. Bennett, iron founder; J.H. Moore, general merchant; and John McNaught, carriage manufacturer. They had for some time disagreed with the north-south transportation strategy of the Buffalo, Brantford and Goderich's route. Instead they wanted integration into an east-west trunk line, preferably in connection with the Great Southern Railway.[23] Sympathetic to their plans were the railroad's creditors, who feared their accounts would never be paid. Most notable was the contracting firm of Mellish, Morrell, and Russell, which had erected the car shops as well as undertaken some of the road work. Along with them were their subcontractors, still waiting for payment. At a public meeting of ratepayers, Wilkes and Moore were elected members of a citizen's committee to investigate the railroad's problems. Their report castigated the "Old Clique" for waste, mismanagement, and generally allowing Buffalo interests to ruin the company.[24]

By 1855 any further rail promotion in Brantford clearly was foolhardy and beyond the town's fiscal resources. The Great Western evinced some interest in taking over the troubled line, but only at the bargain price of two-thirds its construction cost.[25] Even if more money had been offered, it was feared that the Great Western would shut the line down after purchase. Instead Wilkes and friends wanted the existing company to lease the operation of the railroad at a minimal charge to a local company. To facilitate the negotiation of such an arrangement, Wilkes devised an ingenious scheme: town council, which was given representation on the railroad's board in lieu of voting its shares, would sell 4,000 shares to Wilkes for £20,000 on fifteen years' credit. Wilkes would then sell shares to sympathizers, pack the shareholders' meeting, and elect officers and directors sympathetic to Brantford interests. Wilkes's scheme gained favour with another dissatisfied faction. Mayor William Mathews, elected to office in 1855 by the discontented shopkeepers, artisans, and small property owners, persuaded council to adopt a by-law permitting the share sale as proposed by Wilkes. The "Old Clique" fought back and blocked the sale by introducing a suit in Chancery, thereby derailing the take-over bid. Nonetheless, it was apparent that the deference to elite direction of municipal affairs had been seriously weakened.

WILLIAM MATHEWS AND THE CHALLENGE TO DEFERENTIAL POLITICS

Wilkes and company willingly accepted the support that Mathews could give to their railroad manoeuvres, but they were sorely mistaken if they thought he and his followers would fall in behind their leadership. The political ambitions of Mathews and Wilkes conflicted. But more significant were the social dimensions of the positions of each. The insurgency of the Wilkes faction aimed at replacing the municipal leadership of one element of the business elite with that of another. Mathews sought deeper political change which would convey municipal control to representatives of the artisan and shopkeeping stratum in alliance with the labouring class. Even when collaborating with Wilkes, Mathews never hesitated to condemn the rich, to question their business ethics, and to call for better treatment for the common people. For a time through the late 1850s, with the economic distress arising from the railroad collapse and the depression of 1857, Mathews achieved success.

That success united the elite behind a new coalition, a respectable "law and order" party offended by Mathews's willingness to take politics into the streets.

Mathews, an Irish Methodist cordwainer and auctioneer born about 1810, had settled in Brantford in the early 1830s and quickly gained notoriety as a supporter of William Lyon Mackenzie. With the collapse of the western rebellion, Mathews fled to the United States for a time. After his return, he cultivated political support among his Protestant and Catholic countrymen.[26] In 1850 and 1853 through 1857 he was elected to council, which elected him reeve in 1850, deputy reeve in 1854, and mayor in 1855 and 1856. Though unsuccessful in pursuit of municipal office for a decade thereafter, he continued to voice the concerns of the "people" against the municipal stewardship of the wealthy.

Mathews's willingness to collaborate with Catholics and Orangemen gave his populism a distinctive class nature that differed from that described by Barrie Dyster in his study of Captain Bob Moodie of Toronto's St John Ward. As Greg Kealey has remarked about the Orange Order and class politics in Toronto during the same era, bourgeois hegemony required the cultivation of working-class consent rather than the plebeian deference to authority and station which had characterized patrician dominance.[27] Mathews demonstrated that consent was not given easily or unreservedly. His faction on council asserted its independence from elite direction in no uncertain terms. One of his supporters, James Bellhouse, a self-employed carpenter and first-term alderman, in 1855 loudly announced his resentment of the elite's expectation of deference, and protested the lack of respect they gave him in council. Some were "so aristocratic that they would not second the resolution of a working man."[28] Mathews himself espoused a number of causes which needled the commercial elite. In particular, he championed the cause of the volunteer firemen.

Attitudes toward the fire-fighters were an important test of social cohesion, since the wealth of the few frequently depended upon the willingness of the many to risk their lives. Each of the several fire companies was a self-contained and self-disciplined unit, adopting its own rules, electing its own officers, charging dues, fining members who did not turn out for alarms, maintaining and even purchasing its own equipment. The individual companies competed with one another to arrive first at any fire and to contribute the most to extinguishing it. A chief engineer, elected by the companies and approved by town council, co-ordinated their efforts at the scene and on public occasions. Membership in the brigade appealed to young men from a broad middling social stratum – clerks, shopkeepers, and master and journeyman artisans – who wanted adventure, camaraderie, friendly competition, and a chance to enjoy community esteem. In return, the firemen expected respect and municipal funding not just for expensive equipment, such as fire engines, but also to entertain visiting firemen and to travel themselves. They wanted prizes for the first company at a fire, and they wanted property owners to treat them to beer and cheese and oysters after a fire. They wanted uniforms, not for work, but for parade. They wanted parades and gunpowder to celebrate the Queen's birthday. The expenses of fire-fighting to the town were indirect, as much symbolic and social as practical. Young men, many of whom were not property owners, protected the property of others, expecting that with full

maturity they too might at least be small freeholders and independent artisans and shopkeepers. Indeed many of those who in the
1850s owned considerable property had belonged to the brigade in
the 1830s and 1840s. By the late 1850s, with the town in financial
difficulty, many property owners balked at the firemen's requests and
refused to recognize the reciprocity embedded in their voluntary
contribution.[29] William Mathews championed the volunteers' cause.

In 1856 the chief engineer, William Sinon, a thirty-four-year-old
self-employed Irish Catholic carpenter and alderman since 1853, led
a delegation which presented council with a petition requesting a fire
hall for meetings and other occasions. The officers supporting him
included James Hammill, a twenty-six-year-old self-employed stonecutter; Amos Currier, a thirty-three-year-old American blacksmith,
also self-employed; William Morgan, a thirty-two-year-old English
shopkeeper; and John Noble, a thirty-one-year-old self-employed
painter from Ireland.[30] Mathews, himself a former volunteer, supported their request and, as a confirmed temperance man, believed
that the firemen should not have to resort to saloons for their meetings and recreations. The money received from the Clergy Reserves
Fund, about £2,000, he suggested, could be used for the project.[31]
The business and propertied elite were aghast at the suggestion.
Other charges were surely more pressing – roads, sidewalks, the
bridge over the Grand, the gas works. The *Expositor* asked "whether
the first object to be obtained is not the reduction of taxation. ... It
is a mystery how these windy, gassy men are elected to manage
municipal finances in preference to solid men of business habits."[32]
Responding to the protest, council rejected the mayor's recommendation and refused to build a fire hall.

Their low priority offended the firemen. If the council would not
meet their requests, they would not fight fires. On several occasions
over the next seven years, the companies disbanded in protest, and
repeatedly council granted concessions to persuade them to reorganize.[33] Disturbed by what they considered the unpredictable
behaviour of the firemen, the town's major property owners sought
more direct participation in fire-fighting. Their vehicle was a new
engine company, the Washington Independent Fire Co., formed in
early 1860. The company was well funded with donations from the
Brantford prominent, most generously from Ignatius Cockshutt.
While it would be an exaggeration to term this a gentlemen's company, since artisans and shopkeepers joined up, its ranks included
several notable businessmen, like dry goods merchant and militia
officer William Grant, and the sons of property owners, like J.D.
Clement's son, Alex, and James Wilkes's son, George H.[34] A second

engine company was mooted under the auspices of the local YMCA in which Cockshutt and Thomas Shenston were actively involved. Its prospectus is of interest, since its regulations implied what was objectionable in the other companies. The company asked town council to hire a "trustworthy" man to look after its engine. The uniforms would be cheap, just a small red cap, to be provided by the subscribers to the company. Only one meeting a year would be held and that solely to elect officers – no banquets or balls. The men would not turn out for "perambulations" and, when called, would go directly to and from the fire. At the fire they were "to work hard, without the use of any profane language or intoxicating drink." Any offerings received from grateful property owners would be turned over to the YMCA. Town council was interested, but the company never became operational, probably because no red-blooded young men wanted to enlist in such a joyless assembly.[35]

The question of just who was in control of the fire brigades came to a head over the selection of the chief engineer. Both sides claimed the right to elect the chief, the firemen asserting their independence as free volunteers, council because it paid his salary. In early 1864 council ignored the firemen's nominee, William Hunter, a self-employed carpenter, and appointed instead John Turner, a prominent architect and builder. When informed of council's disregard for their wishes, three of the four brigades – the Independent Hook and Ladder Co., the Exchange Engine Co. no. 4, and the Rescue Engine Co. no. 1 – about 150 men in all, resigned. The volunteers organized a protest parade and, headed by their drum and flute band, they marched with burning torches through the streets which they had so recently protected from fire – a vivid spectacle! They then retired to the confectionery shop of Henry Leeming and William Paterson to consider further action.[36] The firemen nominated Paterson as their compromise choice for engineer and decided that if council still refused they would sell their equipment and distribute the proceeds among themselves. To that end, Paterson infuriated council with an offer to sell the Hook and Ladder Co.'s engine to them for $300. How could the firemen sell equipment purchased for them by public subscription, council asked?[37] That was municipal property. To the volunteers, the equipment was their property, bought for them, maintained and repaired by them at their expense, and used by them when they risked their lives to protect others' property.

Through the winter of 1864–5, only the Washington Independent Engine Co. remained in operation. Reluctantly in the spring of 1865 council agreed to accept the services of the reorganized brigade with Paterson as chief.[38] His participation in the dispute made him a target for continuing abuse from several councillors who remained critical of the brigade. Paterson held his position for only a year, although he remained a captain of the Exchange Co. for some time longer.[39] Through his involvement in the fire brigade politics, Paterson developed a reputation as spokesman for the independent artisans and shopkeepers of Brantford.

The disputes arising from the social relations which organized fire protection were symptomatic of the strain between the business elite and the town's shopkeepers, artisans, and workingmen. Yet, the latter groups remained committed to re-establishing a system of reciprocal obligations and deference. William Mathews tested the limits of the challenge to elite leadership when he became embroiled in a controversy over public schooling.

Mathews and his constituency generally supported educational reform, but they objected to the intrusion of the state into family life. Their resistance placed them at odds with the promoters of public education among the elite. Although shopkeeper and artisan representation increased on the school board, the chairmanship through the 1850s remained with the elite: P.C. VanBrocklin chaired it in 1850; Alexander Kirkland, a hardware merchant, in 1851–2; James Wilkes, a merchant, from 1854 to 1857; and Allen Cleghorn in 1858–9.[40]

In May of 1856, Miss Jennings, the head female teacher at Brantford High School, twice strapped thirteen-year-old Jane McKay for truancy and disobedience. The corporal punishment meted out to his daughter so incensed Duncan McKay, a self-employed Scottish saddler, that he laid charges against the teacher. McKay was influential among the town's artisans and had used his influence on Mathews' behalf in the previous municipal elections. Mathews as mayor was also the police magistrate, and he ordered a uniformed constable to serve Miss Jennings with a warrant during school hours. Humiliated before her students, Miss Jennings feared that she would not receive a fair trial before Mathews and so appealed to another justice of the peace, Thomas Shenston, to guarantee the impartiality of the legal proceedings against her. Shenston was sympathetic to the "Old Clique" and offended by Mathews's style of politics. He claimed his right as a magistrate to sit in judgment with Mathews in this or any other case not involving town by-laws. Moreover, he contended that because the conduct of a lady was in question, it was inappropriate to hear the trial in the police station. He would himself prefer to hold proceedings involving women in the privacy of his own house.

Mathews conceded that the case could be tried in the less unsavoury surroundings of the town hall, but he refused to allow Shenston to share the bench, arguing that the latter's intervention at the accused's request rendered his impartiality questionable. Surely a defendant should not hunt around for a magistrate favourably disposed to her cause! Shenston was not easily put off. Once the trial began, he attempted to participate, publicly announcing his right as justice of the peace and trying to examine witnesses over Mathews's objections.

Frustrated by what he took as Mathews's tyranny, Shenston mounted a campaign to impeach the mayor. At its first meeting in June, he presented a petition to council calling for Mathews's removal from office. As chair of the meeting, Mathews tried to rule the petition out of order, but P.B. Long, a lawyer and supporter of Shenston, introduced a motion to accept the petition. William B. Hurst, a "low grocer" and Mathews supporter, moved to amend Long's motion so that the issue of confidence in the mayor would be determined by the ratepayers. The amendment carried ten to four. Anticipating the threat to their tribune, a crowd of three hundred citizens had packed the chambers and when the question was put to them, they gave Mathews a resounding vote of confidence. The *Expositor* doubted that the decision reflected public opinion accurately; "it was clear that Mr. Shenston's friends were by far the most numerous," the paper contended, "but they were not of the class to compete with the characters that had assembled."[41]

The fate of Miss Jennings, sadly, has been lost in the record of Shenston v Mathews. But the affray did establish the prerogative of parents to challenge a teacher's authority. Indeed Duncan McKay shortly thereafter won election to the Board of School Trustees and in 1859 was a member of the board which reprimanded teacher Thomas Muir for expelling a student he judged disobedient. Historians of education have invested this incident with some significance, since it elicited Egerton Ryerson's shrill defence of the teacher's right to enforce discipline. That the trustees had already decided otherwise and that Ryerson's rebuttal was a powerless parting grump has been forgotten. The artisans and shopkeepers on the board, including, besides McKay, shoemaker James Woodyatt, tinsmith Thomas Cowherd, and grocers William Hurst, Thomas James, and George Watt, refused to countenance what they believed to be arbitrary punishment for the sake of the larger cause of classroom order. The merchants on the board, Allen Cleghorn, Robert Sproule, and John Taylor, accepted that Muir had erred, but they feared that a reprimand "would have the effect of ruining the school ... and would encourage insubordination and no teacher would ever be able to maintain discipline."[42] Thus they persuaded the board that an affirmation of the importance of order in the school should balance criticism of an individual teacher. Such a decision permitted unanimity between factions of trustees, though Ryerson accurately perceived it as an affront to teacher authority.

School promotion provoked a certain testiness among artisan and shopkeeper elements in Brantford. They wanted the benefits of schooling for their children, but also wanted control of the institution. Nonetheless, Mathews's treatment of Miss Jennings became an issue in the 1857 municipal election. Even those displeased with the authority assumed by schools and teachers might not wish a young woman subjected to a courtroom spectacle. On the eve of polling, the Brantford *Herald*, controlled by George S. Wilkes, urged the town's artisans and workingmen to choose more moderate representatives who might ally with responsible business leaders: "Should Mr. Mathews and his tools be again returned to the offices they have disgraced by their incapacity, by the suffrages of the workingmen, the prejudices of the anti-popular party will be strengthened and their predictions to a certain extent verified. The election will show that a man may successfully excite the envy and hatred of our people against fellow citizens, *simply because* they have improved their conditions in life, because they have built comfortable houses, wear good clothes, ride in neat equipages or keep a well-bred horse. ... Will you give the enemies of your rights ground for saying that you may be cajoled and deceived by any blatant idler who will flatter you and abuse the class with which you are closely connected and to which you aspire – the employing class?"[43]

Mathews's vote shrank. Even though his strong-arm boys laid siege to the poll, a sufficient number of opposing voters got through to reduce his majority to a single vote. The count so enraged his followers that they wrecked George Fleming's saloon, where earlier in the day opposition forces had been marshalled.[44] The violence of Mathews's campaign and his narrow margin of victory precluded his election to the mayor's chair by the new council. Picked instead was Thomas Botham, partner in the second largest general merchandising firm and one of the wealthiest businessmen.

Though Mathews was kept from the mayor's chair in 1857, his political engagement remained undiminished as he directed his attention to provincial politics. In 1854 he had been touted as a potential Reform candidate for one of the two new ridings in Brant County.[45] His nomination, however, was a remote possibility, given that the county Reform organization was controlled by the "Old Clique" and Clear Grit farmers who were committed to two rural candidates, David Christie and Herbert Biggar. The Liberal-Conservative party, appealing to Hincksite Reformers who believed reform had been achieved in all its essentials, offered a more congenial political home for the former rebel.

Other insurgent elements dissatisfied with the Old Clique's leadership, most notably George S. Wilkes, coquetted with the Liberal-Conservatives. The ambitions of Mathews and Wilkes contended and created difficulties for the party organization. Initially the 1858 campaign for the provincial assembly promised three-cornered races in the two ridings of Brant County. In West Brant, Wilkes intended to run as a hybrid Hincksite Reformer-Independent Ministerialist against Biggar, the incumbent, and Allen Good, an "old fossil Tory". In East Brant, Mathews wanted to run as a Liberal-Conservative against Christie and Daniel McKerlie, a Brantford lawyer who had briefly held the seat in 1854 as a Hincksite supporter of the Conservatives until Christie's protest unseated him.[46] Good was persuaded to resign in favour of Wilkes.[47] Pressure was placed upon Mathews not to run against McKerlie, but he would not give up the campaign and instead decided to run against Wilkes and Biggar. Mathews campaigned aggressively once more. His men disrupted one rural meeting so that Biggar could not speak, creating a disturbance which was, in the *Expositor*'s report, "perfectly disgusting to the farmers present, who are unaccustomed to that kind of ruffianism."[48] Brant's refined agriculturists responded by burning Mathews in effigy. Either the Liberal-Conservative organization got to Mathews or he sensed that the tide was against him, for he did finally withdraw, though not gracefully. He chose first to meet Wilkes in debate – if the series of insults and abuse that the two hurled about can be dignified by the term. At its conclusion, Mathews announced his withdrawal, but in no way expressed favour for Wilkes.

Notwithstanding Mathews's ill-humour, the Liberal-Conservatives met with a degree of success as Wilkes carried Brantford decisively, reversing the landslide which Biggar had enjoyed in 1854 at the urban polls. But Brantford electors cast only about a third of the votes in the constituency, and Biggar's rural support assured his victory. The Liberal-Conservative gains in Brantford, however, did not represent a realignment of social forces, and, in the end, Mathews repelled the insurgent business interests.

In May 1858 several Hincksites, including George S. Wilkes, sought readmission to the Reform fold. They proposed one of their own, James Kerby, hotelkeeper and land speculator, for the Reform nomination for the provincial legislative council. They were rebuffed, however, and on Allen Cleghorn's motion were ejected from the meeting selecting delegates to the Reform convention which would nominate the candidate in Erie Division.[49] Instead of rebounding to the Conservatives, they backed Kerby in his bid as an "independent Ministerialist."

During the campaign the opposition press identified sixty-five of Kerby's backers.[50] Since he received only eighty votes in Brantford, these names make up a fairly complete survey of his support. Sixty were self-employed and were drawn from all levels of the business community: thirteen were merchants or bankers, another thirteen builders and manufacturers, seventeen artisans, and sixteen tavern- and shopkeepers. Dissatisfaction with elite leadership fractured in two separate and hostile ways. The self-employed followed the peregrinations of Wilkes; many journeymen and labourers went with Mathews to the Liberal-Conservatives.

Mathews himself worked vigorously in the campaign for his party's candidate, Robert R. Bown of Bow Park Farm. Most notable was his orchestration of the riot which broke up a public meeting and Reform banquet in late September. Public meetings, convened by municipal officials under the provisions of 7 Vict. c. 12, constituted forums to declare community opinion. Packing meetings, controlling the platform, and disrupting proceedings could be important tactics in cajoling, persuading, and ultimately defining opinion. The Conservatives feared that the presence of leading Reformers George Brown, Oliver Mowat, M.H. Foley, and Luther Holton on the platform with David Christie would draw so many Reform sympathizers that any Conservative resolution would be resoundingly defeated and, conversely, any Reform declaration loudly proclaimed.

Mathews, Daniel Gilkison, a lawyer, and Henry Lemmon, Orange leader and Brantford *Courier* publisher, wrote followers and posted placards calling on all Orangemen and Conservatives to gather. For its annual parades and soirées in the late 1850s, the Orange Lodge could muster as many as five hundred men, making it a potent political force.[51] Rail fares were paid to bring in about fifty men from Dunnville for extra muscle. To work up their men for the meeting, Conservative organizers deposited money at a number of local saloons for drinks through the day. When the county warden, Daniel Anderson, called the meeting to order, Mathews led a charge which forced the platform party to retreat. Another effort to start the meeting at a different location failed when the rioters, some reported to be armed with guns, again rushed the stage, threatening Christie's life. The Reformers beat off their attackers and retreated to the Kerby House, where they were able to hold their banquet, despite occasional disruptions from infiltrators.[52]

Christie won the election, impressively receiving almost twice as many votes as his two opponents combined. He even carried Brantford, though by a plurality. The victory revealed renewed support for the "Old Clique" and some healing in the ranks of the business elite. Indeed, shortly thereafter George S. Wilkes was selected as delegate to the Reform convention of 1859, served on the convention's resolution committee, and spoke emotionally in defence of the Rebellion of 1837.[53]

Though kept from office, Mathews would not relent in denouncing elite political direction. In 1858 he voiced the artisan's traditional concern over the use of convict labour and provoked a government inquiry into the conduct of county sheriff and jailer George Keatchie, an appointee owing his job to the Old Clique–Clear Grit faction controlling county council.[54] Mathews kept up the pressure during the municipal campaign of 1859 by denouncing the predation of the wealthy upon the poor. At a nomination in December 1858, he singled out his old adversary Thomas Shenston for particular abuse, charging him with usury. In 1859 he demanded that municipal council provide relief for the growing number of unemployed. In early March, a hundred men showed up when the town did offer road-grading work at fifty cents a day. Shortly thereafter, Mathews called on the town to sell £5,000 in railway bonds to finance municipal works. When council decided to appropriate only $1,000, a crowd of frustrated job seekers caused such a disturbance that the council meeting had to adjourn.[55] In January 1860 Mathews turned on one of the town's major industrial employers. He charged that a recent fire at Ganson, Waterous and Co.'s foundry and machine works had been arson, set by the financially hard-pressed firm for the insurance coverage.[56] For his continuing service to the cause, Attorney-General John A. Macdonald rewarded the old rebel with a magistracy in 1859.[57]

Despite official approbation, locally Mathews found Conservative businessmen trying to distance themselves from him. When the Reformers staked out the moral high ground by calling themselves the "law and order party," the Conservatives adopted the "moderate" label and proclaimed the business acumen of their candidates as a qualification for public office. Notwithstanding their efforts at moderation, the Conservatives lost both their composure and control of municipal government to the "law and order" elite in 1859. The incumbent "moderate" mayor, Matthew W. Pruyn, a wholesale grocer, liquor merchant, and creditor to most of the town's groceries and groggeries, let it be known that licence renewals were at stake and all efforts to get out the vote would be appreciated. More overtly on election day his rowdies attempted to get unregistered voters accepted at the polls in the East Ward, and in the North Ward his men battled with "law and order" supporters. Thomas Botham, the "law and order" man, had not deigned to solicit votes personally and left the free electors of Brantford to judge for themselves. They chose him and eleven of the fifteen "law and order" candidates for council.[58]

The final achievement in restoring elite political control was the Reform victory in 1863 of E.B. Wood over the independent incumbent, William Ryerson in West Brant.[59] Once more Mathews stirred the mob against the elite candidate. One Tuesday evening in mid-June, Mathews's "ruffians" attacked the Scotland Brass Band and several teams of Wood's supporters as they marched up Dalhousie Street to attend a rally. Rocks were hurled at the marchers, and the Union Jack was torn from the flag bearer and trampled under foot as the two sides fought. Wood began his speech from the balcony of the Brant Hotel overlooking the mêlée. "Big Thunder," as he came to be known in the assembly for his booming voice, could not outshout Mathews who stirred the mob to greater violence by yelling, "Who called Mr. Ryerson an ass?" Wood wisely retreated and achieved victory at the polls if not in the streets.[60]

Despite regaining control of the local political apparatus, the business elite found their freedom of movement constrained by forces beyond their control and outside their community. The elite initially had some reservations about Wood because of his retainer as legal counsel for the Buffalo and Lake Huron, though Wood had for the time assuaged their concerns by pledging himself to uphold the independence of the constituency and to resist the use of government patronage within it.[61]

In the end, Wood proved unable to serve two masters and cleaved to the Buffalo and Lake Huron and, after its takeover, the Grand Trunk. Despite its completion to Goderich and an arrangement with a shipping line for steamship service from there to Chicago and Milwaukee,[62] the Buffalo and Lake Huron barely covered operating costs. By 1863 the railroad could not pay the $11,534 per annum interest it owed on the town's bonds. Its English bondholders agreed first to forego interest for three years on their investment in the company and later to capitalize that interest as additional bondholding.[63] Concessions were also sought from the Town of Brantford, and the company asked the town to surrender its bonds and petition the government to forgive its obligations to the Consolidated Fund.[64]

Even if the town had accepted, and it did not, the railroad would have remained liable for $72,000 in railroad bonds sold by the town to finance various municipal projects. Council did agree, however, to accept a reduced payment of $9,230, the interest required by the fund, and to capitalize the balance at 6 per cent secured by additional bonds.[65]

The railroad's operational difficulties required a more lasting solution. In 1863 it entered a temporary agreement with the Grand Trunk Railway to use the Buffalo to Stratford section as an American link, while details of merger were negotiated.[66] To town council's chagrin, it lost the loyalty of its member of parliament, as E.B. Wood defended the amalgamation and appeared to display little concern for Brantford's interests. Most offensive to the town was the clause that interest payments on the Buffalo and Lake Huron bonds were to be paid only from the net receipts taken by the Grand Trunk from the old Buffalo and Lake Huron line. Reduced operations and imaginative accounting might well reduce these profits to nothing.[67]

LOCAL PROPRIETORS AND OUTSIDE CORPORATIONS: THE GRAND TRUNK RAILWAY AND URBAN POLITICS

As the business elite feared, the amalgamation of the Buffalo and Lake Huron with the Grand Trunk led to reduced rail service. Concerned citizens admitted that the Grand Trunk was not entirely to blame, since the abrogation of the Reciprocity Treaty in 1864 diminished the value of the Buffalo connection. What incensed Brantford businessmen was the disregard for local interests that the Grand Trunk displayed in not providing greater access to east-west transport. The Maritimes, the North-West, and even Japan seemed to beckon as markets for Brant County produce and manufactures. To make matters worse, rumours circulated that the Grand Trunk planned to move the car shops to Stratford on its main line.[68]

Only a challenge to the Grand Trunk's monopoly in Brantford, thought the business elite, would result in better service. In early 1866 several of the major property owners and businessmen – Ignatius Cockshutt, Thomas McLean, C.H. Waterous, J.D. Clement, Alfred Watts, George S. Wilkes, and John Montgomery – formed a company to construct a branch line from Brantford to the Great Western Railway at Harrisburgh. On completion the track would be leased to the Great Western for operation.[69] Municipal subsidies would be critical to the success of this venture. True to his past record of creative financing, George S. Wilkes devised a scheme whereby the road might be constructed without imposing a serious burden upon the town or its ratepayers. Since the Grand Trunk was only obliged to pay the town sufficient bond interest to meet the town's obligations to the Consolidated Fund, those bonds held by the town in excess of the amount necessary to draw that interest, Wilkes argued, might be sold, even at a discount if need be.[70]

To effect this financial sleight-of-hand, the business elite needed to control municipal government. Naturally the Grand Trunk had no desire to see competition financed through the sale of its own securities. While the Buffalo and Lake Huron had generally supported the elite's municipal stewardship earlier, or at least remained aloof from politics, its successor opposed local business leaders and cultivated more sympathetic politicians in whose support it endeavoured to mobilize its employees' votes. Having secured E.B. Wood at the provincial level, the Grand Trunk won an ally at the municipal level by directing a number of contracts to John Elliott, builder and Conservative organizer.[71]

The Grand Trunk "ring," as its critics denounced it, held control of town council with Elliot as mayor in 1866, 1867, and 1868.[72] Direct opposition to the Harrisburgh railroad clearly would have been impolitic. Elliott and his faction on council, therefore, were prepared to endorse resolutions in favour of the branch, but preferred to leave the initiative in other quarters. Council might assist the Great Western if it were to build the line, but without a hefty subsidy in advance that railroad had no intention of building a line which even its promoters confessed was unlikely to pay dividends.[73] Under Elliott's administration, financial assistance was improbable. Criticized for delay, the mayor claimed sound fiscal management as his main concern. He would not jeopardize municipal finances to build a railroad for a few grain dealers, merchants, and manufacturers. If Brantford's business leaders wanted the line so badly, he countered, then why were they not investing their capital in it? In his opinion Brantford's fate depended on the Grand Trunk: "If you would build up the town of Brantford," Elliott argued, "you build up the Grand Trunk Railway."[74]

The business community had no intention of abdicating control over the local economy to any external corporation, and its members pieced together a non-partisan coalition to defend community particularism. Dry goods merchant Thomas McLean headed a "People's Ticket" drafted to unseat the "ring." After the votes were counted, Elliott retained the mayoralty, but "People's" candidates had taken the reeve's and deputy reeve's offices and three of ten aldermanic positions.[75] Despite its name, the "People's Party" in its first campaign was only too clearly the voice of the business elite, mainly Grit with a few Tories. Perhaps to compensate for this, its candidates over the next few years changed the standard lexicon of political rhetoric. Whereas businessmen had previously asserted their commercial acumen as their qualification for public office, increasingly they tempered the record of their achievements with references to their humble origins. Charles B. Heyd, for example, a grocer and son of a Swiss immigrant who had been a foreman in the car shops, was described as "a good businessman, a large property owner ... [and] undoubtedly a working man."[76] Notwithstanding such declarations, the credibility of the "People's Party" was enhanced in late 1868 when the irrepressible William Mathews joined the cause.

That Mathews should unite with his bitter political foes may have smacked of political opportunism on the part of both. If so, no one suggested it. The community particularism they had shared earlier persisted. Accepting Thomas McLean's nomination of him for mayor in 1869, Mathews in his inimitable fashion denied his opposition to the Grand Trunk at the same time as he blamed its management for reducing "this place from the position of a first rate to that of a third rate town." Concluding his acceptance speech, the old man of the people could not resist a parting shot at his old antagonists and criticized Arunah Huntington, by all repute the most tight-fisted of them, for not investing in the town and for never doing anything for the poor or those in distress. His comments elicited a "simultaneous burst of applause from the whole meeting."[77] Mathews defeated Elliott in 1869, was re-elected in 1870 and again by acclamation in 1871. In 1872 he dithered, and when it seemed he would not contest the election, William Paterson accepted the People's call. As so many times before, Mathews changed his mind and belatedly decided to run. The campaign, strangely polite for one engaging the old warrior, raised few issues, the two candidates espousing similar positions and refraining from criticizing one another. Paterson, with his own popular credentials affirmed in fire brigade politics, won the election. Later in 1872 he was elected to the Dominion parliament, and Mathews was again returned as mayor in 1873 and 1874.

During his reborn administration, Mathews adopted a vigorous program to boost the local economy. In August 1870 he reached an agreement with the Great Western, whereby that company agreed to construct and operate the Harrisburgh line for a municipal bonus of $75,000.[78] The Grand Trunk, irritated by the town's negotiations with its rival, threatened to move the car shops to Stratford unless it too was subsidized. The "People's" municipal government elected in reaction to the railroad's indifference to Brantford was hardly

predisposed to acquiesce to blackmail. The Grand Trunk, one suspects, recognized this, since additional pressure was brought to bear
upon council by contractors eager for railroad work. John Elliott,
John H. Stratford, and Henry Yates conveyed the Grand Trunk's
request for $40,000 to the town fathers. Council countered with an
offer of $20,000, a five-year tax exemption, and water services on
condition that the company spend $60,000 itself on the shops and
designate Brantford as the repair centre for its line west of Kingston.
Charles Brydges replied that the offer was interesting, but unacceptable unless Brantford contributed $32,500. In late July 1870,
council agreed.[79] In 1874, the year after the Mowat government had
used the provincial surplus to extinguish the Consolidated Municipal
Loan Fund, Mathews persuaded the town council to subsidize the
construction of the Brantford, Norfolk and Port Burwell Railway to
the sum of $70,000.[80]

In 1871 the bonus policy was extended to manufacturing.
Learning that Alanson Harris was contemplating moving his agricultural implement plant from Beamsville, Mathews offered him a
five-year tax exemption, renewable for a second five years, to locate
in Brantford and employ thirty men. Harris later denied that the
bonus had any influence in drawing him to Brantford, but he made
no effort to reject the offer and even went to court later to make
certain that the town complied with it.[81] In 1879 another council
offered $5,000 to Clayton Slater, who established a cotton mill just
outside Brantford.[82]

Just as the business elite endeavoured to reduce Grand Trunk
influence on municipal politics, its members sought to regain control
at the Dominion and provincial levels, and with some success by the
mid-1870s. The leading businessmen had been increasingly disillu-
sioned with E.B. Wood, who seemed to have been co-opted by the
Grand Trunk and to be gravitating toward the Conservative party.
In 1865 Wood was called to account before a meeting of ratepayers
for his positions on railroad issues.[83] At the 1867 election the Reform
nomination went to H.B. Leeming, William Paterson's business
partner. The votes and muscle of the Grand Trunk workmen gave
Wood the advantage in a disorderly campaign. John Elliott, with the
assistance of Ralph Clench, the town's anti-Fenian detective, organized well-liquored workmen and Orangemen in the disruption of
Reform meetings in Brantford, Mount Vernon, Newport, and
Burtch's Corners.[84] Wood won the election easily, splitting the rural
vote with Leeming, a notable achievement for a Conservative candidate, and receiving a substantial 61 per cent of the Brantford vote.

In the 1871 provincial election Wood again carried Brantford and won the riding.[85]

With William Paterson as their candidate in the 1872 and 1874 Dominion elections, the business elite and the Liberal party recovered dramatically to carry South Brant in both contests. The rural vote remained the old Reform bedrock, but Paterson nonetheless increased the Liberal count in Brantford by slightly more than 50 per cent between 1867 and 1874 and in the latter election won the majority of urban votes.

While Paterson could express with eloquence the ideology of artisan and shopkeeper independence, he and the Liberal party confronted more difficulty in appealing to the increasingly self-aware working class. They lacked the language. At times Reform campaign rhetoric mixed current concerns with archaic analogies. The Liberal response to Paterson's perennial Conservative opponent, Alfred Watts, who ran against him in 1872, 1874, and 1878, sounded anachronistic. (Watts stepped aside in 1872 to allow Francis Hincks to contest the seat.) Watts was derided for being too money-grubbing and uncharitable with his wealth. Moreover, he was "so limited, bigoted, and narrow," in the *Expositor's* judgment, "that he is honestly averse to the liberty of the masses, and believes that government should be in the hands of the few – by an oligarchy and for an oligarchy. He sighs for the days of the family compact."[86] By implying that Watts was heir to Compact Toryism, Liberals misrepresented their opponent's political lineage: a Baldwinite Reformer, subsequently Hincksite, and "People's party" reeve.

The criticism of Watts also offered an implicit critique of the sort of political machine the Conservatives were building through the 1870s to garner working-class votes. Efforts to mobilize the corporate bodies to which workers belonged – the Grand Trunk, the Nine Hours movement, the trade unions – behind the Conservative party were interpreted as "averse to the liberty of the masses," since collective action deprived the individual of his liberty to exercise his free judgment and act independently. This was the great moral danger present in the Grand Trunk especially. During the provincial election campaign in 1871, the car shops closed a half hour early so that workers could pack, and disrupt, a meeting where Edward Blake was to speak on behalf of the Liberal candidate, David Plewes, merchant miller and "self-made man with great practical talents." Blake could not speak over the crowd's shouting.[87] When Macdonald and Hincks arrived in Brantford in mid-July 1872 to campaign, they were greeted at the station by the Grand Trunk band and car shop workers who had been marshalled out of the shops by Mr Hardman, a foreman. Later that day, the rail workers joined with workers from the foundries and machine works to march in procession behind a Nine Hours banner to the fair grounds to hear Macdonald speak. Liberals charged the Grand Trunk with coercing its workers to adopt the company's politics. Those who refused to vote as instructed by their foremen were placed on *per diem* wages rather than piece-work, which was higher paying.[88]

This last criticism implied that wage labour itself might not be conducive to the workingman's exercise of independent decision making. Watts was accused of firing a man who did not vote for him.[89] It was rumoured that the Tory majority on council in 1873 would fire municipal employees who voted Liberal. Workingmen were exhorted to find "the courage and manliness to assert their rights as Britons and freemen," "despite the whip of their masters."[90] . Oliver Mowat himself argued in 1874 that "undue influence between employer and employed, between customers and tradesmen, between landlords and tenants, debtors and creditors, and persons in various positions" made a secret ballot essential for fair elections.[91] However, their critique of the political culpability of those giving and receiving wage labour placed Liberals on potentially dangerous ground, since in Brantford their numbers included the town's major employers.

The working class of Brantford rejected the Liberal agenda of the business elite. Nor were they prepared to defer quietly to their political leadership; 1873–4 was the apogee of the second coming of business control of urban politics. Thereafter Liberal support, at least in relative terms, weakened. Paterson's share of the growing urban vote fell from 52 per cent in 1874 to 44 per cent in 1878. From the mid-1870s a more vigorous partisanship characterized urban politics and something very nearly like a Conservative machine coalesced to take control of the municipal government. The Grand Trunk and its workers remained an integral force in politics, but the bonus issue and freight competition had been resolved to management's satisfaction, so there was less of a corporate imperative to meddle in municipal politics. As well, the growing number of factory workers and marginalized shopkeepers and tradesmen diluted the presence of railroad workers in the Conservative ranks. The Tory cause assumed ever broader and deeper social appeal among the urban working class and petty bourgeoisie.

Conservative politicians perceived the importance of control of municipal government in promoting success at the provincial and Dominion elections. Not only might supporters be promised municipal largesse in the form of licences, contracts, and jobs, but town workers could also be pressured to vote for the appropriate candidate.[92] Not much subtlety attended the making of patronage appointments. The *Expositor* did little to endear the Liberal party to working-class voters when it complained in 1880 that Dr Reginald Henwood, Conservative mayor, had appointed as city auditor a "man whose time is not his own." The appointee, Tom McKenzie, "is a good specimen of the rough, loud-mouthed blustering ward politician, a handy man from his size and huge fist to overawe and gather in the Brant Avenue Valley vote and can, we presume, keep pretty fairly the time list as boss of a gang of half a dozen labourers at the Grand Trunk."[93]

Beyond this was an even more compelling reason to control the municipal apparatus. Council appointed the town assessors, and from the tax rolls the voters' lists for Dominion and provincial elections were compiled. A partisan assessor could slightly increase or decrease the value of property occupied in order to qualify or disqualify voters. He might neglect to identify sympathetic voters as non-residents, thereby giving them votes in the local riding as well as their home riding. He might also enter the name of a son as owner of property actually owned by a father. The Toronto *Mail,* before the 1872 Dominion election, had urged Tory stalwarts not to neglect the importance of urban government.[94]

One should hesitate before decrying a Conservative conspiracy to subvert the electoral process. The Liberals were fully aware of the utility of municipal office and, though they vehemently denounced Tory crimes, they no doubt sought similar advantage when able. In 1881 Oliver Mowat's commissioner of Crown lands and election organizer, T.B. Pardee, prepared a pamphlet for riding associations providing "Instructions for the Correction of the Assessment Rolls and Revision of Voters' Lists in Each Polling Subdivision." Pardee explained, "It is essential that before [the assessors] go round a list of the changes that can properly be made should be prepared. ... By talking over all the names and lots upon it, [Liberal organizers] will soon know whether any can be added as farmers' sons, owners, tenants, occupants or income voters or whether any should be left off." If the assessors were friendly, the list was to be handed over to them; if not, the parties on the list were to be told to request "proper" entry onto the rolls.[95]

Liberals and Conservatives were certain to contest the appointment of assessors, to scrutinize the assessment rolls carefully, and to protest suspicious entries before the Court of Revision and County Court. Ultimately, the rolls would come close to a non-partisan assessment. Thus, timing was of the essence. Elections must be timed so that assessors could retain the rolls long enough to leave too little time for scrutiny before the polling date. Even after that, the election might be contested, but with luck the result would be so clear that protesting a few voters might not be worth the effort.[96]

As municipal politics became more partisan, they also became more decentralized so that politically important decisions were made at the ward level; ward politics replaced mob politics as electoral strategy. The committee system of municipal administration, whereby an alderman chaired a committee responsible for various municipal departments, vested considerable discretion in the hands of ward politicians, especially in working-class wards where casual employment on sidewalks, fencing, and street repairs provided much-needed income.[97] Brantford's East Ward, for example, in the 1870s was under the joint control of Joseph Quinlan, an Irish Catholic grocer and landlord, and Robert Phair, an Irish Anglican limeburner and contractor. Quinlan, who served on council for nineteen years between 1854 and 1875, repeatedly infuriated the business elite while chairman of the Street and Wood Committee. He sold wood below its cost, thus incurring a loss to the town; he expended funds for street work without council authorization and made requests for specific jobs without submitting estimates of costs. Worse still from the elite's perspective, he gave high priority to street and drainage projects which enhanced the value of his own vacant land, disparagingly referred to as "Joseph's Swamp."[98] The North Ward became the bailiwick of the Hawkins brothers, sons of a successful self-employed Irish Catholic carpenter who had settled in Brantford in the 1830s. Either John J. or Dennis Hawkins sat on council regularly from 1872 to 1883. Since councillors were barred from holding liquor licences, the brother who went on council transferred his interest in their grocery and hotel to the one who stayed off that year. The drinks and the credit of their business strengthened their political appeal, as did the influence of a third brother, Arthur, who was president of the Iron Molders' Union.[99] Young Dennis, just twenty-eight years old when first elected to council, quickly became Brantford's most notable "sidewalk politician, who builds walks till his ward is a veritable checker board." Recognizing the power of municipal spending, he unsuccessfully challenged the elite for control of charity expenditures. For over twenty years, council had paid an annual grant for charitable purposes to the Ladies' Aid or Dorcas Society. The society, made up of the wives of leading businessmen, all Protestants, distributed the money among the poor as it saw fit, making sure that aid never went to pay whisky bills run up at establishments like the Hawkins brothers'. In 1879, when council refused a request for assistance from the St Vincent de Paul Society, Dennis demanded an end to support for the Protestant society as well. Henceforth, he argued, a council committee ought to expend charity. That someone, a Catholic liquor seller at that, should assail the impartiality of the good women of the Dorcas Society offended Protestant opinion and assured defeat of his proposal.[100] Somewhat more respectable than Dennis was brother John J. Hawkins, president of the South Brant Liberal-Conservative Association and unsuccessful candidate for provincial and Dominion office. In 1873 he was defeated by Arthur S. Hardy in the provincial by-election to replace E.B. Wood, who had been sent west to become chief justice of Manitoba; he challenged David Mills in Bothwell in the 1878 Dominion election and lost again. For his defeats, Hawkins was granted some influence over patronage appointments in Brantford.[101]

From 1873 through 1881, Conservatives controlled council and the mayor's office. Liberals and the business elite naturally criticized their handling of Brantford affairs and their use of the committee system of administration, "a system of log-rolling, jobbery and municipal corruption."[102] Their protests did result in the appointment of a street overseer in 1877 to superintend road work, although an independent commissioner would have been preferred.[103] But the major Liberal assault on Conservative municipal control took the form of support for city incorporation and temperance. On both issues, local Liberals could draw upon the support of their MLA, Arthur S. Hardy, who was appointed provincial secretary in Oliver Mowat's government in 1877.

City incorporation in 1877 was consistent with the long tradition of Brantford boosterism. As the preamble to the Act of Incorporation (40 Vict. c. 34) declared, "by reason of its increased and extensive railway facilities, its large manufacturing and mercantile trade, and its situation in the midst of a rich agricultural district, [Brantford] is now and will continue to be an important commercial centre." The referendum on city status on 1 Dec. 1876 drew few voters, just 300 of the roughly 1,900 on the voters' list, and resulted in an overwhelming majority of 266 in favour. The Conservatives could not easily oppose such booster sentiment, though city status had some partisan implications. The city franchise, with a higher income qualification of $400 rather than $300 as was required for the town franchise, would reduce the size of the urban electorate, not just for municipal elections but also in provincial and Dominion votes. In a mixed riding like South Brant, the higher qualification protected the strongly Liberal, but numerically stable, rural vote from the growing Conservative urban support.[104] John J. Hawkins, alderman in 1877, sought to contain the damage to his party by leading council to adopt a resolution calling on the provincial government to amend the city charter to retain the town franchise until Brantford's population reached 15,000. Arthur Hardy refused to support the amendment, much to the dismay of South Brant Tories who denounced his obvious partisanship.[105]

Appointed provincial secretary in 1877, Hardy bore responsibility for introducing many of the measures which Mowat promoted to shift power away from municipal government.[106] Most significantly, the Liquor License (Crooks) Act of 1876 took licensing responsibility from municipal councils and gave to the Liberal government the regulation of what had long a critical lubricant for the Conservative machine. In administering the act, Hardy consulted both temperance and liquor interests, apparently neither offending nor fully satisfying either.[107] Hardy knew, however, that the real significance of the act was political.

One of Hardy's first decisions as provincial secretary was to send the whisky detectives into his own riding in September 1877 to enforce the Dunkin Act. In January 1877, in accordance with that act, Brant County had exercised its local option to prohibit the sale of liquor. Although 60 per cent of Brantford voters rejected the county by-law imposing prohibition, the much larger rural vote, 60 per cent in favour, carried the question. The division was not strictly partisan, though prominent Liberals and manufacturers, like William Buck and David Plewes, eagerly campaigned on behalf of the prohibitionist cause.[108] On the other side, the liquor interests, led by J.J. Hawkins, Alfred Watts, and William Imlach of the Licensed Victuallers' Association, were all Conservatives. Indeed, the liquor trade was the major exception to the attraction of leading Brantford businessmen to Liberalism. Alex Fair, a liquor wholesaler, was a Conservative, as was Alfred Watts, a distiller. The latter's whisky, along with other brands of spirits, was distributed by the Conservative liquor wholesaling firm of Hamilton, Dunlop and Co., the main purveyor of refreshments to all the best Conservative election campaigns. Two Conservative grocery and liquor wholesalers, Jackson Forde and the irrepressible Dennis Hawkins, conveyed their liquor business to Hamilton, Dunlop in 1875. A campaign was not a success, either socially or politically, in certain sections of the city unless constituents were liberally treated to drinks in saloons and groceries and unless a keg had been tapped on voting day. As the *Expositor* complained, "Take from the party of Sir John Macdonald the strength which the licensed victuallers of this country give it and it would become a non-entity at once."[109]

Local option proved easier to pass than to enforce. Prohibitionists complained that in Brantford one would scarcely know that the Dunkin Act had been approved. A writer to the editor of the *Expositor* reported that "I found a den in the North Ward ... where the grog and beer are handed out to the poor victims of intemperance by the burly hand of a selfish landlady who says she has the inspectors in a fix."[110] Could one really expect a council controlled by Conservatives and liquor interests to hire a police chief and inspector wholeheartedly committed to the Dunkin Act? Even when charges were laid, convictions were difficult to obtain. A charge of illegally selling liquor was dismissed against Dan Heffernan, the thirty-seven-year-old proprietor of the Great Western Hotel, when witnesses simply denied purchasing drinks. Heffernan, they testified, had given them libations free of charge. Other cases were indefinitely postponed when witnesses called by the prosecution never appeared. When convictions were handed down, the fine of $20 did little to punish and less to deter the offence.[111] In August temperance advocates appealed to Arthur Hardy to do something. He was waiting for the chance.

Early in September, provincial detectives Clarke and Wallace were despatched to Brantford. Quickly they assembled enough information to lay over a hundred charges against twenty-five hotelkeepers, nearly all of those in the trade. Fines for multiple convictions could add up. Heffernan faced nine charges, while Henry Westbrook of the Commercial Hotel and Barney McMonagle of the West Brantford Hotel faced seven each. In retaliation, Heffernan and another hosteler, John Hunter, led a gang of those charged and their sympathizers to the court house, where the two whisky detectives were registering the charges. When they emerged from their business, the mob assaulted them and chased them back to the widow Colter's boarding house. After pelting the house with rocks, the crowd dispersed, and shortly thereafter the detectives quietly slipped out of town. Fearing further violence, the local inspector, James Grace, resigned, explaining that "I have come to the conclusion that it is impossible to enforce the Dunkin Act in the city of Brantford." Following the riot, Hardy compromised by reducing the charges in return for guilty pleas. Heffernan and Hunter pleaded guilty to obstructing the police and paid a $50 fine each. The hotelkeepers each accepted a single count of illegally selling liquor.[112]

City incorporation separated Brantford from the County of Brant and the authority of its county council, and a plebiscite in February 1878 repealed the Dunkin Act in the city.[113] In any case, Hardy had made his point by demonstrating the utility of the licence act in harassing the minions of his political opponents.[114] But the liquor infraction imbroglio and the controversy over city incorporation demonstrated that the business elite and the Liberal party were losing political control of the city.

In the 1878 Dominion election, the Conservatives received a majority of the votes cast in Brantford. Their resurgence did not draw support from the city's leading merchants and manufacturers, however, and Brantford provides little corroboration for Greg Kealey's conclusion from his Toronto study that "by 1879 Canadian industrial capitalists had come to dominate the state."[115] Most of the major industrialists and wealthiest businessmen took a public stand against the protective tariff.

During the campaign, the *Expositor* printed the names of 365 members of the South Brant Liberal Association who served as convention delegates and campaign committee members.[116] If all of them voted on election day, they would have accounted for 62 per cent of the Brantford votes received by William Paterson. Reference to the city directory of 1877 revealed the occupations of 306, or 85 per cent, of these rank-and-file Liberals.[117] Liberalism had a distinctly bourgeois cast to it. Twenty per cent were merchants, manufacturers, and professionals. Fifty per cent were shopkeepers, petty proprietors, or white-collar workers, though the last group totalled only 16 of the 160 in this category. The remaining 30 per cent were mechanics, tradesmen, and labourers. In all, 176 businessmen, equal to 47 per cent of the business population in 1880, declared their Liberal affiliation. Liberal support was not drawn equally across the business community. The commercial sector, 61 per cent of all businessmen in 1880, was under-represented, accounting for 52 per cent of the self-employed Liberals. Large-scale industrialists appear to have been relatively numerous: 16 per cent of Liberals were factory owners, while 10 per cent were builders. The remainder of Liberal businessmen, 23 per cent, were small-scale independent tradesmen and craft producers.

Newspapers reports testified to the opposition to protective tariffs among the leading manufacturers. Three of the four iron founders, William Buck, Charles H. Waterous, and George H. Wilkes, campaigned against the National Policy, as did the city's leading builder and planing-mill owner, William Watt. Agricultural implement manufacturers Alanson and John Harris and their partner, James K. Osborne, supported the Liberals, as did Lyman Melville Jones and Joseph N. Shenston, who were admitted to partnership in A. Harris, Son and Co. shortly after the election. The second largest implement manufacturers, Jesse and Wareham Wisner, and their future partner,

hardware merchant E.L. Goold, shared the Harrises' political affiliation. John Hext and Adam Spence, proprietors of two of the three
largest carriage factories in Brantford, joined the Liberal campaign,
as did pork packer Bernard Heyd, William Welding, owner of the
Brantford Pottery, and George Foster, president of the British American Starch Co. The Liberal candidate, William Paterson, of course,
was an industrialist of note himself.

Brantford's manufacturers did complain about unfair American
competition. But manufacturers rejected tariff protection because of
their own commercial ambitions and because of their analysis of the
economic problems besetting the Canadian economy. Waterous
believed that American engine manufacturers were dumping their
production on the Canadian market. Buck reported that, while
American competition had not adversely affected his business, American goods on the Canadian market "disturbed" him, since he was
"not so strong a believer as some in our capacity to defy American
competition." He attributed the depression of the mid-1870s to
under-consumption: "There is no particular shortness of money," he
explained to the House of Commons Select Committee on the Causes
of the Present Depression in 1876. "People have the money and are
as capable of buying goods as they ever were, but I judge they are
exceedingly economical." The accuracy of his comment remains to
be seen, but his analysis of the economic situation convinced him
that tariff protection, by raising the cost of living, would only exac-
erbate consumer reluctance to spend. An upward revision of tariffs,
others believed, would increase the cost of production beyond the
level of protection imparted by tariffs. So, in the end, Canadian
manufacturers would be at a greater disadvantage. Explaining his
concerns about plant expansion, Alanson Harris declared, "If I
thought Sir John would regain power and carry out his promise of
putting a duty on coal and other raw material, we would not lay one
brick of that building." The challenge confronting Canadian manufacturers, Buck believed, was one of markets: "We can only reach
comparatively few of our people." While Canadians could produce
as efficiently as Americans, they lacked the cheap transportation and
the large markets close at hand enjoyed by their competitors to the
south. Buck had exported ploughs to Michigan and Colorado, but
found the American tariff and customs procedures to be obstacles.
Similarly he had sent ploughs to Jamaica, and expected "an excellent
market for our goods there," but complained of the complications
involved in shipping through New York. Other Brantford manufacturers had tried foreign markets, too. Waterous shipped engines
to Europe, the West Indies, Chile, and Australia, and Hext sold

carriages to customers in England and New Zealand. Probably export sales accounted for only a small share of production, but they did suggest a broadening perspective. Reciprocity seemed to Brantford manufacturers the solution to the limited domestic market.[118]

Protection appealed more to Brantford's workers and to those fearing that their ambitions for self-employment were threatened. Though inferences about individual voting behaviour on the basis of the aggregate characteristics of polling districts are strained, it is apparent that in 1878 the Conservative candidate, Alfred Watts, drew his strongest support from the most working-class polls, while Paterson for the Liberals piled up majorities in the areas housing the city's business elite. The Liberals' loss of a majority of the Brantford vote from 1874 to 1878 resulted in part from a shift in the preference of franchise holders in one poll whose residents were decidedly lower middle class and artisanal in occupation (table 6.2).

The assessment list, from which the voters' list was drawn, provides an occupational profile of electors in 1878. The peripheral areas of the city, division 1 of the North Ward and division 3 of Brant Ward, returned the strongest Conservative vote. North 1 was the centre of the Irish Catholic neighbourhood, a character made visible by St Basil's Church and the separate school. The Grand Trunk Railway station, yard, and car shops were located there, and numerous employees found residential accommodation nearby. Eleven trainmen, fourteen metal tradesmen, and twenty-nine labourers headed households in the division. Brant 3 was another working-class and railroad neighbourhood. The streets there had been laid out in a more regular grid system than in North 1, and though there were more row houses and semi-detached dwellings, housing in the area was somewhat more expensive than in the other neighbourhood, where small frame or rough-cast buildings predominated. About the same number of trainmen as in North 1, ten, lived in Brant 3, though there were more skilled workmen, including twenty metal tradesmen, and fewer labourers, eleven. Three other peripheral, and mainly working-class, areas of the city, divisions 2 and 3 of the East Ward and division 1 of King's Ward, which was on the other side of the Grand River from the main part of Brantford, returned Conservative majorities, though less decisively.

Divisions 2 and 3 of the North Ward were the prime residential sections, and from the boundary of the first division, Pearl Street, to Dumfries Street, where the wealthy built their residences on a height of land overlooking the Grand River, the value and quality of housing increased block by block. "Here, with dollars accumulated generally in little frame buildings, they now erect gorgeous mansions, and live

Table 6.2
Occupation of Voters in Selected Polls, 1878

| | Conservative Majority | | | | | | Liberal Majority | | | |
| | North 1 | | Brant 3 | | Queens 2 | | North 2 | | North 3 | |
Group	%	N	%	N	%	N	%	N	%	N
Merch. Manuf'rs, Prof'nals	**11**	16	**8**	11	17	17	16	28	**31**	53
Grocers, Petty proprietors	4	6	6	8	**15**	15	9	15	6	10
Master artisans	6	9	3	4	6	6	4	7	2	4
Clerical, Sales staff	8	11	15	21	11	11	9	15	12	20
Metal trades	10	14	**14**	20	4	4	10	17	8	14
Railroad workers	**8**	11	7	10			3	6	2	4
Apparel trades	4	6	1	2	**10**	10	5	9	**1**	1
Construction trades	18	26	22	30	10	10	22	38	13	22
Woodworkers	4	6	1	2	3	3	2	3	2	4
Other skilled trades	4	5	7	10	**12**	12	5	8	3	5
Semi-skilled workers	4	5	7	10	9	9	3	6	6	10
Labourers	**20**	29	8	11	**4**	4	14	24	16	27
Total	100	144	100	139	100	101	100	176	100	174
Vote for Winner	68	93	67	70	59	47	55	61	55	73

Note: Percentages in bold type identify groups that are either significantly over- or under-represented.

in dignified repose." The *Expositor* explained, "Dumfries St. is to Brantford what Fifth Avenue is to New York: a very select complacent quarter."[119] Professionals and proprietors were over-represented, and skilled labour under-represented, in this area, especially in division 3. There were slightly more petty proprietors in these two divisions than in the areas of Conservative support, though lumping them together with white-collar workers mutes their presence.

The second division of Queen's Ward, right in the centre of the city, was the "swing" poll, voting 56 per cent Liberal in 1874 and 59 per cent Conservative in 1878. The first section of the city to be settled and containing much of Brantford's commerce and industry, Queen's 2 was by the 1870s somewhat in transition. Factories were expanding, and as the more prosperous businessmen moved to the North Ward, vacant lots that might once have been lawns or gardens were built upon, increasing population density. The occupational profile of voters in the division suggests vulnerability and potential uneasiness. More than a third were white-collar workers and petty proprietors. The white-collar workers – clerks, salesmen, and travellers – had not achieved the security of their more senior counterparts in other areas of the city, and many lived in hotels and rooming houses or over the stores of their employers. The self-employed in general ran small businesses, retail shops, hotels, and various agencies; only two of the seventeen petty proprietors were tradesmen. The majority of the skilled workers in the division plied declining trades as shoemakers, tailors, cigarmakers, cabinetmakers, and coopers. The residents of division 2 of Queen's Ward probably were among the most marginal economically, their businesses the least secure and their occupations holding the least promise for advancement.

Without poll books, questions of who voted for whom remain inconclusive. Yet one can speculate that the Liberal electorate was more prosperous, more secure, and more bourgeois than the Conservative. If so, then voting would seem consistent with the public statements of the business elite. Having survived the depression of the mid-1870s, and profited from the longer-term restructuring of the urban economy, the successful businessmen of Brantford found less of self-interest in tariff protection than did the economically marginal and those depending on wage labour. The National Policy's major appeal in Brantford was to the working class, who hoped for the creation of more and better jobs; its business appeal was to the small shopkeeper and craft producer, and those aspiring to self-employment but doubtful of its attainment. The elimination of foreign competition and the creation of a national market promised to re-create on a larger scale the protective isolation of the self-contained community of the 1840s and 1850s, which had provided the best opportunities for self-employment.

CONCLUSION

The politics of community particularism, attractive in the 1840s and 1850s to those who hoped to prosper along with a rising place, had become by the 1870s associated with unequal results. Moreover, even those who had benefited the most from urban boosterism could see by the 1870s that the locus of essential economic decision making was passing beyond the community. Corporations like the Grand Trunk Railway sought to wring what concessions they could from the municipality by playing one community off against another. Jobs for workingmen and opportunities for self-employment for the petty bourgeoisie could be protected and promoted, it seemed, by a sympathetic and paternal national parliament more effectively than by a community business elite. The mutual self-interest which had bound together diverse social fragments in deferential politics could no longer be sustained, especially when those claiming leadership were also employers reluctant to negotiate collectively with the very men whose votes they sought.

Conclusion

On 19 December 1878, the Montreal branch of the Young Men's Christian Association assembled to hear George Hague, recently appointed general manager of the Merchant's Bank, speak on modern business. Perhaps the ambitious young men of the association were expecting some useful advice on the sorts of qualities that would advance their fortunes in life. If so, they were disappointed, since Hague presented a thoughtful reflection on how business had changed in his lifetime. Born in Rotherham, Yorkshire, England, in 1825, Hague had immigrated in 1854 and had joined the Bank of Toronto, where he served until his appointment to the Merchant's Bank in 1877. In his position at the Merchant's, and earlier as cashier of the Bank of Toronto, he had himself contributed to the substantial changes in banking practices and business conditions. Though he did not comment upon those specific changes, his lecture did reveal why a leading banker had favoured more rigorous credit restrictions.

Formerly, Hague explained, more care was taken in assuming business liabilities, "for men in those times valued their position, their honor, and their credit. The word of an English merchant was his bond. ... As a consequence ... failure was a rare occurrence, and something to be fought against until the very last, as bearing dishonor to themselves and their children. Men succeeded then by far more generally than they do now." The modern businessman was too eager to succeed, too ambitious, and too restless, impatient, dissatisfied, and even ruthless in pursuing his ambition. "The old fashioned mode of conducting business," Hague went on, "was one in which men were content to 'live and let live', to be one of many, to have your own trade, and let your neighbour have his also. But this spirit of aggression, which delights in nothing so much as in trampling down and crushing those who are in the way, is only too common a characteristic of those who have climbed to the highest places in the modern business world. ... The old style led to a moderate and almost uniform success, to the making of a quiet and honest living on the part of the many, the acquiring of a competency on the part of a few, and a respectable fortune for those times ... on the part of one here and there." For Hague, then, modern business was characterized by an excessive competitive ethic which thought nothing of denying others what one sought for oneself. The individualistic commitment to advancement convinced businessmen to ignore their reputations, even if their actions might lower the esteem in which their families were held. The past stood in contrast. Mutual self-respect then allowed more men to achieve modest success and to live in a dignity recognized and accepted by others.[1]

George Hague's history, perhaps not a little nostalgic in its criticism of contemporary business practice, resembled the efforts of Brantford citizens, like the Rev. William Cochrane or Thomas Cowherd or Thomas Shenston, to understand the social significance of recent change. A significant number of self-made men had succeeded in business, often after experiencing earlier failures. In Brantford most of the prominent manufacturers and merchants of the 1870s and 1880s, like the comfortably secure master artisans and self-employed tradesmen, had started with little and had persevered for years in accumulating wealth and status. Their own experiences affirmed the values which they believed to be essential for getting on in life. It was a past in which they wanted sincerely to believe, for it wrapped their own success in communal values of fellowship and respect for others. Moreover, their understanding of the differences between past and present implied that the distance across time could be bridged if men simply acted differently toward one another. An exercise of individual will, of hard work, satisfaction with modest achievements, and concern for others would restore the imagined community of their younger years.

Such reflections and reminiscences articulated one significant element in an emerging bourgeois class identity. Blended together were generalizations from individual experiences, representations of personal qualities, and exhortations for emulation by those ambitious for success. The sum was an ideology intent upon denying exceptionality, not of present condition, but of character and individual potential. Yet, it was also an ideology whose best examples and most earnest advocates belonged to a generation whose allotted time on this earth was approaching its fullness.

Embellished and selective though bourgeois memory was, it none-theless did represent real experiences. Self-employment had indeed been pervasive in the 1830s, 1840s, and 1850s in Brantford. It may not be too indulgent an exaggeration to speculate that during these years more than the one in four adult males identified in 1852 achieved this condition, for a time at least. Were it possible year by year to reconstruct the business community, the proportion would undoubtedly increase. Moreover, a culture valuing independence sup-ported those men seeking it. Co-religionists, kin, and countrymen helped their kind to achieve the condition which had motivated all to seek their futures in new communities. The localism of mutual self-help became reflected in the credit system which relied heavily upon the reputations of men in evaluating risk. Rather than naïveté, such standards of credit-worthiness appreciated that local backers wished to see others achieve independence and that debtors wished to justify the faith of their community in their character by demon-strating their independence.

Independence did indeed reward men beginning with few material advantages. The incidence of this success was such that in the 1840s and 1850s men of modest means were as likely to persist in business as men of more substantial assets. Pursuit of independence through self-employment, valued though it was as a masculine condition, did not, however, bring unalloyed benefits to those who had achieved that status. Invariably through the period under review, half of all businessmen failed to sustain their independence in business for more than ten years. The burden of failure weighed heavily upon those who wanted to believe in the efficacy of individual action and, in consequence, quitting business usually meant leaving town. The absence of failed Brantford businessmen among city residents appar-ently affirmed the truth of self-made success: those in business included men already successful and those endeavouring to be so. Moreover, the assumption that men could determine their fortunes through self-will necessarily led to suspicions about the motives of men fleeing from their business commitments, betraying the trust of their fellows. Ironically then, mutual self-help not only supported pervasive self-employment but also ultimately contributed to its dis-credit, since those who had enjoyed its benefits presumed that those who had not had taken flight because they were frauds and criminals.

By the end of the period under review, the conditions which had permitted independence in business as a particular condition in life had changed as a consequence of transportation improvements and mechanized factory production, but also because of the results of successful, self-made independence. Despite the new opportunities that industrial capitalism elicited for small business, craft production and petty shopkeeping could not nearly absorb the energies or ambitions of as many people in the late 1860s and through the 1870s. Not only were fewer men able to embark upon self-employment, but the older age at which they did so presumed the need of more substantial assets and experiences. Once in business, however, they confronted a much greater likelihood of failure than men already in business, since, unlike their predecessors of twenty years before, they had to compete with established businessmen in and outside Brantford.

It is not inconceivable that the patterns of social transition elsewhere may have differed in detail from those in Brantford. The chain migration of various groups of connections and the mutual self-help that was thereby implied for migrants likely gave to Upper Canadian society peculiar local and community variations in social composition. Still, it seems equally plausible that the process of social change was not unique to Brantford. In a colonial society, like Upper Canada as the first generation of immigrants passed, its members conveyed to their heirs advantages commensurate with their success. For the new generation, that inheritance constituted a new factor, one with which its parent had not had to contend: opportunities could not be pre-empted in the same way by prior arrival. And yet, because of the uneven progress of settlement, especially in its westward progress, in some new place – St Paul, Minnesota, in the 1860s; Winnipeg, Manitoba, in the 1880s, for example – it may have seemed possible to reprise opportunities lost at home. But each frontier was unlikely to reproduce its predecessor exactly. The burden of what remained behind contributed to changes in the regional, national, and international contexts of industrial capitalism. Thus, the inevitable demographic process of generational transition recurred in new social and technological settings.

Besides the structural changes in the nature of opportunity themselves, which are of significance in interpreting the transition to industrial capitalism in Brantford, and by extension in central Canada, there is the social perception and cultural construction of those changes. In conceptualizing early industrial capitalism in Canada, scholars such as H.C. Pentland or Michael Katz, among others, have been tempted to adopt or adapt models of structural change first developed in other social contexts, either to explain modernization or the transition from feudalism to capitalism. The danger in this is the tendency to view change in isolation, as integral to a particular national framework. Thus one social unit is presumed to recapitulate the stages experienced previously by another. But central Canada from the 1820s to the 1850s drew migration from areas already in transition to a new socioeconomic order, and to imagine that, in moving to a geographically more isolated and technologically less sophisticated area, people had reverted to pre-industrial capitalist forms of behaviour and understanding is too simplistic. They were not Hartzian culture fragments, because, just as Thomas Cowherd admitted to fictional – yet, he believed, truthful – embellishment in *The Emigrant Mechanic*, they themselves created imaginatively the culture which they were leaving, and its image in their own minds may well not have been its reality. In Upper Canada, they acted as if it were.

To believe, as George Hague professed, that in earlier England businessmen behaved with a particular sense of honour and responsibility, or, as William Cochrane encouraged, that once men had a knowledge of one another that conduced to trust and support, was to cross boundaries of space and time into a moral utopia. Structural change, the displacement of forms of production and enterprise resembling those of an earlier British or North American era, upset a selective tradition imposed upon a new society by men who had once in their youth confronted what they believed to have been similar change.

. The "poets" of the imagined community who mourned its demise did not go silently into the night. Those who had grown successful had it in their power to deal harshly with their inferiors seeking credit, status, recognition, or mere employment from them, and they issued a warning to men who had lost their values. How could a man act otherwise when all about him engaged in deceit and conspiracy?

As Eric Hobsbawm has remarked, invented traditions often presume an explanation for an authority, newly claimed but absent in the past.[2] What was forgotten, either consciously or unconsciously, in the invention of this tradition was that the solidarity of past community had been negotiated and contingent upon an expectation that individual ambitions would be achieved through collective responsibility. In the New World of Upper Canada at mid-century, deference and mutual self-help rested not on custom and inheritance, for the past was too short to support preferred lineages. Instead shared presumptions about the attractions of particular places, reinforced in many cases by confidence in the perceptions of advantage of kinsmen and former neighbours, encouraged men, especially immigrants, to invest their ambitions for a better life in the advancement of this or that village or town. The interest of those there first was in the success of more recent arrivals, for a prosperous and growing place would benefit all who had a stake in its future. The visions of articulate boosters were supported because it was assumed that their projects would achieve social benefits which others might share.

Those for whom community particularism had proved beneficial clung to it and could not understand the inclination of others – the increasingly marginalized petty bourgeoisie of shopkeepers and master artisans, the tradesmen whose skills were increasingly less marketable, and the wage labourers working for large corporations – to abandon localism in favour of deference to more abstract and impersonal external connections. To the successful, it seemed another abandonment of personal responsibility. There was a social conservatism among the business elite of Brantford that expressed itself in political support for the Liberal party, even though in the long term the National Policy of the Conservatives proved to be compatible with and comfortable to nationalist capitalism. If there was a capitalist design in the protective tariff and other elements of national economy, it was unseen by the capitalists of Brantford.

If the Brantford example can be taken as a representation of processes in larger segments of Ontario society, then capitalism grew within local contexts and did not immediately or uniformly from place to place reach an appreciation of the self-interested utility of a national political economy of protection. Community had spawned and supported that particular condition which for many, beginning humbly in life, had produced success. To accept that that condition, presumed to have been founded in fraternity, could no longer in the 1870s be widely realized was to deny the very self-identity of men who had succeeded.

Occupational Categories

In this study, occupation has been categorized by function, in order to suggest the kinds of business opportunities perceived to be promising in Brantford. Occupation as a status indicator has not been a variable in this study, since self-employment has been taken as the condition giving status to occupations. The categories outlined below are a modification of those developed by Michael Katz and Theodore Hershberg and Robert Dockhorn. Differences with their categorizations relate to peculiarities of Brantford in comparison to the much larger places they studied. In particular, since builders from the early 1850s owned planing mills and stonecutting yards, it seemed appropriate to combine construction and construction materials producers as a single category.

INDUSTRY

Construction and Construction Materials
architect
bricklayer
brick maker
builder
carpenter
civil engineer
contractor
gas fitter
lime burner

mason
marble cutter
paint manufacturer
painter
planing-mill owner
plasterer
plumber
roofer
saw miller
stonemason
stonecutter

Food Processing
baker
beer bottler
brewer
butcher
confectioner
distiller
miller
soda water
   manufacturer
spice miller

starch manufacturer
vinegar maker

Metal Fabricating
agricultural implement
   maker
blacksmith
engine fitter
gunsmith
iron founder
locksmith
machinist
mechanical engineer
millwright
moulder
saw filer
stove fitter
stove manufacturer
stove mounter
tinsmith
wire worker

Apparel Making
cordwainer
cutter
dressmaker

furrier
harnessmaker
hatter
milliner
saddler
shoemaker
tailor

Woodworking
cabinetmaker
carriage maker
carriage manufacturer
carriage painter
carriage trimmer
chair maker
cigar box maker
cooper
fanning-mill maker
furniture manufacturer
pump manufacturer
wheelwright

Other Industrial
artist
bookbinder
broom maker

carpet weaver
chandler
cigarmaker
cotton manufacturer
dyer
gas manufacturer
hairwork manufacturer
jeweller
labourer
liniment manufacturer
manufacturer
newspaper publisher
organ builder
paper box
   manufacturer
paper manufacturer
photographer
picture framer
pottery manufacturer
potash maker
printer
tanner
umbrella manufacturer
watchmaker
weaver
woollen manufacturer

COMMERCE

Staple Commerce
cattle dealer
coal merchant
coal and wood
   merchant
drover
forwarder
grain dealer
grain merchant
horse dealer
ice dealer
leather merchant
lumber dealer
lumber merchant

produce merchant
seedsman
sheepskin merchant
wool dealer

Food Sales
beer merchant
fish dealer
fruiterer
grocer
liquor merchant
milk dealer
spice merchant
tea merchant

Consumer Goods
Merchandising
bookseller
chemist
clothier
commission merchant
druggist
dry goods merchant
fancy goods dealer
florist
furniture dealer
general merchant
glass and crockery
   merchant

hardware merchant
harness merchant
lightning rod dealer
lime dealer
marble dealer
medicine dealer
merchant
merchant tailor
music dealer
nurseryman
oil merchant
pedlar
piano dealer
pump seller
rag dealer
second-hand dealer
sewing machine dealer
shoe dealer
stationer

storekeeper
stove merchant
tobacconist
tree dealer

Service and
Accommodation
accountant
agent
auctioneer
barber
billiard-room keeper
boarding-house keeper
broker
cab man
carter
conveyancer
express agent
hairdresser

hotelkeeper
innkeeper
insurance agent
land agent
livery stable keeper
mail contractor
patent right seller
piano tuner
private banker
real estate agent
restaurant keeper
saloon keeper
shooting gallery keeper
stage proprietor
tavern keeper
teamster
temperance tavern
   keeper
undertaker

Notes

1 Cowherd, *The Emigrant Mechanic*, iii, 5–6, 17–20, 24, 31, 69, 80, 110, 136, 138, 263; Robertson, *History of the Brantford Congregationalist Church, 1820–1920*, 53.
2 Burley, "Shenston, Thomas Strahan," 967–8.
3 *Expositor*, Dec. 1888.
4 Marshall, "Cochrane, William," 201–3.
5 Bauman, *Memories of Class*, 1, 3, 4.
6 Thompson, *The Making of the English Working Class*, 9. Also see the recent theoretical refinements offered in Katznelson, "Working-Class Formation," 13–22.
7 Neale, *Class in English History*, 21.
8 Hobsbawm, "Class Consciousness in History," 6.
9 Neale, *Class in English History*, 45.
10 Crossick and Haupt, "Shopkeepers, Master Artisans and the Historian," 6. Also, Ryan, *Cradle of the Middle Class*, xiii, 13; Blumin, "The Hypothesis of Middle-Class Formation," 299–301.
11 Ossowski, *Class Structure in the Social Consciousness*, 32–3.
12 Crossick and Haupt, "Shopkeepers, Master Artisans and the Historian," 9; Bechhofer and Elliott, "Petty Property," 182–3; Stearns, "The Middle Class," 379, 380; O'Boyle, "The Classless Society," 397–412.
13 Crossick, "The Emergence of the Lower Middle Class in Britain," 12–13.
14 Blumin, "The Hypothesis of Middle-Class Formation," 308–9, 312, 337–8, and *The Emergence of the Middle Class*, 1–16.

15 Katz, Doucet, and Stern, *The Social Organization of Early Industrial Capitalism*, 2–3, 19, 25. Earlier, Katz had argued for a three-class model which placed men with commercial occupations in the entrepreneurial class, masters and journeymen in the artisan class, and unskilled workers in the labouring class. Assumed ideological affinity thereby linked merchants, manufacturers, and white collar workers, while non-manual labour was distinguished from manual, with the latter segmented according to skill. Katz, "Occupational Classification in History," 63–88; Katz, *The People of Hamilton*, 51, 187, 343–8.

16 Gregory Anderson, *Victorian Clerks*, 4, 49.

17 Raymond Williams, "Base and Superstructure," 3–16; Perry Anderson, "The Antinomies of Antonio Gramsci," 20–9, 31–4, 42, 75–8.

18 Katherine A. Lynch has made a distinction betweeen different sorts of quantifiable data, principally those relating to occupation and those relating to marriage. The former are suited to, indeed require, longitudinal study, while the latter by definition are momentary. Her argument is that marriage records, since they document the degree of social class endogamy, provide a useful measure of class boundaries. "The Use of Quantitative Data in the Historical Analysis of Social Class," 230–7.

19 Stephenson, "'There's Plenty Waitin' at the Gates,'" 89–91.

20 E.g., Blumin, *The Emergence of the Middle Class*, 6–7; Mayer, "The Lower Middle Class as Historical Problem," 417, 425.

21 The absence of a complete range of sources for every tenth year has made it necessary to combine 1851 with 1852 and 1880 with 1881. Because the 1852 assessment roll is not extant, the roll of 1851 has been linked to the manuscript census of 1852. In consequence, the assessed business population may be somewhat smaller than it would have been in 1852, since it does not include those men starting business in the interval betweeen the taking of the two sources. Because the 1881 census does not contain enough internal information to permit as complete an identification of the self-employed, especially those in trades, as one would wish, the 1880 directory, which contained extensive business listings, was used and linked to the 1880 assessment. The self-employed identified in the directory and assessment roll were then linked to the 1881 census and to this group were added those clearly self-employed from evidence in the census. The 1880 listing of businessmen is probably more accurate than the 1881 census group, since the latter may include people in business in 1880 but not 1881, as well as some in business in 1881 but not 1880.

22 Ennals, "Cobourg and Port Hope," 183–95; Osborne, "Kingston in the Nineteenth Century," 59–81; Osborne and Swainson, *Kingston*, 169–89;

McCalla, "The Decline of Hamilton as a Wholesale Centre," 247–54; McCallum, *Unequal Beginnings*, 55, 87–90.

23 Hill, "The Grand River Navigation Company"; Walker, "Birth of the Buffalo and Brantford Railway," 81–90.

24 Acheson, "The Social Origins of the Canadian Industrial Elite, 1880–1885," 146–7.

25 McCallum, *Unequal Beginnings*, 90–1; Spelt, *Urban Development in South-Central Ontario*, 76–7, 127–8.

26 Katz, Doucet, and Stern, *The Social Organization of Early Industrial Capitalism*, 3, 12, 20, 31, 43–4.

CHAPTER ONE

1 McCallum, *Unequal Beginnings*, 90–2, 100.

2 Samuel, "Workshop of the World," 8, 58; McKay, "Capital and Labour in the Halifax Baking and Confectionery Industry," 50, 86–7.

3 The business population identified in this study totalled 400 in 1881. As noted in the previous chapter, this number may be inflated by the inclusion of some people identified in the 1880 directory or assessment roll as self-employed who were no longer so occupied in 1881. The 1880 figure probably offers a more accurate count of the overall level of self-employment. Because relatively little personal information is available from 1880 sources, in this and the next chapter the 1881 group has been analysed to explore the more specific characteristics of the self-employed. The rates of self-employment reported, then, should be treated as maximum levels, and the trend to lower rates of self-employment was perhaps more marked than is immediately apparent from the tables.

4 Darroch, "Class in Nineteenth-Century, Central Ontario," 49–72.

5 For a discussion of the problems associated with artisanal occupations, see Thomas Smith, "Reconstructing Occupational Structures," 134–46.

6 The 1852 assessment roll is incomplete, and so the 1851 roll was used.

7 Gagan, "Enumerators' Instructions," 353–64.

8 *Letters from Settlers in Upper Canada*, 8; Pickering, *Inquiries of an Immigrant*, 112.

9 Province of Upper Canada, *Journal of the House of Assembly*, 1830 and 1840, app.: "Assessment Returns" and "Population Returns." On the background of development in the 1820s and 1830s, see McCalla, "The Wheat Staple," 34–46; Johnston, "Introduction," *The Valley of the Six Nations*, lxvi–lxix; Burley, "The Businessmen of Brantford, Ontario," 37–56, 59; McIlwraith, "The Adequacy of Rural Roads," 209

10 Norris, "Household and Transiency in a Loyalist Township," 406.

11 John Brant to Peter Robinson, 3 June 1830, and Jedidiah Jackson to Robinson, 2 Nov. 1830, Department of Indian Affairs, RG 10, vol. 104, NA.

12 McCalla, "Rural Credit," 39.

13 Weaver, "Ferrie, Colin Campbell," 293–5.

14 Aitken, *The Welland Canal Company*; *Gore Gazette*, 18 Dec. 1827; Hill, "The Grand River Navigation Company," 14.

15 Provincial legislation (6 William c. 13) provided for the incorporation of just one mutual fire insurance company in each of the districts of Upper Canada. The Gore District's company remained headquartered in Brantford until 1863, when in response to charges of mismanagement it moved to Galt. *Letter from Allen Good, Secretary of the Gore District Mutual Fire Insurance Co.*, W.C. Good Papers, NA; Young, *Reminiscences of the Early History of Galt*, 126–7.

16 Hill, "The Grand River Navigation Company," 95–6, 99, 110.

17 Osborne, "Trading on a Frontier," 59–82.

18 *Expositor*, 20 Feb. 1857, 14 July 1871.

19 Innis, "Transportation as a Factor in Canadian Economic History," 70–1; Burghardt, "Some Economic Constraints on Land Transportation in Upper Canada/Canada West," 232–6.

20 Forster, "Finding the Right Size," 150–1; Leo A. Johnson, *History of the County of Ontario*, 211–3; Roelens and Inwood, "'Labouring at the Loom,'" 216–7, 221.

21 The growth of Brantford's business population resembled the pattern identified by the Griffens in Poughkeepsie, New York. There the number of firms increased faster than the total population from 1859 to 1870, but slowed to a rate of increase less than the total population from 1870 to 1900. That the decline came sooner in Brantford may have been due to its higher rate of self-employment, although this cannot be stated with certainty, since the Griffens did not report a rate of self-employment for Poughkeepsie. Griffen and Griffen, *Natives and Newcomers*, 104.

22 Paul E. Johnson, *A Shopkeeper's Millennium*, 36.

23 Paterson, "The Long Point Furnace," 70–8.

24 *Canada Gazette*, 23 Mar. 1844; *The History of the County of Brant* ... , 507.

25 Dun, 55.

26 Burley, "Waterous, Charles Horatio," 1090–1; C.H. W[aterous], "Autobiographical Sketch," AO; *In Memoriam: Charles H. Waterous Sr.*, 10; *Expositor*, 13 Mar. 1855.

27 William N.T. Wylie has reported that the average Ontario foundry in 1851 employed 14.7 workers. Only one, in Thorold, had over a hundred employees. "The Blacksmith in Upper Canada," 39, 42.

28 Ball and Phelps, "Williams, James Miller," 929; *Expositor*, 25 Oct. 1853, 4 Jan. 1856, 20 Feb. 1857; Walker, "Birth of the Buffalo and Brantford Railway," 83–4; *Canada Gazette*, 22 Oct. 1853. Craven and Traves have noted that both the Grand Trunk and Great Western Railways adopted similar policies regarding their car shops, first leasing them to private contractors and then taking them over as separate departments. "Canadian Railways as Manufacturers," 255.

29 Dun, 67, 104, 114; *Expositor*, 1 May 1857.

30 *Expositor*, 15 June 1855; Dun, 55, 56.

31 *Expositor*, 8 May 1857; Dun, 24, 48, 55; *The History of the County of Brant* ... , 539.

32 *Expositor*, 27 Jan., 10, 17 Feb. 1860; *Canada Gazette*, 17 May 1851; Dun, 54; *The History of the County of Brant* ... , 96; Cochrane, ed., *The Canadian Album*, 1:232.

33 Deposition of F.P. Goold, 9 Mar. 1860, John H. Moore v. F.P. Goold, Chancery Court Records, Brant County, Case Files, RG 22, series 5, AO; Dun, 108; *Expositor*, 8 May 1857; Newlands, "The Brantford Pottery: The Early Years," 24.

34 *Expositor*, 5 May 1857.

35 Deposition of F.P. Goold, 9 Mar. 1860; Dun, 55, 56, 67.

36 *Canada Gazette*, 1 Aug. 1857; *Expositor*, 24 Mar. 1857; Dun, 52K, 108; Newlands, "The Brantford Pottery: The Early Years," 24.

37 Dun, 57, 83; *Expositor*, 8 Sept. 1871; Newlands, "The Brantford Pottery: The Early Years," 25–7, and "The Brantford Pottery: The Later Years," 5–9; Webster, *The Brantford Pottery*, 8.

38 Agreement between C.H. Waterous and F.P. Goold and G.H. Wilkes, Waterous Papers, BCHM; *The History of the County of Brant* ... , 547.

39 Burrage, *A Pioneer History of South Brant*, 94–5. For a good description of early machine shops, see Anthony F.C. Wallace, *Rockdale*, 147–52.

40 Paul E. Johnson, *A Shopkeeper's Millennium*, 22, 25, 27.

41 Dun, 52D, 64; *Expositor*, 17 Dec. 1854, 2 Jan. 1858; instrument nos. 90 (6 Apr. 1848), 499 (29 Nov. 1852), 571 (13 Dec. 1854), Town of Brantford, Copy Book of Deeds, Municipal Records, RG 21, AO.

42 Bill of Complaint, 23 Aug. 1861, Craig v. Brown and Payne, Chancery Court Records, Brant County, Case Files; Dun, 50–1; *Expositor*, 2 Feb. 1858, 10 Feb. 1871. For a discussion of technical changes in carriage making, see Duggan, "Machines, Markets and Labor," 310.

43 Cochrane, *The Canadian Album*, 1:126.

44 William N.T. Wylie, "The Blacksmith in Upper Canada," 48, 139; James Sutherland, *County of Brant Gazetteer and Directory for 1869–70*, 68.

45 *Expositor*, 12, 26 May 1857.

46 Dun, 81.

47 Risk, "Nineteenth-Century Foundations of the Business Corporation," 272, 299, 301.

48 McCalla, *The Upper Canada Trade.*

49 E.g., *Monetary Times*, 25 Feb. 1868. Also see Careless, "Aspects of Urbanization in Nineteenth-Century Ontario," 71–2; Cruikshank, "The Transportation Revolution," 115–19, 122; Osborne and Pike, "Lowering 'the Walls of Oblivion,'" 201–25.

50 Burley, "The Businessmen of Brantford," 96–8.

51 *The Waterous Engine Works Co.'s Illustrated Catalogue.*

52 *Expositor*, 31 Oct. 1879; Burley, "Wisner, Jesse Oldfield," 1116–17.

53 Evans, *Brantford Town Directory for 1875–6.*

54 A good description of the shops is contained in Craven and Traves, "Canadian Railways as Manufacturers," 273. Also see Bloomfield, "Manuscript Industrial Schedules," 128. Other of Bloomfield's articles are useful in providing general provincial comparisons: "Using the 1871 Census Schedules," 427–41, and "Industry in Ontario Urban Centres, 1870," 279–83.

55 Craven and Traves, "Canadian Railways as Manufacturers," 266–7.

56 Average value added per flour mill in 1871 was $18,000, while average value added per factory was $63,000.

57 *The Waterous Engine Works Co.'s Illustrated Catalogue.*

58 Denison, *Harvest Triumphant*, 67, 79, 82, 117, 206, 255; Bliss, "Harris, John," 386–7; Wallace, *The Macmillan Dictionary of Canadian Biography*, 355.

59 Denison, *Harvest Triumphant*, 79, 82, 88; Irwin, *City of Brantford and County of Brant Gazetteer and Directory for the Year 1880–1.*

60 Cochrane, *The Canadian Album*, 1:144; *Expositor*, 28 Nov. 1879, 16 Dec. 1881; *The History of the County of Brant* ... , 285; *Canadian Manufacturer*, 3 Feb. 1882, cited in Naylor, *History of Canadian Business*, 1:157; Burley, "Cockshutt, Ignatius."

61 *The History of the County of Brant* ... , 297; *Expositor*, anniversary no., 1927; Burley, "Paterson, John," 687.

62 Instrument nos. 4344, 4345, 4346, 4347 (5 July 1867), Copy Book of Deeds.

63 Carriage factories in Brantford were approximately the same size as those in Toronto. Kealey, *Toronto Workers Confront Industrial Capitalism*, 306. For a discussion of technology in carriage making, see Hounshell, *From the American System to Mass Production*, 146–51.

64 Parr, *The Gender of Breadwinners*, 129. Also see John McIntyre, "From Workshop to Factory," 25–35, and Hounshell, *From the American System to Mass Production*, 125–45.

65 Dun, 140.

66 Agreement between John Builder and H.C. Allen, 16 May 1873; Account of John Builder as Interim Receiver, 14 June 1873 to 30 June 1873, and Exhibit C – Statement of Goods Sold, 3 Aug. 1873 to 11 Jan. 1873; Advertisement for Chancery Sale, John Builder and Co., 7 Jan. 1874, John Builder v. H.C. Allen, 1875, Brant County Chancery Court, Case Files; Dun, 70; *Expositor*, 25 Oct. 1878; Evans, *Brantford Town Directory for 1875–6*; Parr, *The Gender of Breadwinners*, 127. On the industrialization of furniture making in Ontario, see Radforth, "Confronting Distance," 75–100; Kealey, *Toronto Workers Respond to Industrial Capitalism*, 19–20, 304.

67 Dun, 52A, 68.

68 *The History of the County of Brant* ... , 545.

69 Dun, 114.

70 Dun, 70, 107; *The History of the County of Brant* ... , 507–8.

71 *Expositor*, 12, 26 May 1871, 2 Apr. 1875.

72 *Daily Expositor*, 11 Dec. 1875; Irwin, *City of Brantford and County of Brant Gazetteer and Directory for the Year 1880–1*; McKay, "Capital and Labour in the Halifax Baking and Confectionery Industry," 59–67.

73 Burley, "The Businessmen of Brantford," 119.

74 Credit reports and court records helped to identify the location of twenty-one wholesalers: fourteen in Hamilton, four in Toronto, three in Montreal, and one in Buffalo. Dun, 40, 52F, 52G, 58, 61, 71, 93, 94, 104, 141; *The History of the County of Brant* ... , 523.

75 Dun, 52G, 59, 94, 107, 113.

76 Glazebrook, *Life in Ontario*, 184–5.

77 Santink, *Timothy Eaton*, 104–6.

78 *Monetary Times*, 8 Dec. 1876, 6 Apr. 1877. Also see Santink on wholesaling, *Timothy Eaton*, 54.

79 *Expositor*, 16 July 1871, 21 May, 2 July 1880.

80 Dun, 141; *Expositor*, 29 July 1870, 2 Apr. 1875, 2 Mar. 1877, 7 June 1878; *The History of the County of Brant* ... , 286.

81 Dom. of Canada, House of Commons, *Journal* (1874), app. 3: "Report of the Select Committee on Manufacturing Interests," 3; ibid. (1876), app. 3: "Report of the Select Committee on the Causes of the Present Depression," iv, 152, 218–21. Also see McCalla, *The Upper Canada Trade*, 38–40; Gervais, "Le commerce de détail au Canada," 521–56; Drummond, *Progress without Planning*, 277–8.

82 *Monetary Times*, 16 Jan. 1874.

83 Dun, 82–2/".

84 *Expositor*, anniversary no., 1927, 77.

85 *Monetary Times*, 10 Nov. 1876; *Expositor*, 30 Aug. 1878; Dun, 111.

86 *Expositor*, 9 June 1871, 10 Apr. 1874, 2 Jan., 10, 24 Sept., 1 Oct. 1875, 25 Aug. 1878.

87 *Expositor*, 23 Dec. 1870, 6 Jan. 1871, 1, 14, 15 Jan., 30 Apr. 1875, 5 Mar., 15 Oct. 1880.

88 Walden, "Speaking Modern," 309; Rosalind H. Williams, *Dream Worlds*, 65–6. Also see McCracken, *Culture and Consumption* 7–8, 22–8.

89 *Expositor*, 25 Dec. 1874, 15 Nov. 1878, 17 Dec. 1880, 16 Dec. 1881.

90 Katz, *The People of Hamilton*, 52.

91 For a discussion of the expansion of commercial activity and the development of retailing in particular, see Blumin, "Black Coats to White Collars," 106, 108, 111.

92 *Expositor*, 27 Feb. 1855.

93 Dun, 54.

94 Dun, 94; Naylor, *The History of Canadian Business*, 1:80.

95 McCalla has explained that difficulty in supervising "a far-flung network of agents" convinced the British America Assurance Co. in the late 1850s to reduce the number of its agencies, especially those at the greatest distance, in the Maritimes, the United States, and Great Britain. "Fire and Marine Insurance in Upper Canada," 143, 147. On salesmanship in insurance, see Boorstin, *The Americans*, 183–4. Also see Schull, *The Century of the Sun*, 15, 18; Bliss, *Northern Enterprise*, 270–7; Weaver and DeLottinville, "The Conflagration and the City," 441–4.

96 Evidence relating to the strike and riots on the Grand River Navigation are found in various files in the records of the provincial secretary for Canada West: vol. 93, no. 4285; vol. 111, no. 6016, 6017; vol. 112, no. 6137, 6174, RG 5, C1, NA. The strikes and riots on the Grand River Navigation were part of the same protest as on other Canadian canal projects. See: Pentland, "The Lachine Strike," 260; Bleasdale, "Class Conflict on the Canals of Upper Canada," 9–39. Weaver has also noted the social disorder in Brantford in "Crime, Public Order, and Repression," 30. The strikes by labourers at various points on the Buffalo, Brantford and Goderich line were reported in: *Expositor*, 1 Oct., 26 Dec. 1854, 20, 27 Mar. 23 Oct., 1 Nov. 1855; *Christian Messenger*, 29 Mar. 1855. Also see Baskerville, "Americans in Britain's Backyard," 67.

97 Cited in Langdon, "The Emergence of the Canadian Working Class Movement," 8.

98 Ibid., 11; Forsey, *Trade Unions in Canada*, 30.

99 Kealey, *Toronto Workers Respond to Industrial Capitalism*, 65–72; Palmer, *A Culture in Conflict*, 78–82. Also see Bischoff's excellent study of the way in which strategies designed to deal with geographical mobility strengthened the organizational capabilities of the iron moulders' union: "'Traveling the Country 'round,'" 37, and "La formation des traditions de solidarité," 21.

100 The backgrounds of Michael Cline and George Middlemass reveal the way in which factory employment brought together men with very dif-

ferent histories. George Middlemass, twenty-seven years old at the time of the strike, had worked at his trade for more than a decade in Brantford. In 1861 he was single and supported himself and his widowed mother, Jane, with his moulder's wages of $300 a year. His father, John, a cooper, had immigrated from Scotland with his wife and eldest son, Peter, in the mid-1820s. They remained in Lower Canada for about a decade, where George was born, before moving to the United States. The Middlemasses arrived in Upper Canada about 1840. John Middlemass found trades for his sons, Peter, a carpenter, Robert, a cooper, and, of course, George, a moulder. Peter, self-employed in 1861, earned the same income as George. Michael Cline, a thirty-four-year-old Prussian Catholic, earned $350 a year as a moulder. He had immigrated to the United States some time before 1848 and had married there when no more than twenty years of age. He had arrived in Brantford some time after 1852 and lived with his wife, two children, and mother-in-law. His four pigs made him, by the standards of his class, a rather large urban stock raiser.

101 Craven, "Workers' Conspiracies," 59, 63–5, 69. Brantford employers on occasion used that other legal instrument, the law of master and servant, to control their workers, charging those who left their employment with breaking their employment contract. E.g., *Expositor*, 18 Aug. 1871. See Craven, "The Law of Master and Servant," 204–5.

102 *Expositor* 3, 10, 24, 31 Aug. 1860, 11 Jan. 1861.

103 Langdon, "The Emergence of the Canadian Working Class Movement," 9, 10; Forsey, *Trade Unions in Canada*, 37–8.

104 In 1870 James Spratt, the owner of the business previous to John Whitroff, was reported to give permanent employment to five hands, while hiring additional help in response to demand for his product. The census enumerator in 1871 reported that Whitroff employed six men and two boys. The employment figures for Leeming and Paterson did not distinguish between their baking and cigarmaking departments, which together employed seventeen men and two boys. Since both shops produced the same number of cigars, I have assumed that their labour force was equal in 1871. *Expositor*, 29 July 1870, 28 July 1871, 4 Jan., 1 Nov. 1878; Langdon, "The Emergence of the Canadian Working Class Movement," 9; Forsey, *Trade Unions in Canada*, 54.

105 Forsey, *Trade Unions in Canada*, 88.

106 *Expositor*, 5, 12 Jan. 1877. Morton, "Taking on the Grand Trunk," 5–34.

107 Kealey, *Toronto Workers Respond to Industrial Capitalism*, 56–7.

108 Ibid., 48; Forsey, *Trade Unions in Canada*, 88; *Expositor*, 18 July 1873.

109 *Ontario Workman*, 16 Jan. 1873. Despite striking and expressing such pride in craft, Brantford printers did not form a local of the Interna-

tion Typographical Union until 1886. Kealey, "Work Control, the Labour Process, and Nineteenth-Century Canadian Printers," 95.

110 *Expositor,* 25 June 1875.

111 Battye, "The 'Nine Hours Pioneers,'" 25–56.

112 *Expositor,* 9 Feb. 1872.

113 Kealey, *Toronto Workers Respond to Industrial Capitalism,* 128–31; Palmer, *A Culture in Conflict,* 131–4.

114 *Expositor,* 1 Mar. 1872; *Ontario Workman,* 9 May 1872.

115 *Expositor,* 16 Feb. 1872.

116 *Ontario Workman,* 16 May 1872.

117 *Ontario Workman,* 30 May, 13 June 1872.

118 *Ontario Workman,* 13 June 1872, 1 Aug. 1872.

119 *Expositor,* 9 Dec. 1881.

120 Langdon, "The Emergence of the Canadian Working Class Movement," 20. McPherson has not noted the early Brantford co-ops, though they may have provided some background for the activities of those Brantford activists, George Keen and W.C. Good, who played such a prominent role in the national movement. *Each for All.*

121 Cited in Kealey, *Toronto Workers Respond to Industrial Capitalism,* 79.

122 *Expositor,* 17 Mar. 1865.

123 *Expositor,* 5, 19 Feb. 1869.

124 Joyce, *Work, Society and Politics,* xvi-xxvii, xx, 4–6, and esp. ch. 3, "Deference, Dependence and Community"; Dutton and King, "The Limits of Paternalism," 59, 72–3. Also see Roberts, *Paternalism in Early Victorian England,* 171–9.

125 Craven and Traves, "Dimensions of Paternalism," 69–70.

126 Ibid., 66.

127 See Joyce's more recent work for a subtler appreciation of the negotiation of paternalism. "The Historical Meanings of Work," 7–8. Also, Gray, "The Languages of Factory Reform in Britain, c.1830–1860," 143, 145.

128 *Expositor,* 4 Jan. 1878.

129 *Expositor,* 14 Jan. 1881.

130 *Expositor,* 8 Jan. 1869.

131 Joyce, *Work, Society and Politics,* 181–6.

132 There may be an analogy in Bushaway's argument that in rural England in the eighteenth and nineteenth centuries rural labourers attempted to maintain customary relations by manipulating ritual and ceremony in such a way as to bind their landowners and wealthy proprietors to their interests. Of course the contractual framework of custom in which negotiations took place in Brantford lacked the history, at least in place, that existed in England, and could not be interpreted as

rooted in folk culture. Still the effort to induce acknowledgment of interest was present in ritual. *By Rite*, 2–5, 22–3, 25.

133 *Expositor*, 7 Dec. 1877.

134 Bischoff notes another example of consciously presented class ambiguity. In 1881, less than a year after moulders struck his Montreal foundry, William Clendenning marched in the St Jean Baptiste Day parade alongside the moulders' union local wearing on his chest a union badge. "La formation des traditions de solidarité," 36–7.

135 *Expositor*, 12 Feb. 1869.

136 *Expositor*, 19 Feb. 1869.

137 *Expositor*, 6 Nov. 1868.

138 *Expositor*, 1 Mar. 1878.

CHAPTER TWO

1 Darroch and Ornstein, "Ethnicity and Class," 136.

2 Elliott, *Irish Migrants in the Canadas*, 231–2.

3 Pentland, *Labour and Capital in Canada*, 71; Yeo and Thompson, eds., *Unknown Mayhew*, 196, 200, 207, 231, 241, 337, 350–1, 440; Dodd, *Days at the Factories*, 2–15. Also see Burnett, ed., *Useful Toil*, 26, 269; Clapham, *An Economic History of Modern Britain*, vol. *1*, 54, 70; Adams, *Ireland and Irish Emigration*, 49, 55; McIntyre, "The Scot as Farmer and Artisan," 163.

4 Levitt and Smout, *The State of the Scottish Working Class*, 247.

5 Pickering, *Inquiries of an Immigrant*, 2.

6 *The Emigrant's Informant*, vi–vii.

7 [Fraser], *The Emigrant's Guide*, 64; *Letters from Settlers in Upper Canada*, 8.

8 Foy, *Canada, the Land of Homes*, 41; Cobbett, *The Picture of Canada for Emigrators*, 12; Pickering, *Inquiries of an Immigrant*, 3.

9 *Canada: The Land of Hope*, 8.

10 [Fraser], *The Emigrant's Guide*, 51.

11 Pickering, *Inquiries of an Immigrant*, 12.

12 *Letters from Settlers in Upper Canada*, 8; Rivington, *In the Track of Our Emigrants*, 7.

13 *Canada: The Land of Hope*, 8.

14 Neilson, *Observations upon Emigration*, 26; *Notes upon Canada*, 85.

15 *Memoirs of Ignatius Cockshutt*, 13–6; Reville, *History of the County of Brant*, 1:76–80.

16 Vincent, *The Formation of the British Liberal Party*, 13; Levitt and Smout, *The State of the Scottish Working Class in 1843*, 161.

17 Yeo and Thompson, eds., *Unknown Mayhew*, 196, 239, 338; Burnett, ed., *Useful Toil*, 250–2, 256.
18 Anthony F.C. Wallace, *Rockdale*, 412; Walsh, *The Manufacturing Frontier*, 59–60, 65; Katz, Doucet, and Stern, *Social Organization of Early Industrial Capitalism*, 16; Hersch, "From Artisans to Manufacturers," 83–9.
19 Hersch, *Roots of the American Working Class*, 7–13. For a useful corrective to Hersch's assumption of unity, see Dobson, *Masters and Journeymen*, 16–18.
20 Anthony F.C. Wallace, *Rockdale*, 51, 55; Griffen, *Natives and Newcomers*, 35.
21 Paul E. Johnson, *A Shopkeeper's Millennium*, 31.
22 Anthony F.C. Wallace, *Rockdale*, 212, 214, 216–19; Calvert, *The Mechanical Engineer*, 6–7, 13. Rorabaugh has suggested that artisans might reveal the secrets of their craft for more personal and less collegial reasons. Authoring books or pamphlets might bring a hard-pressed tradesmen income beyond that earned by a declining craft, while an innovative artisan with capital insufficient to bring his own inventions into production might profit instead through their publication. *The Craft Apprentice*, 33–4.
23 The Mercantile Agency, for example, believed that panic, a "terror inspired by a trifling cause," among the officers of four or five New York banks pushed the contraction of 1857 to unwarranted depths, "putting every one on the rack in order to discover the weakness of the few." "To Our Subscribers," 438. Also see Anthony F.C. Wallace, *Rockdale*, 49, 50.
24 Rodgers, *The Work Ethic in Industrial America*, 28–7.
25 Akenson, *The Irish in Ontario*, 34–40, 338–44; Katz, *The People of Hamilton*, 63–8. Also see Lockwood, "Irish Immigrants and the 'Critical Years,'" 153–4, 176; Duncan, 'Irish Famine Immigration and the Social Structure of Canada West,' 19–41.
26 Darroch and Ornstein, "Ethnicity and Class," 124–7, and "Ethnicity and Occupational Structure," 315. Also see Kevin Burley, "Occupational Structure and Ethnicity in London Ontario," 407, 409; Green, "Immigrants in the City."
27 Gaffield, "The Character and Circumstance of Canada's Industrialization," 223–4, 228–30.
28 Erickson, *Invisible Immigrants*, 276; Wilson, *John Northway*, 26, 33–4; *Letters from Settlers in Upper Canada*, 9–10; Fox, ed., *Letters of William Davies*, 128.
29 *The History of the County of Brant* ... , 300–7; Independent Order of Oddfellows, *History of Oddfellowship in Canada* ... , 119–20; *Expositor*, 15 Feb., 25 Mar., 18 Apr., 8 Aug. 1856, 30 Mar. 1866, 1 May 1868. Also

see Carnes, *Secret Ritual and Manhood*; Brumberg and Dudden, "Masculinity and Mumbo Jumbo," 368.

30 As noted earlier, the 1861 census asked for the value of capital invested. The assumption in this study is that a figure supplied in this column indicated self-employment. Several of the labourers were identified as being self-employed in other sources and at other cross-sections with occupations, such as teamster, carpenter, or mason, which might in some contexts require less skill than would lead a man to give a more specific occupation to the census enumerator.

31 *Expositor*, 25 May 1855.

32 Redlich has argued that individual entrepreneurship was structured by the sanctions upon behaviour imposed by the various groups to which an individual belonged. Accepting that contradictory sanctions might be placed on entrepreneur from different sources, Redlich was somewhat more sophisticated in his cultural theory than other Harvard scholars of entrepreneurship in the 1950s. Redlich, "Sanctions and Freedom of Enterprise," 177, 182. Also see Jenks, "The Role Structure of Entrepreneurial Personality," 108, and Cochran, "Role and Sanction in American Entrepreneurial History," 153.

33 Acheson, "On the Study of Canadian Businessmen," 106–7.

34 Ryan, *Cradle of the Middle Class*, 12–13.

35 Dun, 52c. Also see Fox, ed., *Letters of William Davies*, 54, 82.

36 Duncan, *The Imperialist*, 23. Also see Wilson, *John Northway*, 47.

37 Diary of Rev. William Cochrane (1870–85), 11–12, Rev. William Cochrane Papers, AO; Dun, 99; Clark, *The Developing Canadian Community*, 151; Stedman, *Farringdon Church*, 3, 7, 8, 13; Fox, ed., *Letters of William Davies*, 7, 41, 96–7.

38 Robertson, *History of the Brantford Congregationalist Church*, 67. Also see Fox, ed., *Letters of William Davies*, 86.

39 Ryan, *Cradle of the Middle Class*, 138; Archer, "Family Enterprise in an Industrial City," 67.

40 Farber, *Guardians of Virtue*, 84, 86.

41 Paul E. Johnson, *A Shopkeeper's Millennium*, 25–8, 34–5.

42 On Americans in manufacturing, see Pentland, *Labour and Capital in Canada*, 79–80.

43 Griffen and Griffen, *Natives and Newcomers*, 46, 129–31; Decker, *Fortunes and Failures*, 62, 172, 307.

44 Fingard's discussion of the career of Isaac Sallis documents the progress of one "rough" to respectability along another avenue – tavernkeeping and the liquor trade. *The Dark Side of Life in Victorian Halifax*, 61–74.

45 *Expositor*, 22 Mar. 1861, 16 Dec. 1870, 17 Feb., 12 May, 17 Oct. 1871.

46 Dun, 82 o/=.

47 *Expositor*, 6 Feb., 10 Apr. 1855.

48 *Expositor*, 11 May 1855, 11 Dec. 1857, 1 Sept. 1870, 28 Apr. 1871. Also see Katz, "Blacks in Hamilton," 35; Winks, *The Blacks in Canada*, 146, 356, 367.

49 *Expositor*, 25 Aug. 1871, 8 Sept. 1871, 15 Dec. 1871.

50 Gerber, "Cutting Out Shylock," 201–32; Tulchinsky, "'Said to be a very honest Jew,'" 207–8.

51 Katz, Doucet, and Stern, *The Social Organization of Early Industrial Capitalism*, 27, 32, 44, 50–1, 53.

52 Acheson, *Saint John*, 49, 72–3.

53 Sutherland, "The Merchants of Halifax," 69–71, 170.

54 Griffen and Griffen, *Natives and Newcomers*, 25, 119, 120, 124.

55 Decker, *Fortunes and Failures*, 5, 81, 277, 278.

56 Curti's classic study of Trempeleau County, Wisconsin, has noted that native-born Americans predominated in business in the 1850s and 1860s. But as the frontier filled, the under-representation of the foreign-born diminished. One might conclude that metropolitan connections gave some initial advantage to Americans which dissipated with the establishment of immigrant groups. *The Making of an American Community*, 228, 232, 236.

57 Comparisons with the findings of Darroch and Ornstein are difficult, since they have not explored changes in the distribution of population within the region. Darroch and Ornstein, "Ethnicity and Class," 121–2; Darroch, "Class in Nineteenth-Century, Central Ontario," 64–8.

58 McLeod, *Practical Guide for Immigrants*, 31.

59 Roper, *What Emigration Really Is*, 7–8.

60 *Labour Wants of Canada*, 4, 7.

61 Cowan, *British Emigration to British North America*, 288; Macdonald, *Canada*, 85, 115; Kalbach and McVey, *The Demographic Bases of Canadian Society*, 34–5, 40–1.

62 Brookes, "Family, Youth, and Leaving Home," 104–7, and "Out-migration from the Maritime Provinces," 26–55.

63 Bischoff, "La formation des traditions de solidarité chez les mouleurs Montréalais," 23; Palmer, *A Culture in Conflict*, 77, 127, 151; Kealey, *Toronto Workers Respond to Industrial Capitalism*, 78, and "The Honest Workingman and Workers' Control," 37; Maynard, "Rough Work and Rugged Men," 159–69.

64 Rotundo has identified the need for achievement as one fundamental dimension of nineteenth-century American middle-class masculinity. His study, however, suffers from an unarticulated conceptualization of class and a too easy acceptance of the rise and fall of gender stereotypes. As well, he concentrates upon the significance of gender roles in

child-rearing. Discourse on masculinity, however, not only prescribed socially acceptable behaviour for the rising generation but also was history, an effort to understand and explain the forces which produced and challenged the current generation of men. An awareness of the need to achieve and a fear of not achieving, Byers has suggested, became a form of self-discipline for the American male. Rotundo, "Body and Soul," 23–38, and "Learning about Manhood," 35–51; Byers, "The Making of the Self-Made Man."

65 Cited in Dewar, "Charles Clarke's 'Reformator,'" 244.

66 Will of John Steele, n.d., RG 22, series 6–1, Probate Court Records, AO.

67 Dun, 58, 124.

68 Erickson, *Invisible Immigrants*, 236, 239, 242, 248. Also see Hobsbawm, "The Tramping Artisan," 313.

69 Neilson, *Observations upon Emigration to Upper Canada*, 27.

70 Cochrane, ed., *The Canadian Album* I: 126; *The History of the County of Brant ...* , 505, 537.

71 Redlich articulated a theory of historical generations, or "age coevals," which stated that "men who are born within a nation during a given span of time assume for the rest of their lives certain characteristic ways of thinking, attitudes, and behavior patterns which distinguish them from people who are born as members of the same nation in somewhat earlier or later times." Redlich's seems too deterministic a theory of character formation, and one might might mute its rigidity somewhat by countering that those formative influences constitute the predispositions which an individual must live with, adjust, or reject through life. Redlich, "The Business Leader as 'Daimonic' Figure," 37, and *History of American Business Leaders*, 22–7.

72 Rev. Hugh Johnston, *A Merchant Prince*, 86–9.

73 Katz, Doucet, and Stern have discovered a decline in fertility among business employees (clerks, bookkeepers, etc.) in Hamilton from 1851 to 1871 which they have explained in terms of ambition for upward mobility. The greatest decline within this occupational grouping was among bookkeepers, accountants and salesmen, occupations which they feel were more attractive than clerkships to ambitious men. *The Social Organization of Early Industrial Capitalism*, 337–40. Rosenberg, unlike Maynard cited above, has posited the roots of the crisis of masculinity in the necessity of controlling reproduction in order to enhance prospects in a changing capitalist environemnt. One requirement for business achievement, a small family, contradicted the previously accepted manifestation of patriarchal achievement – many children. "Sexuality, Class and Role in Nineteenth-Century America," 242–3.

74 Dunlop, *Tiger Dunlop's Upper Canada*, 70.

75 Mayhew, *Mayhew's Practical Book-keeping*, 12–14.

76 Inheritance patterns in Brantford appear to differ from the rural
    Ontario norm analysed by Gagan in "The Indivisibility of the Land,"
    126–41, and the situation in New Brunswick explored by Davis in
    "'Patriarchy from the Grave,'" 91–100. Ryan has argued that urban
    and rural inheritance patterns came to differ in the mid-nineteenth
    century as a consequence of the crisis affecting the middle class. More
    or less equal division among children and a growing recognition of the
    claims of widows upon husbands' estates were signs, according to Ryan,
    that inheritance was perceived to be of lesser importance in securing
    the futures of the next generation. *Cradle of the Middle Class*, 27–9, 62–
    3, 176.

77 Will of John Jenkins, 15 Sept. 1885, grant no. 1142, Surrogate Court
    Records, Brant County, RG 22, AO.

78 Leo A. Johnson, "The Political Economy of Ontario Women," 25.

79 Dun, 100, 126.

80 Paul E. Johnson reports that, in Rochester in 1827, 52 per cent of
    master artisans and 39 per cent of merchants and professionals boared
    employees. *A Shopkeeper's Millennium*, 46.

81 Katz, Doucet, and Stern, *The Social Organization of Early Industrial Capi-
    talism*, 312.

82 The association between having an English father and being self-
    employed in the same trade as a father was not significant. However,
    sons of English fathers were most likely to be self-employed in some
    kind of trade or other. The phi coefficient for the association between
    a son of a tradesman being self-employed in any trade and having an
    English father was 0.46.

83 Dun, 128.

84 Bill of Complaint: A.B. Bennett v. Francis Ellis, 18 July 1873, Chan-
    cery Court Records, Brant County, Case Files.

85 On patterns of farm inheritance, see Gagan, *Hopeful Travellers*, 44.

86 T.S. Shenston to Joseph Shenston, 22 Sept. 1894, and Probate of Last
    Will and Testament of Thomas Strahan Shenston, 1895, T.S. Shenston
    Papers, MTRL.

87 Will of Thomas Glassco, grant no. 1134, 16 Nov. 1886, Surrogate
    Court Records, Brant County.

88 Will of Robert Sproule, grant no. 1080, 20 Jan. 1871, Surrogate Court
    Records, Brant County.

89 Will of Frederick Walsh, grant no. 837, 6 June 1878, Surrogate Court
    Records, Brant County.

90 William Gilkison to Jasper Gilkison, 29 Apr. 1832, William Gilkison
    Papers, AO.

91 Henry C. Wilkes to George H. Wilkes, 28 Oct. 1851, 12 Apr. 1852, 6
    Sept. 1852, 19 Aug. 1854, 2 Oct. 1854; Charles R. Wilkes to George

H. Wilkes, 20 Sept. 1852; William A. Wilkes to George H. Wilkes, [?] Apr. 1852, [?] May 1852; James Wilkes to George H. Wilkes, 27 Sept. 1852, 13 and 24 Mar. 1854, James Wilkes Papers, AO; *The History of the County of Brant* ... , 546–7.

92 Ryan has argued that such incessant paternal counsel evidenced an awareness of the crisis confronting the mid-century middle class. *Cradle of the Middle Class,* 173–5.

93 Katz, *The People of Hamilton,* 166–73.

94 The female presence in business was smaller in Brantford than in either Poughkeepsie or Utica. In the former New York city, women accounted for 9 per cent of the business listings in the Dun credit reports; in the latter, female milliners alone accounted for 11 per cent of the listings. Griffen and Griffen, *Natives and Newcomers,* 242; Ryan, *Cradle of the Middle Class,* 205.

95 Bradbury, "Surviving as a Widow," 151, 152.

96 Katz, *The People of Hamilton,* 253; Blumin, "Black Coats to White Collars," 107–8.

97 Dun, 90. On women in business, also see Ryan, *Cradle of the Middle Class,* 205–6.

98 *Expositor,* 20 Mar. 1868.

99 Duncan, *The Imperialist,* 11; *Expositor,* 2 June 1865.

CHAPTER THREE

1 The Mercantile Agency, founded in 1841 by Lewis Tappan of New York, was operated by a succession of firms until 1859 when Robert G. Dun assumed control. For convenience and because he continued to run it until his death in 1900, this study will refer to the Agency as the Dun Co., despite the inaccuracy of the label. See Madison, "The Evolution of Commercial Credit Reporting Agencies," 164–86; and Wyatt-Brown, "God and Dun and Bradstreet," 432–50.

2 Mahony, in his examination of urbanization in the American Midwest at roughly the same time as covered in this study, has noted the significance of the panic of 1857 in contributing to new credit relationships and thereby reshaping the urban economies of that region. *River Towns.*

3 Naylor, "The Rise and Fall of the Third Commercial Empire of the St. Lawrence," 3, 7–8, and *The History of Canadian Business,* 1:4.

4 Tulchinsky, *The River Barons,* 204–5.

5 McCalla, "Tom Naylor's *A History of Canadian Business,*" 249–54; Pollard, "Fixed Capital in the Industrial Revolution," 148–51; McDonald, "Merchants against Industry," 263–81.

6 Katz, *The People of Hamilton,* 201.

7 McCalla, *The Upper Canada Trade*, 38–40, 110, 150–6. Also see Bervin, "Aperçu sur le commerce et le crédit," 527–52.

8 Magill, "The Failure of the Commercial Bank," 169–81; Baskerville, "The Pet Bank," 22–46.

9 Breckenridge, "The Canadian Banking System," 431; McIvor, *Canadian Monetary, Banking and Fiscal Development*, 55, 69–71; Baskerville, *The Bank of Upper Canada*, cxviii.

10 Risk, "The Nineteenth-Century Foundations of the Business Corporation," 270–306; "The Golden Age," 307–46; "The Last Golden Age," 199–239; "The Law and the Economy in Mid-Nineteenth Century Ontario," 403–38.

11 George and Sworden, "The Courts and the Development of Trade," 280.

12 R.J. Burns, "Ridout, Thomas Gibbs," 661–2; Magill, "The Failure of the Commercial Bank," 178.

13 *Canadian Merchants' Magazine and Commercial Review* 2 (Oct. 1857–Mar. 1858): 911.

14 Dun, 45.

15 Dun, 52C, 52D, 52H, 52F, 75, 119.

16 Dun, 37, 48, 67, 82, 82/2, 119.

17 Dun, 45, 52D 67, 82I.

18 Dun, 46, 97, 134, 82/0.

19 Dun, 47, 49, 136.

20 Dun, 52A 52D, 58, 73.

21 Dun, 52L.

22 Dun, 52/0.

23 Dun, 84.

24 Dun, 49, 51, 53, 68, 82.

25 Dun, 56; Ryan, *Cradle of the Middle Class*, 157, 182.

26 Dun, 82.

27 Baskerville, *The Bank of Upper Canada*, ciii–civ. An informative study of one example of unwarranted favouritism is Baskerville, "Donald Bethune's Steamboat Business," 135–50.

28 Acheson, *Saint John*, 57–8.

29 Benson's studies of the efforts of working men and women to supplement their wages through what he has termed "penny capitalism," small-scale buying and selling, attest to the strength of the desire for independence, even among those with the least opportunities for success in business. "Working-Class Capitalism in Great Britain and Canada," 151, and "Hawking and Peddling in Canada," 82–3.

30 Dun, 52D, 58, 70, 91.

31 Dun, 69, 91, 108, 111. Cf. Anthony F.C. Wallace, *Rockdale*, 51, 55, 412; and Griffen and Griffen, *Natives and Newcomers*, 35.

32 Dun, 50, 52, 106.

33 Dun, 52C, 99.

34 Stedman, *Farringdon Church*, 3–13; Cowherd, *The Emigrant Mechanic*, 253.

35 Dun, 52J.

36 Cited in Santink, *Timothy Eaton*, 161.

37 Crossick, *An Artisan Elite*, 144, 156. Also see Faler, "Cultural Aspects of the Industrial Revolution," 388.

38 Thompson, "The Moral Economy of the English Crowd," 83–6; Palmer, "Kingston Mechanics and the Rise of the Pentitentiary," 26–7; . Gray, *The Labour Aristocracy*, 90, 146; Davidoff and Hall, *Family Fortunes*, 15–17, 20, 56.

39 Dun, 70, 101.

40 Dun, 52C, 91, 106.

41 Katz, *The People of Hamilton*, 199, 201, 202–3.

42 Here a very limited and legalistic definition of failure has been employed, including insolvency, assignment of assets for the benefit of creditors, court seizure of assets, court judgments ordering payment of overdue notes, and absconding. Most failures, however, occurred quietly as a man honourably absorbed his losses and quietly closed his shop door.

43 Dun, 65, 78, 82, 94, 102, 112.

44 Dun, 50, 54, 62, 69, 82 1/", 82 3/", 112. Also see Gervais, "Le commerce de détail," 523, 525, 533, 539.

45 E.g., Allen Good to James Coleman, 20 Dec. 1856, Letterbook 1856–61, W.C. Good Papers, vol. 25, NA.

46 Dun, 57.

47 Register of Judgments, 1853–8, County Court Records, Brant County, RG 22, AO.

48 Register of Judgments, 1853–8, Brant County; Allen Good to [?], 4 Mar. 1858, Letterbook 1856–61, Good Papers. Also see Baskerville, *The Bank of Upper Canada*, cxl–cxli, 279.

49 Armstrong, "Austin, James," 42.

50 McCalla, "Morton, Lewis," 745.

51 Copies of the published credit manuals bear the imprint of the Bank of Montreal and of the Brantford saddlery and harness manufacturers, Smith, McKay and Co. The Mercantile Agency also began publishing such useful commercial reference works as *The Mercantile Agency's Legal Guide to the Dominion of Canada*. Also see McCalla, *Upper Canada Trade*, 112; Madison, "The Evolution of Commercial Credit Reporting Agencies," 171–3.

52 On the Bank of Montreal's adoption of a more stringent lending policy, see Rudin, "King, Edwin Henry," 486–7.

53 *Monetary Times*, 24 Oct. 1867. The negative argument was vigorously asserted in Meagher, *The Commercial Agency System*.
54 Dun, 82 3/", 100, 121, 123, 126, 141.
55 Muise, "The Dun and Bradstreet Collection," 23–6.
56 Dun, 52A, 68, 114
57 Shenston to James Pollack, 15 Sept. 1876, 301, Letterbook, Thomas S. Shenston Papers, MTRL.
58 Ibid., "Re: Alfred Watts," 714–20.
59 Ibid., "Re: John Whiting, Sen'r," 503.
60 Ibid., "Re: James Tutt," 171.
61 As Bilak has explained, mortgages in the mid-nineteenth century were less often means to secure financing of real estate purchases than security for business engagements. "The Law of the Land," 177–88.
62 Gagan, "The Security of Land," 137.
63 Cf. Katz, Doucet, and Stern, *The Social Organization of Early Industrial Capitalism*, 132, 144, 156.
64 See Santink's discussion of Timothy Eaton's use of mortgages to finance the expansion of his operations. *Timothy Eaton*, 45.
65 Thompson, "The Moral Economy of the English Crowd in the Eighteenth Century," 131.
66 Fox-Genovese and Genovese, *Fruits of Merchant Capital*, 5–8, 15, 29, 35, 75–6.

CHAPTER FOUR

1 Perry, *Taxes, Tariffs and Subsidies*, 83.
2 Mavor, "Finance and Taxation," 17: 258–61.
3 *Debates of the Legislative Assembly of United Canada* 5 (1846): 191.
4 Ibid., 8, part 2 (1849): 1604.
5 Province of Canada, *Statutes*, 13 and 14 Vict. (1850) c. 67, sec. 13.
6 Hincks, *Reminiscences*, 314.
7 *Debates of the Legislative Assembly of United Canada* 5 (1846): 466.
8 Perry, *Taxes, Tariffs and Subsidies*, 86; Province of Ontario, *Statutes*, 33 Vict. (1869), c. 27, sec. 2; Province of Ontario, Legislative Assembly, *Journals* (1878), app. 4, "Report of Select Committee on Exemptions from Taxation," 22, 25.
9 Province of Canada, Legislative Assembly, *Journal* (1852–3), 176, 707.
10 Province of Canada, *Statutes*, 16 Vict. (1853) c. 182, sec. 3.
11 "Report of Select Committee on Exemptions from Taxation," 26.
12 Darroch, "Occupational Structure, Assessed Wealth and Homeowning," 386, and "Early Industrialization and Inequality," 35–9.
13 Perry, *Taxes, Tariffs and Subsidies*, 87.
14 *Debates of the Legislative Assembly of United Canada* 5 (1846): 464–6.

15 Province of Canada, *Statutes*, 16 Vict. (1853), c. 182, sec. 6.

16 Ibid., sec. 4; 29–30 Vict. (1866), c. 53, sec. 35.

17 "Report of Select Committee on Exemptions from Taxation," 27.

18 Katz, *The People of Hamilton*, 147. In his study of the distribution of assessed wealth in Toronto from 1861 to 1899, Darroch, while recognizing the problem of undervaluation of personal property, has simply summed the real property and personal property/income assessments. "Occupational Structure, Assessed Wealth and Homeowning," and "Early Industrialization and Inequality."

19 Drummond, "Ontario's Industrial Revolution," 286–7, and *Progress without Planning*.

20 Darroch, "Occupational Structure, Assessed Wealth and Homeowning," 389–90, 410, and "Early Industrialization and Inequality," 33, 53–4, 59; Soltow, *Patterns of Wealthholding in Wisconsin*, 31.

21 Darroch, "Early Industrialization and Inequality," 60; Gagan and Gagan, "Working-Class Standards of Living in Late-Victorian Urban Ontario," 173, 178, 185, 192–3. Also see Snell, "The Cost of Living in Canada in 1870," 186–91.

22 Doucet, "Working Class Housing," 90.

23 The formula for calculating the Gini index is explained in Dollar and Jensen, *Historian's Guide to Statistics*, 122–4.

24 Schedule of Town Lots in the Village of Brantford upon which a Value Has Been Placed, 15 May 1830, Department of Indian Affairs, vol. 5, RG 10, NA.

25 Doucet, "Working Class Housing," 90.

26 Instrument nos. 676 (7 June 1855), 1502 (15 June 1857), 3275 (23 July 1863), 3996 (22 Aug. 1866), 7979 (1 Mar. 1875), 9594 (1 Sept. 1874), 11067 (2 Apr. 1880), 11126 (26 Apr. 1880), Town of Brantford, Land Records, Copy Book of Deeds, Municipal Records, RG 21, AO.

27 If Soltow's provincial sample for 1871 is representative, 47 per cent of adult males owned some form of real property, either a home or land. *Men and Wealth in the United States*, 23. Darroch has demonstrated that property ownership varied considerably by occupational grouping and persistence. "Class in Nineteenth-Century, Central Ontario," 58–9, 62–3.

28 Katz, Doucet, and Stern, *The Social Organization of Early Industrial Capitalism*, 134–6.

29 Instrument nos. 4185 (15 Apr. 1867), 4801 (1 Apr. 1869), 4825 (26 May 1869), 5430 (5 June 1869), 5515 (12 Jan. 1871), 6124 (31 Jan. 1872), 6541 (11 Nov. 1872), 6567 (25 Oct. 1872), 6824 (29 May 1873), 8316 (22 Oct. 1875), 9234 (9 Mar. 1877), 10388 (23 Jan. 1879), 10473 (11 Mar. 1879) 11003 (1 Mar. 1880), 11375 (20 Oct. 1880), Copy Book of Deeds.

30 Instrument nos. 7030 (4 Oct. 1873), 7031 (6 Oct. 1873), 7510 (2 July
   1874), 7652 (9 Sept. 1874), 8508 (12 Feb. 1876), 9223 (6 Mar. 1877),
   Copy Book of Deeds.

31 Bacheldor v. Wilkes, Deposition of John A. Wilkes, 14 Oct. 1859,
   Chancery Court Records, Brant County, Case Files, RG 55, series 5, AO.

32 The early holdings of the Wilkes family are somewhat difficult to
   untangle, since in 1840 John A. was granted the right to pre-empt 109
   acres at the upset price. He did not exercise that right at the time of its
   granting, but did so gradually only after land values had escalated so
   that he might mortgage the land for sums which exceeded the upset
   price. He also seems to have conveyed to his sons his pre-emptive right
   to certain portions of his grant.

33 Moyle v. Wilkes, Affadavit of Ignatius Cockshutt [1860] and Affadvit
   of John A. Wilkes, [1860]; Bank of Montreal v. Wilkes, Bill of Complaint, 6 June 1863, Chancery Court Records, Brant County, Case
   Files; instrument no. 7 (10 July 1847), and instrument no. 172 (14 Oct.
   1853), Copy Book of Deeds.

34 Caira R. Wilkins brought to her marriage with George S. Wilkes property inherited from her father and held in trust for the benefit of her
   and her children. Her husband tried to break that trust in 1850 so
   that they might sell the land, much to the chagrin of his mother-in-law,
   who successfully petitioned against their request. Following her separation from George S. in 1869, Caira Wilkes was allowed, by a special
   provincial act of 1874, to sell her property in trust. Presumably at that
   time, the money was needed for her support. "Petition of Maria Wilkins re: Marriage Settlement of Caira R. Wilkins WIlkes and George S.
   Wilkes, 30 May 1850," Provincial Secretary's Office (Canada West)
   Records, vol. 327, no. 898, RG 5, C 1, NA; Province of Ontario, *Statutes,*
   38 Vict. (1874), c. 91.

35 *Expositor,* 26 May 1857.

36 *Canada Gazette,* 18 Sept. 1858.

37 Paton v. Kerby, 1859; Allchin v. Buffalo and Lake Huron Ry., Exhibit T
   – Re: Alex Bunnell, Apr. 1861, Chancery Court Records, Brant
   County, Case Files.

38 Moore v. the Grand River Navigation Co., 1862; Rose v. Tobin, 1866,
   Chancery Court Records, Brant County, Case Files.

39 *Expositor,* 25 Nov. 1870.

40 Petition of Eliza Watts for Letters of Administration, grant no. 244,
   1868, Surrogate Court Records, Brant County, RG 22, AO.

41 Instrument nos. 4294 (2 Mar. 1874), 7511 and 7512 (15 June 1874),
   8294 (15 July 1875), 9115 (4 June 1877), Copy Book of Deeds.

42 Instrument nos. 5676 and 5677 (18 Apr. 1871), Copy Book of Deeds.

43 *Expositor*, 1 Jan. 1871; *History of the County of Brant* ... , 527.
44 Instrument nos. 217 (10 Nov. 1853), 745 (31 July 1855), 1011 (16 Aug. 1856), 1620 (10 Sept. 1857), 1621 (10 Sept. 1857), 2060 (30 Sept. 1858), 2061 (2 Oct. 1858), 2062 (28 Sept. 1858), 2115 (7 Dec. 1858), 2419 (17 Jan. 1860), 3354 (16 Oct. 1863), 3720 (7 Sept. 1865), 4722 (26 Feb. 1869), 5779 and 5780 (1 July 1871), 6277 and 6278 (21 May 1872), 7353 (1 Apr. 1874), 8156 (1 June 1875), 8563 (31 Mar. 1876), 8585 (18 Apr. 1876), 8588 (18 Apr. 1876), 9509 (24 July 1877), 9604 (1 Oct. 1877), 10293 (6 May 1878), 10685 (1 Aug. 1879), 14911 (28 May 1885), Copy Book of Deeds.
45 Dun, 55, 67.
46 *Expositor*, 28 June 1872.
47 The Mercantile Agency, *Reference Book for the Dominion of Canada ... January 1871.*
48 Dun, 83, 85, 107.
49 Regrettably few Canadian studies have been published using probate records to study the inequality of wealth. For a discussion of nineteenth-century Nova Scotian sources, see Saddiq, "The Size Distribution of Probate Wealthholdings in Nova Scotia," 136–9.
50 RG 22, series 6–1A, AO.
51 Grant no. 559, Surrogate Court Records, Brant County.
52 Grant nos. 1131, 1164, Surrogate Court Records, Brant County.
53 Grant nos. 937, 1119, Surrogate Court Records, Brant County.
54 Dun, 46.
55 Gagan, *Hopeful Travellers*, 50–4.

CHAPTER FIVE

1 Shenston to Mrs William Moorhouse, 4 Mar. 1876, Letterbook, 124, Shenston Papers, MTRL.
2 *Expositor*, 9 June 1886, 14 Aug. 1890.
3 Leverenz has pointed to contradictions in the presentation of masculine identity by nineteenth-century American authors and argued that, while three masculine ideals, the patrician, the artisan, and the self-made man, can be identified, the greatest tension existed between the patrician and the self-made man. *Manhood and the American Renaissance.* Canadian authors may have lacked an appealing cultural antecedent for the patrician, especially since the logical referent would have been the Family Compact. Though Morgan's *Sketches of Celebrated Canadians* included politicians and governors, the patrician ideal seems to have been absent from later discourse on masculinity, and, in the success literature at least, the artisan and self-made ideals contended.

4 Hann, "Brainworkers and the Knights of Labor," 52–3.

5 Allen Smith, "The Myth of the Self-Made Man in English Canada," 217. Also see Prentice, *The School Promoters*, 66–84.

6 Irving G. Wylie, *The Self-Made Man in America*, 5, 73–8.

7 Morris, "Samuel Smiles and the Genesis of *Self-Help*," 108. See also Bechhofer and Elliott, "Petty Property," 183–4, 192.

8 Bliss, *A Living Profit*.

9 Cawelti, *Apostles of the Self-Made Man*, 74–5, 98, 122–3; Rex Burns, *Success in America*, vii–viii, 92–4.

10 Mills, "The Business Elite," 20–44; Miller, "American Historians and the Business Elite," 184–204, and "The Recruitment of the American Business Elite," 242–53; Gregory and Neu, "American Industrial Elite in the 1870s," 193–212.

11 Acheson, "The Social Origins of the Canadian Industrial Elite," 150, 152, 171.

12 Gutman, "The Reality of the Rags-to-Riches 'Myth,'" 220–1, 232; Thernstrom, *Poverty and Progress*, 160–5.

13 Katz, *The People of Hamilton*, 147–8. On tax assessment, see Darroch, "Occupational Structure, Assessed Wealth and Homeowning," 384–6; Burley, "The Businessmen of Brantford," 387–95.

14 Griffen and Griffen, *Natives and Newcomers*, 104.

15 No statistically significant relationship existed between being new in business in 1851 and discontinuation before 1861. In the 1860s the relationship was weak (chi square significant at the level of 0.1 probability; phi = 0.1). By the 1870s the relationship was strongly significant and the association was worthy of note (chi square significant at the level of 0.001 probability; phi = 0.34).

16 William W. Johnson, *Sketches of the Late Depression*, 7, 229–31, 233–4.

17 Cited in Houghton, *The Victorian Frame of Mind*, 191.

18 *Monetary Times*, 21 July 1876.

19 J.A.D. Baker to W. Baker, 26 July 1880, Evidence: McKedie vs Watt, Chancery Court Records, Brant County, Case Files, RG 22, series 5, AO.

20 *Expositor*, 17 Apr. 1878.

21 *Expositor*, 11 June 1869, 23, 30 Apr. 1875, 21 Nov. 1879.

22 Dun, 49, 57, 61, 67.

23 Dun, 52D, 112. See also Griffen and Griffen, *Natives and Newcomers*, 108.

24 Hague, *Modern Business*, 16.

25 Griffen and Griffen, *Natives and Newcomers*, 103; Burley, "The Businessmen of Brantford," 318–20.

26 Burton, *A Sense of Urgency*, 27–8.

27 Dun, 62, 82F.

28 On retirement, see Haber, *Beyond Sixty-five*, 109, 117. Little evidence suggests that Brantford businessmen sought the gradual withdrawal from business and the devotion to family and spiritual life that Davidoff and Hall have noted. *Family Fortunes*, 225–7.

29 Dun, 21.

30 His business commitments were such that he could devote more time to philanthropic work and consider his spiritual well-being. As he wrote to a relative, "The great matter for *all to earnestly* consider *how do I stand* in the *sight of the Lord*. Am I resting on the *sure Rock Christ* trusting alone in his precious *Blood* [and] finished work for sinners like *you* and *me*." Ignatius Cockshutt to "My Dear Cousin Clough," 26 Nov. 1888, Ignatius Cockshutt Letterbook, 1888–1901, 19, AO.

31 Palmer, *A Culture in Conflict*, 84.

32 Dun, 74.

33 Phi for the association between quitting business and membership in the bottom rank was 0.13 in the 1850s and 0.30 in the 1860s.

34 For the 1860s: Chi square significant at the level of .001 probability; phi = 0.51. For the 1870s: chi square significant at the level of 0.001 probability; phi = 0.39.

35 Chi square significant at the level of 0.1 probability; phi = 0.29.

36 Chi square significant at the level of 0.1 probability; phi = 0.38.

37 Dun, 50, 82G.

38 *Expositor*, 8 Dec. 1865, 14 July 1871; Dun, 49, 52, 52J, 53, 81, 82, 83, 84, 87, 93, 94, 97, 98, 107, 126.

39 Dun, 83, 84.

40 Dun, 83.

41 Chi square significant at the level of 0.02 probability; phi = 0.36.

42 Gervais, "Le commerce de détail au Canada," 521–56.

43 *Expositor*, 26 Aug. 1881.

44 *The History of the County of Brant* ... passim.

45 Chi square significant at the level of 0.1 probability; phi = 0.14.

46 Dun, 58, 67, 75.

47 Chi square significant at the level of 0.02 probability; phi = 0.33.

48 The phi coefficient for the correlation between declaring insolvency and quitting business for businessmen in rank one was 0.29 in the 1850s, 0.30 in the 1860s and 0.20 in the 1870s. For businessmen in ranks three and four, the coefficients were −0.35 in the 1850s, 0.04 in the 1860s and −0.18 in the 1870s.

49 Hamilton *Spectator*, 2 Apr. 1879.

50 Cochrane, *The Church and the Commonwealth*, 42.

51 Grant, *Life of Rev. William Cochrane*, 21.

52 Marshall, "Cochrane, William," 201–3.

53 Wohl, "The 'Rags to Riches Stories,'" 503.
54 Cochrane, ed., *The Canadian Album. Men of Canada or Success by Example.* 4 vols.
55 Cochrane, *Warning and Welcome*, 78, and *The Church and the Commonwealth*, 317.
56 Cochrane, *The Church and the Commonwealth*, 208.
57 Cochrane, *The Heavenly Vision*, 158.
58 Cochrane, *The Church and the Commonwealth*, 43, 44.
59 Cochrane, *Christ and Christian Life*, 57.
60 Cochrane, *The Church and the Commonwealth*, 48.
61 Ibid., 51, 52–3.
62 Ibid., 52.
63 Cochrane, ed., *The Canadian Album*, 1:4–5.
64 Cochrane, *The Church and the Commonwealth*, 49.
65 Ibid., 43.
66 Cochrane, *Warning and Welcome*, 210.
67 Cochrane, ed., *The Canadian Album*, 1:79, 103, 3:306.
68 Ibid., 1:57, 126.
69 Ibid., 1:216, 232.
70 Ibid., 1:92, 120, 232.
71 Ibid., 2:251, 4:97.

CHAPTER SIX

1 *Expositor*, 26 July 1872.
2 Ibid..
3 Forster, *A Conjunction of Interests*, 4.
4 Craven and Traves, "The Class Politics of the National Policy," 37.
5 Forster, *A Conjunction of Interests*, 155, 175.
6 Forster's claim that workingmen were "squeezable ... deferential" in the 1878 election campaign runs counter to much of the experience in Brantford and to recent labour historiography. Too easily does he assume that similar political positions were reached through similar logic. Ibid., 169–71.
7 Bliss, "The Protective Impulse," 174–88.
8 Gutman, *Power and Culture*, 17, 73–6.
9 Lee A. Johnson, "Ideology and Political Economy," 64.
10 Artibise, *Winnipeg*, 285–6.
11 *Expositor*, 22 Feb. 1855.
12 James Wilkes to Merritt, 15 July 1847, William Hamilton Merritt Papers, AO; Hill, "The Grand River Navigation Company," 95–6, 99, 110.

13 Petition of Inhabitants Comprised within the Twps. of Brantford, Onondaga, Tuscarora, Oakland, and Burford, and Southern Halves of Twps. of Blenheim and Dumfries, [1848], Provincial Secretary's Office (Canada West) Records, vol. 254, no. 565, RG 5, C1, NA; Province of Upper Canada, *Journal of the House of Assembly*, 1834, 49; ibid., 1837–8, 310. Also see Whebell, "Robert Baldwin and Decentralization," 55, 59.

14 Province of Canada, *Journal of the Legislative Assembly*, 1851, app. z: "Return [concerning] Any Company of Persons for the Construction of a Railroad from Fort Erie to Dunnville and Brantford."

15 In their vision, Brantford's boosters were no less optimistic than Francis Hincks when he proposed legislation to finance railroad projects. Piva, "Continuity and Crisis," 198–201; Faucher, "Le Fond d'emprint munic- ipal," 7–32.

16 Petition of the Brantford Town Council, 27 May 1851, Department of Indian Affairs, vol. 327, RG 10, NA; Proceedings of the Board of Direc- tors of the Grand River Navigation Co. and the Town Council of Brantford, 24 Dec. 1851, vol. 796, ibid.; Province of Canada, *Statutes*, 14 and 15 Vict. c. 151.

17 Bill of Complaint: Town of Brantford v. The Grand River Navigation Co., 23 Aug. 1859, Chancery Court Records, Brant County, RG 22, AO.

18 *Reply of the Buffalo and Lake Huron Railway Company.*

19 Quoted in *Expositor*, 13 Mar. 1855.

20 Return to an Address with Report of David Thorburn, 9 Apr. 1855, Department of Indian Affairs, vol. 796.

21 Andrew Steven to David Thorburn, 17 Feb. 1851, Department of Indian Affairs, vol. 1025; Hill, "Grand River Navigation Company," tables 5 and 6.

22 *Expositor*, 10 Jan., 6 Mar., 11, 15 May 1855.

23 The Great Southern, as time revealed, was perhaps even less sound in promotion than the Buffalo and Brantford. G.S. Wilkes to Hon. Jon. Ross, 26 Oct. 1854, Merritt Papers; Province of Canada, *Journals of the Legislative Assembly*, 1857, app. 6, "Report on the Woodstock and Lake Erie Railway and Harbour Company"; Myers, *History of Canadian Wealth*, 195–202; McCalla, *The Upper Canada Trade*, 102–3.

24 *Expositor*, 27 Feb. 1855.

25 *Expositor*, 25 May, 12 June 1855.

26 *Expositor*, 24 June 1856, 17 July 1857; *Brant County Herald*, 2 Dec. 1857. The question of Irish Catholic political participation is part of a larger debate over the integration of the group in early Ontario society. At one pole is the work of Akenson, which has stressed the commonali- ties of Irish Protestant and Catholic experiences within the larger con- text of nineteenth-century society; on the other is the strident riposte

of Nicholson, who has stressed Irish Catholic alienation and the separate cultural identities of Irish Catholics and Protestants. The benefit of work like Kealey's on Protestant and Catholic working-class relations in Toronto is its recognition that negotiation and collaboration can reduce the cultural conflict between groups with a common self-interest. In Brantford, mediation took the person of William Mathews. Akenson, *The Irish in Ontario*; Nicholson, "The Irish Experience in Ontario," 37–49; Kealey, "The Orange Order in Toronto," 13–34.

27 Dyster, "Captain Bob and the Noble Ward," 110–1; Kealey, "Orangemen and the Corporation," 76–7.

28 *Expositor*, 27 Feb. 1855.

29 See Dyster, "Captain Bob and the Noble Ward," 96–7; Weaver and DeLottinville, "The Conflagration and the City," 427–33.

30 *Expositor*, 8 Aug. 1856.

31 On the conversion of Clergy Reserve revenue to municipal funds, see Wilson, *The Clergy Reserves*, 214, 220–1.

32 *Expositor*, 16 May 1856.

33 *Expositor*, 20, 24 Feb., 20 Mar., 15 Dec. 1857; 8, 22 Jan. 1858; 18 Nov. 1859. Faler has noted that firemen in Lynn behaved similarly when they believed that their contributions were not acknowledged with sufficient liberality. *Mechanics and Manufacturers*, 203.

34 *Expositor*, 13 Apr. 1860.

35 *Expositor*, 20 July, 24 Aug. 1860.

36 *Expositor*, 11 Nov. 1864.

37 *Expositor*, 25 Nov. 1864, 3 Feb. 1865.

38 *Expositor*, 3 Feb., 24 Mar., 14 Apr., 19 May, 6 June 1865.

39 *Expositor*, 23 Mar. 1866, 19 July 1867.

40 *Expositor*, 14 Jan. 1859; Reville, *History of the County of Brant*, 1:229.

41 *Expositor*, 3 June 1856; T.S. Shenston, *A Letter ... Respecting the Late Extraordinary Conduct of the Mayor*.

42 Houston and Prentice, *Schooling and Scholars*, 111. The events perhaps give credence to the thesis of Gidney and Lawr that local autonomy was not unable to resist bureaucratic centralization. "Who Ran the Schools?" 140–1.

43 Brantford *Herald*, 3 Jan. 1857.

44 Reville, *History of the County of Brant*, 649.

45 *Expositor*, 4 Apr. 1854.

46 *Expositor*, 25 July 1854, 27 Nov. 1857.

47 *Expositor*, 1 Dec. 1857.

48 *Expositor*, 2 Jan. 1858.

49 *Expositor*, 7, 18, 21 May 1858.

50 *Expositor*, 16 July, 15 Oct. 1858.

51 *Expositor*, 15 July 1856, 14 July 1857, 27 Jan. 1860.

52 *Expositor*, 1, 15 Oct. 1858.

53 *Expositor*, 4 Nov. 1859.

54 Keatchie was a town property owner of some substance. With the informal approval of county council, he had contracted with himself as county jailer to hire prisoners to work on a building he was constructing in Brantford. Though he was exonerated on the grounds that other work was unavailable for prisoners, the affair was an embarrassment for the elite. *Expositor*, 1 June, 15, 23 July, 6 Aug. 58.

55 *Expositor*, 24 Dec. 1858, 14 Mar. 1859.

56 *Expositor*, 27 Jan., 10, 17 Feb. 1860.

57 *Expositor*, 25 Mar. 1859.

58 *Expositor*, 5 Nov. 1858, 7 Jan. 1859.

59 *Expositor*, 29 May 1863. Also see Symons, "Ryerson, William," 640–1, and Livermore, "Wood, Edmund Burke," 934–5.

60 *Expositor*, 19 June 1863.

61 *Expositor*, 5 June, 7 Aug. 1863.

62 Stevens, *Canadian National Railways*, 1:473; Currie, *The Grand Trunk Railway of Canada*, 249.

63 *Expositor*, 11 Dec. 1863.

64 *Expositor*, 3 July 1863.

65 *Report of the Buffalo and Lake Huron Railway Company*; Thomas Botham, "Report on the Town of Brantford," Provincial Secretary's Office (Canada West) Records, RG 5, B 15, NA.

66 *Expositor*, 11 Dec. 1863, 27 Jan., 10 Feb., 1865; A. Cleghorn to A. Brown, 10 Feb. 1865, Buchanan Papers, vol. 21, NA; Weaver, *Hamilton*, 52, 54, 80.

67 *Expositor*, 10 Mar. 1865.

68 *Expositor*, 10 Mar. 1865, 8 Feb., 7 Dec. 1866.

69 *Expositor*, 8 Feb., 7 Dec. 1866, 3 May 1867; *Monetary Times*, 10 Oct. 1867.

70 *Monetary Times*, 10, 24 Oct. 1867.

71 *Expositor*, 9 Dec. 1867, 5 Jan. 1861, 11 Jan. 1861, 25 Dec. 1863.

72 When defeated in 1869, Elliott was rewarded with contracts for two sections of the Intercolonial Railway, no doubt through the influence of Charles Brydges, a member of the supervisory Board of Railway Commissioners. As well, in 1871 he was granted a contract on the construction of Toronto Central Prison, perhaps through the intercession of E.B. Wood. *Expositor*, 4 June 1869; Construction Accounts, Central Prison, Toronto, Department of Public Works, RG 15, series V-2, AO.

73 *Expositor*, 21 Aug. 1868.

74 *Expositor*, 16 July 1869.

75 *Expositor*, 15, 20 Dec. 1867, 24 Jan. 1868.

76 *Expositor*, 13 Dec. 1872.

77 *Expositor*, 21 Dec. 1868.
78 *Expositor*, 12 Aug. 1870; Province of Ontario, *Statutes*, 34 Vict. (1871), c. 55.
79 *Expositor*, 15, 22, 29 July 1870.
80 Evans, "Oliver Mowat and Ontario," 427–9; Province of Ontario, *Statutes*, 37 Vict.(1874) c. 53.
81 *Expositor*, 22 Mar. 1878.
82 *Expositor*, 28 Nov. 1879; *Canadian Manufacturer*, 3 Feb. 1882; *Monetary Times*, 3 Mar. 1882. For a discussion of municipal bonusing, see Bloomfield, "Municipal Bonusing of Industry," 59–76, and "Building the City on a Foundation of Factories," 207–43.
83 *Expositor*, 31 Mar. 1865, 19 Feb. 1869.
84 *Expositor*, 26 July, 10 Aug. 1867. For a reference to Fenianism in Brantford, see Sheppard, "'God Save the Green,'" 133.
85 *Expositor*, 24 Mar. 1871.
86 *Expositor*, 19 July 1872.
87 *Expositor*, 17 Mar. 1870.
88 *Expositor*, 2 Aug. 1872.
89 *Expositor*, 13 Feb. 1874.
90 *Expositor*, 24 Mar. 1871.
91 Evans, "Oliver Mowat and Ontario, 1867–1896," 246.
92 *Expositor*, 2 May 1873.
93 *Expositor*, 23 June 1880.
94 *Expositor*, 18 July, 17 Oct. 1873, 30 Jan. 1874.
95 T.B. Pardee, Confidential Circular to Presidents of Riding Associations, 30 Nov. 1881, Edward Blake Papers, AO.
96 *Expositor*, 16, 23 May, 11, 18 July 1873.
97 On ward politics and politicians, see Weaver, *Shaping the Canadian City*, 56–7.
98 *Expositor*, 20 June, 5, 17 Dec. 1873, 20, 27 Nov. 1874.
99 *Expositor*, 5 Aug. 1881.
100 *Expositor*, 21 Dec. 1877, 14 Dec. 1879.
101 *Expositor*, 14 June 1878, 19 Mar. 1880; Hamilton *Spectator*, 25 May 1878; J.C. Aikins to Hawkins, 14 June 1881, James Cox Aikins Papers, P 471, Letterbook B, 260, PAM.
102 *Expositor*, 20 Nov. 1874.
103 *Expositor*, 20 June 1873, 6 Apr. 1877.
104 For a rather uncritical discussion of the Mowat's government's franchise legislation, see Evans, "Oliver Mowat and Ontario, 1867–1896," 264–6, and *Sir Oliver Mowat*, 93–8.
105 *Expositor*, 2, 9, 23 Feb. 1877.
106 Noel, "Dividing the Spoils," 77.

107 Province of Ontario, *Statutes* (1881) c. 27, (1884) c. 34, (1886) c. 39; Debate of 15 Feb. 1881, in Toronto *Globe*, 16 Feb. 1881; Evans, "Oliver Mowat and Ontario, 1872–1896," 305, 321–2.

108 *Expositor*, 15, 22 Feb. 1877.

109 *Expositor*, 19 Feb., 12 Mar. 1875, 12, 19 Jan., 3 Aug. 1877, 1 Mar., 11 June 1878, 26 Mar. 1880.

110 *Expositor*, 8 June, 13 July 1877.

111 *Expositor*, 22, 29 June, 3, 10, 17 Aug. 1877.

112 *Expositor*, 14, 21 Sept., 28 Nov. 1877, 15 Mar. 1878; Toronto *Globe*, 14, 18 Sept. 1877.

113 Toronto *Globe*, 26 Feb. 1878.

114 *The Bystander* 3 (1883): 18; Brantford *Courier*, 27 Dec. 1886; Cartwright, *Reminiscences*, 169.

115 Kealey, *Toronto Workers Respond to Industrial Capitalism*, 16–17.

116 *Expositor*, 7 June, 23 Aug. 1878, 20 May 1879.

117 Evans, *Brant County Gazetteer and Business Directory for 1877*.

118 Dominion of Canada, House of Commons, *Journal, 1876*, app. 3, "Report of the Select Committee on the Causes of the Present Depression," 185–8; *Expositor*, 7 Jan., 30 Aug. 1878, 25 Apr., 2 May, 25 July, 31 Oct. 1879, 28 May 1880, 9 Dec. 1881.

119 *Expositor*, 11 Nov. 1870.

CONCLUSION

1 Hague, *Modern Business*, 13–14, 22.

2 Hobsbawm, "Introduction: Inventing Traditions," 8.

Bibliography

ARCHIVAL SOURCES

ARCHIVES OF ONTARIO [AO]
Blake, Edward, Papers
Church Records Collection. West St. Baptist Church, Brantford. Building
    Committee Records, 1853–72
Cochrane, Rev. William, Papers
Cockshutt, Ignatius, Letterbook, 1888–1901
Court Records (RG 22)
    Brant County, Chancery Court
    Brant County, Judgment Book, 1853–7
    Brant County, Surrogate Court
    Probate Court
Crown lands Department Records (RG 1)
Department of Public Works Records (RG 15)
Gilkison, William, Papers
Manuscript Census Schedule, 1842, Brantford Township
Merritt, William Hamilton, Papers
Municipal Records, Brantford (RG 21)
    Abstract Index to Deeds
    Assessment Rolls
    Copy Book of Deeds
    Minute Book of Municipal Council
Shenston, Thomas S., Papers
Street, Samuel, Papers

W[aterous], C.H., "Autobiographical Sketch"
Wilkes, James, Papers

BAKER LIBRARY, HARVARD UNIVERSITY [DUN]
Dun and Bradstreet Collection, R.G. Dun and Co., Credit Ledger, vol. 13, Brant County

BRANT COUNTY HISTORICAL SOCIETY MUSEUM [BCHM]
Waterous Company Records

CITY OF BRANTFORD ARCHIVES [BA]
Municipal By-laws
Municipal Journals

METROPOLITAN TORONTO REFERENCE LIBRARY [MTRL]
Shenston, Thomas S., Papers

NATIONAL ARCHIVES OF CANADA [NA]
Buchanan Family Papers
Canada West. Provincial Secretary's Office Records (RG 5)
Department of Indian Affairs (RG 10)
Department of Public Works (RG 11)
Good, W.C., Papers
Manuscript Census Schedules, Brantford and Brantford Township, 1852–81
Upper Canada State Papers (RG 1)

PROVINCIAL ARCHIVES OF MANITOBA [PAM]
Aikins, James Cox, Papers

PRINTED PRIMARY SOURCES

Barrister-at-Law. *Foundations of Success and Laws of Trade*. London, Ont.: S. Smith, 1877.
Brantford and Buffalo Joint Stock Railway Company. Toronto: Hugh Scobie, 1851.
Brantford Board of Trade. *Report on Grand River Navigation*. Brantford: Courier Office, 1867.
Burnett, John, ed. *Useful Toil: Autobiographies of Working People from the 1820s to the 1920s*. London: Allen Lane, 1974.
Canada, Dominion of. House of Commons, *Journals*, 1867–81.
– *Sessional Papers*, 1867–81.
Canada, Province of. *Journals of the Legislative Assembly*.
– *Statutes*.
– *Sessional Papers*.

Canada: The Land of Hope for the Settler and Artisan, the Small Capitalist, the Honest and Persevering ... London: Algar and Street, 1857.

The Canada Directory ... 1857. Montreal: John Lovell, 1857.

Canada Gazette

The Canadian Biographical and Portrait Gallery of Eminent and Self-Made Men. Ontario Volume. Toronto: American Biographical Publishing Co., 1880.

Cartwright, Richard. *Reminiscences.* Toronto: Briggs, 1912.

Cobbett, Joseph M. *The Picture of Canada for Emigrators.* London: Wittenoom and Cremer, 1832.

Cochrane, Rev. William, ed. *The Canadian Album. Men of Canada or Success by Example.* 5 vols. Brantford: Bradley, Garretson and Co., 1891–6.

– *Christ and Christian Life. Sermons Preached in Zion Church, Brantford, 1875.* Brantford, 1876.

– *The Church and the Commonwealth: Discussions and Orations on Questions of the Day.* Brantford: Bradley, Garretson and Co., 1887.

– *The Heavenly Vision; and Other Sermons (1863–73).* Toronto: Adam, Stevenson and Co., 1874.

– *Warning and Welcome: Sermons Preached in Zion Presbyterian Church, Brantford, during 1876.* Brantford: John Sutherland, 1877.

Cowherd, Thomas. *The Emigrant Mechanic and Other Tales in Verse, by ... the Brantford Tinsmith Rhymer.* Jackson, Mich.: Daily Citizen and Job Printing House, 1884.

Debates of the Legislative Assembly of United Canada, 1841–1869. 12 vols. Elizabeth Abbott [Nish] Gibbs, gen. ed. Montreal: Centre de Recherche en Histoire Economique du Canada Français, 1970–.

Dodd, George. *Days at the Factories, or the Manufacturing Industry of Great Britain Described ... Series I: London.* London: Charles Knight and Co., 1843; reprint ed., New York: Augustus M. Kelley, 1967.

Duncan, Sara Jeanette. *The Imperialist.* Toronto: McClelland and Stewart, 1971.

Dunlop, William. *Tiger Dunlop's Upper Canada.* M. Ross, ed. Toronto: McClelland and Stewart, 1967.

The Emigrant's Informant or a Guide to Upper Canada. London: G. Coure, 1834.

Evans, W.W. *Brant County Gazetteer and Business Directory for 1877.* Brantford: J.T. Johnson, Brantford Union Office, 1877.

– *Brantford Town Directory for 1875–6.* Brantford: J.T. Johnson, Brantford Union Office, 1875.

Ferrie, Adam. *Autobiography of the Late Adam Ferrie.* n.p., 1864.

Fox, W. Sherwood, ed. *Letters of William Davies, Toronto, 1854–1861.* Toronto: University of Toronto Press, 1945

Foy, Charles. *Canada, the Land of Homes. Facts for Emigrants.* Belfast: W. and G. Baird, 1874.

[Fraser, William] A Scottish Minister, *The Emigrant's Guide, or Sketches of Canada ... from 1831 to 1867.* Glasgow: Porteous Bros., 1867.

Freedley, Edwin T. *The Secret of Success in Life*. Whitby: J.S. Robertson, 1881.

Good, Allen. *Extract from the Address of the Warden of the County of Brant to the Council Assembled on 18th June, inst., on Prisons Generally*. Brantford: Herald, 1855.

– *Letter from Allen Good, Secretary of the Gore District Mutual Fire Insurance Co.* Brantford, 1863.

Grant, R.N. *Life of Rev. William Cochrane*. Toronto, 1899.

Harvey, Arthur. "The Census of 1871." *Canadian Monthly and National Review* 1 (1872): 97–104.

Hague, George. *Modern Business: A Lecture*. Montreal: D. Bentley, 1879.

Hincks, Francis. *Reminiscences*. Montreal: Drysdale, 1884.

The History of the County of Brant ... Toronto: Warner, Beers, 1883.

Illustrated Historical Atlas of the County of Brant, Ont. Toronto: Page and Smith, 1875; reprint ed., Stratford: Cumming Atlas Reprints, 1972.

In Memoriam: Charles H. Waterous Sr. Brantford: n.p., 1892.

Independent Order of Oddfellows. *History of Oddfellowship in Canada ...* Brantford: Expositor, 1879.

Irwin, W.H., and Co., *City of Brantford and County of Brant Gazetteer and Directory for the Year 1880–1*. Brantford: Expositor Steam Printing House, 1880.

Johnson, William W. *Sketches of the Late Depression: Its Causes, Effect and Lessons, with a Synoptic Review of the Leading Trades during the Past Decade*. Montreal: J.T. Robinson, 1882.

Johnston, C.M., ed. *The Valley of the Six Nations: A Collection of Documents on the Indian Lands of the Grand River*. Toronto: University of Toronto Press, 1964.

Johnston, Rev. Hugh. *A Merchant Price: Life of Hon. Senator John Macdonald*. Toronto: William Briggs, 1893.

Kealey, Gregory S., ed. *Canada Investigates Industrialism: The Royal Commission on the Relations of Capital and Labour, 1889*. Toronto: University of Toronto Press, 1964.

Labour Wants of Canada. Ottawa: Department of Agriculture, 1873.

Letters from Settlers in Upper Canada. London: Marchant, 1833.

Linscott, T.S. *The Path of Wealth, or Light from my Forge: A Discussion of God's Money Laws, the relation of Giving and Getting, Cash and Christianity*. Brantford: Bradley, Garretson and Co., 1888.

Macdonald, John. *Business Sense: What It Is and How to Secure It*. Toronto: Adam, Stevenson, 1872.

– *Elements Necessary to the Formation of Business Character*. Toronto: W. Briggs, 1886.

– *To the Young Men of the Warehouse*. Toronto: Hunter, Rose, 1876.

Mackay, Robert W.S. *The Canada Directory: Containing Names of the Professional and Businessmen of Every Description in the Cities, Towns and Principal Villages of Canada*. Montreal: John Lovell, 1851.

McCabe, James Dabney. *The Encyclopaedia of Business and Social Forms*. London: S. Smith, 1882.

McLeod, Malcolm. *Practical Guide for Immigrants to the United States and Canada*. Manchester: A. Ireland and Co., 1870.

Mayhew, Ira. *Mayhew's Practical Book-keeping, Embracing Single and Double Entry, Commercial Calculations, and the Philosophy and Morals of Business*. 16th ed., Boston: Nichols and Hall 1860.

Meagher, Thomas F. *The Commercial Agency System of the United States and Canada Exposed: Is the Secret Inquisition a Curse or Benefit?* New York, 1876.

Memoirs of Ignatius Cockshutt, Consisting Chiefly of His Own Reminiscences, Collected and Arranged by a Member of His Family. Brantford: n.p., 1903.

The Mercantile Agency. *Reference Book for the Dominion of Canada ... January 1871*. Montreal: Dun, Wiman and Co., 1871.

– *Reference Book for the Dominion of Canada ... 1881*. Montreal: Dun, Wiman and Co., 1881.

– *The Mercantile Agency's Legal Guide to the Dominion of Canada*. Montreal: J. Lovell, 1868.

– "To Our Subscribers." *Business History Review* 37 (1963): 437–43.

Milner, Thomas S. *How to Make Business Pay; or the Principles of Success in Trade*. Montreal: George Nolan, 1865.

Morgan, Henry J. *Sketches of Celebrated Canadians and Persons Connected with Canada*. Quebec: Hunter, Rose and Co., 1862.

Neufeld, E.P., ed. *Money and Banking in Canada: Historical Documents and Commentary*. Toronto: McClelland and Stewart, 1967.

Neilson, Joseph. *Observations upon Emigration to Upper Canada, Being the Prize Essay ... from the Upper Canadian Celtic Society*. Kingston: n.p., 1837

Notes upon Canada and the United States of America in the Year 1835. Toronto: W.G. Coates, 1835.

Pickering, Joseph. *Inquiries of an Immigrant, Being the Narrative of an English Farmer from ... 1824 to 1830*. London: Effingham Wilson 1832.

Ontario, Province of. *Journals of the Legislative Assembly*, (1878), app. 4, "Report of Select Committee on Exemptions from Taxation."

Ontario, Province of. *Statutes*, 1867–81.

Reply of the Buffalo and Lake Huron Railway Company to the Objections of the Town of Brantford to the Bill Now Before the House of Assembly, for the Confirmation of the Agreement between the Company and the Grand Trunk Railway [1865].

Rivington, Alex. *In the Track of Our Emigrants. The New Dominion as a Home for Englishmen*. London: Sampson Low, Maiston Low and Searle, 1872.

Roper, Edward. *What Emigration Really Is*. London: Graphotyping Co., 1870.

Rordans, Joshua. *The Canadian Conveyancer and Hand-book of Legal Forms ... with an Introductory treatise on the Law of Real Property in Ontario*. Toronto: J. Rordans, 1879.

Scobie and Balfour's Municipal Manual for Upper Canada for 1850. Toronto: Scobie and Balfour, 1850.

Shenston, Benjamin. *Minutes in Reference to my Leaving England.* Chicago: Donnelly, 1937.

Shenston, Thomas S. *An Appeal to the Unthinking.* Toronto: Standard Publishing Co., 1886.

– *The Berean.* Brantford: T. Shenston, (Amateur) Printer, 1862.

– *Gleanings.* Guelph: James Hough, 1893.

– *A Jubilee Review of the First Baptist Church, Brantford, 1833 to 1884.* Toronto: Bingham and Webber, 1890.

– *A Letter to the Inhabitants of the Town of Brantford, Respecting the Late Extraordinary Conduct of the Mayor.* Brantford, 1856.

– *Letter: As Many of the Creditors Did Not Attend Any of the Meetings.* Brantford: n.p., 1866.

– *The Oxford Gazetteer: Containing a Complete History of the County of Oxford.* Hamilton: Chatterton and Helliwell, 1852.

– *Private Family Register of the Shenston and Lazenby Families.* Brantford: T. Shenston, printer, 1864.

– *The Sinner and his Savior.* London: Elliott Stock, 1879.

– *Tellogoo Mission Scrap Book.* Brantford: Expositor, 1888.

Smith, W.H. *Canada: Past, Present and Future. Being a Historical, Geographical and Statistical Account of Canada West.* Toronto: Thomas Maclear, 1852; reprint ed., Belleville: Mika Publishing, 1973.

– *Smith's Canadian Gazetteer: Comprising Statistical and General Information Respecting All parts of the Upper Province or Canada West.* Toronto: H. and W. Rowsell, 1846.

Sutherland, James. *County of Brant Gazetteer and Directory for 1869–70.* Toronto: Hunter, Rose and Co., 1869.

Thomas, David. *The Practical Philosopher: A Daily Monitor for Businessmen.* Toronto: Adam, Stevenson, 1873.

Upper Canada, Province of. *Journal of the House of Assembly,* 1830–40.

The Waterous Engine Works Co.'s (Limited) Illustrated Catalogue of Steam Engines, Saw and Grist Mill Machinery, Waterous' Improved System of Fire Protection and Water Supply, Saws and Saw Mill Furnishings. Brantford, 1875.

Wilkes, George S. "Banking and the Currency." *Hunt's Merchant Magazine and Commercial Review* 39 (1858): 191–7.

Yeo, Eileen, and E.P. Thompson, eds., *The Unknown Mayhew: Selections from the "Morning Chronicle," 1849–1850.* Harmondsworth: Penguin, 1971.

Young, James. *Reminiscences of the Early History of Galt and the Settlement of Dumfries in the Province of Ontario.* Toronto: Hunter, Rose and Co., 1880.

NEWSPAPERS

Brantford. *Brant County Herald*
- *The Christian Messenger*
- *Courier*
- *Expositor*
- *The River Roarer; or the Snapping Turtle*
Toronto. The *Canadian Merchants' Magazine and Commercial Review*
- *The Monetary Times*
- *The Ontario Workman*

SECONDARY SOURCES

Acheson, T.W. "On the Study of Canadian Businessmen." *Acadiensis* 9 (Spring 1980): 101–8.
- *Saint John: The Making of a Colonial Urban Community.* Toronto: University of Toronto Press, 1985.
- "The Social Origins of the Canadian Industrial Elite, 1880–1885." In *Canadian Business History: Selected Studies, 1497–1971.* D.S. Macmillan, ed. Toronto: McClelland and Stewart, 1972.
Adams, W.F. *Ireland and Irish Emigration to the New World from 1815 to the Famine.* New Haven: Yale University Press, 1932.
Aitken, H.G.J. *The Welland Canal Company: A Study in Canadian Enterprise.* Cambridge, Mass.: Harvard University Press, 1954.
Akenson, Donald H. *The Irish in Ontario: A Study in Rural History.* Kingston and Montreal: McGill-Queen's University Press, 1984.
Anderson, Gregory. *Victorian Clerks.* Manchester: Manchester University Press, 1976.
Anderson, Perry. "The Antinomies of Antonio Gramsci." *New Left Review* 100 (Nov. 1976–Jan. 1977): 5–80.
Archer, Melanie. "Family Enterprise in an Industrial City: Strategies for the Family Organization of Business in Detroit, 1880." *Social Science History* 15 (Spring 1991): 67–95.
Armstrong, Christopher. "Austin, James." *Dictionary of Canadian Biography, XII: 1891 to 1900.* Toronto: University of Toronto Press, 1990.
Artibise, Alan F.J. *Winnipeg: A Social History of Urban Growth, 1874–1914.* Montreal: McGill-Queen's University Press, 1975.
Ball, Norman R., and Edward Phelps. "Williams, James Miller." *Dictionary of Canadian Biography, XI: 1881 to 1890.* Toronto: University of Toronto Press, 1982.
Baskerville, Peter. "American's in Britain's Backyard: The Railway Era in Upper Canada, 1850–1880." In *The Development of Canadian Capitalism:*

Essays in Business History. D. McCalla, ed. Toronto: Copp Clark Pitman, 1990.
- *The Bank of Upper Canada.* Ottawa: Carleton University Press, 1987.
- "Donald Bethune's Steamboat Business: A Study of Upper Canadian Commercial and Financial Practice." *Ontario History* 67 (1975): 135–50.
- "The Pet Bank, the Local State and the Imperial Centre, 1850–1864." *Journal of Canadian Studies* 20 (1985): 22–46.
Battye, John. "The 'Nine Hours Pioneers': Genesis of the Canadian Labour Movement." *Labour/Le Travailleur* 4 (1980): 25–56.
Bauman, Zygmunt. *Memories of Class: The Pre-History and After-life of Class.* London: Routledge and Kegan Paul, 1982.
Bechhofer, Frank, and Brian Elliott. "Petty Property: The Survival of a Moral Economy." In *The Petite Bourgeoisie: Comparative Studies of the Uneasy Stratum.* F. Bechhofer and B. Elliott, eds. New York: St Martin's Press, 1981.
Benson, John. "Hawking and Peddling in Canada, 1867–1914." *Histoire sociale – Social History* 18 (May 1985): 75–83.
- "Working-Class Capitalism in Great Britain and Canada, 1867–1914." *Labour/Le Travailleur* 12 (Fall 1983): 145–54.
Bervin, George. "Aperçu sur le commerce et le credit à Québec, 1820–1830." *Revue d'histoire de l'Amérique française* 36 (1983): 527–52.
Bilak, Dennis A. "The Law of the Land: Rural Debt and Private Land Transfer in Upper Canada." *Histoire sociale – Social History* 20 (May 1987): 177–88.
Bischoff, Peter. "La formation des traditions de solidarité chez les mouleurs Montréalais: la longue marche vers syndicalisme." *Labour/Le Travail* 21 (Spring 1988): 9–42.
- "'Traveling the Country 'round': migrations et syndicalisme chez les mouleurs de l'Ontario et du Québec membres de l'Iron Molders Union of North America, 1860 à 1892." *Journal of the Canadian Historical Association/Revue de la Societé historique du Canada,* new series, 1 (1990): 37–72.
Bleasdale, Ruth. "Class Conflict on the Canals of Upper Canada in the 1840s." *Labour/Le Travailleur* 7 (Spring 1981): 9–39.
Bliss, Michael. "Harris, John." *Dictionary of Canadian Biography, XI: 1881 to 1890.* Toronto: University of Toronto Press, 1982.
- *A Living Profit: Studies in the Social History of Canadian Business, 1883–1911.* Toronto: McClelland and Stewart, 1974.
- *Northern Enterprise: Five Centuries of Canadian Business.* Toronto: McClelland and Stewart, 1987.
- "The Protective Impulse: An Approach to the Social History of Oliver Mowat's Ontario." In *Oliver Mowat's Ontario.* D. Swainson, ed. Toronto: Macmillan, 1972.
Bloomfield, Elizabeth. "Building the City on a Foundation of Factories: The 'Industrial Policy' in Berlin, Ontario, 1870–1914." *Ontario History* 75 (1983): 207–43.

– "Industry in Ontario Urban Centres, 1870." *Urban History Review* 15 (Feb. 1987): 279–83.
– "Manuscript Industrial Schedules of the 1871 Census of Canada: A Source for Labour Historians." *Labour/Le Travail* 19 (Spring 1987): 125–31.
– "Municipal Bonusing of Industry: The Legislative Framework in Ontario to 1930." *Urban History Review* 9 (Feb. 1981): 59–76.
– "Using the 1871 Census Schedules: A Machine-Readable Source for Social Historians." *Histoire sociale – Social History* 19 (Nov. 1986): 427–41.
Blumin, Stuart M. "Black Coats to White Collars: Economic Change, Non-manual Work, and the Social Structure of Industrializing America." In *Small Business in American Life*. S. Bruchey, ed. New York: Cambridge University Press, 1980
– *The Emergence of the Middle Class: Social Experience in the American City, 1760–1900*. Cambridge, Mass.: Harvard Univesity Press, 1989.
– "The Hypothesis of Middle-Class Formation in Nineteenth-Century America: A Critique and Some Proposals." *American Historical Review* 90 (1985): 299–338.
Boorstin, Daniel J. *The Americans: The Democratic Experience*. New York: Vintage Books, 1973.
Bradbury, Bettina. "Surviving as a Widow in Nineteenth-Century Montreal." *Urban History Review* 17 (Feb. 1989): 146–60.
Breckenridge, R.M. "The Canadian Banking System, 1817–1890." *Journal of the Canadian Bankers' Association* 2 (1894–5): 105–96, 267–366, 431–502, 571–660.
Brookes, Alan A. "Family, Youth, and Leaving Home in Late-Nineteenth-Century Rural Nova Scotia: Canning and the Exodus, 1868–1893." In *Childhood and Family in Canadian History*. J. Parr, ed. Toronto: McClelland and Stewart, 1982.
– "Out-migration from the Maritime Provinces, 1860–1900." *Acadiensis* 5 (Spring 1976): 26–55.
Brumberg, Joan Jacobs, and Faye E. Dudden. "Masculinity and Mumbo Jumbo: Nineteenth-Century Fraternalism Revisited." *Reviews in American History* 18 (Sept. 1990): 363–70.
Burghardt, Andrew F. "Some Economic Constraints on Land Transportation in Upper Canada/Canada West." *Urban History Review* 18 (Feb. 1990): 232–6.
Burley, David G. "The Businessmen of Brantford, Ontario: Self-employment in a Mid-Nineteenth Century Town." Ph.D. thesis, McMaster University, 1983.
– "Cockshutt, Ignatius." *Dictionary of Canadian Biography, XIII: 1901 to 1910*. Toronto: University of Toronto Press, forthcoming.
– "Paterson, John." *Dictionary of Canadian Biography, VIII: 1851 to 1860*. Toronto: University of Toronto Press, 1985.

– "Shenston, Thomas Strahan." *Dictionary of Canadian Biography, XXII: 1891 to 1900.* Toronto: University of Toronto Press, 1990.

– "Waterous, Charles Horatio." *Dictionary of Canadian Biography, XII: 1891 to 1900.* Toronto: University of Toronto Press, 1990.

– "Wisner, Jesse Oldfield." *Dictionary of Canadian Biography, XII: 1891 to 1900.* Toronto: University of Toronto Press, 1990.

Burley, Kevin. "Occupational Structure and Ethnicity in London Ontario, 1871." *Histoire sociale – Social History* 11 (Nov. 1978): 390–410.

Burns, Rex. *Success in America: The Yeoman Dream and the Industrial Revolution.* Amherst: University of Massachusetts Press, 1976.

Burns, R.J. "Ridout, Thomas Gibbs." *Dictionary of Canadian Biography. Vol. IX: 1861 to 1870.* Toronto: University of Toronto Press, 1976.

Burrage, Walter. *A Pioneer History of South Brant and Adjacent Townships.* n.p, n.d.

Burton, C.L. *A Sense of Urgency: Memoirs of a Canadian Merchant.* Toronto: Clarke Irwin, 1952.

Bushaway, Bob. By *Rite: Custom, Ceremony and Community in England, 1700–1880.* London: Junction Books, 1982.

Byers, Ronald P. "The Making of the Self-Made Man: The Development of Masculine Roles and Images in Ante-Bellum America." Ph.D. dissertation, Michigan State University, 1979.

Calvert, Monte. *The Mechanical Engineer in America, 1830–1910: Professional Culture in Conflict.* Baltimore: Johns Hopkins University Press, 1967.

Careless, J.M.S. "Aspects of Urbanization in Nineteenth-Century Ontario." In *Aspects of Nineteenth-Century Ontario: Essays Presented to James J. Talman.* F.H. Armstrong, H.A. Stevenson, and J.D. Wilson, eds. Toronto: University of Toronto Press, 1974.

Carnes, Mark C. *Secret Ritual and Manhood in Victorian America.* New Haven: Yale University Press, 1989.

Cawelti, Joseph. *Apostles of the Self-Made Man: Changing Concepts of Success in America.* Chicago: University of Chicago Press, 1965.

Clapham, J.H. *An Economic History of Modern Britain, vol. 1: The Early Railway Age, 1820–1850.* Cambridge: Cambridge University Press, 1939.

Clark, S.D. *The Developing Canadian Community.* Toronto: University of Toronto Press, 1966.

Cochran, Thomas C. "Role and Sanction in American Entrepreneurial History." In *Change and the Entrepreneur.* Cambridge, Mass.: Harvard University Press, 1949.

Cowan, Helen I. *British Emigration to British North America: The First Hundred Years.* Toronto: University of Toronto Press, 1961.

Craven, Paul. "The Law of Master and Servant in Mid-Nineteenth-Century Ontario." In *Essays in the History of Canadian Law, I.* D.H. Flaherty, ed. Toronto: University of Toronto Press, 1981.

- "Workers' Conspiracies in Toronto, 1854–72." *Labour/Le Travail* 14 (Fall 1984): 49–70.
Craven, Paul, and Tom Traves. "Canadian Railways as Manufacturers, 1850–1880." Canadian Historical Association, *Historical Papers* (1983): 254–81.
- "The Class Politics of the National Policy, 1872–1933." *Journal of Canadian Studies* 14 (Fall 1979): 14–38.
- "Dimensions of Paternalism: Discipline and Culture in Canadian Railway Operations in the 1850s." In *On the Job: Confronting the Labour Process in Canada*. C. Heron and R. Storey, eds. Montreal and Kingston: McGill-Queen's University Press, 1986.
Crossick, Geoffrey. "The Emergence of the Lower Middle Class in Britain: A Discussion." In *The Lower Middle Class in Britain, 1870–1914*. G. Crossick, ed. London: Croom Helm, 1977.
- *An Artisan Elite in Victorian Society: Kentish London, 1840–1880*. London: Croom Helm, 1978.
Crossick, Geoffrey, and Heinz-Gerhard Haupt. "Shopkeepers, Master Artisans and the Historian: The Petite Bougeoisie in Comparative Focus." In *Shopkeepers and Master Artisans in Nineteenth-Century Europe*. Crossick and Haupt, eds. London: Methuen, 1984.
Cruikshank, Ken. "The Transportation Revolution and Its Consequences: The Railway Freight Rate Controversy of the Late Nineteenth Century." Canadian Historical Association, *Historical Papers* (1987): 112–37.
Currie, A.W. *The Grand Trunk Railway of Canada*. Toronto: University of Toronto Press, 1957
Curti, Merle. *The Making of an American Community: A Case Study of Democracy in a Frontier County*. Stanford: Stanford University Press, 1959.
Darroch, Gordon. "Class in Nineteenth-Century, Central Ontario: A Reassessment of the Crisis and Demise of Small Producers during Early Industrialization, 1861–1871." In *Class, Gender, and Region: Essays in Canadian Historical Sociology*. Gregory S. Kealey, ed. St John's, Nfld.: Committee on Canadian Labour History, 1988.
- "Early Industrialization and Inequality in Toronto, 1861–1899." *Labour/Le Travailleur* 11 (Spring 1983): 31–61.
- "Occupational Structure, Assessed Wealth and Homeowning during Toronto's Early Industrialization, 1861–1899." *Histoire sociale – Social History* 26 (Nov. 1983): 381–410.
Darroch, Gordon, and Michael Ornstein. "Ethnicity and Class, Transitions over a Decade: Ontario, 1861–1871." Canadian Historical Association, *Historical Papers* (1984): 111–37.
- "Ethnicity and Occupational Structure in Canada in 1871: The Vertical Mosaic in Historical Perspective." *Canadian Historical Review* 61 (1980): 305–31.

Davidoff, Leonore, and Catherine Hall. *Family Fortunes: Men and Women of the English Middle Class, 1780–1850*. London: Hutchinson, 1987.

Davis, Nanciellen. "'Patriarchy from the Grave': Family Relations in Nineteenth Century New Brunswick." *Acadiensis* 13 (Sept. 1984): 91–100.

Decker, Peter R. *Fortunes and Failures: White Collar Mobility in Nineteenth-Century San Francisco*. Cambridge, Mass.: Harvard University Press, 1978.

Denison, Merrill. *Harvest Triumphant: The Story of Massey-Harris*. Toronto: Collins, 1949.

Dewar, Kenneth C. "Charles Clarke's 'Reformator': Early Victorian Radicalism in Upper Canada." *Ontario History* 78 (Sept. 1986): 233–52.

Dobson, C.R. *Masters and Journeymen: A Prehistory of Industrial Relations, 1717–1800*. London: Croom Helm, 1980.

Dollar, Charles M., and Richard J. Jensen. *Historian's Guide to Statistics: Quantitative Analysis and Historical Research*. New York: Holt, Rinehart and Winston, 1971.

Doucet, Michael J. "Working Class Housing in a Small Nineteenth Century Canadian City: Hamilton, Ontario, 1852–1881." In *Essays in Canadian Working Class History*. G.S. Kealey and P. Warrian, eds. Toronto: McClelland and Stewart, 1976.

Drummond, Ian M. "Ontario's Industrial Revolution, 1867–1941." *Canadian Historical Review* 69 (Sept. 1988): 283–99.

– *Progress without Planning: The Economic History of Ontario from Confederation to the Second World War*. Toronto: University of Toronto Press, 1987.

Duggan, Edward P. "Machines, Markets and Labor: The Carriage and Wagon Industry in Late Nineteenth-Century Cincinnati." *Business History Review* 51 (Fall 1977): 308–28.

Duncan, Kenneth. "Irish Famine Immigration and the Social Structure of Canada West." *Canadian Review of Sociology and Anthropology* 2 (Feb. 1965): 19–41.

Dutton, H.I., and J.E. King. "The Limits of Paternalism: The Cotton Tyrants of North Lancashire, 1836–54." *Social History* 7 (Jan. 1982): 59–74.

Dyster, Barrie. "Captain Bob and the Noble Ward: Neighbourhood and Provincial Politics in Nineteenth-Century Toronto." In *Forging a Consensus: Historical Essays on Toronto*. V.L. Russell, ed. Toronto: University of Toronto Press, 1984.

Elliott, Bruce. *Irish Migrants in the Canadas: A New Approach*. Kingston and Montreal: McGill-Queen's University Press, 1988.

Ennals, Peter. "Cobourg and Port Hope: The Struggle for Control of 'The Back Country.'" In *Perspectives on Landscape and Settlement in Nineth Century Ontario*. J.D. Wood, ed. Toronto: McClelland and Stewart, 1975.

Erickson, Charlotte. *Invisible Immigrants: The Adaptation of English and Scottish Immigrants in Nineteenth-Century America*. Coral Gables, Fla.: University of Miami Press, 1972.

Evans, A. Margaret. "Oliver Mowat and Ontario, 1872–1896: A Study in Political Success." Ph.D. thesis, University of Toronto, 1967.
– *Sir Oliver Mowat*. Toronto: University of Toronto Press, 1992.
Faler, Paul G. "Cultural Aspects of the Industrial Revolution: Lynn, Mass., Shoemakers and Industrial Morality, 1830–1860." *Labor History* 15 (1974): 367–94.
– *Mechanics and Manufacturers in the Early Industrial Revolution: Lynn, Massachusetts, 1780–1869*. Albany: State University of New York Press, 1981.
Farber, Bernard. *Guardians of Virtue: Salem Families in 1800*. New York: Basic Books, 1972.
Faucher, Albert. "Le Fond d'emprint municipal dans le Haut-Canada, 1852–1867." *Recherches sociographiques* 1 (1960): 7–32.
Fingard, Judith. *The Dark Side of Life in Victorian Halifax*. Porter's Lake, NS: Pottersfield Press, 1989.
Forsey, Eugene. *Trade Unions in Canada*. Toronto: University of Toronto Press, 1982.
Forster, Ben. *A Conjunction of Interests: Business, Politics and Tariffs, 1825–1879*. Toronto: University of Toronto Press, 1985.
– "Finding the Right Size: Markets and Competition in Mid- and Late Nineteenth-Century Ontario." In *Patterns of the Past: Interpreting Ontario's History*. R. Hall et al., eds. Toronto: Dundurn Press, 1988.
Fox-Genovese, Elizabeth, and Eugene Genovese. *Fruits of Merchant Capital: Slavery and Bourgeois Property in the Rise and Expansion of Capitalism*. New York: Oxford University Press, 1983.
Gaffield, Chad. "The Character and Circumstance of Canada's Industrialization." *Labour/Le Travail* 24 (Fall 1989): 219–30.
Gagan, David P. "Enumerators' Instructions for the Census of Canada, 1851 and 1861." *Histoire sociale – Social History* 7 (1974): 353–65.
– *Hopeful Travellers: Families, Land and Social Change in Mid-Victorian Peel County, Canada West*. Toronto: University of Toronto Press, 1981.
– "The Indivisibility of the Land: A Microanalysis of the System of Inheritance in Nineteenth-Century Ontario." *Journal of Economic History* 26 (1976): 126–41.
– "The Security of Land: Mortgaging in Toronto Gore Township, 1835–1885." In *Aspects of Nineteenth-Century Ontario: Essays Presented to James J. Talman*. F.H. Armstrong, J.D. Wilson, H.A. Stevenson, eds. Toronto: University of Toronto Press, 1974.
Gagan, David, and Rosemary Gagan. "Working-Class Standards of Living in Late-Victorian Urban Ontario: A Review of Miscellaneous Evidence on the Quality of Material Life." *Journal of the Canadian Historical Association/ Revue de la Societé historique du Canada* new series, 1 (1990): 171–94.
George, Peter, and Philip Sworden. "The Courts and the Development of Trade in Upper Canada, 1830–1860." *Business History Review* 60 (1986): 258–80.

Gerber, David. "Cutting Out Shylock: Elite Anti-Semitism and the Quest for Moral Order in the Mid-Nineteenth Century American Marketplace." In *Anti-Semitism in American History*. D.A. Gerber, ed. Urbana: University of Illinois Press, 1986.

Gervais, Gaetan. "Le commerce de détail au Canada (1870–1880)." *Revue d'histoire de l'Amérique française* 33 (Mar. 1980): 521–56.

Gidney, R.D., and D.A. Lawr. "Who Ran the Schools? Local Influence on Education Policy in Nineteenth-century Ontario." *Ontario History* 72 (1980): 131–43.

Gilkison, Augusta. "Captain William Gilkison." Ontario Historical Society, *Papers and Records* 8 (1907): 147–8.

– "Reminiscences of Earlier Days in Brant." Ontario Historical Society, *Papers and Records* 12 (1914): 81–8.

Glazebrook, G.P. de T. *Life in Ontario: A Social History*. Toronto: University of Toronto Press, 1968.

Gray, Robert Q. *The Labour Aristocracy in Victorian Edinburgh*. Oxford: Clarendon Press, 1976.

– "The Languages of Factory Reform in Britain, c.1830–1860." In *The Historical Meanings of Work*. P. Joyce, ed. Cambridge: Cambridge University Press, 1987.

Green, A.B. "Immigrants in the City: Kingston as Revealed in the Census Manuscripts of 1871." In *To Preserve and Defend: Essays on Kingston in the Nineteenth Century*. G. Tulchinsky, ed. Kingston and Montreal: McGill-Queen's University Press, 1976.

Gregory, Frances, and Irene Neu. "American Industrial Elite in the 1870s." In *Men in Business*. W. Miller, ed. Cambridge, Mass.: Harvard University Press, 1952.

Griffen, Clyde and Sally. *Natives and Newcomers: The Ordering of Opportunity in Mid-Nineteenth Century Poughkeepsie*. Cambridge, Mass.: Harvard University Press, 1978.

Gutman, Herbert G. *Power and Culture: Essays on the American Working Class*. New York: Pantheon Books, 1987.

– "The Reality of the Rags-to-Riches 'Myth': The Case of Paterson, New Jersey, Locomotive, Iron, and Machinery Manufacturers, 1830–1880." In *Work, Culture, and Society in Industrializing America: Essays in American Working-Class and Social History*. New York: Pantheon, 1976.

Haber, Carole. *Beyond Sixty-five: The Dilemma of Old Age in America's Past*. New York: Cambridge University Press, 1983.

Hann, Russell. "Brainworkers and the Knights of Labor: E.E. Sheppard. Phillips Thompson and the Toronto News, 1883–1887." In *Essays in Canadian Working Class History*. G.S. Kealey and P. Warrian, eds. Toronto: McClelland and Stewart, 1976.

Hersch, Susan E. "From Artisans to Manufacturers: Industrialization and the Small Producer in Newark." In *Small Business in American Life*. Stuart Bruchey, ed. New York: Columbia University Press, 1980.

– *Roots of the American Working Class: The Industrialization of Crafts in Newark, 1800–1860.* Philadelphia: University of Pennsylvania Press, 1978.

Hershberb, Theodore, and Robert Dockhorn. "Occupational Classification." *Historical Methods Newsletter* 9 (Mar./June 1976): 59–98.

Hill, Bruce E. "The Grand River Navigation Company." MA thesis, University of Western Ontario, 1964.

Hobsbawm, Eric. "Class Consciousness in History." In *Aspects of History and Class Consciousness*. I. Meszaros, ed. London: Routledge and Kegan Paul, 1971.

– "Introduction: Inventing Traditions." In *The Invention of Tradition*. E. Hobsbawm and T. Ranger, eds. Cambridge: Cambridge University Press, 1984.

– "The Tramping Artisan." *Economic History Review* series 2, 3 (1950): 299–320.

Hooker, H.L. *Descendants of James McMichael (1772–1821) and Roseanna DeMott (1785–1856).* New York: n.p., 1942.

Houghton, Walter E. *The Victorian Frame of Mind, 1830–1870.* New Haven: Yale University Press, 1957.

Hounshell, David A. *From the American System to Mass Production, 1800–1932: The Development of Manufacturing Technology in the United States.* Baltimore: Johns Hopkins University Press, 1984.

Houston, Susan, and Alison Prentice. *Schooling and Scholars in Nineteenth-Century Ontario.* Toronto: University of Toronto Press, 1988.

Innis, H.A. "Transportation as a Factor in Canadian Economic History." *Essays in Canadian Economic History.* M.Q. Innis, ed. Toronto: University of Toronto Press, 1956.

Jenks, Leland H. "The Role Structure of Entrepreneurial Personality." In *Change and the Entrepreneur.* Cambridge, Mass.: Harvard University Press, 1949.

Johnson, Leo A. *History of the County of Ontario, 1615–1875.* Whitby: County of Ontario, 1973.

– "Ideology and Political Economy in Urban Growth." In *Shaping the Urban Landscape: Aspects of the Canadian City-Building Process.* G.A. Stelter and A.F.J. Artibise, eds. Ottawa: Carleton University Press, 1982.

– "The Political Economy of Ontario Women in the Nineteenth Century." In *Women at Work: Ontario, 1850–1930.* J. Acton, P. Goldsmith, and B. Shepard, eds. Toronto: Canadian Women's Educational Press, 1974.

Johnson, Paul E. *A Shopkeeper's Millennium: Society and Revivals in Rochester, New York, 1815–1837.* New York: Hill and Wang, 1978.

Johnston, C.M. *Brant County: A History, 1784–1945.* Toronto: Oxford University Press, 1967.

Joyce, Patrick. "The Historical Meanings of Work: An Introduction." In *The Historical Meanings of Work*. P. Joyce, ed. Cambridge: Cambridge University Press, 1987.
– *Work, Society and Politics: The Culture of the Factory in Later Victorian England*. New Brunswick, NJ: Rutgers University Press, 1982.
Kalbach, Warren E., and Wayne W. McVey. *The Demographic Bases of Canadian Society*. Toronto: McGraw-Hill, 1971.
Katz, Michel B. "Blacks in Hamilton, 1851–1861." Canadian Social History Project, *Report* 5 (1973–4), working paper no. 5.
– "Occupational Classification in History." *Journal of Interdisciplinary History* 3 (Summer 1972): 63–88.
– *The People of Hamilton, Canada West: Family and Class in a Mid-Nineteenth-Century City*. Cambridge, Mass.: Harvard University Press, 1974.
Katz, Michel B., Michael Doucet, and Mark Stern. *The Social Organization of Early Industrial Capitalism*. Cambridge, Mass.: Harvard University Press, 1982.
Katznelson, Ira. "Working-Class Formation: Constructing Cases and Comparisons." In *Working-Class Formation: Nineteenth-Century Patterns in Western Europe and the United States*. I. Katznelson and A.R. Zolberg, eds. Princeton: Princeton University Press, 1986.
Kealey, Gregory S. "The Honest Workingman and Workers' Control: The Experiences of Toronto's Skilled Workers, 1860–1892." *Labour/Le Travailleur* 1 (1976): 32–68.
– "The Orange Order in Toronto: Religious Riot and the Working Class." In *Essays in Canadian Working Class History*. G.S. Kealey and P. Warrian, eds. Toronto: McClelland and Stewart, 1976.
– "Orangemen and the Corporation: The Politics of Class during the Union of the Canadas." In *Forging a Consensus: Historical Essays on Toronto*. V.L. Russell, ed. Toronto: University of Toronto Press, 1984.
– *Toronto Workers Confront Industrial Capitalism, 1867–1892*. Toronto: University of Toronto Press, 1980.
– "Work Control, the Labour Process, and Nineteenth-Century Canadian Printers." In *On the Job: Confronting the Labour Process in Canada*. C. Heron and R. Story, eds. Kingston and Montreal: McGill-Queen's University Press, 1986.
Langdon, Steven. "The Emergence of the Canadian Working Class Movement, 1845–75." *Journal of Canadian Studies* 7 (1971): 3–31.
Leverenz, David. *Manhood and the American Renaissance*. Ithaca: Cornell University Press, 1989.
Levitt, Ian, and Christopher Smout. *The State of the Scottish Working Class in 1843: A Statistical and Spatial Enquiry Based on the Data from the Poor Law Commission Report of 1844*. Edinburgh: Scottish Academic Press, 1979.

Livermore, J. Daniel. "Wood, Edmund Burke." *Dictionary of Canadian Biography, XI: 1881 to 1890.* Toronto: University of Toronto Press, 1982.

Lockwood, Glenn J. "Irish Immigrants and the 'Critical Years' in Eastern Ontario: The Case of Montague Township, 1821–1881." *Canadian Papers in Rural History, IV.* D.H. Akenson, ed. Gananoque, Ont.: Langdale Press, 1984.

Lynch, Katherine A. "The Use of Quantitative Data in the Historical Analysis of Social Class." *Historical Methods* 17 (Fall 1984): 230–7.

Macdonald, Norman. *Canada: Immigration and Colonization.* Toronto: Macmillan, 1968.

Madison, James H. "The Evolution of Commercial Credit Reporting Agencies in Nineteenth-Century America." *Business History Review* 47 (1974): 164–86.

Magill, Max. "The Failure of the Commercial Bank." In *To Preserve and Defend: Essays on Kingston in the Nineteenth Century.* G. Tulchinsky, ed. Montreal: McGill-Queen's University Press, 1974.

Mahony, Timothy R. *River Towns in the Great West: The Structure of Provincial Urbanization in the American Midwest, 1820–1870.* New York: Columbia University Press, 1990.

Marshall, David. "Cochrane, William." *Dictionary of Canadian Biography, XII: 1891 to 1900.* Toronto: University of Toronto Press, 1990.

Mavor, James. "Finance and Taxation." In *Canada and Its Provinces ...* A. Shortt and A.G. Doughty, eds. Toronto: Glasgow, Brook and Co., 1914.

Mayer, Arno J. "The Lower Middle Class as Historical Problem." *Journal of Modern History* 47 (1975): 409–36.

Maynard, Steven. "Rough Work and Rugged Men: The Social Construction of Masculinity in Working-Class History." *Labour/Le Travail* 23 (Sept. 1989): 159–69.

McCalla, Douglas. "The Decline of Hamilton as a Wholesale Centre." *Ontario History* 65 (Dec. 1973): 247–54.

– "Fire and Marine Insurance in Upper Canada: The Establishment of a Service Industry, 1832–68." In *Canadian Papers in Business History, I.* P. Baskerville, ed. Victoria: University of Victoria, 1989.

– "Morton, Lewis." *Dictionary of Canadian Biography, XII: 1891 to 1900.* Toronto: University of Toronto Press, 1990.

– "Rural Credit and Rural Development in Upper Canada, 1790–1850." In *Patterns of the Past: Interpreting Ontario's History.* R. Hall et al., eds. Toronto: Dundurn, 1988.

– "Tom Naylor's *A History of Canadian Business, 1867–1914.*" Canadian Historical Asociation, *Historical Papers* (1976): 249–54.

– *The Upper Canada Trade, 1834–1872: The Buchanans' Business.* Toronto: University of Toronto Press, 1979.

- "The Wheat Staple and Upper Canadian Development." *Canadian Historical Association, Historical Papers* (1978): 34–46.

McCallum, John. *Unequal Beginnings: Agriculture and Economic Development in Quebec and Ontario until 1870.* Toronto: University of Toronto Press, 1980.

McCracken, Grant. *Culture and Consumption: New Approaches to the Symbolic Character of Consumer Goods and Activities.* Bloomington: University of Indiana Press, 1988.

McDonald, L.R. "Merchants against Industry: An Idea and Its Origins." *Canadian Historical Review* 56 (1975): 263–81.

McIlwraith, Thomas F. "The Adequacy of Rural Roads in the Era before Railways: An Illustration from Upper Canada." In *People, Places, Patterns and Processes: Geographical Perspectives on the Canadian Past.* G. Wynn, ed. Toronto: Copp Clark Pitman, 1990.

McIntyre, J.A. "The Scot as Farmer and Artisan." In *The Scottish Tradition in Canada.* W. Stanford Reid, ed. Toronto: McClelland and Stewart, 1976.

McIntyre, John. "From Workshop to Factory: The Furnituremaker." *Material History Bulletin* 19 (1984): 25–35.

McIvor, R. Craig. *Canadian Monetary, Banking and Fiscal Development.* Toronto: Macmillan, 1961.

McKay, Ian. "Capital and Labour in the Halifax Baking and Confectionery Industry during the Last Half of the Nineteenth Century." In *Essays in Canadian Business History.* T. Traves, ed. Toronto: McClelland and Stewart, 1984.

McPherson Ian. *Each for All: A History of the Co-operative Movement in English Canada, 1900–1945.* Toronto: Macmillan, 1979.

Miller, William. "American Historians and the Business Elite." *Journal of Economic History* 9 (1949): 184–204.

- "The Recruitment of the American Business Elite." *Quarterly Journal of Economics* 64 (1950): 242–53.

Mills, C. Wright. "The Business Elite: A Collective Portrait." *Journal of Economic History* 5 (supplement 1945): 20–44.

Morris, R.J. "Samuel Smiles and the Genesis of *Self-Help*: The Retreat to a Petit Bourgeois Utopia." *Historical Journal* 24 (1981): 89–109.

Morton, Desmond. "Taking on the Grand Trunk: The Locomotive Engineers Strike of 1876–7." *Labour/Le Travailleur* 2 (1977): 5–34.

Muise, D.A. "The Dun and Bradstreet Collection: A Report." *Urban History Review* 3–75 (Feb. 1976): 23–6.

Myers, Gustavus. *History of Canadian Wealth, vol. I.* Toronto: J. Lewis and Samuel, 1972.

Naylor, Tom. *The History of Canadian Business, 1867–1914.* 2 vols. Toronto: Lorimer, 1975.

– "The Rise and Fall of the Third Commercial Empire of the St. Lawrence."
In *Capitalism and the National Question in Canada.* Gary Teeple, ed. Toronto:
University of Toronto Press, 1972.

Neale, R.S. *Class in English History, 1680–1850.* Oxford: Basil Blackwell, 1981.

Newlands, David L. "The Brantford Pottery: The Early Years, 1849–1867."
Canadian Collector, (Jan./Feb. 1977): 22–7.

– "The Brantford Pottery: The Later Years, 1855–1906." *Canadian Collector*
(Mar./Apr. 1977): 22–7

Nicholson, Murray. "The Irish Experience in Ontario: Rural or Urban?"
Urban History Review 14 (June 1985): 37–49.

Noel, S.J.R. "Dividing the Spoils: The Old and New Rules of Patronage in
Canadian Politics." *Journal of Canadian Studies* 22 (Summer 1987): 72–95.

Norris, Darrell. "Household and Transiency in a Loyalist Township: The
People of Adolphustown, 1784–1822." *Histoire sociale – Social History* 13
(Nov. 1980): 399–415.

O'Boyle, Lenore. "The Classless Society: Comment on Stearns." *Comparative
Studies in Society and History* 21 (1979): 397–412.

Osborne, Brian S. "Kingston in the Nineteenth Century: A Study in Urban
Decline." In *Perspectives on Landscape and Settlement in Nineteenth Century
Ontario.* J.D. Wood, ed. Toronto: McClelland and Stewart, 1975.

– "Trading on a Frontier: The Function of Peddlers, Markets, and Fairs in
Nineteenth Century Ontario." *Canadian Papers in Rural History, II.* D.H.
Akenson, ed. Ganonoque, Ont.: Langdale Press, 1980.

Osborne, Brian S., and Robert Pike. "Lowering 'the Walls of Oblivion': Postal
Communications in Central Canada, 1851–1911." In *Canadian Papers in
Rural History, IV.* D.H. Akenson, ed. Gananoque, Ont.: Langdale Press,
1984.

Osborne, Brian S., and Donald Swainson, *Kingston: Building on the Past.*
Westport, Ont.: Butternut Press, 1988.

Ossowski, Stanislaw. *Class Structure in the Social Consciousness.* London: Routledge and Kegan Paul, 1963.

Palmer, Bryan D. *A Culture in Conflict: Skilled Workers and Industrial Capitalism
in Hamilton, Ontario, 1860–1914.* Montreal: McGill-Queen's University
Press, 1979.

– "Kingston Mechanics and the Rise of the Pentitentiary, 1833–1836." *Histoire sociale – Social History* 8 (May 1980): 7–32.

Parr, Joy. *The Gender of Breadwinners: Women, Men and Change in Two Industrial
Towns, 1880–1950.* Toronto: University of Toronto Press, 1990.

Paterson, W.J. "The Long Point Furnace." *Ontario Historical Society Papers and
Records* 36 (1944): 70–8.

Pentland, H. Clare. *Labour and Capital in Canada, 1650–1860.* Paul Phillips,
ed. Toronto: Lorimer, 1981.

– "The Lachine Strike of 1843." *Canadian Historical Review* 29 (Sept. 1948): 255–77.

Perry, J.H. *Taxes, Tariffs and Subsidies: A History of Canadian Fiscal Development.* Toronto: University of Toronto Press, 1955.

Piva, Michael. "Continuity and Crisis: Francis Hincks and Canadian Economic Policy." *Canadian Historical Review* 66 (June 1985): 185–210.

Pollard, S. "Fixed Capital in the Industrial Revolution." In *Capital Formation in the Industrial Revolution.* F. Crouzet, ed. London: Methuen, 1972.

Prentice, Alison. *The School Promoters: Education and Social Class in Mid-Nineteenth Century Upper Canada.* Toronto: McClelland and Stewart, 1977.

Radforth, Ian. "Confronting Distance: Managing Jacques and Hay's New Lowell Operations, 1853–73." *Canadian Papers in Business History, I.* Peter Baskerville, ed. Victoria: University of Victoria, 1989.

Redlich, Fritz. *History of American Business Leaders: A Series of Studies, vol. 1, Theory – Iron and Steel, Iron Ore Mining.* Ann Arbor: Edwards Bros.1940.

– "Sanctions and Freedom of Enterprise" and "The Business Leader as 'Daimonic' Figure." *Steeped in Two Cultures: A Selection of Essays.* New York: Harper and Row, 1971.

Reville, F.D. *History of the County of Brant.* 2 vols. Brantford: Hurley Printing Co. 1920.

Risk, R.C.B. "The Golden Age: The Law about the Market in Nineteenth-Century Ontario." *University of Toronto Law Journal* 26 (1976): 307–46.

– "The Last Golden Age: Property and the Allocation of Losses in Ontario in the Nineteenth Century." *University of Toronto Law Journal* 27 (1977): 199–239.

– "The Law and the Economy in Mid-Nineteenth Century Ontario." *University of Toronto Law Journal* 27 (1977): 403–38.

– "The Nineteenth-Century Foundations of the Business Corporation in Ontario." *University of Toronto Law Journal* 23 (Summer 1973): 270–306.

Roberts, D. *Paternalism in Early Victorian England.* London: Croom Helm, 1979.

Robertson, John. *History of the Brantford Congregationalist Church, 1820–1920.* Brantford: n.p., 1920.

Rodgers, Daniel T. *The Work Ethic in Industrial America, 1850–1920.* Chicago: University of Chicago Press, 1978.

Roelens, Janine, and Kris Inwood. "'Labouring at the Loom': A Case of Rural Manufacturing in Leeds County, Ontario, 1871." *Canadian Papers in Rural History, VII.* D.H. Akenson, ed. Gananoque, Ont.: Langdale Press, 1990.

Rorabaugh, W.J. *The Craft Apprentice.* New York: Oxford University Press, 1986.

Rosenberg, Charles. "Sexuality, Class and Role in Nineteenth-Century America." In *The American Man.* E.H. Pleck and J.H Pleck, eds. Englewood Cliffs, NJ: Prentice-Hall, 1980.

Rotundo, E. Anthony. "Body and Soul: Changing Ideals of American Middle Class Manhood, 1770–1920." *Journal of Social History* 16 (1983): 23–38.

– "Learning about Manhood: Gender Ideals and the Middle-Class Family in Nineteenth-Century America." In *Manliness and Morality: Middle-Class Masculinity in Britain and America.* J.A. Mangan and J. Walvin, eds. New York: St Martin's Press, 1987.

Rudin, Ronald. "King, Edwin Henry." *Dictionary of Canadian Biography, XII: 1891 to 1900.* Toronto: University of Toronto Press, 1990.

Ryan, Mary P. *Cradle of the Middle Class: The Family in Oneida County, New York, 1790–1865.* Cambridge, Mass.: Harvard University Press, 1981.

Saddiq, Fazley. "The Size Distribution of Probate Wealthholdings in Nova Scotia in the Late Nineteenth Century." *Acadiensis* 18 (Fall 1988): 136–47.

Samuel, Raphael. "Workshop of the World: Steam Power and Hand Technology in Mid-Victorian Britain." *History Workshop Journal* 3 (Spring 1977): 6–72.

Santink, Joy. *Timothy Eaton and the Rise of His Department Store.* Toronto: University of Toronto Press, 1990.

Schull, Joseph. *The Century of the Sun: The First Hundred Years of the Sun Life Assurance Company of Canada.* Toronto: Macmillan, 1971.

Sheppard, George. "'God Save the Green': Fenianism and Fellowship in Victorian Ontario." *Histoire sociale – Social History* 20 (May 1987): 129–44.

Smith, Thomas. "Reconstructing Occupational Structures: The Case of the Ambiguous Artisans." *Historical Methods Newsletter* 8 (1975): 134–46.

Smith, Allen. "The Myth of the Self-Made Man in English Canada, 1850–1914." *Canadian Historical Review* 59 (1978): 189–219.

Snell, J.G. "The Cost of Living in Canada in 1870." *Histoire sociale–Social History* 12 (May 1979): 186–91.

Soltow, Lee. *Men and Wealth in the United States, 1850–1870.* New Haven: Yale University Press, 1975.

– *Patterns of Wealthholding in Wisconsin since 1850.* Madison: University of Wisconsin Press, 1971.

Some Papers Read during the Years 1908–1911 at the Meetings of the Brant Historical Society. Brantford: n.p., n.d.

Spelt, Jacob. *Urban Development in South-Central Ontario.* Toronto: McClelland and Stewart, 1972.

Stearns, Peter. "The Middle Class: Toward a Precise Definition." *Comparative Studies in Society and History* 21 (1979): 377–96.

Stedman, Mary B. *Farringdon Church: Its History and Background from 1833 to 1977.* Brantford: n.p., 1977.

Stephenson, Charles. "'There's Plenty Waitin' at the Gates': Mobility, Opportunity and the American Worker." In *Life and Labor: Dimensions of American Working-Class History.* C. Stephenson and R. Asher, eds. Albany: State University of New York Press, 1986.

Stevens, G.R. *Canadian National Railways*. Toronto: Clarke Irwin, 1962.

Sutherland, David. "The Merchants of Halifax, 1815–1850: A Commercial Class in Pursuit of Metropolitan Status." Ph.D. dissertation, University of Toronto, 1975.

Symons, Thomas H.B. "Ryerson, William." *Dictionary of Canadian Biography, X: 1871 to 1880*. Toronto: University of Toronto Press, 1972.

Thernstrom, Stephan. *Poverty and Progress: Social Mobility in a Nineteenth Century City*. New York: Atheneum, 1974.

Thompson, E.P. *The Making of the English Working Class*. Harmondsworth: Penguin, 1968.

– "The Moral Economy of the English Crowd in the Eighteenth Century." *Past and Present* 50 (1971): 76–136.

Tulchinsky, Gerald J.J. *The River Barons: Montreal Businessmen and the Growth of Industry and Transportation, 1837–1853*. Toronto: University of Toronto Press, 1977.

– "'Said to be a very honest Jew': The R.G. Dun Credit Reports and Jewish Activity in Mid-Nineteenth Century Montreal." *Urban History Review* 18 (Feb. 1990): 200–9.

Vincent, John. *The Formation of the British Liberal Party, 1857–1868*. Harmondsworth: Penguin 1972.

Walden, Keith. "Speaking Modern: Language, Culture, and Hegemony in Grocery Window Displays." *Canadian Historical Review* 70 (Sept. 1989): 285–310.

Walker, Frank N. "Birth of the Buffalo and Brantford Railway." *Ontario History* 47 (Spring 1955): 15–30.

Wallace, Anthony F.C. *Rockdale: The Growth of an American Village in the Early Industrial Revolution*. New York: Alfred A. Knopf, 1978.

Wallace, W. Stewart. *The Macmillan Dictionary of Canadian Biography*. 3rd edition. Toronto: Macmillan, 1963.

Walsh, Margaret. *The Manufacturing Frontier: Pioneer Industry in Antebellum Wisconsin, 1830–1860*. Madison: State Historical Society of Wisconsin, 1972.

Weaver, John C. "Crime, Public Order, and Repression: The Gore District in Upheaval, 1832–1851." In *Lawful Authority: Readings on the History of Criminal Justice in Canada*. R.C. McLeod, ed. Toronto: Copp Clark Pitman, 1988.

– "Ferrie, Colin Campbell." *Dictionary of Canadian Biography, VIII: 1851 to 1860*. Toronto: University of Toronto Press, 1985

– *Hamilton: An Illustrated History*. Toronto: Lorimer, 1982.

– *Shaping the Canadian City: Essays on Urban Politics and Policy, 1890–1920*. Monographs on Canadian Urban Government, no. 1. Toronto: Institute of Public Administration of Canada, 1977.

Weaver, John C., and Peter DeLottinville. "The Conflagration and the City: Disaster and Progress in British North America during the Nineteenth Century." *Histoire sociale – Social History* 13 (Nov. 1980): 417–49.

Webster, D.B. *The Brantford Pottery, 1849–1907: History and Assessment of the Stoneware Pottery at Brantford, Ontario.* Art and Archeology Occasional Paper no. 13. Toronto: Royal Ontario Museum, 1968.

Whebell, C.F.J. "Robert Baldwin and Decentralization, 1841–9." *Aspects of Nineteenth-Century Ontario: Essays Presented to James J. Talman.* F.H. Armstrong, H.A. Stevenson, and J.D. Wilson, eds. Toronto: University of Toronto Press, 1974.

Williams, Raymond. "Base and Superstructure." *New Left Review* 82 (Nov.-Dec. 1973): 3–16.

Williams, Rosalind H. *Dream Worlds: Mass Consumption in Late Nineteenth-Century France.* Berkeley: University of California Press, 1982.

Wilson, Alan. *The Clergy Reserves of Upper Canada: A Canadian Mortmain.* Toronto: University of Toronto Press, 1968.

– *John Northway, A Blue Serge Canadian.* Toronto: Burns and MacEachern, 1965.

Winks, Robin. *The Blacks in Canada: A History.* Montreal: McGill-Queen's University Press, 1971.

Wohl, Robert. "The 'Rags to Riches Stories': An Episode of Secular Idealism." In *Class, Status, and Power: Social Stratification in Comparative Perspective.* R. Bendix and S.M. Lipset, eds. New York: Free Press, 1966.

Wyatt-Brown, Bertram. "God and Dun and Bradstreet, 1841–51." *Business History Review* 40 (1966): 432–50.

Wylie, Irvin G. *The Self-Made Man in America: The Myth of Rags to Riches.* New York: Free Press, 1954.

Wylie, William N.T. "The Blacksmith in Upper Canada, 1784–1850: A Study of Technology, Culture and Power." *Canadian Papers in Rural History, VII.* D.H. Akenson, ed. Gananoque, Ont.: Langdale Press, 1990.

Index

Acheson, T.W., 13, 73, 83, 109, 173
Adams, Francis P., shoe dealer, 94
Adams, George, shoe dealer, 94
Adolphustown, Ontario, 22
Afro-American businessmen, 81–2
Age: debt, 121–2; ideology and life cycle, 19, 65–6, 85; self-employment and stage of life, 4, 13, 85–91; wealth, 164–8
Agnew, James, hardware merchant, 37
Agricultural implement manufacturers, 35, 37, 156, 220, 228
Akenson, Donald H., 67
Allen, H.C., physician, 40
American immigrants: age, 88–9; rates of self-employment, 68; types of businesses, 78, 80
Anderson, Gregory, 9
Apprenticeship, 3–4, 81
Archer, Melanie, 76
Artibise, Alan, 200

Assessment rolls: as indicators of wealth, 127; municipal tax legislation, 128–33; use in compiling voters' lists, 223

Babcock, George, stage proprietor, 162
Baker, J.A.D., grocer, 176
Bakers and confectioners, 19, 22, 43, 182–3
Banks: of British North America, 152; of Montreal, 109, 152, 183; of Upper Canada, 105, 106, 108, 203; Baring Brothers, 204; Commercial Bank, 105
Barrett, Richard, jeweller, 179
Baskerville, Peter, 105, 108
Batchelor, Thomas, tailor, 161
Batchelor, William, tailor, 161
Bauman, Zygmunt, 5–6
Bechhofer, Frank, and Brian Elliott, 8

Beck, William F., moulder, 53
Bellhouse, James, carpenter, 207
Bennett, A.B., iron founder, 27, 29, 56, 95, 205
Bennett, A.B., Jr, druggist, 95
Benson, John, 262n29
Biggar, Herbert, politician, 213
Bischoff, Peter, 86, 255n134
Blacksmiths, 22, 33, 156
Bliss, Michael, 172, 200
Blumin, Stuart M., 9
Bond, Francis, street vendor, 82
Botham, Thomas: merchant, mayor, 160, 183, 212, 216
Boulton, Henry John, 129
Bown, Robert R., farmer, 214
Bradley, Abram, livery keeper, 28
Brantford, industries, 35, 38, 46, 57; Alanson Harris, Son and Co., 35, 37, 156, 220; Brant

Carriage Factory, 39;
Brantford Foundry and
Steam Engine Works,
28–9; Brantford Gas
Works, 146; Brantford
Iron Works, 30; Brant-
ford New Grist Mill,
152, 154; Brantford
Pottery, 29, 45, 146;
Brantford Steam
Planing Mill, 34; C.H.
Waterous and Co., 30,
35, 36; Cockshutt
Plough Co. Ltd., 37,
184; Craven Cotton
Co., 38, 220; Depot
Foundry (Butler and
Jackson), 27, 52–3;
Dominion Starch
Works, 36; F.P. Goold
and Co., pottery, 29;
Goold, Bennett and
Co., 27, 28; Goold,
VanBrocklin and Co.,
26; Holmedale Mer-
chant Mills, 35–6, 149,
152, 153; Hoyt
Brothers' Steam Planing
Mill, 34; Ganson,
Waterous and Co.,
foundry, 28, 29, 215;
Mohawk Paper Mill,
163; Ontario Planing
Mills, 36; Waterous
Engine Works Co. Ltd.,
37, 55–6, 146, 229;
Williams, Butler and
Co., 26
Brantford, municipal
politics: boosterism
and politics of commu-
nity particularism, 12,
17, 23, 201–6, 239;
city incorporation,
225; municipal bonus-
ing of industry, 13,
26, 38, 220; munic-
ipal finance, 202–5,
208; ward politics,
224–5

Brantford, population,
12–13, 22, 24
Breckenridge, R.M., 105
Brendon, Frederick, drug-
gist, 39
Brethour, Henry, dry
goods merchant, 37,
42, 45, 143, 186
Bromwich, Fred,
machinist, 54
Bromwich, John, builder,
56
Brophey, Edward, saddler,
35
Brophey, Michael, shoe
dealer, 94, 147
Brumberg, Joan Jacobs,
and Faye E. Dudden,
70–1
Buchanan, Donald, Nine
Hour leader, 54, 55
Buck, C.A., stationer, 48
Buck, William, iron
founder, 28, 30, 36, 37,
46, 52, 195, 226, 228,
229
Builder, John, furniture
manufacturer, 36, 40
Builders, 98–9, 155
Bunnell, Alexander, mer-
chant miller, 24, 148,
149, 152, 183
Bunnell, Enos, merchant
miller, 148
Burns, M.A., planing mill
owner, 36
Burns, Rex, 172
Burton, C.L., 179
Bushaway, Bob, 254n132
Business failure, 15, 234–
5, 263n32; role of char-
acter, 172, 176; busi-
ness discontinuation,
175; suicide, 176–7;
transiency, 16, 177–8;
insolvency and property
seizures, 114–15, 188–90
Business organization:
partnership, 25–34;
incorporation, 37–9

Butler, Matthew, founder,
26, 27, 52–3

Cabinetmakers, 40, 141,
158
Calvert, Monte, 66
Campbell, George, Nine
Hour leader, 55
Canadian-born business-
men: age, 88–9; self-
employment, 16, 62,
68, 83–5, 89; types of
business, 78, 81;
wealth, 167–8
Carlton, Henry, co-opera-
tive organizer, 56
Carlyle, Thomas, 176
Carnes, Mark, 71
Carriage makers, 31–3,
39, 127, 158, 185
Cawelti, John, 172
Christie, David, politician,
202, 213, 215
Clarke, Charles, Elora
merchant, 86
Class, definitions, 5–7, 21,
246n15
Cleghorn, Allen, hard-
ware merchant, 44, 47,
202, 210, 213
Cleghorn, James, hard-
ware merchant, 44, 47
Clelland, William, liquor
merchant, 184
Clement, J.D., innkeeper,
202, 208, 217
Clench, Ralph, anti-
Fenian detective, 220
Clergy Reserves Fund,
208
Clerks, 9–10, 98, 99
Cline, Michael, moulder,
53, 252n100
Cobbett, Joseph M., 64
Cochrane, Rev. William,
5, 76, 235; co-operative
society, 56; success ide-
ology, 171–2, 191–6
Cockshutt, Ignatius, 45,
65, 69, 93, 109, 149,

160, 184, 199, 202, 217; cotton mill, 38, 49; fire company, 208, 209; foundry interests, 26, 28, 29–30, 37; mortgage investment, 146; rental properties, 138–40; retirement, 179, 269n30

Cockshutt, James G., plough manufacturer, 37, 184

Cockshutt, James, merchant, 23, 28, 64–5, 109

Cockshutt, Jane, merchant, 65

Coleman, James, merchant miller, 35, 152

Colver, John M., carriage maker, 31

Comerford, John, grocer, 72–3

Commerce: estates of merchants, 163; investment in manufacturing, 34, 37, 146–7; occupational inheritance, 94–5, 98; persistence, 23, 183–4; retail, 15, 20, 34–5, 36, 47–51, 186; self-employment in, 49; wealth, 158, 160–1; wholesale, 44–6, 104, 112, 251n74

Competition, 31, 65–6, 234–5, 256n22

Conservative party, support in 1870s, 199, 200, 231–2

Consolidated Municipal Loan Fund, 203, 205, 216

Construction trades, 22, 43, 101, 155–6, 180, 185

Cooke, Thomas, grain merchant, 153

Co-operatives, 56–7, 254n120

Coopers, 34

Cowherd, Christopher, tinsmith, 156–7

Cowherd, James, tinsmith, 156–7

Cowherd, Thomas, "Tinsmith Rhymer," 3–4, 69, 110, 156–7, 211, 235

Cowherd, Thomas, Jr, tinsmith, 156–7

Cowherd, William, machinist, 55, 157

Craft production: credit, 118; immigrants in, 78; persistence, 185; replacement, 33–4

Craig, Joseph R., wagonmaker, 32

Craven, Paul, 53; and Tom Traves, 57, 199

Credit, 4, 15, 46–7; based on character, 106–11, 193–4; and control of workers, 120; exemption of inventories held on credit from assessment, 132; and family limitation, 108; mercantile, 15, 104–5, 109; real estate, 108; social politics of credit relations, 23, 109, 114; and wealth, 115–18, 186

Credit agencies, Canada Trade Protection Society, 115

Credit agencies: R.G. Dun, and Co., 177, 261n1; basis for ratings, 103–4, 106–11, 115–16; depression of 1857, 115; reliability of ratings, 111–13

Crooks, Peter H.S., shoemaker, 157–8

Crossick, Geoffrey, 9, 111; and Heinz-Gerhard Haupt, 8

Currier, Amos, blacksmith, 208

Curti, Merle, 258n56

Cutterson, Albert E., grocer, 87

Dalrymple, William, cabinetmaker, 141, 157, 158

Darroch, Gordon, 20, 131, 134, 265n18; and Michael Ornstein, 63, 67, 84

Davies, Edwin, millwright, 55

Decker, Peter, 83

Deference: negotiated, 4, 58–61; in politics, 14, 201–2, 207, 212

Depression of 1857, 12, 14, 29, 103, 105, 114–15, 122, 148, 261n2

Depression of 1873, 175

Dodd, George, 63

Donovan, Joseph, grocer, 87

Doucet, Michael, 134, 136

Draper, Thomas, miller, 154, 155

Draper, William Henry, 128

Druggists, 44, 45, 46–7

Drummond, Ian, 133–4

Dry goods merchants, 41–2, 50, 78, 143, 185, 186

Duncan, Charles, dry goods merchant, 44, 47, 76, 186

Duncan, Henrietta, milliner, 101

Duncan, Sara Jeanette, 76, 102

Dunn, Patrick, carriage maker, 32

Dutton, H.I., and J.E. King, 57

Dyster, Barrie, 207

Eaton, Timothy, 45, 111

Economic rank: credit,
116–17; landlords, 140,
methodology, 128, 132–
3; mortgages, 121, 147;
social mobility, 181–2;
transiency, 177
Edgar, George, glass and
crockery merchant, 160
Edgar, John, glass and
crockery merchant, 46,
160
Elections, Dominion: of
1872, 198, 221; of
1874, 222; of 1878,
228–32
Elections, municipal: of
1855, 206; of 1857,
212; of 1866, 218; of
1869, 219
Elections, provincial: of
1858, 213–15; of 1863,
216; of 1873, 225
Elliott, Bruce, 63, 69
Elliott, John, builder, 88,
218, 220, 273n72
Ellis, Francis H., druggist,
44, 95
Endorsement of promis-
sory notes, 113–14
England, class conflict
and decline of middle
class, 63–4
English immigrants: age,
88–9; self-employment,
68, 88–9; types of busi-
nesses, 78
Erickson, Charlotte, 69,
87
Ethnic stereotypes in
credit reporting, 107,
111

Fair, Alex, merchant,
cigar manufacturer, 45,
46, 80, 186, 226
Farber, Bernard, 77
Family size, 90–1
Ferrie, Colin Campbell,
and Co., Hamilton mer-
chants, 23
Firemen, 207–10

Fleming, George, saloon
keeper, 212
Fletcher, William, carriage
maker, 32
Flour millers and milling,
22, 24, 34, 35–6, 43,
128, 148–54
Forde, Jackson, grocer, 48,
80, 94, 186
Forde, Robert, grocer, 94
Forde, William, grocer, 94
Foreman, Isaac, milk
dealer, 82
Forster, Ben, 24, 199,
270n6
Foster, George, grocer,
starch manufacturer,
147, 186, 229
Fox-Genovese, Elizabeth,
and Eugene Genovese,
126
Fraternal organizations,
69–70
Furniture factories, 39–40

Gaffield, Chad, 68
Gagan, David P., 120; and
Rosemary Gagan, 134
Galt, Alexander, 24
Ganson, Joseph, iron
founder, 27
George, Peter, and Philip
Sworden, 105
Gerber, David, 82
German immigrants, 107,
109
Gilkison, Daniel, lawyer,
214–15
Glass, Alex, baker, 176
Glassco, George, hatter,
95
Glassco, Thomas, hatter,
95, 143
Glazebrook, George, 45
Good, Allen, farmer, 213
Goold, Edward L.,
partner in J.O. Wisner,
Son and Co., 37, 46,
229
Goold, Franklin P., iron
founder, 26, 27, 28, 29

Goold, Ralph W., iron
founder, 27, 29
Gordon, McKay and Co.,
Toronto dry goods
wholesaler, 44
Gore District Mutual Fire
Insurance Co., 23,
248n15
Grain merchants, 152–3
Grand River Navigation
Co., 12, 23–4, 152,
201–2, 204
Grant, Robert, tailor, 42
Grant, William, dry goods
merchant, 42, 44, 76,
208
Griffen, Clyde and Sally,
83, 174, 179
Griffith, James, watch-
maker, 48
Grocers, 45, 50, 80, 107,
109, 101, 112, 140,
159, 164, 185, 186
Gunsmiths, 22, 33
Gutman, Herbert, 173,
200

Hague, George, general
manager, Merchant's
Bank, 178, 234–5
Hall, Thomas W.,
machinist, 30
Hamilton, Joshua, liquor
merchant, 46, 226
Hann, Russell, 171
Hardware merchants, 44,
45
Hardy, Arthur S., lawyer,
MLA, 54, 225, 226, 227
Hardy, Russell, merchant,
44
Harper, John, blacksmith,
56
Harris, Alanson, agricul-
tural implement manu-
facturer, 156, 184, 195,
228, 229
Harris, John, agricultural
implement manufac-
turer, 156, 163, 184,
228

Hatters, 22
Hawkins, Arthur, moulder, 224
Hawkins, Dennis, grocer, 224–5, 226
Hawkins, John J., grocer, 80, 224, 225, 226
Heaton, John, merchant, 160
Heeney, Thomas, carriage maker, 32
Heffernan, Dan, hotel-keeper, 227
Henry, Robert, merchant, 143, 154
Helper, A., moulder, 53
Henwood, Reginald, mayor, 223
Hersch, Susan E., 65
Hext, John, carriage maker, 32, 35, 39, 229
Hext, Thomas, carriage maker, 32, 39
Heyd, Bernard, grocer, 43, 147, 164, 229
Heyd, Charles B., grocer, 219
Hill, Moore, miller, 154
Hincks, Francis: assessment legislation, 129, 130; candidate in South Brant Riding, 200, 221
Hobsbawm, Eric, 8, 238
Hooper, Jacques and Co., Montreal merchants, 97
Hunter, John, hotelkeeper, 227
Hunter, William, carpenter, 209
Huntington, Arunah, shoemaker and merchant, 22, 26, 28, 57, 163, 219
Hurst, William B., grocer, 176, 211

Imlach, William, starch manufacturer, 36, 226
Immigrants: group assistance, 4, 14, 68, 69; occupational structure and ethnic stratification, 66–7, 78–85; rates of self-employment, 70; wealth, 167–8
Immigration: chain, 63, 69; class conflict as reason, 64; family, 87; search for independence, 21–2, 63, 64, 69, 83
Immigration literature, 4, 12, 63–4
Independence as cultural value, 14, 31, 69
Independentists (Farringdon Church), 4, 109
Inglis, John Henry, alias "Joe Ringo," barber, 82
Insolvency and property seizure, 104, 114–15, 188–90
Innkeepers, 23
Irish immigrants, 67; age, 89; Catholics, 71–2, 98, 107; political unity, 206–7, 271n26; Protestants, 73; self-employment, 69, 71, 89; types of businesses, 80–1

Jackson, Jedidiah, merchant, 22
Jackson, Robert, carriage maker, 33, 39
Jackson, Royal G., founder, 27, 52–3
James, Thomas, grocer, 211
Jenkins, John, merchant tailor, 42, 92, 185
Jewellers, 44
Jex, Johnson, blacksmith, 183
Johnson, "Doc," hat blocker, 82
Johnson, Leo, 92, 200
Johnson, Paul E., 24, 31, 66, 77
Jones, Hugh, dry goods merchant, 58, 143, 160
Jones, Lyman Melvin, partner in Alanson Harris, Son and Co., 37, 228
Jones, Terence, broker, 184
Joyce, Patrick, 57, 58

Katz, Michael, 67, 97, 105, 111, 132–3, 237; and Mark Stern and Michael Doucet, 9, 10, 83, 93, 144–5, 259n73
Kealey, Gregory, 52, 207, 228
Keatchie, George, sheriff, 215
Ker, Adam, merchant miller, 35, 152
Kerby, Abraham T., merchant miller, 148, 153, 183
Kerby, James, hotelkeeper, 213–14
Kerby, John, merchant miller, 148
Kerby, William, miller, 148
Kester, Erastus, sewing machine dealer, 48, 101
Kirkland, Alexander, hardware merchant, 210

Labourers, self-employed, 71–2, 257n30
Ladies' Aid (Dorcas) Society, 224–5
Landon, W.E., tinsmith, 28, 29, 30
Langdon, Steven, 56
Lathrop, Holester, iron founder, 27, 29
Laycock, James, merchant, 65
Leeming, Henry B., confectionery manufacturer, 43, 53, 60, 209, 220
Leitch, John A., insurance agent, 195

Lemmon, Henry, newspaper publisher, 214
Leonard, Elijah, St Thomas iron founder, 25
Lethbridge, J.W., piano dealer, 48
Leverenz, David, 267n3
Liberal party: party of the successful, 199, 228; appeal to workingmen, 198, 221, 222
Licensed Victuallers' Association, 226
Lines, William, merchant, 114, 160
Long, P.B., lawyer, 211
Long, William, shoemaker, 41
Lowry, Rev. T., 54
Luke, S.M.L., printer, 54
Lynch, Katherine A., 246n
Lyons, Woods, carriage maker, 32, 39

McCalla, Douglas, 23, 34, 104, 252
McCallum, John, 12, 13, 19
McDonald, John, Toronto wholesaler, 89
Macdonald, John A., 221
McInnis, D., and Co., Hamilton wholesaler, 44
McIlwraith, Thomas F., 22
McIvor, R. Craig, 105
McKay, Donald B., saddler, 185
McKay, Duncan, saddler, 210, 211
McKay, Ian, 19, 43
McKenzie, Tom, city auditor, 223
McKerlie, Daniel, lawyer, 213
McLaughlin, John, moulder, 53
McLean, Thomas, dry goods merchant, 41,

42, 44, 47, 58, 76, 217, 218
McMaster, William, Toronto dry goods wholesaler, 44
McMonagle, Barney, hotelkeeper, 227
McNaught, John, carriage maker, 31, 205
McQuillan, James, labourer, 72
McQuillan, Richard, grocer, 72
Magill, Max, 105
Martin, Thomas, bookseller, 176
Masculinity, 65, 71, 85–6, 92, 106, 236, 258n, 259n, 267n
Mathews, William, shoemaker, politician, 22, 206–17, 219
Mayer, Arno J., 11
Mayhew, Henry, 63
Mayhew, Ira, 91
Maynard, Steven, 86
Mellish, William, 27, 52, 205
Mellish, Morrell, and Russell, railroad contractors, 205
Merican, Andrew, broker, 82
Metal fabricating industries, 25–31, 34, 35–7, 55–6, 78, 94, 124, 127, 156, 215, 229
Metal tradesmen, 20, 30–1, 52–3, 156–7
Middlemass, George, moulder, 53, 252n100
Mills, C. Wright, 173
Mobility, geographic, 4, 16, 88; in 1830s, 22–3; in 1840s, 24; from rural to urban areas, 84, 193; transiency, 177–8
Mobility, intergenerational, 13, 17, 96–7;

wills and inheritance, 86, 95, 260n76; business families, 93–4, 154, 155–6, 156–7, 160–1, 163; occupational inheritance, 94–5, 97–9
Mobility, social, 16; persistent self-employment as measure, 11, 173–4; change in relative wealth as measure, 174; relation to wealth, 181–6; merchants, 183–4; manufacturers, 184–5; significance of debt, 187
Monter, William, blacksmith, 32
Montgomery, John, dry goods merchant, 217
Moore, J.H., general merchant, 42, 205
Moral economy, 106, 111, 126, 238
Morgan, William, shopkeeper, 208
Morphey, Samuel, jeweller, 44
Morris, R.J., 172
Mortgage debt: age and, 121; capital formation and, 15–16, 123–5; credit and, 120, 264n61; social mobility and, 187; wealth and, 121–2
Mortgages: investment exempt under assessment legislation, 131–2; merchant investment in manufacturing and, 16, 146–7
Mowat, Oliver, 222
Muir, Thomas, teacher, 211
Muirhead, Andrew, merchant, 44
Muirhead, William, merchant, 23

Muirhead, William, and Co., carriage makers, 31, 176

National Policy, 17–18, 199, 228–30, 232
Naylor, Tom, 104
Neale, R.S., 8
Nine Hour movement, 17, 54–6, 221, 222
Noble, John, painter, 155–6, 208
Noble, Thomas A., painter, 47, 156
Norris, Darrell, 22

Occupation: categories, 241–3; inheritance, 97–9
Osborne, Brian, 24
Osborne, James K., partner in Alanson Harris, Son and Co., 37, 156, 228
Ossowski, Stanislaw, 8

Palmer, Bryan D., 52
Pardee, T.B., 223
Paris, Ontario, 22
Park, Seth, photographer, 190–1
Parr, Joy, 39
Partnership: religion as basis, 76; family, 93–4
Paternalism: rituals of, 57–60; craft life cycle and, 66
Paterson, William, confectionery manufacturer and MP, 43, 53, 54, 184; election of 1872, 198–9, 221, 222; municipal politics, 209–10, 219
Payne, James, carriage maker, 32
Pentland, H.C., 63, 67, 237
Percy, E.A., newspaper publisher, 54

Personal property assessment, 143
Petite bourgeoisie: definitions, 8–11; and bourgeois elite, 14, 200–2, 210; and labouring class, 206; proletarianization, 20
Pickering, Joseph, 63
Phair, Robert, contractor, 224
Planing mills, 34, 36
Plewes, David, merchant miller, 36, 153, 154, 221
Poe, William, grain merchant, 153
Potts, J. and W., tinsmiths, 29
Potts, Thomas, stove dealer, 48
Pruyn, Matthew W., merchant, 183, 215

Quinlan, Joseph, grocer, 159–60, 164, 184, 185, 224

Rackham, John, wheelwright, 32
Railroads: Brantford and Harrisburgh Railway, 35, 217–18, 219; Brantford, Norfolk and Port Burwell Railway, 35; Canadian Pacific Railway, 35; Canadian Southern Railway, 35; Credit Valley Railway, 35; Great Southern railway, 205; Great Western railway, 35, 205, 217–18
Railroads: Buffalo and Lake Huron Railway, 26, 52, 205; take-over by Grand Trunk Railway, 35
Railroads: Buffalo, Brantford, and Goderich Railway, 12, 26, 29; investors in, 202–3; municipal finance, 203–4; sold to bondholders, 205
Railroads: Grand Trunk Railway, car shops, 13, 36, 219, 249n28; politics, 199, 200, 218, 221–2; strike of 1876–7, 54; takeover of Buffalo and Lake Huron Railway, 35, 199, 216–17
Raymond, William G., piano tuner, 195
Read, Samuel G., real estate agent, 195
Real estate: as restraint upon geographical mobility, 108, 180; rate of ownership, 122, 143, 265n; distribution of ownership, 136–8; use value, 144–5; owned by ex-businessmen, 180; business premises, 25
Rebellion of 1837, 206, 215
Redlich, Fritz, 257n32, 259n71
Reid, Henry, cooper, 54
Religion: congregational support for businessmen, 4, 76; evangelicalism as self-control, 76; partnership among co-religionists, 76–8; reinforcement of immigrant identities, 73
Rental property investments, 138
Residence, separation from place of business, 93, 143–4, 159–60
Respectability, 4; basis for credit, 106–7
Responsibility as basis for credit, 107–8
Retirement, 179

Ridout, T.G., Toronto banker, 106
Riots, 214, 227, 252n96
Risk, R.C.B., 105
Robson, Thomas, miller, 154
Roman Catholic Church, attitude to display of wealth, 72–3
Rorabaugh, W.J., 256n22
Rosenberg, Charles, 259n73
Ross, Mitchell and Co., Toronto wholesaler, 44
Rotundo, E. Anthony, 258n64
Roy, George, carriage maker, 32
Royal Loan and Savings Co., 95, 171
Russell, John, railroad contractor, 52, 162
Ryan, Mary P., 74–5, 76, 108
Ryerson, Egerton, 211
Ryerson, William, politician, 216

St Thomas, Ontario, 25
St Vincent de Paul Society, 225
Samuel, Raphael, 19
Santink, Joy, 45
School politics, 210–12
Scottish immigrants, 111; self-employment, 68, 69; religion, 73; types of businesses, 78
Self-employment: business morality and, 65; definition of class, 6–7, 11; immigrants, 68–9; Irish Catholics, 71–3; methodology, 21, 246n, 247n, 257n; rate, 14, 15, 20, 24, 36, 248n21; rate by occupational group, 25; rate in commerce, 49

Self-made success, 5, 16; ideology, 170–3, 190–6, 235–6; as solution to class conflict, 192–3
Shaw, Alex, engine fitter, 55
Shenston, Joseph N., partner in Alanson Harris, Son and Co., 37, 95, 228
Shenston, Reuben, 95
Shenston, Thomas S., county registrar, 5, 56, 95, 209, 235; Bank of Commerce credit agent, 119–20; self-help advocate, 171; politics, 210–11, 215
Sherwood, Henry, 131
Shoemakers, 22, 29, 40–1, 47, 81, 98, 118, 141–2, 157–8
Sinon, William, carpenter, 208
Six Nations Indians, 22
Slater, Clayton, cotton manufacturer, 30, 220
Slingsby, William, woollen manufacturer, 39
Small towns, as places for self-employment, 64
Smith, Allen, 172
Smith, Arthur, carriage maker, 31
Smith, James, saddler, 35, 185
Smith, Margaret, grocer, 101
Smith, "Second Hand," and Eliza, pawnbrokers, 101
Soltow, Lee, 134, 265n27
Spelt, Jacob, 13
Spence, Adam, carriage maker, 32, 39, 59–60, 88, 195
Spence, David, miller, 154
Spence, James, miller, 152, 154

Spratt, James, cigar manufacturer, 46, 253n104
Sproule, George, druggist, 48, 160
Sproule, Robert, merchant, 39, 95, 160, 211
Stapleton, John, shoemaker, 141–2
Stearns, Peter, 9
Standard of living, 133–5
Steele, John, merchant, 28, 86, 162
Stephenson, Charles, 10
Storey, Robert, cigar manufacturer, 58
Stratford, William H., drug merchant, 45, 143, 184
Stratford, John H., railway contractor, 155, 163, 220
Stratford, Joseph, drug merchant, 143, 184
Street, Joshua, shoe dealer, 47
Strikes: canal labourers, 52; iron moulders, 52; locomotive engineers, 54; coopers, 54; Nine Hour Strike, 54–6; printers, 54, 253n109; volunteer firemen, 208–10
Strobridge, Richard S., merchant, 160, 183
Strong, Thomas, shoemaker, 142
Stubbs, William, blacksmith, 32
Sutherland, David, 83

Tailors, 22, 41, 78, 98, 157, 161, 185, 190
Tanners, 22
Taylor, John, baker, 43, 44
Taylor, John, dry goods merchant, 58, 211
Tedball, Hugo, barber, 82
Temperance movement, 54, 208, 209, 226–7

Thernstrom, Stefan, 173
Thompson, David, 129–30
Thompson, E.P., 8, 10, 111, 126
Tisdale, Bradford G., iron founder, 27, 30, 37, 94
Tobin, John, miller, 152
Trade unions, 192–3; Amalgamated Society of Engineers, 52; Brotherhood of Locomotive Engineers, 54; Canadian Labor Protective and Mutual Improvement Association, 55; carpenters, 54; carriage makers, 54; cigarmakers, 53; dry goods clerks, 54; Iron Molders' Union, 52, 53, 224; Knights of St Crispin, 54; Nine Hour Workingman's League, 55
Tulchinsky, Gerald, 82, 104
Tupper, John M., carriage maker, 31, 32, 114
Turner, John, architect, 209
Tutt, James, builder, 120

Undertakers, 50

VanBrocklin, Philip C., iron founder, 25, 26, 27, 114, 202, 210
Vann, King, carpenter, 55
Vincent, John, 65

Wadleigh, Jerome, carriage maker, 32, 33
Walden, Keith, 48
Walkinshaw, William, Jr, foreman, 56
Wallace, Anthony F.C., 66
Wallace, James, leather merchant, 160

Wallace, James A., druggist, 160
Walsh, Fred, hotelkeeper, 95–6, 160
Walsh, Percival, tobacconist, 96, 160
Walsh, William, tobacconist, 96, 160
Watchmakers, 22
Waterous, Charles H., iron founder, 26, 27, 29, 30, 35, 36, 37, 55–6, 184, 195, 217, 228, 229
Watt, George, grocer, 45, 80, 94, 176, 211
Watt, William, builder, 34, 155, 228
Watts, Alfred, merchant, distiller, manufacturer, and miller, 36, 45, 46, 54, 55, 143, 153–4, 184, 217, 221, 226, 230
Watts, Charles, merchant, distiller, 154
Weinaug, John, grocer, 43
Wealth, probate records as evidence, 161–4
Wealth, assessed: change in proportion held by businessmen, 134–5; distribution, 136–45; distribution by occupational groups, 145–61
Welding, William E., pottery manufacturer, 45
Weyms, James, shoemaker, 41
Whan, McLean and Co., Toronto wholesaler, 44
Whitham, Matthew, baker, 182–3
Whittemore, E.F., Toronto private banker, 114
Whitroff, James, cigar manufacturer, 53, 253n104
Wilkes, Charles, merchant, 96

Wilkes, George H., iron founder, 30, 37, 96–7, 208, 228
Wilkes, George S., iron founder, merchant miller, 30, 97, 148, 149, 152; debts, 113–14, 266n34; politics, 205–6, 212, 213, 217
Wilkes, James, merchant, miller, 149, 96–7, 210
Wilkes, John A., merchant, miller, 23, 148, 149, 266n32
Wilkes, William, merchant, 96
Williams, James Miller, Hamilton manufacturer, 26, 88
Williams, Rosalind H., 48
Winer, J., and Co., Hamilton wholesaler, 44
Winter, Thomas, iron founder, 26, 27
Wisner, Jesse O., agricultural implement manufacturer, 35, 37, 228
Wisner, Wareham, agricultural implement manufacturer, 228
Wives: place in husbands' business, 91; as executors of estates, 91–2
Wohl, Robert, 191
Women, self-employed, 99–102, 261n94; widows, 100; wage labour, 42, 49, 101
Wood, E.B., lawyer, 216, 217, 220
Woodyatt, James, shoemaker, 211
Wylie, Irvin G., 172
Wylie, William, 33, 248n

Yates, Henry, railway contractor, 52, 57–8, 155, 220